Pharmaceutical Patent Protection and World Trade Law

Patents, including pharmaceutical patents, enjoy extended protection for twenty years under the TRIPs Agreement. The Agreement has resulted in creating a two-tier system of the World Trade Organisation Member States, and its implementation has seen the price of pharmaceutical products skyrocket, putting essential medicines beyond the reach of the common man. The hardest hit populations come from the developing and least developed countries, which have either a weak healthcare system or no healthcare at all, where access to essential and affordable medicines is extremely difficult to achieve.

Pharmaceutical Patent Protection and World Trade Law studies the problems faced by these countries in obtaining access to affordable medicines for their citizens in light of the TRIPS Agreement. It explores the opportunities that are still open for some developing countries to utilise the flexibilities available under the TRIPS Agreement in order to mitigate the damage caused by it. The book also examines the interrelationship between the world governing bodies, and the right to health contained in some of the developing country's national constitutions.

Jae Sundaram is Senior Lecturer in International Trade and Maritime Law at the University of Buckingham, UK.

Routledge Research in Intellectual Property

Available:

The Object of Copyright
A conceptual history of originals and copies in literature, art and design
Stina Teilmann-Lock

Well-Known Trade Marks
A comparative study of Japan and the EU
Hiroko Onishi

Contemporary Issues in Pharmaceutical Patent Law
Setting the framework and exploring policy options
Bryan Mercurio and Daria Kim

Intellectual Property, Finance and Corporate Governance
Janice Denoncourt

Protecting Intellectual Property in the Arabian Peninsula
The GCC states, Jordan and Yemen
David Price and Alhanoof AlDebasi

Biodiversity, Genetic Resources and Intellectual Property
Developments in access and benefit sharing
Charles Lawson and Kamalesh Adhikari

Pharmaceutical Patent Protection and World Trade Law
The unresolved problem of access to medicines
Jae Sundaram

Patent Pools, Competition Law and Biotechnology
Devdatta Malshe

For a full list of titles in this series, please visit www.routledge.com

Pharmaceutical Patent Protection and World Trade Law

The unresolved problem of access to medicines

Jae Sundaram

Routledge
Taylor & Francis Group
LONDON AND NEW YORK

First published 2018
by Routledge

2 Park Square, Milton Park, Abingdon, Oxfordshire OX14 4RN
52 Vanderbilt Avenue, New York, NY 10017

Routledge is an imprint of the Taylor & Francis Group, an informa business

First issued in paperback 2020

British Library Cataloguing-in-Publication Data
A catalogue record for this book is available from the British Library

Library of Congress Cataloging-in-Publication Data
Names: Sundaram, Jae, author.
Title: Pharmaceutical patent protection and world trade law: the unresolved problem of access to medicines/Jae Sundaram.
Description: New York: Routledge, 2018. | Series: Routledge research in intellectual property | Includes bibliographical references and index.
Identifiers: LCCN 2018000566 (print) | LCCN 2018000722 (ebook) | ISBN 9781315267692 (Master) | ISBN 9781351973830 (Web PDF) | ISBN 9781351973823 (ePUB 3) | ISBN 9781351973816 (Mobipocket/Kindle) | ISBN 9781138288768 (hardback)
Subjects: LCSH: Drugs—Patents. | Drug accessibility. | Patent laws and legislation. | Foreign trade regulation. | Pharmaceutical industry—Moral and ethical aspects.
Classification: LCC K1519.D78 (ebook) | LCC K1519.D78 S86 2018 (print) | DDC 346.04/86—dc23
LC record available at https://lccn.loc.gov/2018000566

ISBN: 978-1-138-28876-8 (hbk)
ISBN: 978-0-367-59091-8 (pbk)

Typeset in Goudy
by Apex CoVantage, LLC

To my family, who have been very patient and kind to me, while I spent time away from them researching and writing this monograph.

Contents

Cases

1. *Actavis UK Ltd v. Merck & Co Inc.* [2008] EWCA Civ. 444
2. *Bayer Corpn. v. Union of India*, (2014) SCC OnLine Bom 963: AIR 2014 Bom 178
3. *BDR Pharmaceuticals International Pvt Ltd v. Bristol-Myers Squibb Co* CLA No. 1 of 2013, Controller of Patents, Patent Office, Mumbai, India
4. *Darcy v. Allen* (1603) 74 Eng Rep 1131
5. *Diamond v. Diehr* case 450 U.S. 175, 185–187 (1981)
6. *Government of the Republic of South Africa and Others v. Grootboom and Others* (2000), (11) BCLR 1169 (CC)
7. *Hospira UK Ltd and Generics UK Ltd v. Novartis AG* [2013] EWCA Civ 1663
8. *Les Laboratoires Servier v. Apotex Inc.* [2008] EWCA Civ 445
9. *Lee Pharma Ltd. v. AstraZeneca*, CLA No 1 of 2015, The Controller of Patents, Patent Office, Mumbai, India
10. *Minister of Health v. Treatment Action Campaign (No 2)* 2002 (5) SA 721 (CC)
11. *Minister of Health v. New Clicks South Africa (Pty) Ltd* 2006 (2) SA 311 (CC)
12. *Minister of Health and Others v. Treatment Action Campaign and Others* (2002), (10) BCLR 1033 (CC)
13. *Novartis Ag v. Union of India and Others* (2007) 4 MLJ 1153
14. *Novartis Ag v. Union of India and Others* (2013) 6 SCC 1
15. *Okunda and Another v. Republic* [1970] EA 453
16. *PAO and 2 Others v. Attorney General* [2012] eKLR
17. *Paschim Banga Khet Mazdoor Samity and Others v. State of West Bengal* (1996) AIR SC 2426
18. *Schering Corp. v. Geneva Pharm., Inc.*, 339 F.3d 1373 (Fed Cir 2003)
19. *Soobramoney v. Minister of Health, KwaZulu-Natal* (1997) (12) BCLR 1696 (CC)
20. WTO, *India-Patent Protection for Pharmaceutical and Agricultural Chemical Products – Report of the Appellate Body* (19 December 1997) WT/DS50/AB/R
21. WTO, *Canada – Patent Protection of Pharmaceutical Products* – Report of the Panel (17 March 2000) WT/DS114/R

Acronyms

A2M	Access to Medicines
ACE	Advisory Committee on Enforcement
ACTN	Advisory Committee on Trade Negotiations
ACP	African, Caribbean and Pacific Countries
ACTA	Anti-Counterfeiting Trade Agreement
ACT UP	AIDS Coalition to Unleash Power
APEC	Asian Pacific Economic Cooperation
ARVs	Antiretroviral medicines
BASCAP	Business Coalition to Stop Counterfeiting and Piracy
BRICS	Brazil, Russia, India, China, and South Africa
BSA	Business Software Alliance
CEO	Chief Executive Officer
CEDAW	Convention on the Elimination of Discrimination Against Women
CIEC	Center for Innovation and Economic Change
CII	Confederation of Indian Industry
DIIP	Database on International Intellectual Property Crime
DMCA	Digital Millennium Copyright Act
DSU	Dispute Settlement Body
EPA	Economic Partnership Agreement
FAO	Food and Agricultural Organization
FBI	Federal Bureau of Investigation
FDI	Foreign Direct Investment
FTA	Free Trade Agreement
G8	Group of Eight
GATT	General Agreement on Trade and Tariffs
GMO	Genetically Modified Organism
GSP	Generalized System of Preferences
ICC	International Chamber of Commerce
ICESCR	International Covenant on Ecnomic, Social and Cultural Rights
IFPMA	International Federation of Pharmaceutical Manufacturers' Associations
IIAS	International Investment Agreements

IIPA	International Intellectual Property Alliance
IIPI	International Intellectual Property Institute
IMF	International Monetary Fund
IMPACT	International Medicinal Products Anti-Counterfeit Taskforce
INPI	Brazilian Patent and Trademark Office
INTA	International Trademark Association
IP	Intellectual Property
IPC	Intellectual Property Committee
IPI	Institute for Policy Innovation
ISP	Internet Service Provider
IT	Information Technology
LDCs	Least Developed Countries
LPI	Industrial Property Law
MFN	Most Favoured Nation
MPA	Motion Picture Association
MPAA	Motion Picture Association of America
NACC	National AIDS Control Council
NAFTA	North American Free Trade Agreement
NGO	Non-Governmental Organization
OECD	Organization of Economic Cooperation and Development
PCT	Patent Cooperation Treaty
PhRMA	Pharmaceutical Research and Manufacturers of America
PRO-IP	Prioritizing Resources and Organization for Intellectual Property
RIAA	Recording Industry Association of America
RTA	Regional Trade Agreement
SECURE	Standards to be Employed by Customs for Uniform Rights Enforcement
SPLT	Substantive Patent Law Treaty
SSA	Sub-Saharan Africa
STOP	Strategy Targeting Organized Piracy
TNPCs	Transnational Pharmaceutical Corporations
TPP	Trans-Pacific Partnership
TRIPS	Agreement on Trade-Related Intellectual Property
TTIP	Trans Atlantic Trade and Investment Partnership
UK	United Kingdom
UN	United Nations
UNDP	United Nations Development Programme
UNESCO	United Nations Educational, Scientific and Cultural Organization
UNIDO	United Nations Industrial Development Organization
US	United States
USCC	United States Chamber of Commerce
USPTO	United States Patent and Trademark Office
USTR	United States Trade Representative
WB	World Bank

WCO	World Customs Organization
WHO	World Health Organization
WPPT	WIPO Performances and Phonograms Treaty
WTO	World Trade Organization
WIPO	World Intellectual Property Organization

Preface

The seeds of the current book were sown while carrying out a series of studies between 2013 and 2015 on the implementation of the TRIPS Agreement in developing countries, which also included a jurisprudential enquiry into the legal and philosophical foundations of the current model of international intellectual property protection. The TRIPS Agreement, which is contained in 73 articles, has come under legal and academic scrutiny on its policy implications, been roundly criticised from some quarters, and also received plaudits from others. This book is not aimed at presenting yet another commentary on its policy implications, or a forensic deconstruction of the provisions of TRIPS, but more about its failure to address a fundamental problem which had been raised before various forums from the time it was negotiated in the late 1980s and 1990s. The purpose of this book is not to close the debate surrounding the enforcement of the TRIPS Agreement in developing countries and its direct link to the problems associated with access to affordable medicines. Rather, it is to continue engaging in the pursuit for solutions by exploring other avenues, as the problems persist.

The remit of the current book is to study the changing landscape of pharmaceutical patents and the continuing impact of the intellectual property (IP) rights policies and regulations developed and introduced by the WTO through the TRIPS Agreement on access to affordable medicines in developing countries and least developed countries (LDCs). The advent of the TRIPS Agreement only made the situation acute, despite being clearly identified during the negotiation phase, and in later discussions at the highest levels. It will analyse how, although the battle lines drawn in the 1990s and early 2000s have come to be modified since the Doha Declaration, the reality on the ground for those in need of affordable medicines remain almost unchanged, and in some cases have worsened.

This work, while advocating a rethink of the TRIPS Agreement (with regard to the policy on pharmaceutical patent protection), or a complete revision of the Agreement as a whole, also seeks to explore ways to improve access to affordable medicines through alternate avenues available to users and patent holders by using TRIPS flexibilities. This requires a more critical analysis of the interpretation and implementation of the TRIPS Agreement, through the lens of human rights laws (contained in both international conventions and domestic laws), in those developing countries where access to affordable medicines is still a major issue, affecting health policies and actual deliverance of affordable medicines by the respective governments. One should bear in mind that the question of access to affordable medicines had been around for decades, including when the TRIPS Agreement was being negotiated at the Uruguay Round of negotiations, and was known to all international institutions and agencies of the United Nations (UN). Although the debate has continued – at times with intensity and at times with less intensity – the problems have not gone away. The situation requires us to assume a more proactive and pragmatic approach to finding solutions for the problems.

This book does not seek to present a solution to the whole set of problems in relation to the TRIPS Agreement and access to affordable medicines, but nevertheless seeks to explore a number of avenues and present the reader with options to look at and explore further. The legal framework introduced by the TRIPS Agreement has now come to be changed through the introduction of TRIPS-plus provisions in free trade agreements (FTAs), which effectively take away the use of any flexibilities contained in the TRIPS Agreement for developing countries. The use of TRIPS-plus provisions in regional trade agreements (RTAs) and FTAs have not only narrowed the flexibilities available under the Agreement but has also severely restricted the policy space available for manoeuvre in discussions on IP rights protection *vis-à-vis* access to affordable medicines. The obligation brought under the TRIPS Agreement is burdensome, and TRIPS-plus adds to the burden by raising the threshold of compliance originally envisaged under the Agreement. The premise of the book remains that the introduction of the TRIPS Agreement resulted only in aggravating the problems in accessing affordable medicines in developing countries and least developed countries.

Jae Sundaram
Buckingham, UK
November 2017

1 Introduction

Contents

1 Globalising intellectual property rights

The World Trade Organization (WTO), which is at the forefront of promoting and delivering the agenda on the global economy, is an intricate network of multilateral legal agreements entered into by its Member States. The last quarter of the twentieth century witnessed the birth of the globalised economy administered by the WTO through a series of agreements drawn up amongst the Member States of the Organization. The WTO, which is the custodian of several multilateral agreements, is linked in profound ways to the international economic order and is now the principal institution for international trade. The agreements were the products of negotiations which were carried out over lengthy periods of time in various rounds with the participation from developed, developing and least developed countries. The agreements came to be defined by their primary objective within the multilateral trading system introduced by the WTO, and some were classified as covered, core agreements that were compulsory in nature and a prerequisite for membership in the Organization. One such agreement is the TRIPS Agreement, a product of the Uruguay Round of negotiations (Jackson, 2006),[1] which also saw the creation of the WTO. Since the entry in 1995, the

1 The Uruguay Round of negotiations, the most complex of all the GATT trade rounds, was also probably the largest and most complex economic multilateral treaty negotiation in history. Its final text is approximately 26,000 pages long, with most pages containing detailed schedules of concessions and obligations, and about 1,000 pages consisting of reasonably dense and complex treaty general norms.

membership of the WTO has swelled to over 160,[2] with the promise of being part of a globalised economy which is more predictable and committed to reducing tariffs.

The Agreement on Trade-Related Aspects of Intellectual Property Rights (TRIPS)[3] is one of the covered agreements under the multilateral trading system administered by the WTO. The Agreement, which entered into force on 1 January 1995,[4] is largely built upon a long tradition of intellectual property (IP) rights protection found in both domestic and international law of developed Western market economies (Cottier, 2005). Originally conceived as a minor agreement relating to border enforcement measures against counterfeiting and piracy, TRIPS evolved into becoming the third pillar of the multilateral trading system. The Agreement is viewed by IP rights holders as integral to the international legal environment, but in sharp contrast has prompted systemic questions from advocates of better public health; human rights lawyers; advocates of food security, biodiversity, access to medicines, access to cultural works; advocates of better agricultural policies, advocates of international economic laws, to identify a few. The origins of the TRIPS Agreement are clearly traceable to the 1970s when there was a growing trade in counterfeit goods, leading to the formation of the Anti-Counterfeiting Coalition, an alliance comprising 100 multinational corporations (Matthews, 2002). Among the Agreement's distinctive features are the requirement that the member states provide regulatory standards – which is considered a positive prescription; recognize IP as inherently present in commercially traded products but also in creative ideas, information or expressions – and found embodied in such products; provide for the creation of private rights in economic operators (unlike in a state); establish legal mechanism for enforcement of such rights; and also incorporate substantive rules from pre-existing international agreements on IP rights. Some of the above features are a 'first time' in terms of rule-making in international law, and the Agreement also has a distinctive enforcement capability attached to the soft law framework. The TRIPS Agreement is not without its shortcomings, as it sets very high standards of protection for IP rights, leaving little room for flexibility for any developing country member state that had sought to implement it (Cottier, 2005).[5]

2 As of February 2018, the membership of the WTO stands at 164.

3 Agreement on Trade-Related Aspects of Intellectual Property Rights (Annex 1C to the Agreement establishing the World Trade Organization of 15 April 1994).

4 The TRIPS Agreement, being one of the multilateral agreements, is binding on all member states of the WTO and a 'condition precedent' of membership for any country wishing to join the WTO. This is a significant condition; for example, the People's Republic of China (PRC), which was not a founding member but was to join later, implemented the TRIPS Agreement before becoming a member.

5 The author opines that one of the important concepts, namely progressive liberalization (which is considered an incremental goal and to be achieved in multilateral rounds of trade negotiations), is not in the field of IP protection, and that any flexibility available is limited only to transitional periods.

The TRIPS negotiations, commenced in the Uruguay Round of negotiations (Van Dijk, 2005; Martin, 1994),[6] reframed both the international governance of IP and multilateral trade through the ingenious linking of the concept of 'trade-related aspects' of IP rights and the very conception of 'trade' within the multilateral trading system (Taubman, 2015). In one single stroke, the TRIPS Agreement changed the landscape of international IP governance by being implemented through the multilateral trading system and making it one of the covered agreements, with only a small window of transition period for developing countries and a longer period for the least developed countries (LDCs). Some commentators hold the view that not enough attention has been paid to the concept of 'trade-relatedness' in the TRIPS Agreement by legal scholars, and that the 'concept' in the past decade has migrated to a number of bilateral trade agreements, where TRIPS-plus standards have been incorporated (Drexl, 2016).[7] The then CEO of Pfizer Corporation, Edmond Pratt Jr., termed the introduction of the TRIPS Agreement a victory brought about by hard-fought efforts of the US government and US businesses (Drahos and Braithwaite, 2002).[8] The Agreement's emergence is to be seen as an example of corporate capture of international law-making (Gopakumar, 2016; Sell, 2003).[9]

A strong view exists among scholars that transnational corporations from the US were primarily responsible for the lobbying that brought the TRIPS Agreement into existence (Sell, 2003).[10] The creation of an international IP rights

6 The Uruguay Round, which was the eighth round, is considered as the most ambitious round of all the multilateral trade negotiations undertaken under the GATT. It has been described as a victory for the rules-based multilateral trading system and a milestone in the evolution of international economic relations. The agreements introduced in the Uruguay Round had the effect of removing several distortions that had previously weakened the integrity of the trading system.

7 Drexl views the concept as needing a reassessment in order to judge the appropriateness of IP bilateralism, which had emerged in the post-TRIPS era, and argues for a reconsideration of trade policies that are strongly predicated on trade concessions as a bargaining chip for higher intellectual property standards.

8 Former CEO of Pfizer, Edmond Pratt Jr. (1971–91), made the following remarks at the US Council of International Business: 'The current GATT Victory, which established provisions for intellectual property, resulted in part from the hard-fought efforts of the US government and US businesses, including Pfizer, over the past three decades. We've been in it from the beginning, taking a leadership role,' as quoted by Wallach, Woodall and Public Citizen Foundation (2004). For a more detailed discussion on the role played by US corporations in promoting an international intellectual property regime, see Drahos (2003) and Sundaram (2015a).

9 The actions of the Intellectual Property Committee (IPC) formed in the United States, through its manoeuvres, succeeded in getting the IP rights protection as an item on the agenda of the Uruguay Round of negotiations, which eventually saw the birth of the TRIPS Agreement, offering important lessons about the increasing role of private power in international rule-making and politics.

10 Sell notes that the IPC from the United States, comprising of twelve chief executive officers (representing pharmaceutical, entertainment and software industries), successfully developed international support for strengthening the global protection of intellectual property rights. See also Drahos and John Braithwaite (2002); Matthews (2002). The United States was the principal *demandeur* in the area of TRIPS and was represented by a large and specialized team during the negotiations. See also Watal and Taubman (2015).

regime was clearly a victory for the patent-holding transnational corporations, which were determined to raise international IP rights standards globally, and in particular in developing countries (Deere, 2009). In short, the Agreement globalised IP rights, without allowing the developing country and the LDC member states of the WTO to comprehend fully the consequences of an international IP rights regime. This view may have sounded a bit exaggerated if it had been made in the 1990s (in the immediate aftermath of the entry of the TRIPS Agreement), or in the early part of the 2000s, but with over two decades of the TRIPS Agreement, there is sufficient evidence to prove it right. As Sell noted, the TRIPS Agreement is hardly the end of the story, and in many ways, it is just the beginning (Sell, 2003). TRIPS, in her view, is only the machinery; the domestic and international institutions have been enlisted for its enforcement, with the private sector activists continuing to play a central role in monitoring implementation and enforcement efforts. With the establishment of the TRIPS Agreement, the mission of strengthening and expanding the international IP rights of transnational corporations commenced. The past two decades have witnessed the transnational corporations successfully implementing their private rights at the cost of public rights, with one such right being the right to health and access to affordable medicines.

1.1 *Knowledge: the new capital*

Advances made in various scientific fields in the second part of the twentieth century, including pharmaceuticals, computing and electronics, biotechnology, information technology and digitisation, to mention a few, has ushered in a new era in creativity. The developments are heavily reliant on the foundations of a sound knowledge economy and science-intensive products, and knowledge economy is referred to by some as the third industrial revolution (Mowrey, 2009). The knowledge components of the goods produced can be distributed without diminishing their real value with exceptional ease (Dinwoodie and Dreyfuss, 2012). The knowledge one owns, or controls becomes capital, allowing for the same to be licenced or traded across national borders for a fee. Patents, also referred to as industrial property, are viewed as the key component of the knowledge economy. Patent rights fall under the broad spectrum of IP rights and have a very high commercial value in a consumer-driven economy, where rights holders seek to enforce their rights globally. Patent right is a monopoly right granted to a person who has invented a new and useful product, and it prohibits the unauthorised exploitation of the patented product by third parties.[11] The justification for an exclusive monopoly right is strongly grounded on the premise that rewarding the inventor for the skill and effort expended will encourage innovation – although

11 'A patent is the right granted to an inventor by a State, or by a regional office acting for several States, which allows the inventor to exclude anyone else from commercially exploiting his invention for a limited period, generally 20 years.' Idris (2008).

no clear evidence is available to lend support to this rhetoric (Basheer, 2012), and is strongly contested (Chien, 2003).[12]

The regime set out by the TRIPS Agreement largely governs knowledge as capital, while paying little attention to how this arrangement affects the provision of the many public goods that rely on knowledge and innovation. The global IP rights regime that was to emerge was premature, as it left unresolved the many complex tensions inherent in governing IP rights. As TRIPS treats IP protection as a trade matter, it effectively marginalises the many other areas where IP rights impact, *viz.*, health, education, human rights and technology transfer, to name a few (Muzaka, 2011). The patent-holding developed countries have lauded the success of globalising IP rights, but the developing countries and least developed countries have found the going extremely difficult in their pursuit of access to affordable medicines, as a direct result of the implementation of the Agreement. The developing countries were required to introduce TRIPS-compliant IP legislation into their domestic laws, which over the past two decades has had the effect of unsettling established domestic laws and health policies which were primarily designed to safeguard the interests of the general public in accessing both affordable treatment and medicines (Sundaram, 2014a, 2014b).[13] The Agreement's implementation became a complex political game, played out mostly outside the WTO, with the institution having little or no oversight. Muzaka notes that since the introduction of TRIPS through the multilateral trading system, rules on IP had been negotiated bilaterally and plurilaterally by member states and issued through various international organisations, including the WTO, WIPO, WHO, United Nations Industrial Development Organization (UNIDO), Food and Agricultural Organization (FAO), World Bank, United Nations Development Programme (UNDP), *etc.* (Muzaka, 2011). This position only goes to demonstrate that IP rights governance cannot be presented as a trade matter and be encapsulated in one agreement, *i.e.*, TRIPS Agreement, without actually addressing the other areas that it impinges on, *viz.*, health, education and human rights. Long prior to the entry of the TRIPS Agreement, developing countries like India did not grant product patent protection for pharmaceutical patents, and granted only a process patent protection. India decided to recognise product patents on the back of the Justice Ayyangar Committee Report,[14] which strongly recommended the process patent protection of pharmaceutical and chemical patents, with the objective of making medicines affordable and accessible to the general public.

12 Chien argues that the studies available only indicate that licenses do not have any significant demonstrable effects on the rate and pace of innovation.

13 For example, in the case of Brazil and India, the governments came under pressure from transnational pharmaceutical corporations (TNPCs) as opposed to WTO member states, to implement TRIPS-compliant intellectual property legislation.

14 The Ayyangar Committee Report, 'A Report on the Revision of the Law in India Relating to Patents for Inventions' (September 1959), paved the way for the generics industry to be developed in India.

Under the scheme envisaged in the Agreement, patents (including pharmaceutical patents) enjoy an extended global protection for a period of twenty years. The current study is more concerned with the protection afforded, in particular, to pharmaceutical patents under the Agreement. Sponsored by the patent-holding developed nations, it has resulted in creating a two-tier system of the WTO member states, and its implementation has also witnessed the price of pharmaceutical products skyrocket, putting essential medicines beyond the reach of the patients in developing and least developed countries. The hardest hit populations by the implementation of the Agreement are to be found in developing countries and LDCs that have a weak healthcare system (or no healthcare system at all in some cases), and where access to essential and affordable medicines is extremely difficult to achieve even in the absence of the Agreement due to weak infrastructure to produce affordable medicines, poor governance and weak socio-economic conditions.

2 Access to medicines and the TRIPS Agreement

The TRIPS Agreement's 'one size fits all' policy ignores the diversity of the world population and the problems that confront them, which is exemplified in the difficulties that developing nations confront (Siew-Kuan Ng, 2010), in their pursuit to access affordable medicines. With such diversity at socio-economic and cultural levels prevalent amongst the member states, a level playing field was not in sight for the implementation of an international IP regime. One of the primary areas of coverage sought under the Agreement was pharmaceutical patent law enforcement in developing countries, which had witnessed the growth of generic medicines to the disadvantage of patented/branded medicines. The prerequisites for implementing an international IP regime required a strong institutional setup including a sound legal system, a healthcare system, and the appropriate level of infrastructure to produce medicines in the domestic markets, which factors were largely absent in most developing countries. Although in theory the Agreement affords flexibility, this is hardly ever allowed to be properly exercised by developing countries in times of need. As allowing the flexibilities to be implemented would mean a reduction in the price of patented medicine, patent-holding transnational corporations go to extremes to protect their 'private' rights as against a public good.[15] India, Brazil and South Africa are some of the developing countries that have faced pressure from both pharmaceutical corporations and developed countries when seeking to exercise their rights under the Agreement.[16]

15 For example, the use of compulsory licensing as provided in the TRIPS Agreement has been used successfully only in a few instances since 1995. In most cases it had followed lengthy negotiations, court battles, the involvement of NGOs and a strong developing country government prepared to stand up for its rights.

16 The three countries which form part of the five-country BRICS alliance (Brazil, Russia, India, China, and South Africa) have been waging their own battle against HIV/AIDS, and as a result

Developing countries, generally, do not have a good track record for innovation, especially on the pharmaceutical front, due to weak socio-economic conditions, a weak knowledge economy and a lack of proper industrial infrastructure, as the priorities for any key spending are focused elsewhere. In the above environment, the introduction of TRIPS-compliant pharmaceutical patent protection has had some highly adverse distributive consequences (Reichman and Dreyfuss, 2007). The result was, needless to say, a manifold increase in the price of branded essential medicines in the developing countries and in some cases a decrease in the supply of generics, which combined with weak healthcare has made access to affordable medicines an extremely difficult goal to achieve. Pharmaceutical patent protection introduced under TRIPS has put medical treatment beyond the reach of the populace living in the developing countries, where the healthcare system is weak. In contrast, the TRIPS Agreement supports a system/model prevalent amongst the patent-holding developed nations, which is defined by a strong healthcare system. It is not an exaggeration to postulate that the patent system mandated by TRIPS effectively shifts wealth from developing countries to the patent-holding developed countries (Sundaram, 2015). Although the principles and objectives of the Agreement clearly acknowledge the importance of interests and the necessity to promote social welfare and protect public health, the ground realities of implementing the rules contained in the Agreement seem to bypass the fundamental problem of access to affordable medicines. Commentators have also observed that the outcomes from the WTO Dispute Settlement Body (DSB) lean towards the 'one size fits all' theory of TRIPS (Dinwoodie and Dreyfuss, 2004a, 2004b), which does not take into consideration the diversity of member states and their requirements. Another criticism of the DSB is that the adjudicators lack the 'judicially manageable standards' that are required to convert the aspirations found in the TRIPS Agreement into concrete legislative safeguards for public interest concerns (Dreyfuss and Lowenfeld, 1997; Dreyfuss, 2010).

In an environment where branded medicines come at a premium, generics are the saviours, as they consist of the same chemical compounds as branded products. Generics are produced by pharmaceutical companies after the expiry of the patent (twenty years under TRIPS), which is not prohibited under law. Most sub-Saharan African (SSA) countries still rely on generics to meet their day-to-day medical requirements. Transnational pharmaceutical corporations (TNPCs), on the other hand, often portray generics as inferior copies of patented medicines, implying that they could be harmful, and seek to outlaw them from international markets. Further, to avoid entry of generics, the TNPCs also engage in 'evergreening', which is the practice of extending the period of patent exclusivity by carrying out cosmetic changes to the chemical composition of pharmaceutical products to bring them within the patentable category. The use of the data exclusivity provisions (non-disclosure of test data) under the

access to medicines has always been high on the agenda. The case studies presented in later chapters cover the implementation of the TRIPS Agreement in the above countries and others.

TRIPS Agreement coupled with the practice of evergreening by the TNPCs together makes it extremely difficult for the entry of any generic drugs into the market at the earliest possible time under TRIPS. With opportunities for entry of affordable generics lessening, the average consumer in developing countries is driven to seek branded patented drugs, which are beyond their reach. One can even visualise a future when generics will dry out, and the only pharmaceutical products on the market will be branded medicine, for which, the knowledge component/patent right will be held by transnational corporations, with little or no say in any negotiation process from developing countries whatsoever. As the world witnesses, people die of diseases not from the want of a cure, but from a want of affordable medicines. Simply put, the deaths occur not because science has not found a cure, but because the prices put on the 'cure', (or medicines) are too expensive to afford.

International governing bodies, including the United Nations (UN) and the World Health Organization (WHO), have highlighted the plight of the disadvantaged populace living in developing countries and LDCs, with very little or no access to affordable medicines, who continue to suffer as a direct result of the extended pharmaceutical patent granted under the TRIPS Agreement. Attempts to find a solution by the TRIPS Council at the WTO in 2001 and 2003 resulted in the Doha Declaration,[17] but very little benefits were achieved, as the transnational pharmaceutical corporations, with the active participation from patent-holding developed countries, were able to successfully thwart any attempts by developing countries from utilising the flexibilities under the Agreement and the Doha Declaration. Currently, the LDCs do not have to meet any of the obligations under the TRIPS Agreement, as they have until 2033 to implement the Agreement. But with patented medicines getting pricier and the generics getting more and more difficult to access due to restrictions imposed by the TRIPS Agreement, the LDCs' position appears to be vulnerable. The transnational pharmaceutical industry has sought to further extend their monopolies by using data exclusivity (non-disclosure of test data), which helps lengthen the patent life of the drug.

2.1 *Twenty years of TRIPS and the proliferation of RTAs*

For the patent-holding transnational corporations and developed countries, twenty years of the TRIPS Agreement is a step in the right direction, as it offers protection to their private rights at an international level, coupled with institutional oversight and enforceability of any claims at the domestic level. One could not have negotiated and gotten a better legal framework before an international organisation, *viz.*, the WTO. As mentioned earlier, in the post-TRIPS era, the patent-holding developed countries have sought to expand trade by using

17 The 2001 Doha Declaration and the 2003 Decision on Implementation of paragraph 6 of the TRIPS Agreement recognises the right of a country to gain access to medicines. See WTO General Council (1 September 2003).

free trade agreements (FTAs), regional trade agreements (RTAs), bilateral trade agreements, economic partnership agreements (EPAs) and the like, with developing nations. The use of TRIPS-plus provisions or IP provisions in FTAs, RTAs and EPAs have clearly disadvantaged the developing nations, as they nullify the use of compulsory licencing, parallel imports and any flexibilities provided under the TRIPS Agreement to access affordable medicines. The patent-holding developed countries, under the leadership of the US, have set the twenty-year patent protection period under the TRIPS Agreement as a benchmark from where they have proceeded to build a strong position by forging FTAs and RTAs, which contain TRIPS-plus or special IP provisions. In recent years, large-scale FTAs have emerged on the horizon, *viz*., Trans-Pacific Partnership (TPP), Trans Atlantic Trade and Investment Partnership (TTIP) (the failed Anti-Counterfeiting Trade Agreement (ACTA)), *etc*., which could result in both developing country partners and third parties suffering as a result of TRIPS-plus and/or special IP provisions drafted into them. Yet another threat for access to medicines, apart from the FTAs and RTAs, is the proliferation of economic partnership agreements and international investment agreements (IIAs), which invariably do contain provisions that increase/extend the IPR protection beyond the WTO-TRIPS minimum standards by introducing additional obligation under the IP chapter. Here, the multilateral trading system has failed to find a clear-cut solution to the problem of access to affordable medicines in developing countries, and had instead actively supported the creation of a global IP rights protection system and a mechanism for the enforcement of such rights.

The WTO has also failed to contain the proliferation of RTAs and FTAs, as they are not prohibited under the existing laws of the WTO. Simply put, it is a growing conundrum for developing countries, as the position on access to affordable medicines has only worsened in the post-TRIPS era. Access to affordable medicines is as yet an unresolved problem, which seems to grow multifold on a daily basis through the actions of patent-holding developed countries and transnational pharmaceutical corporations, who are very keen to enforce a private property right against a public right to health. The inability of the WTO to control and question the proliferation of FTAs, and the unbridled lobbying powers enjoyed by the transnational pharmaceutical corporations to lobby their parent countries to negotiate TRIPS-plus provisions into the FTAs with developing countries, appear to have the effect of taking away any flexibilities or advantages the developing countries may come to enjoy under the TRIPS Agreement, leaving them with little choice.

Attempts by the developing countries to draft TRIPS-compliant legislation to meet their domestic requirements, against the above backdrop, have also come under severe criticism from TNPCs, with patent-holding developed nations (mostly the US) playing proxy for the pharmaceutical industry, and preventing the implementation of any domestic laws (Brazil, India, and South Africa being instances) which would allow greater access to affordable medicines. This has also seen national governments dragged to court, life-saving affordable generic drugs confiscated, disputes raised before the WTO against member states, and last but not least, political pressure exerted through listing the developing countries with capabilities to produce generic drugs under 'trade watch lists' to present them as rogue nations – all in the name of IP rights protection of pharmaceutical patents.

2.2 Organisation of the book and areas of enquiry

This book covers one of the key areas of IP protection under the TRIPS Agreement, *viz*., pharmaceutical patent protection, the problems of access to affordable medicines in developing countries' and the failed attempts to find a solution. The book touches upon lost opportunities, from both sides of the divide, to improve access to medicines, and also the failure of developing countries (and regional groups) to utilise TRIPS flexibilities in some cases. The book seeks to enhance the debate on TRIPS and access to medicines by discussing the role of world governing bodies, who are entrusted with the task of global health governance, and their failure in achieving the goal of access to affordable medicines in the developing world. It will call into question the WHO's commitment to global health; the interrelationship between the world governing bodies, namely, the WHO, the World Bank and the WTO; the role of international law and the right to health contained in some of the developing country's national constitutions.

This book seeks to give shape to some of the debates surrounding the following issues: (i) the subject of pharmaceutical patent protection as introduced by the TRIPS Agreement and the crises of access to affordable medicines in developing countries and LDCs (through case studies); (ii) the justification of patent protection for pharmaceutical patents (jurisprudential enquiry); (iii) the responsibility and obligation of the governing institution over international IP protection, *viz*. the WTO, and (iv) the role and responsibilities of developed nations within the multilateral trading system as lead nations in the negotiation process. One of the issues covered will be the restrictive nature of the current IP laws (relating to pharmaceutical patents), as promoted through the WTO' on access to medicines in developing countries, and to the broader policy debate on the need for a complete rethink of the TRIPS Agreement *vis-à-vis* the need for a global pharmaceutical patent protection.

The book is organised into ten chapters and spread over three parts. The introductory chapter presents an overview of the entry of the TRIPS Agreement and how an extended patent protection of pharmaceutical patents have intensified the problem of affordable access to medicines in the post-TRIPS era, and how patent-holding developed nations and transnational pharmaceutical corporations have utilised TRIPS as a benchmark to ratchet up IP rights protection in the developing countries. If the extended pharmaceutical patent protection, as administered and overseen by the multilateral trading system, is to be identified as one of the principal reasons for the problem of access to affordable medicines in developing countries, then it becomes essential to have a philosophical/jurisprudential enquiry into the foundations of the IP protection. Part I contains chapters 2 to 4. Chapter 2 takes up for study the justification for an extended

IP rights protection under the TRIPS Agreement, which is presented through an analysis of the philosophical/legal justification to grant exclusive rights to IP rights, and pharmaceutical patents in particular. The chapter will include the analysis of IP rights from utilitarian and economic principles, which helped in broadening private rights, as well as an analysis of human rights and right-to-health principles to establish the public rights argument. It will be argued that access to medicines is to be considered a human right, and it was a grave mistake to have included the IP rights protection within the multilateral trading system without striking a clear balance between private legal rights (IP protection) and the public legal right to health of the citizens. The chapter concludes with the advent of the TRIPS Agreement and an enquiry of its principle of broadening the private right/one-size-fits-all mantra.

Chapter 3 takes up for study the forum shifting resorted to by transnational pharmaceutical corporations by successfully lobbying patent-holding developed countries to move the international IP agenda from the World Intellectual Property Organization (WIPO) to the WTO even before its formation, by including global IP rights protection as a major item for negotiation in the Uruguay Round of negotiations. This chapter also presents a critical study of the flexibilities (compulsory licencing, *etc.*) contained in the TRIPS Agreement and the Doha Declaration, which were both intended to assist the developing nations and LDCs in the quest for affordable medicines in times of need. It will be argued that they had not produced the desired effect in most parts of the developing world, and the problem of access to medicines continue. It will also be argued that the entry of the TRIPS Agreement had seen the profits of pharmaceutical corporations go up, but at the same time access to medicines have only become increasingly difficult in most parts of the developing world.

Chapter 4 takes up for discussion how FTAs and TRIPS-plus provisions have nearly rendered useless the flexibilities contained in the TRIPS Agreement. It will be argued that the patent-holding developed countries have proceeded to strengthen their position by forging FTAs with partner countries (both, developed and developing) which contain TRIPS-plus provisions. In recent years, large-scale FTAs have emerged on the horizon (TTP, TTIP – not fully ratified yet) led by the US, which could see developing country partners and third parties suffer as a result of TRIPS-plus provisions contained therein. The inability of the WTO to control and question the proliferation of FTAs, and the unbridled lobbying powers enjoyed by the TNCPs to lobby their parent countries to insert TRIPS-plus provisions into the FTAs with developing countries, appear to have the effect of taking away any flexibilities or advantages the developing countries may come to enjoy under the TRIPS Agreement. The developing countries, who are parties to the FTAs, do not have the same powers as their developed country counterparts during negotiations and are forced to accept such TRIPS-plus provisions. This chapter will analyse how FTAs result in the violation of international norms on commitment to health and the status of generics in the market, which provide an effective and much affordable alternate for patented drugs.

Part II of the book covers the implementation phase of the TRIPS Agreement in a selection of developing countries, including Brazil, China, India, South

Africa and Kenya. Some of the countries identified have slightly stronger economies and knowledge economies than other developing countries. This part discusses the difficulties encountered in the implementation of the Agreement into the domestic IP legislation in the above jurisdictions. Chapter 5 covers a case study of Brazil and how it had coped with pressure from the US, whilst implementing the Agreement ahead of its deadline. Chapters 6 and 7 take up for study two of the Asian neighbours, *viz.*, the People's Republic of China (PRC) and India. In the case of PRC, it was not only the sudden transitioning from a socialist/Marxist notion of property to that of a westernised notion of market economy, but also to be WTO compliant to do business with the rest of the world. In the case of India, the analysis will focus on how the country had to face an uphill task to move from a well-established process patent regime to a product patent regime, while desperately trying to preserve its advantage of being a key global producer of generics. Chapters 8 and 9 cover the case studies of South Africa and Kenya, respectively, from sub-Saharan Africa, and how the two nations have struggled to implement domestic IP legislation to meet their own local requirements and at the same time being TRIPS compliant in the eyes of TNPCs. It will also cover the actions of TNPCs backed by patent-holding developed nations in trying to thwart the efforts of the developing countries to produce generics and access affordable medications for their own use. Part III of the book, following from the case studies carried out in Part II, looks at the future of access to affordable medicines in developing countries and LDCs. Chapter 10 discusses the findings from the preceding chapters, whilst also covering the key questions of whether the TRIPS Agreement is for everybody's benefit, whether developing countries actually need the Agreement, *etc.* The chapter will argue how the imposition of an enhanced IP protection through the multilateral-trading system, and the requirement to introduce a TRIPS-compliant IP regulation at the domestic level, had strained the existing legal and other institutions of developing member states of the WTO. This part of the chapter will also discuss the ways in which to work towards improving access to affordable medicines in disadvantaged communities while still pursuing the goal of a complete rethink in the legal policy of granting patent protection to essential medicines. The chapter will then investigate one of the primary questions that had repeatedly featured in the discussions for over a decade, *viz.*, whether an amendment to the TRIPS Agreement in relation to pharmaceutical patent protection helps achieve the goal of access to affordable medicines, and suggest the way forward for developing country and LDC member states before the multilateral trading system.

Bibliography

1 Arup, Christopher. *The World Trade Organization Knowledge Agreements* (Cambridge University Press, 2008) 286–287.

2 Ayyangar Committee Report. 'A Report on the Revision of the Law in India Relating to Patents for Inventions' (September 1959) <http://spicyip.com/wp-content/uploads/2013/10/ayyangar_committee_report.pdf> accessed 29 November 2017.

3 Basheer, Shamnad. 'India's First Compulsory License: Patents vs. Public Health?' *IP Osgoode* (2 April 2012) <www.iposgoode.ca/2012/04/india%E2%80%99s-first-compulsory-license-patents-vs-public-health/> accessed 29 November 2017.
4 Chien, Colleen. 'Cheap Drugs at What Price to Innovation: Does Compulsory Licensing of Pharmaceuticals Hurt Innovation?' *Berkeley Tech Law Journal* Vol. 18 (2003) 853, 896–907.
5 Cottier, Thomas. 'The Agreement on Trade-Related Aspects of Intellectual Property,' in Macrory, P.F.J., A.E. Appleton, and M.G. Plummer (eds.) *The World Trade Organization: Legal, Economic and Political Analysis*, Vol. I (Springer, 2005) 1043.
6 Deere, Carolyn. *The Implementation Game: The TRIPS Agreement and the Global Politics of Intellectual Property Reform in Developing Countries* (Oxford University Press, 2009).
7 Dinwoodie, Graeme, and Rochelle C. Dreyfuss. 'Intellectual Property Law and the Public Domain of Science,' *Journal of International Economic Law* Vol. 7 (2004a) 431.
8 Dinwoodie, Graeme, and Rochelle C. Dreyfuss. 'TRIPS and the Dynamics of International Property Lawmaking,' *Case Western Reserve Journal of International Law* Vol. 36 (2004b) 95.
9 Dinwoodie, Graeme, and Rochelle C. Dreyfuss. 'The Challenges of TRIPS Agreement,' in Dinwoodie, Graeme, and Rochelle C. Dreyfuss (eds.) *A Neofederalist Vision of TRIPS: The Resilience of the International Intellectual Property Regime* (Oxford University Press, 2012) 3–4.
10 Drahos, Peter, and John Braithwaite. *Information Feudalism: Who Owns the Knowledge Economy?* (Earthscan, 2002).
11 Drahos, Peter. 'Expanding Intellectual Property's Empire: The Role of FTAs,' *Regulatory Institutions Network, Research School of Social Sciences, Australian National University* (2003).
12 Drexl, Joseph. 'The Concept of Trade-Relatedness of Intellectual Property Rights in Times of Post-TRIPS Bilateralism,' in Ullrich, Hanns, Retro M. Hilty, Matthias Lamping, and Jose Drexl (eds.) *TRIPS Plus 20: From Trade Rules to Market Principles* (Springer, 2016).
13 Dreyfuss, Rochelle C., and Andreas Lowenfeld. 'Two Achievements of the Uruguay Round: Putting TRIPS and Dispute Settlement Together,' *Virginia Journal of International Law* Vol. 37 (1997) 275.
14 Dreyfuss, Rochelle C. 'TRIPS and Essential Medicines: Must One Size Fit All? Making the WTO Responsive to the Global Health Crisis,' in Pogge, Thomas, Matthew Rimmer, and Kim Rubenstein (eds.) *Incentives for Global Public Health: Patent Law and Access to Essential Medicines* (Cambridge University Press, 2010).
15 Gopakumar, K.M. 'Twenty Years of TRIPS Agreement and Access to Medicine: A Development Perspective,' *Indian Journal of International Law* Vol. 55, No. 3 (2016) 367–404.
16 Idris, Kamil. *WIPO Intellectual Property Handbook: Policy, Law and Use*, Publication No. 489 (WIPO, 2008) <www.wipo.int/edocs/pubdocs/en/intproperty/489/wipo_pub_489.pdf> accessed 29 November 2017.
17 Jackson, John H. *Sovereignty, the WTO and Changing Fundamentals of International Law* (Cambridge University Press, 2006) 99.
18 Martin, Will, and Winters L. Alan. *The Uruguay Round: Widening and Deepening the World Trading System Directions in Development* (World Bank Publication, 1994).
19 Matthews, Duncan. *Globalising Intellectual Property: The TRIPS Agreement* (Routledge, 2002) 9.
20 Mowrey, David C. 'Plus Ça Change: Industrial R&D in the "Third Industrial Revolution,"' *Industrial and Corporate Change* Vol. 18, No. 1 (2009) 1–50.

21 Muzaka, Valbona. *The Politics of Intellectual Property Rights and Access to Medicines* (Palgrave MacMillan, 2011).
22 Reichman, Jerome, and Rochelle C. Dreyfuss. 'Harmonization Without Consensus: Critical Reflections on Drafting a Substantive Patent Law Treaty,' *Duke Law Journal* Vol. 57 (2007) 85.
23 Sell, Susan K. *Private Power, Public Law: The Globalization of Intellectual Property Rights* (Cambridge University Press, 2003).
24 Siew-Kuan Ng, Elizabeth. 'Global Health and Development: Patents and Public Interest,' in Pogge, Thomas, Matthew Rimmer, and Kim Rubenstein (eds.) *Incentives for Global Public Health: Patent Law and Access to Essential Medicines* (Cambridge University Press, 2010).
25 Sundaram, Jae. 'India's Trade-Related Aspects of Intellectual Property Rights Compliant Pharmaceutical Patent Laws: What Lessons for India and Other Developing Countries?' *Information & Communications Technology Law* Vol. 23, No. 1 (2014a) 1–30.
26 Sundaram, Jae. 'Brazil's Implementation of TRIPS Flexibilities: Ambitious Missions, Early Implementation, and the Plans for Reform,' *Information & Communications Technology Law* Vol. 23, No. 2 (2014b) 81–116.
27 Sundaram, Jae. 'Analysis of TRIPS Agreement and the Justification of International IP Rights Protection in the WTO's Multilateral Trading System, With Particular Reference to Pharmaceutical Patents,' *Information & Communications Technology Law* Vol. 24, No. 2(2015) 1–43.
28 Taubman, Antony. 'Thematic Review: Negotiating "Trade-Related Aspects" of Intellectual Property Rights,' in Watal, Jayashree, and Antony Taubman (eds.) *The Making of the TRIPS Agreement: Personal Insights From the Uruguay Round Negotiations* (World Trade Organization, 2015) 15.
29 Van Dijk, Meine Pieter. 'Introduction: The Results of the Uruguay Round and the Agenda for the World Trade Organisation,' in van Dijk, Meine Pieter, and Sandro Sideri (eds.) *Multilateralism Versus Regionalism: Trade Issues After the Uruguay Round*, Vol. 5 (Routledge, 2005).
30 Wallach, Lori, Patrick Woodall, and Public Citizen Foundation (Washington DC). *Whose Trade Organization?: A Comprehensive Guide to the WTO* (The New Press, 2004).
31 Watal, Jayashree, and Antony Taubman. 'Revisiting the TRIPS Agreement: Genesis and Structure of This Book,' in Watal, Jayashree, and Antony Taubman (eds.) *The Making of the TRIPS Agreement: Personal Insights from the Uruguay Round Negotiations* (World Trade Organization, 2015) 8.
32 WTO General Council. 'Implementation of Paragraph 6 of the Doha Declaration on the TRIPS Agreement and Public Health,' *Decision of the General Council* [WT/L/540 and Corr.1] (1 September 2003).
33 World Trade Organization. *The Legal Texts: The Results of the Uruguay Round of Multilateral Trade Negotiations* (Cambridge University Press, 2010).

Part I

Evolution of intellectual property laws, and the introduction of IP protection in the multilateral trading system

Introduction

To fully understand the problems associated with access to affordable medicines in the developing countries and LDCs it is essential to understand the arguments underlying the justification for grant of patents, and more particularly IP protection for pharmaceutical products. This takes us on a jurisprudential enquiry into the justification of IP rights protection of pharmaceutical patents as recognised by the WTO. Not stopping with a jurisprudential enquiry, it is also incumbent upon us to study the political economy of trade at the multilateral trading system, which witnessed 'forum shifting' resorted to by the TNCs and was stage-managed by the developed nations, who stood to benefit from such a move. The patent-holding developed countries successfully shifted the forum of discussion from the WIPO – the natural home of the IP rights – to that of the WTO, a move which was seen as more beneficial to developed nations who had stronger knowledge economies with more patent rights.

Part I, besides presenting a juriprudential enquiry into the foundations of IP laws, and pharmaceutical patents in particular, also takes up for study the forum shifting resorted to by the developed nations during the WTO negotiation process, besides carrying out an analysis of the role of FTAs, economic partnership agreements, TRIPS-plus provisions and other factors that undermine the flexibilities available under the TRIPS Agreement to developing countries and LDCs. Commentators view TRIPS-plus provision as a serious hindrance to the enjoyment of flexibilities provided under the Agreement. The three chapters in Part I serve as the necessary background study of the complex landscape of pharmaceutical patent rights, and as a precursor to the study of TRIPS implementation in the developing countries. Each of the chapters presented in part I highlights some of the common arguments that will be encountered in the case studies to follow in part II of the book.

2 A jurisprudential enquiry into the justification of international IP rights protection, with particular reference to pharmaceutical patents

Contents

1 Introduction

When the agenda for a global IP rights protection was introduced at the Uruguay Round of negotiations, one of the primary objections raised was that of the fear of increase in the price of pharmaceutical products in developing countries and LDCs, where the incident of HIV/AIDS was posing a major problem and the situation was worsening. The key protagonist behind the move to introduce IP rights protection into the multilateral trading system was the patent-holding pharmaceutical corporations from developed nations. The next objection was that the entry of the TRIPS Agreement would see the developing countries and the LDCs suffer from the excessive burden of obligations imposed under the Agreement to embrace and implement a higher standard of IP protection. The author views the obligation set under the Agreement as not only excessive, but also unnecessary and cumbersome, as the developing countries had to carry out seismic changes to their existing legal framework and health policies, and in that process aggravating the problem of access to medicines. The Doha Declaration does not seem to have resolved the problem, and can only be seen as a window dressing. TRIPS has become a burden for two fundamental reasons – the first one purely legal and jurisprudential, and the second one, socio-economic. Most developing countries struggled to change their laws as the notion of IP rights protection as laid out in the Agreement was excessive and did not fit with the reality of their socio-economic needs. In some cases, it required a paradigm shift of their existing domestic laws in order to make way for a TRIPS-compliant IP law regime.

This chapter seeks to carry out a jurisprudential enquiry into the justification for an extended international IP rights protection under the TRIPS Agreement. The enquiry commences with an analysis of the development of IP rights over the centuries in Europe, and the philosophical underpinnings of the patent regime – pharmaceutical patent protection in particular – and how it had alternated between process patent and product patent before the commencement of the Uruguay Round of negotiations. The analysis will also include the study of the benefits of the Agreement under the principles of economic law; seek justification from a human rights perspective to the question of whether it was wise to equate private rights of pharmaceutical patent rights holders with right to health (which includes the right to access affordable medicines), especially when there was an overwhelming body of evidence that the implementation of the TRIPS Agreement would see the price of essential drugs rise exponentially; and investigate whether there was a level playing field in the negotiations when many member countries did not even have elementary levels of IP standards due to a weak national economy, knowledge economy, industrial infrastructure, and poor governance with weak institutions.

This chapter is divided into four sections, with the first presenting the premise of the current research, and the second analysing the emergence of IP rights and the legal justification in the seventeenth century, the philosophical and legal basis of modern IP rights under the economic law principles to argue that it benefits only a handful of rights-holding developed member states of the WTO, while depriving the non-rights-holding member states of any benefits. The third section will briefly outline the background to the introduction of IP rights in the former colonies during the colonial era, which largely facilitated the implementation of an expanded IP rights regime through the TRIPS Agreement. The third section will also closely analyse the TRIPS Agreement from a human rights perspective and its impact on access to medicines in developing countries and LDCs. It will be argued that the international IP rights protection regime, as it stands today, does not benefit and cannot benefit the developing countries and the LDCs, and that it is primarily designed to benefit the rights holders and not the end users in developing countries and LDCs as the rights comes at a very high premium. The fourth part will discuss the findings and conclude the chapter, suggesting a way forward for the WTO community, including a complete rethink of the TRIPS Agreement, if not a comprehensive review.

2 Patent rights: origins, traditional views and economic foundations

The foundations of economic theories are deeply entrenched in utilitarianism, which was instrumental in creating the framework for development of IP rights, and in particular patent rights. Utilitarian theorists strongly supported the creation of IP rights as an appropriate means to foster innovation, while non-utilitarian theorists relied on the creator's moral rights to have control over their work (Menell, 2000). Rights associated with real and personal property, grant perpetual ownership; in contrast, rights available under prominent forms of IP, *i.e.*, patents and copyrights, offer rights only for a limited time (Menell and Scotchmer, 2007).[1] IP laws, as it stands today, are made up of a system of policy levers and law, tailored by the legislators and interpreted by the courts, which is aimed at promoting innovation and protecting the private property (or knowledge) interest contained therein. The modern IP landscape comprises distinct legal regimes, including patent rights, copyrights, trade secrets, trademarks, *etc.* The Anglo-American traditions more broadly define IP laws, combining industrial property law, copyright and neighbouring rights to the area of IP, while the Continental traditions have treated patent laws as part of industrial property laws (Lemley, Menell, and Merges, 2016). The rights identified in the legal regimes are different, and the duration of protection conferred as well are limited. The remit of the current chapter is restricted to an enquiry into the origins of patent rights, with particular focus on pharmaceutical patents.

Historically, the first administrative apparatus for granting a patent originated during the Renaissance, with the Venetian Senate's 1474 Act, under which the inventor's monopoly right extended to a period of ten years (Mandich, 1948).[2] Some scholars opine that the practice of granting patents might have existed as early as in 500 BC in Sybaris, Greece, where monopolies were granted to new dishes for a period of one year (Adams, 2008). The Venetian concept of recognising an inventor's legal right spread across Europe, quickly. For rulers in the middle ages, it mattered little whether industrial development was achieved by inducing inventions in their own realm, or by importing knowledge from abroad (Hestermeyer, 2008; Walterscheid, 1994a). Walterscheid notes that English patent custom took root and flourished during the reign of Queen Elizabeth I, who granted at least fifty-one patents between 1561 and 1600 (Walterscheid, 1994b). Walterscheid also points out that the official series of granting patents and cataloguing them did not begin before 1617, although the grant of patents had been in vogue for over fifty years prior to the said date (Walterscheid, 1996).[3] The English practice under the above custom required the patentee to work the patent, failing which the patent was liable to be revoked, and when granted to a foreigner, it was liable to be revoked if the patentee failed to teach a native the new art. But this custom came to be abused as monopolies were granted to the favourites of the

1 In the case of copyrights, the term is longer than for patents. The authors also note that the principal objective of IP law is to promote new and improved works, and also to ensure the integrity of the marketplace.

2 Besides granting a monopoly right, the Act also authorised any violator to pay a sum of one hundred ducats to the patent holder and the destruction of any unauthorised copies of the patented work. See also Mandich (1960) and Sichelman and O'Connor (2012).

3 The author also argues that during the middle of the nineteenth century the standards of 'patentability' employed on behalf of the crown in England were low, and this may well have meant that the number of patents issued 'overstated' the level of inventive activity.

court, even for well-established industries (Hestermeyer, 2008).[4] The legal recognition of the grant of a patent started in England with the passing of the Statute of Monopolies of 1623 (Machlup and Penrose, 1950),[5] which also laid down the principle that only a 'true and first inventor' should be granted a monopoly patent. Under section 6 of the statute, patent monopolies were allowed for a period of fourteen years, which appears to be based on economic policies rather than the motive to do justice to the inventor (Adams, 2008). Later, in the seventeenth and eighteenth centuries, the laws in England no longer required the patentee to teach apprentices but to submit written specifications, which would in turn enable others to learn the new skill through reading (Walterscheid, 1995).

Just over two hundred years after the passing of the Statute of Monopolies of 1623, the subject of patent reform was raised before the English Parliament, for the reason that the procedure for obtaining a patent was expensive, clumsy and uncertain (Machlup and Penrose, 1950). This move before the Parliament triggered off a debate in England and soon spread to the Continent, where economists too joined in to create pro-patent and anti-patent lobbies (Machlup and Penrose, 1950).[6] The lobbying and debating brought about a number of changes to the laws on patents both in England and on the Continent, besides witnessing the emergence of economic theories on the subject, with notable ones coming from England and France. During the above period, the classical writers in England almost completely fell in line with the traditional principles contained in the Statute of Monopolies of 1623 that justified the grant of temporary monopolies for the exploitation of innovations, due to their special character and function, and hence being exempt from the prohibition of monopoly.

Jeremy Bentham, regarded as the founder of modern-day utilitarianism and also a jurist, held the view that there was

> one species of privilege certainly very advantageous: the patents which are granted in England for a limited time, for inventions in arts and manufactures. Of all the methods of existing and rewarding industry, this is the least burthensome, and the most exactly proportioned to the merit of the invention.
>
> (Bentham, 1843)

4 See also *Darcy v. Allen* (1603) 74 Eng Rep 1131, 1139, where the King's Bench held that patent monopolies should only be granted where the product was previously unknown in England. This case also struck down the grant of a monopoly in the manufacture of playing cards.

5 It is widely accepted that the policy of granting privileges of monopoly under the royal prerogative in England culminated in the Statute of Monopolies of 1623.

6 Select committees of the English Parliament and Royal commissions investigated the operation of the patent system in 1851–1852, in 1862–1865, and again in 1869–1872. Some of the testimonies before the two commissions were so damaging to the repute of the patent system that leading statesmen in the two houses of Parliament proposed the complete abolition of patent protection. The Patent Bill 1874, although passed in the House of Lords, was to be withdrawn in the House of Commons.

A strong supporter of the English patent system, he further observed that the privilege conferred under a patent had nothing in common with monopolies (Bentham, 1843; Bentham, 1825; Machlup and Penrose, 1950).[7] Adam Smith, recognised as the pioneer of political economy, whilst referring to the risks that a company of merchants undertake and the expenses they incur to establish a new trade, held the view that the state should compensate the merchants by granting them

> a monopoly of the trade for a certain number of years . . . [to] recompense them for hazarding a dangerous and expensive experiment, of which the public is afterwards to reap the benefit. A temporary monopoly of this kind may be vindicated upon the same principles upon which a like monopoly of a new machine is granted to its inventor, and that of a new book to its author.
> (Smith, 2012)

Adam Smith was of the opinion that such monopolies for inventions could be defended on the grounds of equity,[8] and as far as extending the similar rights to new books was concerned he argued that such exclusive privilege could be regarded as 'an encouragement to the labours of learned men' and being beneficial to the society.[9] The views of both Bentham and Smith were key to the development of the law on patents both in England and in the New World.

John Stuart Mill, yet another proponent of utilitarianism, took a similar stance and lent his support for the patent system as follows: 'the condemnation of monopolies ought not to extend to patents' (Mill, 2004). Mill also observed that 'the originator of an improved process is allowed to enjoy, for a limited period, the exclusive privilege of using his own improvement', and that inventors should be both compensated and rewarded. He was yet cautious about the duration of the privilege and argued that

> an exclusive privilege, of temporary duration, is preferable; because it leaves nothing to anyone's discretion; because the reward conferred by it depends upon the invention's being found useful, and the greater the usefulness, the greater the reward; and because it is paid by the very persons to whom the services is rendered, the consumers of the commodity.
> (Mill, 2004)

7 Bentham notes that 'With respect to a great number of inventions in the arts, an exclusive privilege is absolutely necessary in order that what is sown may be reaped. . . . He who has no hope that he shall reap will not take the trouble to sow'.

8 Adam Smith observed, 'if the legislature should appoint pecuniary rewards for the inventors of new machines, *etc.*, they would hardly ever be so precisely proportional to the merit of the invention as this is. For here, if the invention be good and such as is profitable to mankind, he will probably make a fortune by it; but if it be of no value he will also reap no benefit.'

9 Adam Smith argued that such exclusive privileges granted to authors could be beneficial 'if the book be a valuable one the demand for it in that time will probably be a considerable addition to his fortune. But if it is of no value the advantage he can reap from it will be very small.'

The advocates of utilitarian philosophy viewed the patent system as being responsible for the greater part of inventing activity (Taussig, 1915).

In contrast, French economist Michel Chevalier was more emphatic in his opposition of both patents and tariffs, declaring that both originate from the same doctrine and result in the same abuses (Chevalier, 1878).[10] The opponents of the privileges and monopolies were able to ideologically link patent protectionism with tariff protectionism and patent monopoly to argue against monopoly privileges, which was clearly exemplified in the views expressed by Michel Chevalier. The advocates of a strong patent protection, on the other hand, were able to separate the idea of patent protection from the monopoly issue and the free trade issue to present the case of patent protection as one of natural law and private property, and of man's right to live by his work (Machlup and Penrose, 1950).[11] David Hume argued that property has no purpose where there is abundance; it arises, and derives its significance, out of the scarcity of the objects that become appropriated in a world in which people desire to benefit from their own work and sacrifice (Hume, 1902). For Hume, systems of justice protected property rights solely because of their utility. Criticising the protectionist arguments, Arnold Plant notes that when the security of property is adequately assured, property owners generally see to it that scarce means are directed to those uses, which within their knowledge and judgment are most productive of what they want (Plant, 1934).

Another strand of thought to emerge in the eighteenth century that was to play an important role in the centuries to come was the notion that man had a 'natural property right' in his own ideas. France enacted its first patent laws in 1791, which captured the spirit of the 'natural property right'. The Patent Act was later amended in 1800 and 1844. The preamble to the 1791 Act read as follows:

> that every novel idea whose realization or development can become useful to society belongs primarily to him who conceived it, and that it would be a violation of the rights of man in their very essence if an industrial invention were not regarded as the property of its creator.[12]

One of the main arguments put forth by Stanislas de Bouffle at the time of presenting the bill to the French Constitutional Assembly in 1790 was that a man's property in his ideas was more sacred than his property in things material. The above preamble, to a greater degree, captured and encapsulated the spirit of the arguments of the eighteenth-century pro-patent economists, who favoured the

10 As cited in Machlup and Penrose (May 1950) 9. See also Plant (1934) 30–51, where the author notes that Isambard Kingdom Brunel, one of the pioneering engineers in British history from the nineteenth century, believed that workers wasted their time and ruined themselves trying to think out patentable inventions, when development would be quicker if they were distracted from making improvements.

11 The authors, writing in 1950, observe that these arguments were still being used in the twentieth century in debates on the issue.

12 Schuller (1843), as cited in Machlup and Penroes (1950). See also Recht (1969), as cited in Bouckaert (1990) 791–792.

grant of a patent monopoly. Interestingly, under the French patent laws the inventors could decide if they wanted a patent for a period of five, ten or fifteen years, with the term being extendable through legislative action (Adam, 2008). Under this French law, the right of the author to act freely with his intellectual product was linked with the generalisation of the exclusivity for reproduction previously granted by the king to individual publishers. The legal protection of this exclusivity was granted to authors during their lifetimes and to their heirs for ten additional years. The protection afforded under the patent laws did not include theoretical or scientific discoveries without practical application, financial methods, medicines and items that could be covered by copyright (Adam, 2008).[13]

The leading powers in Europe were keen to recognise the rights of inventors and reward them with monopoly rights from an economic perspective. It should also be borne in mind that the laws introduced coincided with the industrial revolution, which was sweeping through Europe and across the Atlantic. In 1790, the US Congress introduced the new Patent Act, based on the copyright provisions contained in its Constitution.[14] Most importantly, the 1790 Act also effectively abolished patents for the importation of knowledge (Walterscheid, 1998).[15] The framers of the US Constitution perceived the patent system as one of incentives and rewards. In a letter written on 13 August 1813 to the inventor Isaac McPherson, Thomas Jefferson noted that

> [i]f nature has made any one thing less susceptible than all others of exclusive property, it is the action of the thinking power called an idea, which an individual may exclusively possess as long as he keeps it to himself; but the moment it is divulged, it forces itself into the possession of everyone, and the receiver cannot dispossess himself of it. Its peculiar character, too, is that no one possesses the less, because every other possesses the whole of it.[16]

He further added that

> ideas should freely spread from one to another over the globe, for the moral and mutual instruction of man, and improvement of his condition, seems to

13 The author opines that France was probably the first country to introduce systematic examinations of applications for privileges.

14 Article I, Section 8, Clause 8 of the United States Constitution expressly vests the US Congress to create patent and copyright laws upon a utilitarian foundation, and reads as follows: 'To promote the Progress of Science and useful Arts, by securing for limited Times to Authors and Inventors the exclusive Rights to their respective Writings and Discoveries.' This clause is also referred to as the 'Copyright Clause.' Although the actual author of the copyright clause is still unknown, most commentators believe that it was either James Madison or Charles C. Pinckney. See Fenning (1929) 438. See also Donner (1992). Here, the author observes that at the time of the US Constitutional Convention, twelve of the thirteen states had already enacted copyright laws.

15 The author notes that importation of patents faced criticism, and was abolished in the House and Senate debates, allowing patents only 'for matters not before known or used'.

16 The Letters of Thomas Jefferson 1743–1826.

> have been peculiarly and benevolently designed by nature, when she made them, like fire, expansible over all space, without lessening their density in any point, and like the air in which we breathe, move, and have our physical being, incapable of confinement or exclusive appropriation.
>
> (David, 1993)

Interestingly, Jefferson was not in favour of the argument of the French philosophers that inventors and authors had a 'natural rights' claim to property in their creations. He was clear in his view that inventions cannot be a subject of property in nature.[17] His comments came two decades after the passing of the first US laws on the subject in 1790. The fact that Jefferson was the principle author of the US Declaration of Independence and the third president of the United States cannot be ignored here.

The nineteenth and twentieth centuries were to witness a proliferation of inventions across the fields of science, a further expansion to the rights of inventors through the introduction of industrial properties in more countries across Europe, and the introduction of such laws into colonies of European powers (which will be discussed in later chapters of the book). James Watts, the eighteenth-century inventor, stated that he 'feared that an engineer's life without patent was not worthwhile'(Walterscheid, 1996), which summed up the growing sense of importance of inventors during the industrial revolution and the need for recognition of their contribution to the society's economic growth through the issue of patents. The leading European nations along with the US were to forge international conventions to protect both patents and copyrights in the nineteenth century, which was to later on become a compulsory component of the TRIPS Agreement.

2.1 *Intellectual property rights and the control of 'knowledge'*

The term 'IP right' has come to denote a whole set of intangible property rights which can be identified broadly under patents, copyrights, trademarks and trade secrets. As mentioned earlier, the foundations of economic theories are deeply entrenched in utilitarianism, which also provides the philosophical basis for property rights, both tangible and intangible. In this section, the author seeks to analyse some of the key economic theories to emerge in the twentieth century on the subject of IP rights, which lay the foundations for the creation of an international IP rights protection regime to come in the form of the TRIPS Agreement under the auspices of the WTO. This section will also briefly study some of the views on the subject expressed in the twenty-first century. Currently, as it stands, the

17 Jefferson also argued, '[i]nventions then cannot, in nature, be a subject of property. Society may give an exclusive right to the profits arising from them, as an encouragement to men to pursue ideas which may produce utility, but this may or may not be done, according to the will and convenience of the society, without claim or complaint from anybody.' See David (1993); The Letters of Thomas Jefferson 1743–1826.

principal policy objective of IP laws is the promotion of new and improved works through the recognition and creation of property rights, regardless of whether it is in the realm of expressive media, chemicals and pharmaceuticals, technology, or other forms of creative work. Hence, it will be beneficial for our purposes to present a more contemporary analysis of the economic foundations of IP rights and the justification for the grant of exclusive rights for inventions and other similar intangibles. The study will initially focus on IP in general, and thereafter proceed to focus on patent rights, and more particularly on pharmaceutical patents.

The mainstream economics profession has consistently argued that inventors need support and protection from the government for their innovations in order to maintain an incentive for creative inquiry. The economic justification for protection of IP rights is founded on the premise that unless an invention or a creation is compensated at its full social value, there will be very little incentive to undertake or engage in such activities (Trebilcock, 2013).[18] Patent rights are deliberate creations of statue law, and it is the intention of the legislators that the beneficiary shall be placed in a position to secure an income from the monopoly conferred upon him by placing restrictions on the supply of the information (Plant, 1934). Grant of such rights is intended to stimulate innovation by allowing the rights holder to work his/her patented product for a definite period to recover the investment, and also to make a profit. Such exclusive rights are designed to empower the rights holder to prevent third parties from unauthorised use of the subject matter. So, one can assume that the statutes creating and granting patent rights monopolies would not have continued to remain in statute books, in the absence of a widespread expectation of public advantage from their operation. The dissenting tradition has maintained the position that government action of any kind, including the awarding of copyrights and patents, is unnecessary to stimulate such activity (Plant, 1934). The picture that emerges is a debate of polarised views, with one side arguing that ideas should benefit the public and the other side arguing that individuals should benefit from their ideas.

There had been a fundamental shift in conventional thinking of trade as only goods-oriented, which was brought about as a result of the sheer significance of IP to developed economies (Marcellin, 2010) in the latter part of the twentieth century. The modern-day IP rights principles are strongly modelled on the US IP rights regime, which in turn is severely influenced by the pharmaceutical, computing, and music and motion picture industries. Today, much of the value of the leading corporate bodies in the world is estimated by their portfolio of intangible assets, which range from the better-defined forms of IP – patents and copyrights, to the least tangible of the intangibles – trade secrets and trademarks (Menell and Scotchmer, 2007). Calandrillo explains the justification behind the US IP regime as being built on the hypothesis that it is socially desirable to encourage and produce many types of information, whose value to society far exceeds its

18 The authors observe that 'in terms of neo-classical trade theory, whether a particular country will want stronger or weaker intellectual property protection will depend on whether its comparative advantage lies more in innovation or in the imitation and adaptation of others' innovations.'

developmental costs (Calandrillo, 1998). Calandrillo asserts that most supporters of the US incentive system ignore the exorbitant costs it involves and the restrictions placed upon the availability of information generated by the system. Needless to say, IP rights confer an exclusive right to exploit the protected subject matter, or in other words, confer a right on the titleholder to prevent third parties from using the protected knowledge without authorisation (Correa, 2003). Non-rivalrous goods, which include knowledge (Stiglitz, 1999), can be made available for public use, usually at low cost and sometimes at no cost.[19] Joseph Stiglitz, the Nobel laureate, argues that Thomas Jefferson anticipated the modern concept of public good when he wrote to Isaac McPherson, the inventor in 1813, as follows: 'he who receives an idea from me, receives instruction himself without lessening mine; as he who lights his taper at mine, receives light without darkening me'.[20] But knowledge can be made excludable through actions by its possessor or through legal means.[21] Menell and Scotchmer posit the argument that knowledge is 'non-excludable' in its natural state; even if someone claims to own the knowledge, it is difficult to exclude others from using it. IP laws attempt to solve this problem by legal means, by granting exclusive use of the protected knowledge or creative work to the creator (Menell and Scotchmer, 2007). Through the device of 'intellectual property', the inventor can control entry and exclude users from the intangible assets. Knowledge and intellectual products are intangible and not appropriable, unlike tangible goods which are appropriable and separable from the commons (Muzaka, 2011). Also, the 'consumption' of intangible goods would leave the same quantity and quality of such goods to be consumed and enjoyed by others (Hughes, 1988).[22]

As it stands, laws relating to IP rights are based on the premise that it encourages innovation. Some commentators, though, have expressed their reservations to this argument. First, it is difficult to establish this position, and second, IP rights

19 Lemley (1997) 995, notes that public goods are 'nonrivalrous' as everyone can benefit from them once they are produced. See also Gruner (2011), where the author argues that patents are mistakenly described as 'nonrivalrous' property, and patent rights actually govern nonrivalrous actions of parties using patented inventions, besides regulating highly rivalrous allocations of scarce resources to the production of patented inventions.

20 See David (1993), where it is argued by the author that Jefferson grasped the essential point that the cost of transmitting useful knowledge in codified form is negligible, when compared with the cost of creating it, and that for society's need to encourage the pursuit of ideas, such information should be distributed freely.

21 See for example Correa (2003), who opines that a company may prevent its competitors from knowing how a particular manufacturing process operates by tightly controlling access to its physical premises and preventing the disclosure of relevant data by its employees. See also Kinsella (2001), who strongly argues that in today's world, the institution of intellectual property rights deliberately creates scarcity when none existed before to enable the commodification and appropriation of otherwise plentiful, nonrivalrous intellectual goods.

22 The author also observes that much of the IP generated 'is produced only after considerable financial investment, whether it be in the research laboratory or in the graduate education of the scientist using the facility.' And that '[o]ne cannot call the history of intellectual property a purely proletarian struggle.'

attempt to restrict the use of knowledge in one way or another and pose potential impediments to diffusion and cumulative innovation (Stiglitz, 2008; Menell and Scotchmer, 2007). The number of patents granted in a technologically fast-growing world, especially set against the backdrop of a globalised economy, requires a different philosophical basis and a clear set of theories to justify their grant than what was presented in the nineteenth century US and Europe, as the rationale for grant of a monopoly has changed significantly.[23] Until the early part of the 1990s, very little empirical research was done on the impact of economics on public policy in the area of IP rights, especially in comparison to the influence of professional writings in areas such as antitrust and taxation (Besen, 1991). Of all the IP rights within the legal system, the patent right is considered the most powerful, as it enables the rights holder (patentee) to exclude all others from making, selling or using the subject matter of a valid patent for a prescribed period of time (Besen, 1991).[24] In practice, the patent offers the rights holder the incentive of a statutory right to exclude others from use as a means of inducing activity. It can be observed that the right of the patent owner is conditioned on the disclosure of the subject matter to the public when the patent is issued. Also, such rights allow the patentee to obtain the reward for the innovation by sale of the right conferred for a fee/royalty, or to retain the exclusive exploitation rights (Katz and Shapiro, 1985).[25] Currently, under the TRIPS Agreement the term of the patent granted is for a period of twenty years, but some pharmaceutical patent holders are known to extend this term beyond the said period through the practice of evergreening.[26]

2.2 *Patents: an economic analysis*

An economic analysis of law takes into account the affordability, and at times the justification, of the introduction/implementation of a particular law into a legal

23 For instance, significant changes have taken place in the legal approach to the grant of patents to software since the late 1970s. When VisiCalc was developed as the first computer spreadsheet program in 1979, the US Patent Office, relying upon US Supreme Court case laws, took the position that the mathematical algorithms in computer programs were incapable of being protected as a subject matter. This position was to change when the US Supreme Court in the *Diamond v. Diehr* case 450 U.S. 175, 185–187 (1981) held that controlling the execution of a physical process, by running a computer program, did not preclude patentability of the invention as a whole, and found patentable subject matter in a process utilizing a computer algorithm.

24 The patentee can even prevent an independent subsequent discoverer of the same subject matter from making, using or selling it.

25 The authors argue that major innovations are not normally licensed, but equally efficient firms will tend to license minor innovations, and that for some innovations, licensing is both privately and socially undesirable.

26 Patent-holding TNPCs are known to extend the period of patent through the practice of evergreening, which is also referred to as 'patent-layering' and 'life-cycle management.' This practice effectively blocks the entry of generics into the market. See generally Glasgow (2001). India, a developing country and a big player in the generics market, introduced provisions in its domestic patent legislation to check the practice of evergreening. See chapter 7 for a discussion on the legislative measures taken by India to check the practice of evergreening.

environment. Such an analysis of any laws enacted, or that which is sought to be enacted, can always present an interesting insight into the political and economic policy objectives for the introduction of the law in question. In the 1960s, Guido Calabresi and Ronald Coase were the first to attempt and apply economic analysis in a systematic way to areas of law that did not purport to regulate economic relationships (Calabresi, 1961; Ronald Coase, 1960).[27] Edmund Kitch, a legal scholar and economist, thinks that although good progress was made in the understanding of the economics of IP rights in the twentieth century, much still remains to be done (Kitch, 2000). Kitch, while identifying recurring errors in the literature on the subject matter, posits the strong view that writers over time had repeatedly analysed IP rights on the assumption that they confer an economic monopoly on the rights holder, protecting him/her from competition and also allowing to sell into a market with a downward sloping demand curve.[28] He further argues that the characterisation of patents as a monopoly can only be true if the claims cover all of an economically relevant market, *i.e.*, there is no alternative way for competitors to provide the same economic functionality to their customers without infringing on the claims. The key error that Kitch identifies in most analyses on the subject is the use of the basic diagram/graph to study the competitive market in which the parameters are not clearly identified, and thus, according to him 'the market reflected in the diagram is not the market for the IP right itself'.[29] For Kitch, the empirical question of whether IP rights confer any economic monopoly, although persistently raised in the literature, is not properly addressed.[30] It is hard to brush aside the arguments of Kitch on the issue, as it questions the very premise of the justification for the grant of a monopoly right for patents (Kitch, 1977, 2000).

Kitch also notes that much of the analysis of IP rights proceeds on the footing that an author or inventor creates a work or an invention and then wishes to exploit it commercially. This analysis, according to Kitch, conveniently leaves out of the equation the interaction between IP rights on any one work or invention and the creation of other works and inventions – in other words, it omits or ignores the fact that authors make use of existing cultural elements, and likewise,

27 Both Calabresi and Coase are considered as pioneers in the field of new economic analysis of law. See also Posner (1975) 759–760.

28 Kitch argues that a clear distinction is to be made 'between the issue of whether intellectual property rights confer an economic monopoly, and thus impose the social welfare cost associated with monopoly, and the fact that intellectual property rights systems have costs – as does any system of property rights.'

29 Kitch opines that all systems of property rights involve costs to define the scope of their rights, in detecting and preventing trespass, and also 'in foreclosing particular productive opportunities that might be possible if the property system did not exist. Any system of property rights is appropriately subject to examination as to whether the benefits of the property system outweigh these costs, but that examination has nothing to do with the social welfare loss caused by economic monopolies.'

30 See Lemley (1997), where the author makes an interesting observation that while some IP rights 'may in fact give their owner power in an economically relevant product market, most do not; they merely prevent others from competing to sell copies of a particular product, not from selling different products that compete with the original' (p. 996).

inventors build on the work of inventors who preceded them (Kitch, 2000).[31] Suzzane Scotchmer posits a similar, but more emphatic argument on the point by stating that most innovators 'stand on the shoulders of giants, and never more so than in the current evolution of high technologies, where almost all technical progress builds on a foundation provided by earlier innovators' (Scotchmer, 1991). Scotchmer's primary argument is that later-day innovators simply bettered previous technologies, presenting examples from molecular biology, pharmaceuticals, computers and the cotton gin. She also observes that most economic literature on patenting has proceeded to

> study innovations in isolation, without focusing on the externalities or spillovers that early innovators confer on later innovators. But the cumulative nature of research poses problems for the optimal design of patent law that are not addressed by that perspective
>
> (Scotchmer, 1991: 30)

Arguments presented by both Kitch on the grant of monopoly rights and Scotchmer on innovation as opposed to invention cannot be taken lightly. One is tempted to raise the question, if it is indeed cumulative research leading to innovation, which 'invention' is patentable in the eye of the law and results in the 'inventor' being rewarded with exclusive patent rights?

Stiglitz also notes that many of the most important ideas, such as the mathematics that underlie the modern computer, the fundamentals behind atomic energy, lasers, *etc.*, are not protected by IP rights and have been used freely by academics and researchers, and also that academics disseminate their research findings without charging for them (Stiglitz, 2005). He is of the opinion that products of immediate commercial value can be produced without IP protection. Stiglitz strongly argues that an IP regime rewards innovators by creating a temporary monopoly power, which allows the rights holder to charge far higher prices than they could possibly charge if there were to be a competition, and in the above process, ideas are used and disseminated far less than they would be otherwise. For Stiglitz, once a monopoly is established under an IP regime it may be hard to dislodge it, as a monopoly can use its market power to crush competitors; he cites Microsoft as a classic example (Stiglitz, 2005). Machlup, in a study carried out on the US patent system for the Subcommittee on Patents, Trademarks, and Copyrights, observes that there is a general perception that 'property' and 'monopoly' are one and the same from an economic perspective, and the rights holder of an invention has a 'monopoly' over its use just as the owner of a house has a 'monopoly' of the use of the house, which according to Machlup could encumber economic analysis (Machlup, 1958).[32] In his view, 'property' and

31 Isaac Newton, when writing to Robert Hooke in 1676, noted that 'If I have seen a little further it is by standing on the shoulders of Giants.'

32 The author also observes that there is some confusion regarding the meaning and object of 'property' and 'property rights', which again is more troublesome to lawyers than economists, and how

'monopoly' have almost nothing to do with each other, for a seller owning his wares will have property but not monopoly, if others sell similar things in the same market. Likewise, a seller who controls the price of what he sells in a certain market may have a monopoly but not property (if he does not own what he sells), as there is no serious competition (Machlup, 1958). What one needs to be mindful of is that the term property, although used frequently in discussions, is indeed complex and highly political (besides being in every way legal), as it vests the individual with both tangible and intangible rights.

For Landes and Posner, the standard rationale of patent law is its efficiency of enabling the benefits of research and development to be internalised, and thereby promoting innovation and technological progress (Landes and Posner, 2003). According to them, the rationale for granting legal protection to inventions is the difficulty that a manufacturer may encounter whilst trying to recover the fixed costs of research and development when the product or process that embodies a new invention is readily 'copiable'. But this protection presents a greater danger, as the inventor would be enabled to charge a much higher price than he/she needs to recover for the actual costs of the invention, which will restrict access to the invention more than is necessary.[33] Landes and Posner also argue that the greater the patent protection afforded, the smaller the benefit to competitors, as there will be very little information available to them and any costs of working around the patent will be higher. They also assert that a patentee's monopoly mark-up, which is influenced by the degree of protection afforded, bears no direct relation to the fixed costs that the patentee incurred in the creation of the patented product. They also postulate that legislation and policy are for the most part for non-excludable public goods (Landes and Posner, 2003),[34] and that in contrast IP is an excludable public good. While the above argument appears to be the position as regards economic analysis of IP rights, the public-choice theory, seen as the driving force behind policy decisions, had neither succeeded in explaining the forces that brought into being the system of property rights that is fundamental to a capitalist economy nor said anything about the extension of that system to encompass IP (Landes and Posner, 2003).

Writing in 1934, the economist Arnold Plant expressed the view that property rights in patents, unlike other properties, do not arise out of scarcity of the objects which become appropriated, as they were not the 'consequences of scarcity', and that that they were deliberate creations of statute law (Plant, 1934). Plant also opined that property rights in patents made possible the creation of a scarcity of the products appropriated, which could not otherwise be maintained. David

---

quite often the controversial idea of property right in an invention is confused with the non-controversial idea of a property right in a patent.

33 Landes and Posner also note that this fear may explain the reason for the term of a patent being shorter than the term of a copyright.

34 The authors observe that a person can enjoy the full benefit of the statute, regulation or other policy in question without having to contribute monetarily to the collective effort that was necessary to get it passed in the first place.

Hume, the eighteenth-century philosopher, had earlier argued that property had no purpose where it is found in abundance, as it derives its significance through the scarcity of the objects which become appropriated, and that systems of justice were keen to protect property purely due to their utility (Hume and Beauchamp, 2006). Richard Posner, in a more recent contribution made to a blog, expresses the concern that both patent and copyright protection, particularly the former, may be excessive. Posner argues that the cost of inventing must be comparable to the cost of copying in order to determine the optimal patent protection for an inventor, and that when patent protection is too strongly in favour of the inventor, market efficiency is decreased (Posner, 2012). Posner also avers that pharmaceutical drugs are the 'poster child' for patent protection, and that few other products in the market have the same characteristics that make patent protection indispensable to the pharmaceutical industry (Posner, 2012).[35] The most interesting, if not scathing, comment to come from Posner concerns the twenty-year duration of the patent protection, which he feels confers no real benefit – except to enable the producer to extract licence fees from firms wanting to make a different product that incorporates the invention. Posner concludes the brief with a parting shot that the need for reform of both patent and copyright laws is sufficiently acute to warrant serious attention from the US Congress and the courts (Posner, 2012). In his view, the long protection given to patents under current US laws leads to profiteering by the rights holder, which defeats the very basis for the grant of a patent protection. This strong criticism can be extended to the twenty-year patent protection granted under the TRIPS Agreement, which was in turn shaped by US-led developed countries during the Uruguay Round of negotiations. Gary Becker, who jointly wrote the blog with Posner, made similar comments by noting that the patent system might in fact discourage innovations (Becker, 2012).

From the preceding discussions, one can postulate the argument that economic theorists are yet to succeed in producing a convincing and coherent set of principles to justify IP protection for intangible rights, and any protection that IP (*i.e.*, patents) enjoys currently is driven by a state's interest to protect its knowledge base/patent base, which in turn is the source for its various industrial activities. This argument can be extended to IP rights' global applications too, as the American IP protection policy narrative has been embraced by developed nations and applied internationally through the WTO to its member states. What one witnesses under the TRIPS Agreement is the enshrinement of IP laws, which were developed by schools of thought based on 'wealth maximisation' (Posner, 1983),[36] and the establishment of an international regime providing

35 For Posner, the pharmaceutical and software industries are the extremes as far as the social benefits and costs of patent protection are concerned. Posner opines that patent protection is overall excessive and that major reforms are necessary.

36 Posner advocates and argues for 'wealth maximization,' which he views as the guiding principle of common law. He puts forth the argument that the basic function of law from an 'economic, or wealth-maximization perspective is to alter incentives.'

strong IP rights protection for innovations, which are held and exploited by patent-holding developed nations, to the detriment of non-owners through the multilateral trade institution of the WTO. This approach to IP rights protection goes even beyond the utilitarian principles expounded by Jeremy Bentham, as it completely disregards other human values, including the needs of the society. One cannot ignore the fact that we live in an information-driven society, where developed economies are strong information producers and would naturally be inclined to support the establishment of strong laws to protect their IP rights and serve their own interests.

One can also argue that information is knowledge and *vice versa*. IP rights are the tools, or building blocks, of a sound knowledge economy, and anyone that controls knowledge has a greater say in the sustenance of the knowledge economy. In an information-driven, knowledge-based economy, the contours of the landscape are hence determined by IP rights policies which are viewed as fundamental to the organizational principles. IP rights policies determine the way in which knowledge relations are structured and governed in a given environment (Ghafele, 2008). The modern, or contemporary, perception of IP rights is strongly influenced and shaped by US expansionist economic policies and lawmaking. It has its foundations in utilitarianism, Lockean model of natural laws, besides being strongly influenced by the common law notions of property rights and mercantilism. This understanding of IP rights, as propagated by Anglo-Saxon jurisprudence, and later to be developed by Anglo-American jurisprudence (which in turn is influenced by Posnerian economic analysis from the 1970s), has paved the way for a winner-take-all 'wealth maximisation' policy of IP lawmaking. One should note that the US and its allies (developed countries with a similar vision) have a strong knowledge-based economy and can afford to promote an IP rights regime which grants the rights holder an extended term of monopoly over information/knowledge, which makes any IP product relying on such information scarce and unaffordable in the developing world. This approach to IP rights has, most notably, a significant impact on pharmaceutical products and affects access to medicines in developing countries and LDCs, as most pharmaceutical patents are held in the strong knowledge-based economies of developed countries.

2.3 *Expansion of intellectual property laws: the haunting colonial legacy*

IP rights, which evolved in the Middle Ages (Correa, 2003; Machlup and Penrose, 1950),[37] was introduced by the European colonial powers into their respective colonies and dominions in the nineteenth century. It will be beneficial for the purposes of the current study to cast our thoughts backwards in time to understand how colonisation facilitated the expansion of IP laws (industrial property,

37 Machlup and Penrose (1959) observe that apart from its expression in statute form (Statute of Monopolies of 1623), the patent system is not chiefly an English creation.

copyrights and trademarks) of the European colonial powers in the nineteenth century (Deere, 2009; Okediji, 2003).[38] This part of the enquiry becomes necessary, as some of the difficulties in accessing affordable medicines in the developing countries are still rooted in the colonial past, especially in the realm of IP laws introduced during the colonial era. The international movement on IP standards started in the nineteenth century from developed countries to developing countries, or from key industrialised Western states to developing countries/former colonies (Drahos, 2002).[39] Carolyn Deere notes that those IP laws introduced into colonies during the colonial era embodied concepts alien to many traditional and indigenous approaches to knowledge and innovation, as Western conceptions of privately held rights over intellectual assets had no local cultural or legal roots. Besides, the colonial administrators held the traditional laws of their dominions in low regard, as they did not serve the commercial interests of the colonizers (Okediji, 2003).[40]

The IP laws were introduced in the colonies to protect the interests of the colonial administrators, or the interests of the native citizens of the colonial powers over the natives of the colonies. The IP laws imposed were purely aimed at extracting wealth from the colonies rather than seeking to educate or promote knowledge in the colonies. Deere makes an interesting observation that Britain, during the colonial era, was keen to emphasise the promotion of the common law legal profession in its colonies to generate an English legal culture, but this practice was rarely extended to the realm of IP laws. Following their independence from colonial rule, most developing countries in Africa chose to retain the legal system, laws and institutions of governance established during the colonial era by the colonial powers, including IP laws (Okediji, 2003).[41] In most of the former colonies, the establishment of national IP laws only started in the wake of independence from colonial rule (Deere, 2009).[42] Deere notes that in the Americas,

38 Britain introduced its then prevailing laws (including IP laws) to its colonies. Likewise, France too applied its own IP laws to its colonies.

39 The author refers to the case of Philippines, where Spanish patent laws were introduced, only to be later replaced by US patent laws. Similarly, in Korea, Japanese patent laws were introduced and replaced later by US patent laws. Likewise, in India and Malaysia, Britain introduced English patent laws in the late nineteenth century and early twentieth century.

40 The author notes that when the Paris Convention for the Protection of Industrial Property was concluded in 1883, the respective colonial masters swept non-Western societies in Africa and Asia under the aegis of the IP property system through the agency of colonial rule. The author also notes that despite a limited membership to the Paris Convention of 1883 and the Berne Convention of 1886 by developed countries, the colonies and foreign territories controlled by a few European sovereigns made the geographic scope of the treaties significant.

41 After independence, countries and many developing LDCs continued to have as their own domestic laws the old, antiquated Acts and ordinances of the colonial era. The author notes that given the socio-economic conditions in most of the former colonies, existing IP laws were not a reform priority, as they were either not beneficial to the domestic industries or deemed irrelevant to the domestic public.

42 In Latin America and the Caribbean, IP laws were established in the wake of independence from the Spanish and Portuguese in the early nineteenth century, as opposed to Africa, Asia and the

and in some of the former Asian colonies, the era of decolonisation also sparked efforts to substantially revise their IP laws and related policies.

A number of countries that emerged from colonial rule in the twentieth century promulgated IP laws that still closely resembled earlier colonial laws, or those of the erstwhile colonial powers (Deere, 2009),[43] and in most cases, did not reflect on-the-ground realities (Kongolo, 2000).[44] A few former colonies, such as India, moved towards a product patent regime during the 1970s (Sundaram, 2014a)[45] and, as a result, also emerged as a key player in the generic drugs market. In the Americas, countries such as Brazil, Mexico and Argentina, whilst revising their IP laws, also lowered standards of patent protection to stimulate local production of generic medicines. Deere also notes that the Andean Community,[46] comprising Chile, Colombia, Bolivia, Ecuador and Peru, followed a reformist agenda, in pursuit of a vision for industrial development and regional integration, and adopted common rules on foreign direct investment (FDI), IP rights and technology transfer (Deere, 2009). One can observe that in the post-colonial era, the former colonies adopted different approaches towards their IP laws and policies, where again the policies were shaped by the prevalent colonial legal system, besides other factors including social, economic and political objectives of the newly emerged sovereign states. The post-colonial era restructuring and legal reformation of laws in the former colonies was not a complete purge of the laws introduced by erstwhile colonial powers, but was a process through which efforts

---

Pacific, where IP laws were introduced by colonial powers in the late nineteenth century. The author points out that several countries in the Americas promulgated formal IP laws far earlier than did other developing countries, and indeed earlier than many developed countries.

43 Deere notes that the former British colonies enacted copyright laws based on the same 1911 British Copyright Act that served as the foundation for their colonial laws. Similarly, a number of former French colonies in Africa adopted copyright laws that replicated those of France at the given point in time, and others chose to keep the laws introduced during colonial rule.

44 The author, discussing the two major African regional IP organisations, *viz*., African Regional Industrial Property Organization (ARIPO) and Organisation Africaine de la Propriété Intellectuelle (OAPI), makes an interesting observation that the systems of protection provided under the said organisations do not reflect the African realities. This, in Kongolo's view, is down to the fact that the organisations are modelled after the Western style of IP protection, which does not always correspond to and fit the African realities and environment.

45 India in the 1970s moved away from the IP laws introduced under British rule, based on the recommendations contained in the Justice Iyyengar Committee Report, and successfully introduced a process patent system as opposed to a product patent system with regards to chemical and pharmaceutical patents. But this position was to change with its membership in the WTO and the introduction of TRIPS-compliant IP laws. See chapter 7 for a detailed discussion.

46 In 1969, the Cartagena Agreement (the 'Pact') was signed by Bolivia, Chile, Colombia, Ecuador and Peru. The objective for the Pact was the creation of a Customs Union and a Common Market. In 1996, through the Protocol of Trujillo, the Pact was renamed as the Andean Community. Venezuela joined the Pact in 1973, but under the leadership of Hugo Chavez it withdrew its membership in 2006, claiming that Free Trade Agreements (FTAs) signed by Colombia and Peru with the US caused damage to the spirit of the community. Likewise, under the leadership of Augusto Pinochet, Chile withdrew from the Pact in 1976. Currently, it has four members, five associate members and one observer country.

were made to remove laws that were not relevant to the newly emerged state, while retaining some of the colonial-era laws that were still relevant for practical purposes.

As regards the introduction of former colonies to international conventions, the methodology adopted by the colonial powers were procedural in nature. It is also important to bear in mind that the international conventions in turn were drafted at the behest of former colonial powers. In the latter part of the nineteenth century, the two key international conventions, *viz.*, the Paris Convention[47] and the Berne Convention,[48] were codified and designed to enhance the degree of protection that IP rights holders from developed countries enjoyed in overseas jurisdictions (Deere, 2009).[49] With very few developing nations participating in the negotiations, only a handful became parties to the two conventions. Interestingly, almost half of the original signatories to the Paris Convention lacked national patent regimes at the time of ratification of the conventions (Roffe and Vea, 2008; Deere, 2009). Brazil, one of the original signatory nations and a former colony of Portugal, was an exception, as it had established a patent system in the early part of the nineteenth century (Sundaram, 2014b).[50] Through the provisions contained in Article 19 of the Berne Convention,[51] the former colonial powers of Britain, France, Italy, Belgium, Portugal and Spain acceded their colonies to the Convention (Deere, 2009; Okediji, 2003; Roffe and Vea, 2008).[52] Through this mechanism, the colonial powers were also able to pick and choose the colonies and dominions that would be covered in their document of accession (Okediji, 2004). In short, during the colonial era, the colonies and dominions did not have a say in their accession process to the conventions. In many cases, post-independence, the former colonies continued to be signatories

47 The Paris Convention for the Protection of Industrial Property 1883, as amended on 28 September 1979.

48 The Berne Convention for the Protection of Literary and Artistic Works 1883, as amended on 28 September 1979.

49 The two treaties were also aimed at replacing the loose network of reciprocal IP arrangements that European colonial powers had in place in some of the bilateral commercial treaties in the nineteenth century. Notably, both the Paris and Berne Conventions enshrined the principle of national treatment, which provides that signatory countries shall extend to foreign nationals the same advantages, rights and legal remedies against infringement as enjoyed by their own nationals.

50 Brazil, one of the original signatories to the Paris Convention, had a patent regime traceable to the nineteenth century. In 1809, Dom João VI, to stimulate invention in an economy primarily driven by agriculture, introduced a system of licensing, or *alvará*. Later, in 1830, Brazil passed laws recognising the rights of inventors.

51 The original Article 19 of the Berne Convention 1886 reads as follows: '[1] Countries acceding to this Convention shall also have the right to accede thereto at any time on behalf of their colonies or foreign possessions. [2] They may for this purpose make either a general declaration of adhesion that includes all their colonies or possessions, or expressly indicate only those which are included, or which are excluded.' See also *Guide to the Berne Convention for the Protection of Literary and Artistic Works (Paris Act, 1971)*, WIPO Publication No 615 (E) (1978).

52 As a French protectorate, Tunisia was one of the original signatories to the Paris Convention through adherence.

without the actual need to be part of the regime, as they were mostly unaware of the necessity to have such legislations in their statute books, which were originally designed to serve their former colonial masters. In the post-colonial era, a number of larger developing countries were able to delay their accession to international IP conventions (Deere, 2009).[53] A majority of developing countries in the Americas postponed accession to the Paris Convention until the 1990s, as they were sceptical of the merits and benefits of IP conventions (Roffe and Vea, 2008).[54] In most of their former colonies and dominions, the colonial powers left behind a network of legal systems and institutions, which would in later years assist in the introduction of a much wider and far-reaching IP rights regime with the creation of the WTO in the latter part of the twentieth century.

3 IP rights policy *vis-à-vis* human rights: an analysis

One key area of law that is constantly overlooked in the debates surrounding the importance of IP policy and legislation in facilitating and promoting innovation in society is how IP rights – in particular the grant of patent rights – possibly affect the human rights of the individuals who constitute the same society. The lacuna in both legal and policy debates on the justification for grant of property rights for intangibles has particularly gained in significance in the case of pharmaceutical patents, as access to medicines has become a major issue since the entry into force of the TRIPS Agreement. The importance of balancing human rights with private rights, especially in granting pharmaceutical patent rights, had been well highlighted in academic debates in recent times. However, it was not considered seriously and embraced at the national level in developed countries in the lead-up to the entry of the WTO to shape any serious policy outcomes on IP rights. As a result, there is an inadequate understanding of the complex justification of IP rights policy, legislation, conventions and, most importantly, the TRIPS Agreement, which while extending the period of patents on pharmaceutical and other patents to twenty years, has effectively outlawed process patents of pharmaceuticals.

It will benefit our enquiry to start with an analysis of the relevant provisions of the international human rights conventions where creators' rights are recognised. Firstly, the Universal Declaration of Human Rights 1948 (UDHR) provides as follows:

> Everyone has the right to the protection of the moral and material interests resulting from any scientific, literary or artistic production of which he [or she] is the author.

53 India became a member of the Paris Convention only in 1998, and Pakistan in 2004.

54 Roffe and Vea point out that the general view prevailing in Latin America was that there was no benefit in joining a convention that was not flexible enough to accommodate the needs of the local economy. Also, the national treatment principle of the Paris Convention was viewed as a barrier to the design of national regimes dealing with industrial property. They were to become signatories to the conventions following the entry of the TRIPS Agreement.

The UDHR, seen as a milestone in the history of human rights, arose directly from the experience of World War II (Helfer and Austin, 2011).[55] The creators' rights are also identified and recognised in the International Covenant on Economic, Social and Cultural Rights 1966 (ICESCR).[56] These solemn assertions are to be found in the international conventions passed post–World War II. Some commentators have even speculated that the protection of creators' rights found in the above international instruments was no accident (Torremans, 2004; Helfer and Austin, 2011).[57] Similarly, commitment to the guarantee of the right to good health is also to be found in the constitutions of developing nations. These guarantees, or undertakings, made at the highest levels of governance have now been jeopardised by the development of international instruments, through both the WTO under multilateral trade agreements and other plurilateral agreements negotiated by developed nations and their trading partners. There is no reference to human rights in the Paris Convention or the Berne Convention, which is not surprising, as both conventions were created in the nineteenth century, during the colonial era. More worryingly, the Rome Convention[58] and the WTO TRIPS Agreement do not contain any reference to human rights in the body of the text. The TRIPS Agreement requires all member states to comply with pre-existing international agreements on IP laws, including the Paris Convention and Berne Convention. But all the above treaties do refer to the protections granted to authors and inventors as 'rights'. Helfer and Austin take the position that the principal justification for such rights lies not in deontological claims about the inalienable liberties of human beings, but rather in the economic and instrumental benefits that flow from the protection of IP across national borders (Helfer and Austin, 2011).

IP rights protection is alluded to in the human rights protection found in the cultural rights of Article 25 of the UDHR and Article 15 of the ICESCR. Principles of human rights demand that all individuals are granted or,

55 Helfer and Austin note that UDHR came to be drafted less than three years after the end of World War II, and that science and technology as well as copyright-based propaganda was abused for atrocious purposes during the war by those who lost the war. It was felt that the best way to avoid repeating such an abuse was to recognize that everyone had a share in the benefits of such technological advances and that, at the same time, those who made valuable contributions were entitled to protection. See also generally Torremans (2004) 5.

56 ICESCR entered into force on 3 January 1976, and as of July 2015 has been ratified by 164 countries. Although the US signed the Covenant, it has not ratified it.

57 Commenting on the inclusion of Article 27 in the UDHR, legal scholars note that the strong initial criticism that IP was not properly speaking a human right, or that it had already attracted sufficient protection under property rights in general, was eventually defeated by the coalition who voted in favour, as they felt that moral rights deserved and needed protection and met the human rights standard, and by those who felt the ongoing internationalization of copyright needed a boost and that this could be a tool in this respect.

58 International Convention for the Protection of Performers, Producers of Phonograms and Broadcasting Organizations 1961 (adopted at Rome, Italy on 26 October 1961), also referred to as the Rome Convention.

are presumed to have the right to good health. Article 25(1) of the UDHR provides as follows:

> Everyone has the right to a standard of living adequate for the health and well-being of himself and of his family, including food, clothing, housing and medical care and necessary social services, and the right to security in the event of unemployment, sickness, disability, widowhood, old age or other lack of livelihood in circumstances beyond his control.

Likewise, Article 15.1(c) of the ICESCR recognises the right of the creator to 'benefit from the protection of the moral and material interests resulting from any scientific, literary or artistic production of which he is the author', and such expression entitles 'both individuals or groups or communities to a right to IP protection for his own creation' (Xiong, 2012; Chapman, 2001).[59] Similar expressions are to be found in Article 27 of the UDHR regarding the individual's right to 'the protection of the moral and material interest resulting from any scientific, literary or artistic production of which he is the author'.[60] What is glaringly missing here is the exact scope of the right to 'scientific, literary or artistic production', and it is also unclear if it includes inventors and patent protection (Xiong, 2012). While examining the implications of IP rights over human rights, policymakers, inter-governmental and non-governmental organizations, international bureaucrats and scholars usually employ the conflict approach or the coexistence approach (Helfer, 2003).[61] The conflict approach views the two sets of rights as being in fundamental conflict, and the coexistence approach considers them as essentially compatible.[62] Professor Peter Yu notes that while the two approaches may have their own benefits and drawbacks, both ignore or overlook the fact that some of the attributes of IP rights are indeed protected in international instruments and/or regional human rights instruments, while other attributes do not have any human rights basis at all (Yu, 2006). The UN Sub-Commission on the Promotion and Protection of Human Rights and the WTO have adopted the conflict approach and the coexistence approach respectively. Yu presents a third approach and strongly argues that instead of inquiring whether human rights and

59 Chapman expresses a strong view that the inventor can be a group or a community as well as an individual, which is in contrast with the individualism of IP.

60 Article 27, Universal Declaration of Human Rights 1948.

61 The author argues that allowing greater opportunities for airing a human rights perspective on IP issues will strengthen the legitimacy of the WTO and the WIPO.

62 For example, the UN Sub-Commission on the Promotion and Protection of Human Rights has adopted the 'conflict approach,' noting that 'actual or potential conflicts exist between the implementation of the TRIPS Agreement and the realization of economic, social and cultural rights'. See UN Commission on Human Rights, Sub-Commission on the Promotion and Protection of Human Rights, 'Intellectual Property Rights and Human Rights', Resolution 2000/7, Preamble, Recital 1 (17 August 2000) [Document E/CN.4/Sub.2/2000/2000/7]. In contrast, the WTO has adopted the 'coexistence' approach, emphasising the availability of built-in flexibilities in existing international trade agreements. See World Trade Organization (27 November 2000).

IP rights conflict or coexist with each other, one should most importantly identify the human attributes of IP rights and distinguish them from the non-human rights aspects of IP protection (Yu, 2006). The third approach suggested by Yu, to a certain degree, advances the position of the advocates of human rights and also those who seek a balance between the grant and protection of private rights and human rights.

The existing tensions between IP rights and human rights was summarised by the United Nations Committee on Economics, Social and Cultural Rights in 2001 as the 'allocation of rights over IP has significant economic, social and cultural consequences that can affect the enjoyment of human rights'.[63] These tensions are obviously driven by the manner in which creative works, cultural heritage and scientific knowledge are turned into property at an alarming pace, which has significant human rights implications (Matthews, 2010). Audrey Chapman opines that IP rights should be considered as human rights, as the three provisions of Article 15.1(c) of the ICESCR were viewed by drafters as intrinsically interrelated to one another, that the rights of authors and creators were understood as essential preconditions for cultural freedom, participation and scientific progress, and not as goods in themselves (Chapman, 2001). Chapman also argues that in order to be consistent with the provisions of Article 15, IP laws must assure that IP protections complement, fully respect and promote other components of Article 15. This caveat is served so that the rights of authors and creators facilitate rather than constrain cultural participation on the one hand, and scientific progress and access on the other. For Chapman, under the human rights approach, an author, artist or creator can be a group or a community as well as an individual. This approach strikes a balance between the rights of inventors and creators and the interests of the wider society within the IP paradigms and makes it far more explicit and exacting, which means the rights of the creator are not absolute but conditional on contributing to the common good and welfare of society (Chapman, 2001).[64] Yet another argument says that some aspects of IP rights have potentially adverse implications for human rights (Matthews, 2010), which finds support in the observations made in the study carried out by the High Commission on Human Rights on the impact of TRIPS Agreement on human rights. This study acknowledges that Article 15 of the ICESCR clearly identifies the need to balance the protection of both public and private interests.[65]

The UNHCR Committee on Economic, Social and Cultural Rights adopted General Comment 17, which elaborates on the right of everyone to benefit from

63 Statement by the United Nations Committee on Economic and Cultural Rights (UNCECR), *Substantive Issues Arising in the Implementation of the International Covenant on Economic, Social and Cultural Rights* – Follow-up session to the day of general discussion on Article 15.1(c), Monday 26 November 2001, Human Rights and Intellectual Property. United Nations Committee on Economic, Social and Cultural Rights, 14 December 2001, para 1 [Document E/C.12/2001/15].

64 Chapman takes the position that unless human rights advocates provide an effective intellectual and organizational counterweight to economic interests, the IP landscape in the coming years will be reshaped without adequate consideration of the impact of IP on human rights.

65 United Nations Commission on Human Rights (27 June 2001) p. 5.

the protection of the moral and material interests resulting from any scientific, literary or artistic production of which he/she is the author, as set out in Article 15.1(c), of the Covenant.[66] It is noted in General Comment 17 that human rights are fundamental and inalienable and are universal entitlements belonging to individuals and, under certain circumstances, groups of individuals and communities. It further elaborates that human rights are inherent to the human person as such, whereas IP rights are means through which states seek to provide incentives for inventiveness and creativity, encourage the dissemination of creative and innovative productions as well as the development of cultural identities, and preserve the integrity of scientific, literary and artistic productions for the benefit of society as a whole.[67] The most interesting comments come in paragraph 2 of the General Comments, where it is noted that human rights are timeless expressions of fundamental entitlements of the human person, whereas IP rights are of a temporary nature and can be revoked, licenced or assigned to third parties, and can also be allocated, limited in time and scope, traded, amended and even forfeited.[68] Besides, the scope of protection of the moral and material interests of an author provided for by Article 15.1(c), does not necessarily coincide with what is referred to as IP rights under national legislations or international instruments, and hence, it is important that IP rights are not sought to be balanced with the human rights recognised in Article 15.1(c).[69] A bare reading of the above international instruments causes confusion, as IP rights are identified as human rights, which has a far wider scope than the narrow private proprietorial right envisaged under modern instruments on IP rights, including the TRIPS Agreement. This has undermined the position of the advocates of human rights who witness IP rights being given preference over the human right to good health and life in the debate on access to affordable medicines. While the debate rages on, the expanded IP rights protection imposed through the WTO had caused unnecessary hardship and suffering in the developing countries and LDCs due to scarcity of access to affordable medicines. What is obvious from the foregoing discussion is that the relationship between IP rights and human rights remains unclear (Helfer, 2003; Helfer and Austin, 2011), which is to the greatest disadvantage of the real sufferers from the exploitation of IP rights by transnational pharmaceutical corporations.

Most member states of the WTO that have undertaken to implement the minimum standards of IP rights protection in the TRIPS Agreement have also ratified the ICESR, which means the member states have a double duty to implement – the minimum standards of the Agreement, and the human rights obligation under

66 General Comment No. 17: The right of everyone to benefit from the protection of the moral and material interests resulting from any scientific, literary or artistic production of which he is the author (Article 15(1)(c) of the Covenant), adopted by the UNHCR Committee on Economic, Social and Cultural Rights on 21 November 2005 (E/C.12/2005/GC/17).

67 General Comment 17 (no 163) para 1.

68 General Comment 17 (no 163) para 2.

69 General Comment 17 (no 163) paras 2–3.

ICESR (Dutfield and Suthersanan, 2008). The question we ask is, Should the member states interpret the Agreement as only safeguarding trade interests, or should it be read in the light of the importance of upholding the needs and interests of all market actors, including corporations and individual human beings? Importantly, do all international instruments, including the specialist TRIPS Agreement, strike the right balance between human rights and IP rights? Sadly, the literature available on the point seems to indicate that they do not strike a balance, and one can assume that IP rights have a more favoured position than human rights in this debate. Finding a link between the standards of TRIPS and human rights is not the same as saying that TRIPS takes a human rights approach to IP protection.[70] So, the primary question is whether TRIPS strikes a balance that is consistent with a human rights approach. Resolution 2000/7 of the UN Commission on Human Rights on intellectual property and human rights goes as far as to state that the WTO is 'a veritable nightmare' for certain sectors of humanity (UN Commission on Human Rights, 2000), in that the TRIPS Agreement in some ways encourages, or has as a side effect, some human rights violations (Papadopoulou, 2011). The report concludes thus:

> Since the implementation of the TRIPS Agreement does not adequately reflect the fundamental nature and indivisibility of all human rights, including the right of everyone to enjoy the benefits of scientific progress and its applications, the right to health, the right to food and the right to self- determination, there are apparent conflicts between the intellectual property rights embodied in the TRIPS Agreement, on the one hand, and international human rights law on the other.

The above resolution of the Sub-Commission on the Promotion and Protection of Human Rights also identifies the areas of actual or potential conflict between human rights and IP rights as an impediment resulting from the application of IP rights to the transfer of technology to developing countries; the consequences of plant variety rights and the patenting of genetically modified organisms for the enjoyment of the basic right to food; the reduction of control by communities (especially indigenous communities) over their own genetic and natural resources and cultural values, leading to accusations of 'biopiracy'; and restrictions on access to patented pharmaceuticals and the implications for the enjoyment of a basic right to health.[71] The resolution goes further to affirm the right to protection of the moral and material interests resulting from any scientific, literary or artistic production as a human right, which is however, subject

70 See for example The Report of the UN High Commissioner for Human Rights, *The Impact of the Agreement on Trade-Related Aspects of Intellectual Property Rights on Human Rights*, E/CN.4/Sub.2/2001/13, pp. 7–11.

71 UN Commission on Human Rights, Sub-Commission on the Promotion and Protection of Human Rights, Resolution 2000/7.

to limitations in the public interest. A year later in 2001, Resolution 2001/21[72] was adopted, wherein it was noted that the implementation of TRIPS did not adequately reflect the fundamental nature and indivisibility of all human rights, including the right of everyone to enjoy the benefits of scientific progress and its applications, and that there are apparent conflicts between the IP rights regime embodied in TRIPS, on the one hand, and international human rights law, on the other. The resolution also recommended that an assessment be made to study whether the patent 'as a legal instrument' was compatible with the promotion and protection of human rights, and the impact of the TRIPS Agreement on the rights of indigenous peoples. It is important to stress here that both Resolutions 2000/7 and 2001/21 of the Sub-Commission observe that human rights prevailed over all economic rights and should be taken into account in the drafting of economic rights policies.[73] Sadly, not much progress has been made since the making of the above two resolutions, as several economic policies have come to be drafted at the WTO, followed by subsequent agreements at the multilateral level on trade involving IP rights, and it is doubted if the above observation of the Sub-Commission was given serious consideration.

It is abundantly clear that a conflict exists between the 'private' interests of IP rights holders, which is contained in the TRIPS Agreement, and the 'social' or 'public' concerns found in international human rights law (Mwangi, 2007). Mwangi notes that the TRIPS Agreement has successfully tilted the balance inherent in IP laws away from the public interest, and in favour of IP rights holders. One of the major shortcomings of the TRIPS Agreement is that it does not have the promotion and protection of human rights at the heart of the aim of IP protection, but rather more as an exception. The promotion of health, nutrition, *etc.*, which are links to human rights, are all generally expressed in terms of exceptions to the rule. Further, the TRIPS Agreement only recognises individual rights by clearly stating in the preamble that IP rights are private rights, which ignores the creativity and innovation of groups and communities (Mwangi, 2007). This position undoubtedly weakens the objectives on human rights contained in the Agreement. The resolutions and reports produced by the UN Commission on Human Rights in the area of IP rights have been unanimous in their view, and note that there was a need for lawmakers to take international human rights into account in international economic policy formulation to emphasise the primacy of the former over the latter (Dutfield and Suthersanan, 2008). Dutfield and Suthersanan also note that none of the resolutions and reports suggest that IP rights *per se* conflict with human rights, but rather that the problems lie in the implementation of the TRIPS Agreement. The implication is that a concerted attempt must be made to interpret TRIPS as human rights norms.

72 UN Commission on Human Rights, Sub-Commission on the Promotion and Protection of Human Rights, 'Intellectual Property Rights and Human Rights', Resolution 2001/21, 16 August 2001 [Document E/CN.4/Sub.2/Res/2001/21].

73 UN, Sub-Commission Resolution 2000/7 at point 2 and Sub-Commission Resolution 2001/21 at point 7.

The right to health as found in international instruments, due to its indeterminacy and vagueness, makes it appear more aspirational rather than justiciable and renders it difficult to implement at the national level (Forman, 2005; Xiong, 2012).[74] Consequently, it is important to clarify the position of the right to health and its remit in international instruments. UDHR and other international instruments view IP rights as part of human rights, or in other words, IP rights are seen as being contained in human rights. This position only favours those seeking a much stronger and wider IP rights protection, which effectively sidelines all other social and public concerns at the heart of the human rights argument. As Santoro points out, negative rights require others to forbear from interfering with the right holder, whereas positive rights like the right to healthcare will require someone to act for or provide something to the right holder (Santoro, 2006). This, according to Santoro, also raises the question as to who exactly has the duty to honour the human right to drugs (Santoro, 2006; Forman, 2005). The problem clearly appears to be the mistake of trying to balance private rights (negative rights) with the right to health (positive right). Here, the right to health suffers a setback, as the private right that is sought to be balanced with the 'right to health' is also described as a human right, which it is not in actual terms. Thomas Pogge argues that the current international rules shaped by developed/wealthier countries contribute to massive deprivations among the disadvantaged and are therefore unjust, and those responsible for the design and imposition of the said rules are not merely failing to protect human rights but are actively violating the rights of billions (Pogge, 2008a). He further urges the developed nations to work toward reform or to compensate for the harm caused.

3.1 *Access to medicines as human right*

Improving access to affordable medicines in the developing countries and LDCs had been on the agenda of international bodies for well over four decades, resulting in the adoption of resolutions and declarations. These resolutions and declarations meant a clear commitment from developed nations and developing nations to devote time and resources to address the issue of access to medicines in developing countries and to draft relevant policies that facilitate access to healthcare in developing countries. In the 1980s, HIV/AIDS, a previously unknown disease, affected populations across the globe, with the most vulnerable populace coming from the developing and least developed parts of the world. While progress has been made in the treatment of the disease with the development of antiretroviral drugs (ARVs) in developed countries, they remain inaccessible to a majority of the populace in the developing countries due to the exorbitant pricing of the medicines. HIV/AIDS patients in developed countries have access to the best treatment options, and still live relatively healthily, but

74 Forman is of the strong opinion that the inclusion of the right to health in human rights treaties show that the right to health is a legal right, which entails obligations on states.

patients in developing countries and LDCs have little or no access to ARVs and proper medical treatment. The TNPCs in developed countries hold the patent rights to most medicines which offer the best options possible for the treatment of HIV/AIDS. By moving the protection of IP rights (which importantly includes pharmaceutical patents) from the remit of the WIPO to the WTO and extending the patent protection to twenty years, the developed countries have made access to life-saving medicines even more difficult to achieve, both in the short and long term. These changes proposed in the late 1980s to ensure IP rights protection was granted at a global level, saw the introduction of the TRIPS Agreement through the WTO. Although the Agreement, in some ways, seeks to strike a balance between IP rights and access to medicines, it falls short. The Agreement instead struck a discord, and has made access to life-saving medicines an even more difficult task to achieve in developing countries and LDCs.

It can be argued that the clash between human rights and IP is clearly epitomised by the issue of access to patented medicines, which only worsened with the advent of the WTO and the introduction of an extended global IP rights protection regime under the TRIPS Agreement. The problems faced by those in developing countries and LDCs in accessing medicines present the stark realities of the ills of an extended international protection regime for IP rights, specifically pharmaceutical patent protection. The cost of access to affordable medicines, as opposed to an available cure, has clearly contributed to the loss of innocent lives. The developed nations who advocated the wider, global IP protection at the WTO are not being affected by the rising costs of medicines, as they have in place a robust healthcare system through which citizens access both affordable healthcare and medicines. For instance, in developed countries, ARVs have 'transformed AIDS from a death sentence to a chronic illness and saved thousands of lives'; in sharp contrast, even at the reduced price of $300 per year, the drugs remain out of reach for the 25 million sub-Saharan Africans suffering from HIV and AIDS.[75] Many of the diseases and health conditions that account for a large part of the disease burden in low- and middle-income countries are far less common in high-income countries (Jamison, Breman, Alleyne, Claeson, Evans, Jha, Mills, and Musgrove, 2006).[76] Unfortunately, for AIDS patients in developing countries and LDCs, the ARVs for frontline treatment are inaccessible due to its exorbitant price, which again is fixed by TNPCs.[77] The only option available in

75 'Paying the Price' (Television Trust for the Environment, U.S. Release 2002). See also McClellan (2005) 154.

76 According to the authors, just eight diseases and conditions account for 29 percent of all deaths in low- and middle-income countries, namely TB, HIV/AIDS, diarrheal diseases, vaccine-preventable diseases of childhood, malaria, respiratory infections, maternal conditions and neonatal deaths.

77 UNAIDS, Joint UN Programme on HIV/AIDS Staff, 2006 Report on the Global AIDS Epidemic (World Health Organization, 2006) 13–14. The report states that millions of people have died of this terrible disease – 2.6 million in 2003 and 2.8 million in 2005, of which sub-Saharan Africa contributed 1.9 million and 2.0 million respectively. For the measures taken by Brazil to procure ARVs for its anti-AIDS programme, see chapter 5.

such countries is affordable generics, the procurement of which in some instances has become highly problematic (Sundaram, 2014a). It should also be noted that the production and procurement of generics has almost been outlawed through the implementation of the TRIPS Agreement. Patients from developing countries and LDCs suffer most from the impact of TRIPS, as the implementation of the Agreement has seen the price of patented drugs rise exponentially in a very short time, defying any logic.

Commentators identify poverty as the primary reason for not being able to access medicines, and governments, even those that are not corrupt or otherwise woefully dysfunctional, lack the resources and infrastructure to get medicines to those who need them but cannot afford them (Dutfield, 2008; Jones, 2006; Ferreira, 2002).[78] One other important reason for the lack of access to medicines in many cases is the high prices of drugs which acts as a barrier to much-needed treatments, and that prohibitive drug prices are often the result of strong IP protection ('t Hoen, 2003). These factors, according to Dutfield, are used cleverly by the pharmaceutical industry to stave off any argument that patent rights allow them to set high prices that keep life-saving drugs out of the reach of the poor (Dutfield, 2008; Jones, 2006). In the twenty-first-century globalised economy, the existence of medicines, or a cure, does not guarantee their accessibility to the poor and needy in developing countries and LDCs, who were compelled to embrace the IP rights protection regime under the TRIPS Agreement. For Thomas Pogge, the idea of withholding life-saving drugs from individuals suffering from fatal or debilitating diseases when the means exist to distribute those drugs cheaply and effectively is anathema to all notions of morality (Pogge, 2008a). Pogge refers to TRIPS as a 'notorious' Agreement that globalised a monopoly patent regime, which keeps the prices of advanced medicines much higher than the long-run cost of production by suppressing generic competition. He also strongly argues that this excludes the global poor from access to vital medicines for the sake of enhancing the incentives to develop new medicines for the affluent (Pogge, 2008a).

Under international human rights laws, the right to health includes elements related to healthcare, *viz.*, access to medicines, curative and preventive healthcare, and other aspects related to a number of 'underlying preconditions for health' (Toebes, 1999). In this regard, the Committee on Economic, Social and Cultural Rights (CESCR) interpreted the understanding of the 'highest attainable standard of health' as 'a right to the enjoyment of a variety of facilities, good, services and conditions necessary for the realisation of the highest attainable standard of health',[79] and access to necessary medicines should be understood in light of the above interpretation. This means that the 'right to highest attainable standard of health' should include the 'provision of equal and timely access to basic preventive, curative, rehabilitative health services and health

78 Ferreira argues that poverty is a potent cause of death in developing countries with a significantly poor population, and that a vast proportion of patients in developing countries may die because the medicines to control the progression of diseases are unaffordable.

79 See Council on Economic, Social and Cultural Rights (CESR) (4 July 2000) para 9.

education; . . .; appropriate treatment of prevalent diseases, illness, injuries and disabilities; [and] the provision of essential drugs'. Following from the above, one can say that medicines, as a basic means for the guarantee of people's enjoyment of health, should be made available to ensure the realisation of the right to health, which implies that the right to health encompasses a minimum and universal right to affordable essential medicines (McClellan, 2005).

It can be argued that the developing countries and LDCs had their chance to put their cases across when the TRIPS Agreement was negotiated in the Uruguay Round of negotiations prior to its entry in 1995, and that the negative effects of the TRIPS Agreement, if any on access to medicines, was addressed by the TRIPS Council, and subsequently offset through the Doha Declaration in 2001. Unfortunately, this argument is not sustainable, as a level playing field was glaringly absent during the Uruguay Round of negotiations (a factor discussed elsewhere in this book), which effectively handed over any advantage to the advocates of the international IP rights protection regime. The negotiation and entry of TRIPs in 1995 resulted in empowering a particular group of actors, namely developed countries led by the US, to successfully embed their preferred way of governing IP rights in the TRIPs agreement (Muzaka, 2011). This in fact disadvantaged the developing countries and LDCs, who unlike the developed countries did not possess knowledge-intense economies. Also, the IP policy template of the developed nations were at loggerheads with the still struggling developing country economies, some of which were still emerging from their colonial pasts. Pogge also posits the argument that the Agreement cannot be just, highlighting the fact that representatives of a number of acceding governments included individuals such as Suharto (Indonesia), Mugabe (Zimbabwe), Sani Abacha (Nigeria), Mobutu Sese Seko (Democratic Republic of Congo) and Burma's SLORC junta, who could not have represented the best interests of the people they were ruling (Pogge, 2008a). One can also add that large democracies such as India, Brazil, *etc*., represented by democratically elected governments, opposed the very entry of patent protection into the WTO on the grounds that the right place to debate matters relating to IP rights protection was the WIPO, while also warning that a global IP regime could cause serious harm to the populace residing in developing countries and LDCs in their access to affordable medicines. The developing countries were in for a rude shock when the negotiated trade-off agreed with the developed countries to sign the TRIPS Agreement failed to materialise (Dreyfuss, 2009).[80] Pogge also argues that by globalising the pharmaceutical patent regime, the advanced nations have imposed a costly loss of freedom on the global poor, thereby cutting off poor patients from their generics drug supply and exposing billions of vulnerable people to heightened risk of death and disease (Pogge, 2008b).

Stiglitz observes that while serving in the Council of Economic Advisors under the Clinton Administration, it was clear that there was more interest for the

80 Dreyfuss argues that the trade-off was access to foreign markets in exchange for raising domestic IP levels, which was a losing proposition.

government in pleasing the pharmaceutical and entertainment industries than in forging an IP regime that would be good for innovation, let alone for developing countries (Stiglitz, 2005). Stiglitz also notes that the trade negotiators who framed the IP agreement of the Uruguay Round of negotiations in the early 1990s were either unaware of all the issues surrounding the IP rights or, more likely, uninterested in knowing the issues. These shocking observations shed light on the general mood prevalent at the highest level of trade negotiation, where the framers, while unaware of such problems of access to medicines, were also not so keen to discuss such issues. Several investigations carried out in the pre-WTO era had clearly demonstrated that the protection of IP rights is disproportionately more important to the chemical and pharmaceutical industries than any other industries (Siebeck, Evenson and Braga, 1990). It is obvious that at the root of the TRIPS Agreement lies the persistent tension between the economic powerhouses who seek to commodify and appropriate more intellectual goods into the private property realm and those who seek the dissemination of such intellectual goods into the 'intangible commons' for public use and the protection of the public domain more generally (Muzaka, 2011). The TRIPS Agreement in terms of the magnitude of harm caused in exacerbating the problems relating to access to medicines in developing countries and LDCs can be viewed as an institutionalised human rights violation.

3.2 *Pharmaceutical corporations and the right to life-saving medicines*

From the foregoing discussions, it is clear that one of the key players behind the creation of a global IP rights protection was the TNPCs, who hold patent rights to pharmaceutical patents for all modern medicines required in the treatment of diseases around the world. Importantly, the consumers of patented pharmaceutical goods are spread all over the world, and more so in the developing countries and LDCs, which have a greater population and higher incidents of mortality due to poor/weak healthcare systems. Patients in developing countries and LDCs suffer most from the impact of the TRIPS Agreement, as its implementation has seen the price of patented drugs rise exponentially within a very short time. This situation has resulted in medicines becoming unaffordable and beyond the reach of even governmental agencies in developing countries. As mentioned earlier, the most affected populations of the HIV/AIDS pandemic come from developing countries and LDCs, where frontline treatment is unaffordable due to the above factor. Stiglitz posits the argument that one of the reasons for high costs of medicines is the patent system, which clearly impedes access to lifesaving drugs for billions (Stiglitz, 2005). Stiglitz also argues that the key motive for the transnational pharmaceutical industry to push for TRIPS was that their desire to reduce access to generic medicines, as generic drugs are priced very low (affordable) and are favoured over the much higher-priced patented drugs. Also, any competition with generic drugs would drive down the price of brand-name drugs. Stiglitz notes that the lower prices in turn lower the profits of the brand-name pharmaceutical companies, and that it is understandable why the TNPCs pushed so hard for and contributed to the negotiations on international IP rights protection.

Patients in developed countries do not face the same fate as those in developing countries and LDCs, as they benefit from a well-defined healthcare system, where not only are prescription medicines affordable, but also medical treatment which is well regulated by the respective states. The developing countries and LDCs can boast of neither a healthcare system nor affordable medical treatment. Importantly, the voice one hears from the developing countries is not for free medicines but for access to affordable medicines. It can only be considered a failure of the WTO that they have not developed an adequate solution to the AIDS issue, which is emblematic of a broader truth about global IP rights and the developing world (Drahos and Braithwaite, 2003). The WTO, as an agency of the United Nations (UN) and the world governing body that administers the TRIPS Agreement, must be made accountable for its failure to find an effective solution for access to medicines in most of its member states, and more particularly in developing countries and LDCs, where patent protection is compulsorily extended to pharmaceutical products through the TRIPS Agreement. The argument that the Doha Declaration was especially formulated to address this issue and that flexibilities were built into the TRIPS Agreement to address the specific issue cannot be sustained, as problems have persisted.

As Stiglitz observes, the TNPCs and FTAs have made the grant of compulsory licences difficult. He further argues that had the negotiators only intended to retain access to lifesaving generic medicines for developing countries, TRIPS would have provided for an automatic right, facilitating the issue of compulsory licences for expensive, life-saving medicines. Stiglitz also holds the strong view that when the trade ministers signed the TRIPS Agreement in the 1994, they were effectively signing the death warrants of thousands of people living in sub-Saharan Africa and in the developing countries elsewhere (Stiglitz, 2005). Marcellin also notes that the making of the patent provision under the TRIPS Agreement represents an instance of institutional capture by private interests, dominated by American industry (Marcellin, 2010). This position, in fact, gives the pharmaceutical corporations almost dictatorial powers not only in fixing the price, but also in controlling the supply of medicines to any part of the world. As mentioned earlier in this chapter, the introduction of the TRIPS Agreement has almost seen the outlawing of generic medicines. One of the chief suppliers of generic medicines, *viz.*, India, has come under severe attack since 2000 from both transnational pharmaceutical corporations and the US, as generics made in India are seen as posing a real threat to the profits that patented branded drugs make. It is to be noted here that the generic medicines are made with outdated patents – the original patent holder does not have any more rights to the composition – and are perfectly legal.

The debate that surrounds the grant of pharmaceutical patent rights (private rights), which violates the human right of an individual's right to medicine is intense. This brings us to the question of whether any duties are owed by TNPCs for access to medicines in developing countries and LDCs. Should TNPCs be obligated to prioritise the primary goal of healthcare policy in order to promote access to medicine (Wu,2012)? The patent-holding corporations, including TNPCs, were able to carve out an extraordinary deal during the Uruguay Round of negotiations, which resulted in the TRIPS Agreement. This deal granted them the right to hold a twenty-year patent right, a negative private right, as against all consumers of medicines living across the globe – be it an over-the-counter paracetamol or an expensive ARV. From what has been discussed, it can be concluded that this right was granted to the pharmaceutical patent holders at the cost of global consumers losing their human right to access affordable medicines and medical treatment. In response to the above position, it can be argued that human rights apply to states, and only in limited cases to corporations (Muchlinski, 2003), as a corporation's activities are normally governed by domestic laws, and that it may not be possible to hold a corporation accountable for compliance of the right to health (Wu, 2012). Wu argues that due to the enormous profits generated by TNPCs through their global operations, one has to reconsider the boundaries between the private and public sphere. With mounting evidence of human rights abuses by TNPCs, one is also led to the conclusion that they should be legally bound, or at least morally guided, by international human rights norms. He further believes that the problem of access to medicines cannot be solved by the governments/states concerned or by the market/TNPCs.

If prospective member states engaged in the trade negotiations and the institutions (GATT/WTO) responsible for such negotiations were aware that the problem of access to medicines could be exacerbated by the recognition and grant of an expanded private negative right, why was the grant of such a private right not put on hold? This only makes us raise the following further questions relating to the issue, *viz.*, (i) were the developing countries *made to* trade away the human rights of their citizens during the GATT trade negotiations? (ii) Did the developing countries trade away the human rights of their citizens during the trade negotiations? (iii) Did the GATT/WTO trade negotiations *tacitly* facilitate this process? (iv) Were the developing countries hoodwinked into signing the TRIPS Agreement? (v) What responsibilities do the institutions that are the precursors to the WTO – World Health Organization (WHO), World Bank (WB), the United Nations (UN) – have for the resulting Agreement which has caused problems in access to affordable medicines (and to other matters relating to IP)?

4 Public right to health *v.* private right to restrict

The neoclassical worldview that what is good for business is also good for the society cannot be sustained, as the economic foundations of the patent system, or the justification for a monopoly protection for private rights at the cost of the public good and human rights, is ill-founded. Jagdish Bhagwati, the renowned economist and an advocate of free trade, argues that the TRIPS Agreement does not belong in the WTO, as it enforces payment by the poor countries (consumers) to the rich countries (IP producers), and that by introducing TRIPS through the WTO, we collectively legally authorise the WTO to extract royalty payments

(Bhagwati, 2002). Bhagwati, declaring support for the NGO statement 'asking for the IP leg of the WTO to be sawn off', also observed that the WTO must be about mutual gains in trade. IP protection introduced through the TRIPS Agreement, however, is a tax on poor countries, constituting a wealth transfer to the rich countries, that has turned the WTO into a royalty-collection agency (Bhagwati, 2001). As observed by Stiglitz, the importance of IP rights is exaggerated; such rights form only one part of our innovation system and should only be considered as being part of a portfolio of instruments (Stiglitz, 2005). Stiglitz further argues that there is an immediate need to strengthen the other elements of this portfolio and redesign the current IP regime to increase its benefits and reduce its costs. Martin Khor, while advocating for a review of the TRIPS Agreement, argues that the agenda should include the question of whether IP rights should be removed from the WTO so that the multilateral trading organisation can return to its stated mission of promoting balanced trade options (Khor, 2002).

As discussed elsewhere in this book, transnational corporations, led by patent-holding pharmaceutical corporations and ably backed by developed countries, successfully shifted the forum for international IP rights protection from the WIPO to the WTO during the Uruguay Round of negotiations. Not stopping with the shift in the forum, as argued by Marcellin, the patent-holding pharmaceutical corporations, through developed country representation, have resorted to an 'institutional capture' (Marcellin, 2010), which in effect had resulted in a stalemate with the prospect of renegotiation of the TRIPS Agreement at the WTO appearing remote. Not only have the transnational patent-holding corporations been successful in shifting the forum from the WIPO to the WTO, and in the eventual creation of the TRIPS Agreement, but also in taking absolute control of the administering body through developed country member states. In the foregoing paragraphs, we discussed the access to medicines/public health implications of an enforced international IP rights protection regime on the member states of the WTO, and also that there is no real consensus concerning the impact of patent protection on the growth of technology (Kitch, 1986). Instead of engaging in a debate on whether IP rights protection will lead to increased innovation and foreign investment in developing countries (Sherwood, 1999), or whether current drug prices are justified by the need for future research and development (Bale, 1997; Grabowski, 2002), it would be hugely beneficial to engage in a serious study of the harms of an expanded international IP rights protection on global public health concerns as a human right. The need of the hour is a thorough examination of the philosophical foundations that justify an international IP rights protection *vis-à-vis* that of the foundations to the public right to health, as the utilitarian basis of IP rights protection seems to completely neglect the rights of the individual to the enjoyment of the public good.

5 Conclusion

The economic analysis of IP laws is inconclusive with regards to their benefit to society, as a division exists in the perception of what constitutes a public good; if IP rights would actually constitute a public good; and in particular if a negative private right could constitute a public good when it only goes to enrich the individual holding the said right to the exclusion of others. From the preceding discussion, it becomes clear that the current international IP rights protection regime, which is modelled on the US IP laws and policy and promoted by the WTO through the TRIPS Agreement, has caused and continues to cause enormous difficulties for developing countries and LDCs through its implementation. The entry of the TRIPS Agreement has also helped the pharmaceutical corporations create a false demand and increase the price of patented pharmaceutical products. This raises the real question of whether the international IP rights protection regime's economic justification to society's welfare has been overstated, and overshadows the harm it causes to societies in developing countries and LDCs. What is clear, though, is that under the current regime, information is patentable (and heavily patented) and comes at a very high price, and consumers from developing countries pay taxes and royalties to the developed countries on everything they consume on a daily basis. Information is knowledge, and it does not come free but at a high price. This leads us to the question, was it at all necessary for the WTO to move towards a global product patent regime in the first place? As discussed earlier, the idea, or more precisely the template, was mooted by TNPCs ably backed by other patent-holding corporations and developed countries to move towards a product patent regime. This model was designed to create a two-tier system, which comprises of the patent holders and consumers amongst the WTO member states, where consumers across the globe (mostly located in developing countries and LDCs) pay a royalty to the patent holders based in developed countries. The TRIPS regime also effectively outlaws the generic drugs industry through the introduction of a product patent system, which had been the mainstay for developing countries and LDCs, offering access to affordable medicine for their healthcare needs.

The argument that IP rights are important for the society will become unacceptable if the right to access affordable medicine is not addressed by the WTO clearly. The model of multilateral trade promoted and practiced under the WTO through the covered agreements is such that it does not allow the WTO to either contain or respond quickly to any social inequalities created by the operation of the covered agreements. What one has to note is that IP rights, through their close association with the growth of technology and the media, hold a popular position and have been glamorised by its proponents. Unfortunately, human rights and related issues do not enjoy the same luxury that IP rights enjoy. Human rights arguments have come to be associated with images of the poor and suffering in the Third World and might not have the same glamour, or public appeal as IP rights.

Bibliography

1 Adams, John N. 'History of Patent System,' in Takenaka, Toshiko (ed.) *Patent Law and Theory: A Handbook of Contemporary Research* (Edward Elgar Publishing, 2008) 101.

2 Bale, Harvey E., Jr. 'Patent Protection and Pharmaceutical Innovation,' *New York University Journal of International Law and Politics* Vol. 29 (1997) 95.

3 Becker, Gary. 'Reforming the Patent System Toward a Minimalist System,' *The Becker-Posner Blog* (30 September 2012) <www.becker-posner-blog.com/2012/09/

reforming-the-patent-system-toward-a-minimalist-system-becker.html> accessed 25 November 2017.

4 Bentham, Jeremy. *Rationale of Reward* (John & HL Hunt, 1825).

5 Bentham, Jeremy. 'Observation on Parts of the Declaration of Rights, as Proposed by Citizen Sieyes,' in *The Works of Jeremy Bentham*, Vol. II (Simpkin, Marshall & Co, London, 1843) 533.

6 Besen, Stanley M., and Leo J. Raskind. 'An Introduction to the Law and Economics of Intellectual Property,' *The Journal of Economic Perspectives* Vol. 5, No. 1 (1991) 3–27.

7 Bhagwati, Jagdish. Letter to The Editor, *Financial Times* (14 February 2001) <www.columbia.edu/~jb38/papers/pdf/FT_Letter_on_IPP.pdf> accessed 25 November 2017.

8 Bhagwati, Jagdish. 'Afterword: The Question of Linkage,' *American Journal of International Law* Vol. 96, No. 1 (2002) 126–134, 127.

9 Bouckaert, Boudewijn. 'What Is Property?' *Harvard Journal of Law & Public Policy* (1990) 775–816.

10 Calabresi, Guido. 'Some Thoughts on Risk Distribution and the Law of Torts,' *Yale Law Journal* (1961) 499–553.

11 Calandrillo, Steve P. 'Economic Analysis of Property Rights in Information: Justifications and Problems of Exclusive Rights, Incentives to Generate Information, and the Alternative for a Government-Run Reward System,' *Fordham Intellectual Property Media & Entertainment Law Journal* Vol. 9 (1998) 301–360.

12 Chapman, Audrey R. 'Approaching Intellectual Property as a Human Right: Obligations Related to Art 15.1(c),' *UNESCO Copyright Bulletin* Vol. 35, No. 3 (2001) 6.

13 Chevalier, Michel. *Les brevets d'inventions dans leurs relations au principe de la liberté, du travail et de l'égalité* (1878) 38. As cited in Machlup Fritz, and Edith Penrose, 'The Patent Controversy in the Nineteenth Century,' *The Journal of Economic History* Vol. X, No. 1 (May 1950) 1–29, 9.

14 Coase, Ronald. 'The Problem of Social Cost,' *Journal of Law and Economics* Vol. 3 (1960) 1.

15 Correa, Carlos M. 'Managing the Provisions of Knowledge: The Design of Intellectual Property Management,' in Kaul, Inge, Pedro Conceição, Katell Le Goulven, and Ronald U. Mendoza (eds.) *Providing Global Public Goods: Managing Globalization* (Oxford University Press, 2003).

16 Council on Economic, Social and Cultural Rights (CESR), General Comment No 14, 22nd Sess, (4 July 2000) para 9 [Document E/C.12/2000/4].

17 *Darcy v. Allen* (1603) 74 Eng Rep 1131, 1139.

18 David, Paul A. 'Intellectual Property Institutions and the Panda's Thumb: Patent, Copyrights, and the Trade Secrets in Economic Theory and History,' in Wallerstein, Mitchel B., Mary E. Mogee, and Robin A. Schoen (eds.) *Global Dimensions of Intellectual Property Rights in Science and Technology* (National Academy Press, 1993) 19–61, 20, 26.

19 Deere, Carolyn. *The Implementation Game: The Global Politics of Intellectual Property Reform in Developing Countries* (Oxford University Press, 2009) 35.

20 *Diamond v. Diehr* case [450 U.S. 175, 185–187 (1981)].

21 Donner, Irah. 'The Copyright Clause of the US Constitution: Why Did the Framers Include It with Unanimous Approval,' *The American Journal of Legal History* Vol. 36, No. 3 (1992) 361–378, 361–362.

22 Drahos, Peter. 'Developing Countries and International Intellectual Property Standard-Setting,' *The Journal of World Intellectual Property* Vol. 5, No. 5 (2002) 765–789.

23 Drahos, Peter, and John Braithwaite. 'Three Tests of US Trade Policy on Intellectual Property Rights,' *Nthposition* (July 2003) <www.nthposition.com/threetestsofustrade.php> accessed 25 November 2017.

24 Dreyfuss, Rochelle C. 'The Role of India, China, Brazil and Other Emerging Economies in Establishing Access Norms for Intellectual Property and Intellectual Property Law Making,' *IILJ (Institute of International Law and Justice) Working Paper 2009/5* (2009) 9–53, 4.
25 Dutfield, Graham. 'Delivering Drugs to the Poor: Will the TRIPS Amendment Help?' *American Journal of Law & Medicine* Vol. 34 (2008) 107–124.
26 Dutfield, Graham, and Uma Suthersanan, *Global Intellectual Property* (Edward Elgar Publishing, 2008) 224–225.
27 Fenning, Karl. 'The Origin of the Patent and Copyright Clause of the Constitution,' *Journal of Patent Office Society* Vol. 11 (1929) 438–445, 438.
28 Ferreira, Lissett. 'Access to HIV/AID Drugs: The Human Rights Obligations of Multinational Pharmaceutical Corporations,' *Fordham Law Review* Vol. 71, No. 3 (2002) 1133–1180, 1133–1135.
29 Forman, Lisa. 'Ensuring Reasonable Health: Health Rights, the Judiciary, and South African HIV/AIDS Policy,' *The Journal of Law, Medicine & Ethics* Vol. 33, No. 4 (2005) 711–724, 711–714.
30 General Comment No. 17: The right of everyone to benefit from the protection of the moral and material interests resulting from any scientific, literary or artistic production of which he is the author (Article 15(1)(c) of the Covenant), adopted by the UNHCR Committee on Economic, Social and Cultural Rights on 21 November 2005 (E/C.12/2005/GC/17). Available in 'Human Rights Instruments, Vol. I, Compilation of General Comments and General Recommendations Adopted by Human Rights Treaty Bodies' HRI/GEN/1/Rev.9 (Vol. I) 123–138.
31 Ghafele, Roya. 'Perceptions of Intellectual Property: A Review,' University Library of Munich, Germany (2008).
32 Glasgow, Lara J. 'Stretching the Limits of Intellectual Property Rights: Has the Pharmaceutical Industry Gone Too Far?' *IDEA* Vol. 41 (2001) 227.
33 Grabowski, Henry. 'Patents, Innovation and Access to New Pharmaceuticals,' *Journal of International Economic Law* Vol. 5, No. 4 (2002) 849–860.
34 Gruner, Richard. 'Dispelling the Myth of Patents as Non-Rivalrous Property: Patents as Tools for Allocating Scarce Labor and Resources,' *Colum Science & Technology Law Review* Vol. 13 (2011) 1–70.
35 *Guide to the Berne Convention for the Protection of Literary and Artistic Works (Paris Act, 1971)*, WIPO Publication No 615 (E) (1978).
36 Helfer, Laurence R. 'Human Rights and Intellectual Property: Conflict or Coexistence?' *Minnesota Intellectual Property Review* Vol. 5, No. 1 (2003) 47–61.
37 Helfer, Laurence R. and Graeme W. Austin. *Human Rights and Intellectual Property: Mapping the Global Interface* (Cambridge University Press, 2011) 32.
38 Hestermeyer, Holger. *Human Rights and the WTO: The Case of Patents and Access to Medicines* (Oxford University Press, 2008).
39 Hughes, Justin. 'The Philosophy of Intellectual Property,' *Georgetown Law Journal* Vol. 77 (1988) 287–366.
40 Hume, David. *Enquiries Concerning the Human Understanding and Concerning the Principles of Morals*, Section III, Part II (Oxford University Press, 1902) 192–204.
41 Hume, David, and Tom L. Beauchamp. *An Enquiry Concerning the Principles of Morals: A Critical Edition* Vol. 4 (Oxford University Press, 2006).
42 Jamison, Dean T., Joel G. Breman, Anthony R. Measham, George Alleyne, Mariam Claeson, David B. Evans, Prabhat Jha, Anne Mills, and Philip Musgrove. 'Cost-Effective Strategies for the Excess Burden of Disease in Developing Countries,' in *Priorities in Health* (World Bank, 2006) 59–95.

43 Jones, Trevor. Commentary, in *Public Health, Innovation and Intellectual Property Rights: Report of the Commission on Intellectual Property Rights, Innovation and Public Health* (World Health Organization, 2006) 202.
44 Katz, Michael L., and Carl Shapiro. 'On the Licensing of Innovations,' *The RAND Journal of Economics* Vol. 16, No. 4 (1985) 504–520.
45 Khor, Martin. 'Rethinking Intellectual Property Rights and TRIPS,' in Drahos, Peter and Ruth Mayne (eds.) *Global Intellectual Property Rights: Knowledge, Access and Development* (Palgrave Macmillan, 2002) 201–213, 212.
46 Kinsella, N. Stephen. 'Against Intellectual Property,' *Journal of Libertarian Studies* Vol. 15, No. 2 (2001) 1–53.
47 Kitch, Edmund W. 'The Nature and Function of the Patent System,' *Journal of Law and Economics* Vol. 20, No. 2 (1977) 265–290.
48 Kitch, Edmond W. 'Patents: Monopolies or Property Rights?' *Research in Law & Economics* Vol. 8 (1986) 31–49.
49 Kitch, Edmond W. 'Elementary and Persistent Errors in the Economic Analysis of Intellectual Property,' *Vanderbilt Law Review* Vol. 53 (2000) 1727–1741, 1728.
50 Kongolo, Tshimanga. 'The African Intellectual Property Organizations: The Necessity of Adopting One Uniform System for All Africa,' *The Journal of World Intellectual Property* Vol. 3, No. 2 (2000) 265–288.
51 Landes, William M., and Richard Posner. *The Economic Structure of Intellectual Property Law* (Harvard University Press, 2003) 294.
52 Lemley, Mark A. 'The Economics of Improvement in Intellectual Property Law,' *Texas Law Review* (1997) 989–1084, 995.
53 Lemley, Mark A., Peter S. Menell and Robert P. Merges. *Intellectual Property in the New Technological Age: 2016, Vol. I: Perspectives, Trade Secrets and Patents* (University of California, 2016).
54 McClellan, Melissa. 'Tools for Success: The TRIPS Agreement and the Human Rights to Essential Medicine,' *Washington & Lee Journal of Civil Rights & Social Justice* Vol. 12 (2005) 153–175, 154.
55 Machlup, Fritz, and Edith Penrose. 'The Patent Controversy in the Nineteenth Century,' *The Journal of Economic History* Vol. X, No. 1 (May 1950) 1–29, 3.
56 Machlup, Fritz. 'An Economic Review of the Patent System,' No. 15, US Government Printing Office (1958).
57 Mandich, Giulio. 'Venetian Patents (1450–1550),' *Journal of the Patent Office Society* (1948) 166–224, 177.
58 Mandich, Giulio. 'Venetian Origins of Inventors' Rights,' *Journal of the Patent Office Society* (1960) 378–382.
59 Marcellin, Sherry S. *The Political Economy of Pharmaceutical Patent: US Sectional Interests and the African Group at the WTO* (Ashgate Publishing, 2010) 3.
60 Matthews, Duncan. 'Intellectual Property Rights, Human Rights and the Right to Health,' in Grosheide, F. Willem (eds.) *Intellectual Property and Human Rights: A Paradox* (Edward Elgar Publishing, 2010) 118–139, 118.
61 Menell, Peter S. 'Intellectual Property: General Theories' in Bouckaert, B. and G. De Geest (eds.) *Encyclopedia of Law and Economics: The History and Methodology of Law & Economics* Vol. 1 (Edward Elgar Publishing, 2000) 129. <http://encyclo.findlaw.com/1600book.pdf> accessed 23 November 2017.
62 Menell, Peter S., and Suzanne Scotchmer. 'Intellectual Property Law,' in Mitchell A. Polinsky and Steven Shavell (eds.) *Handbook of Law and Economics* Vol. 2 (Elsevier BV, 2007) 1473.

63 Mill, John Stuart. *Principles of Political Economy With Some of Their Applications to Social Philosophy*, Book V Chapter X, Section 4 (Hackett Publishing, 2004).
64 Muchlinski, Peter. 'The Development of Human Rights Responsibilities for Multinational Enterprise,' in Sulliven, Roy (ed.) *Business and Human Rights: Dilemmas and Solutions* (2003) 33.
65 Muzaka, Valbona. *The Politics of Intellectual Property Rights and Access to Medicines* (Palgrave Macmillan, 2011) 18.
66 Mwangi, Jeannette. 'TRIPS and Agricultural Biotechnology: Implications for the Right to Food in Africa,' in Sinjela, Mpazi (ed.) *Human Rights and Intellectual Property Rights: Tensions and Convergences* Vol. 2 (Martinus Nijhoff Publishers, 2007) 265.
67 Okediji, Ruth L. 'The International Relations of Intellectual Property: Narratives of Developing Country Participation in the Global Intellectual Property System,' *Singapore Journal of International & Comparative Law* Vol. 7 (2003) 315–385, 316.
68 Okediji, Ruth L. 'Africa and the Global Intellectual Property System: Beyond the Agency Model,' *African Year Book of International Law* Vol. 12, No. 1 (2004) 207–251, 216–217.
69 Panichas, George E. 'Hume's Theory of Property,' in K. Mackinnon (ed.) *Hume and Law* (Ashgate, 2012) 225–239.
70 Papadopoulou, Frantzeska. 'TRIPS and Human Rights,' in Kur, Annette (ed.) *Intellectual Property Rights in a Fair World Trade System: Proposals for Reform of TRIPS* (Edward Elgar Publishing, 2011) 262.
71 'Paying the Price' (Television Trust for the Environment, U.S. Release 2002). <http://tve.org/film/paying-the-price/>; <https://youtu.be/vZIrnwAAzmQ> accessed 26 November 2017.
72 Plant, Arnold. 'The Economic Theory Concerning Patents for Inventions,' *Economica*, New Series, Vol. 1, No. 1 (1934) 30–51.
73 Pogge, Thomas. 'Access to Medicines,' *Public Health Ethics* Vol. 1, No. 2 (2008a) 73–82, 74.
74 Pogge, Thomas. 'Medicines for the World: Boosting Innovation Without Obstructing Free Access,' *SUR – International Journal on Human Rights*, Vol. 8 (2008b) 117–140.
75 Posner, Richard A. 'The Economic Approach to Law,' *Texas Law Review* (1975) 757–782, 759–760.
76 Posner, Richard. *The Economics of Justice* (Harvard University Press, 1983) 75–115.
77 Posner, Richard. 'Do Patent and Copyright Law Restrict Competition and Creativity Excessively?' *The Becker-Posner Blog* (30 September 2012) <www.becker-posner-blog.com/2012/09/do-patent-and-copyright-law-restrict-competition-and-creativity-excessively-posner.html> accessed 24 November 2017.
78 Recht, Pierre. 'Le Droit d'Auteur, Une Nouvelle Forme de *Propriété: Histoire et Théorie*,' Paris Librarie Générale de Droit et de Jurisprudence (1969) 39, as cited in Bouckaert, Boudewijn. 'What Is Property?' *Harvard Journal of Law & Public Policy* (1990) 775–816, 791–792.
79 Roffe, Pedro, and Gina Vea. 'The WIPO Development Agenda in a Historical and Political Context,' in Netanel, Netanel W. (ed.) *The Development Agenda: Global Intellectual Property and Developing Countries* (Oxford University Press, 2008) 83.
80 Santoro, Michael A. 'Human Rights and Human Needs: Diverse Moral Principles Justifying Third World Access to Affordable HIV/AIDS Drugs,' *NCJ International Law & Commercial Regulation* Vol. 31 (2006) 923–942, 940.

81 Schuller, Anton. *Handbuch der Gesetze über ausschliessende Privilegien auf neue Erfindungen*, Entdeckungen und Verbesserungen im Gebiete der Industrie (Vienna, 1843), as cited in Machlup and Penrose (1950) 11.
82 Scotchmer, Suzzane. 'Standing on the Shoulders of Giants: Cumulative Research and the Patent Law,' *The Journal of Economic Perspectives* Vol. 5, No. 1 (1991) 29–41, 29–30.
83 Sherwood, Robert M. 'A Larger Context for Considering Pharmaceutical Patents in Developing Countries,' *World Bull* Vol. 15 (1999) 76.
84 Sichelman, Ted, and Sean O'Connor, 'Patents as Promoters of Competition: The Guild Origins of Patent Law in the Venetian Republic,' *San Diego Law Review* Vol. 49 (2012) 1267.
85 Siebeck, Wolfgang E., Robert E. Evenson, and Carlos A. Primo Braga. 'Strengthening Protection of Intellectual Property in Developing Countries: A Survey of the Literature,' *World Bank Discussion Papers* 112 (1990) 48.
86 Smith, Adam. *An Inquiry Into the Nature and Causes of the Wealth of Nations* – Book V, Ch. 1 Part 3 (Wordsworth Classics of World Literature, 2012) 753–754.
87 Stiglitz, Joseph E. 'Knowledge As a Global Public Good,' in Kaul, Inge, Isabelle Grunberg and Marc A. Stern (eds.) *Global Public Goods: International Cooperation in the 21st Century* (Oxford University Press, 1999) 308–325, 325.
88 Stiglitz, Joseph E. 'Intellectual-Property Rights and Wrongs,' *Project Syndicate* (5 August 2005) <www.project-syndicate.org/commentary/intellectual-property-rights-and-wrongs> accessed 24 November 2017.
89 Stiglitz, Joseph E. 'Economic Foundations of Intellectual Property Rights,' *Duke Law Journal* 57 (2008) 1693–1724.
90 Sundaram, Jae. 'India's Trade-Related Aspects of Intellectual Property Rights Compliant Pharmaceutical Patent Laws: What Lessons for India and Other Developing Countries?' *Information & Communications Technology Law* Vol. 23, No. 1 (2014a) 1–30.
91 Sundaram, Jae. 'Brazil's Implementation of TRIPS Flexibilities: Ambitious Missions, Early Implementation, and the Plans for Reform,' *Information & Communications Technology Law* Vol. 23, No. 2 (2014b) 81–116, 94.
92 Taussig, Frank William. *Inventors and Money-Makers* (The MacMillan Company, 1915).
93 't Hoen, Ellen. 'TRIPS, Pharmaceutical Patents and Access to Essential Medicines: Seattle, Doha and Beyond,' in Moatti, Jean-Paul, Benjamin Coriat, Yves Souteyrand, Rony Barnett, Jérôme Dumoulin, and Yves-Antoine Flori (eds.) *Economics of AIDS and Access to HIV/AIDS Care in Developing Countries: Issues and Challenges* (ANRS, Collection Science Sociales et SIDA, Paris, 2003) 39–67.
94 The Berne Convention for the Protection of Literary and Artistic Works 1883, as amended on 28 September 1979.
95 The Founders' Constitution [A website maintained by the University of Chicago, USA] <http://press-pubs.uchicago.edu/founders/documents/a1_8_8s12.html> accessed 29 November 2017.
96 The Letters of Thomas Jefferson 1743–1826, *American History: From Revolution to Reconstruction and Beyond* [A website maintained by the University of Groningen, The Netherlands] <www.let.rug.nl/usa/presidents/thomas-jefferson/letters-of-thomas-jefferson/jefl220.php> accessed 29 November 2017.
97 The Paris Convention for the Protection of Industrial Property 1883, as amended on 28 September 1979.
98 The Report of the UN High Commissioner for Human Rights, *The Impact of the Agreement on Trade-Related Aspects of Intellectual Property Rights on Human Rights*, E/CN.4/Sub.2/2001/13, pp. 7–11.

99 Toebes, Brigit. 'Towards an Improved Understanding of the International Human Right to Health,' *Human Rights Quarterly* Vol. 21, No. 3 (1999) 661–679, 665–671.

100 Torremans, Paul (ed.), *Copyright and Human Rights: Freedom of Expression, Intellectual Property, Privacy* (Kluwer Law International, 2004) 5.

101 Trebilcock, Michael J., Robert Howse, and Antonia Eliason. *The Regulation of International Trade* (Routledge, 2013) 515–516.

102 UN Committee on Economic and Cultural Rights (UNCECR), *Substantive Issues Arising in the Implementation of the International Covenant on Economic, Social and Cultural Rights* – Follow-up session to the day of general discussion on Article 15.1(c), Monday 26 November 2001, Human Rights and Intellectual Property. United Nations Committee on Economic, Social and Cultural Rights, 14 December 2001, para 1 [Document E/C.12/2001/15].

103 UN Commission on Human Rights, Sub-Commission on the Promotion and Protection of Human Rights, 'Intellectual Property Rights and Human Rights,' Resolution 2000/7, 17 August 2000, para 1 [Document E/CN.4/Sub.2/2000/2000/7].

104 UN Commission on Human Rights, 'Economic, Social and Cultural Rights: The impact of the Agreement on Trade-Related Aspects of Intellectual Property Rights on Human Rights. Report of the High Commissioner,' 27 June 2001, E/CN.4/Sub.2/2001/13, p. 5.

105 UN Commission on Human Rights, Sub-Commission on the Promotion and Protection of Human Rights, 'Intellectual Property Rights and Human Rights,' Resolution 2001/21, 16 August 2001 [Document E/CN.4/Sub.2/Res/2001/21].

106 UNAIDS, *Joint UN Programme on HIV/AIDS Staff, 2006 Report on the Global AIDS Epidemic* (World Health Organization, 2006) 13–14.

107 Walterscheid, Edward C. 'The Early Evolution of the United States Patent Law: Antecedents (Part 1),' *Journal of Patent & Trademark Office Society* Vol. 76 (1994a) 697 706–707.

108 Walterscheid, Edward C. 'The Early Evolution of the United States Patent Law: Antecedents (Part 2),' *Journal of Patent & Trademark Office Society* Vol. 76 (1994b) 849–880.

109 Walterscheid, Edward C. 'The Early Evolution of the United States Patent Law: Antecedents (Part 3),' *Journal of Patent & Trademark Office Society* Vol. 77 (1995) 771–802, 777.

110 Walterscheid, Edward C. 'The Early Evolution of the United States Patent Law: Antecedents (Part 4),' *Journal of Patent & Trademark Office Society* Vol. 78 (1996) 77.

111 Walterscheid, Edward C. *To Promote the Progress of Useful Arts: American Patent Law and Administration, 1798–1836* (FB Rothman, 1998) 121–137.

112 World Trade Organization, *Protection of Intellectual Property Under the TRIPS Agreement* (27 November 2000) [UN.Doc.E/C.12/2000/18].

113 Wu, Cheng-Feng. 'Transnational Pharmaceutical Corporations' Legal and Moral Human Rights Responsibilities in Relations to Access to Medicines,' *Asian Journal of WTO & International Health Law & Policy* Vol. 7 (2012) 77.

114 Xiong, Ping, *An International Law Perspective on the Protection of Human Rights in the TRIPS Agreement* (Martinus Nijhoff Publishers, 2012) 57.

115 Yu, Peter K. 'Ten Common Question About Intellectual Property and Human Rights,' *Georgia State University Law Review* Vol. 23 (2006) 709–753, 709–710.

3 Intellectual property in the multilateral trading system

Forum shifting, TRIPS Agreement, Doha Declaration and TRIPS flexibilities

Contents

1 Introduction

This chapter takes up for study the forum shifting resorted to by TNPCs by successfully lobbying patent-holding developed countries to move the international IP agenda from the WIPO to the WTO (even before the formation of the WTO), and by including global IP rights protection as a major item for negotiations in the Uruguay Round of negotiations.[1] Besides dealing with the issue of forum shifting by TNPCs and developed countries, this chapter will also present a critical study of the flexibilities (compulsory licencing, *etc.*) contained in the TRIPS Agreement and the Doha Declaration, which were both intended to assist the developing nations and LDCs in the quest for affordable medicines in times of need. It will be argued that the flexibilities did not produce the desired effect in most parts of the developing world, as a direct result of the swap in forums, and that the problem of access to medicines only got worse. It will also present the argument that the entry of the TRIPS Agreement had only witnessed the profits of pharmaceutical corporations go up, and at the same time access to medicines have become increasingly difficult in

1 The Uruguay Round was the eighth round of multilateral trade negotiations, and it took over seven years to complete. Launched in Punta Del Este in September 1986, it was finally concluded in Geneva in January 1995 with the creation of the World Trade Organization. WTO. 'The Uruguay Round' <www.wto.org/english/thewto_e/whatis_e/tif_e/fact5_e.htm> accessed 25 November 2017.

most parts of the developing world – in short, the trajectories move in opposite directions.

Forum shifting is primarily aimed at achieving a desired/preferred result by resorting to a change to the game. This is normally achieved by key players moving an agenda from one forum to another – which could also involve leaving a forum altogether (Braithwaite and Drahos, 2000; Drahos, 2004), or even pursuing a particular agenda before multiple forums (Drahos, 2004; Sell, 2009).[2] Braithwaite and Drahos note that this practice was started in the post–WW II era, in which the US was the key player. They note that when staring at defeat on a given regulatory agenda before an international forum, the US would shift the same agenda to another forum, or simply abandon that forum. This was based on the thinking that the abandoned international organization will be shocked into a more compliant mood of behaviour and would put in the maximum efforts to woo back the world's powerful state with more favourable policies. The authors also cite the instance in which the US left the United Nations Educational, Scientific and Cultural Organization (UNESCO). Later, UNESCO was also to become the victim of 'forum-blocking' due to its stance on copyrights (Braithwaite and Drahos, 2000).[3] It should not be forgotten that the US is a chief financial contributor to key international forums. We will in this chapter discuss how forum shifting, or regime shifting, has enormously helped the US-led developed nations, in conjunction with TNPCs, to relocate IP rights rule-making to the WTO; how that process helped the development of a new international IP rights regime as a trade-related agenda; and how the same was developed to the detriment of the other countries who were not in the 'developed countries' bloc, resulting in exacerbating the problems of access to medicines. In the instant case, the obvious reason for the shift appears to be to weaken the opposition and to achieve the goal of an international IP rights regime with its home as the WTO, and not the WIPO.

1.1 *The quest for stronger IP rights protection and forum shifting*

The vision for an international IP rights protection was initially conceived and promoted by patent rights holding transnational corporations from developed countries, which had campaigned relentlessly for the inclusion of an agreement on IP rights in the Uruguay Round of Multilateral Trade Negotiations (Drahos, 2003). It was claimed by US industries, which included pharmaceutical corporations and computer software industries, that they suffered heavy losses from the absence of adequate protection of their IP rights in foreign markets (Adede,

2 Drahos notes that strong states like the US shift forums to optimise their power and advantages, as well as to minimise opposition.

3 The authors note that the strategy of 'forum-blocking' is adopted to ensure that an international forum does not become a stage for an agenda that threatens the interest of the particular state. The above strategy was adopted by the US, as the UNESCO's position on 'copyrights' was untenable.

2003). For purposes gaining an understanding of the regime complexities that existed before the formation of the WTO and the TRIPS Agreement. Prior to the entry into force of the TRIPS Agreement, IP rights were regulated through a patchwork of treaties administered by the WIPO, including the Paris Convention on Industrial Property and the Berne Convention on Literary and Artistic Works (ICTSD, 2005). For instance, the Paris Convention[4] administered by the WIPO was focused on procedures to streamline patent applications in countries already providing patents and to ensure equal treatment of foreign applicants alongside domestic ones (Ho, 2011).

As discussed in chapter 2, developing countries and least developed countries (LDCs) have had little or no involvement, or input, in the development of the above core international IP treaties, as most of them were negotiated in the colonial era. Developing country concerns about international IP regulations started to emerge only in the post-colonial era, culminating in a North–South standoff on reform of the international IP system in the 1970s and 1980s (Deere, 2009). The TRIPS Agreement was negotiated at a time when there was a deadlock between developed countries on the one hand, and the developing countries and LDCs on the other hand over the revision of the Paris Convention for the Protection of Industrial Property, before the WIPO (Yu, 2004).[5] Instead of resolving the deadlock on the matter, the developed nations pushed to shift the entire IP rights agenda from the WIPO to the GATT trade negotiations. Also, a number of developing countries which sought membership at the WTO were not granting patent monopolies for pharmaceutical products (Correa, 2009) at the time when the Uruguay Round of negotiation was taking place (Correa, 2008). Both the TNPCs and the developed countries considered the WIPO as a forum where the voice of the developing countries were more pronounced, drowning the voice of the developed countries which spoke for incentivising innovation, and that any efforts to introduce an international IP rights regime with a clear enforcement mechanism at the WIPO would be met with strong opposition and end in failure. On the other hand, there was a general feeling amongst the developing countries that the IP rights concerns raised by the US government was being put forth on behalf of its industry (which clearly held a large pool of global IP rights), and that efforts towards the creation of an international IP rights regime was aimed at furthering the interests of the Western business and not those of the developing countries (Adede, 2003). Without a doubt, the TNPCs played a key role in bringing the agenda of IP rights to be treated as a trade-related issue for discussion and negotiation at the Uruguay Round of negotiations. This particular strategy of

4 The Paris Convention for the Protection of Industrial Property 1883, as amended on 28 September 1979; The Patent Cooperation Treaty, June 19, 1970, 28.7 U.S.T. 7645, 1160 U.N.T.S. 232 (providing a streamlined process for submitting patent applications in multiple jurisdictions).

5 The 1980s and 1990s saw the shift in the administration of international IP rights from the WIPO to the GATT through the lobbying of transnational corporations (TNCs). The TNCs were convinced that renegotiation of the Paris Convention under the aegis of the WIPO will never give them the level of protection they sought.

identifying IP as a trade-related issue facilitated the activation of new institutions to parties seeking to ration IP (Sell, 2009).

The modern global economy is knowledge based, and the policies built around IP invariably affects most fields – economic development, access to medicines, access to knowledge (education at all levels), human rights, innovation, technology, agriculture, *etc*. Sell notes that the US had shifted the forum 'horizontally' from the WIPO to the GATT as early as the mid-1980s with a view to seeking higher global IP standards, and as well as vertically through bilateral trade agreements and RTAs (Sell, 1998), requiring higher standards of IP protection from partner countries. The recurring theme from the US was the exertion of continued pressure on developing countries through the threat of trade sanctions to reduce any opposition to the agenda in the Uruguay Round of negotiations (Sundaram, 2014a).[6] When the US and its developed country allies moved the agenda on IP rights from the WIPO to the GATT trade negotiations as a trade related matter at the Uruguay Round of negotiations, it was with a view to measure the IP rules using the economic yardstick (Menescal, 2005; Gervais, 2005).[7] Here, Gervais notes that by bringing the IP rights protection agenda to the GATT negotiations, IP rights as a variation on the classic theme of property rights, or even as a human rights notion, was bound to fail (Gervais, 2005). To this day, the US, along with EU, bypasses multilateral debates and successfully pressures weaker countries to adopt TRIPS-plus IP standards in bilateral and regional trade agreements, instances of which will be discussed in chapter 4 in more detail.

Developing countries, led by India, Brazil and Argentina, were strongly opposed to the proposal of a change in forum, as they were of the firm view that the GATT mandate did not allow for the discussion of substantive issues on IP, and that it was the WIPO that had the institutional competence to discuss such issues (Watal, 2001; Drahos, 2002). The developing countries were also aware that once the IP rights agenda was taken out of WIPO and moved to the newly emerging multilateral trading system as a trade-related matter, they would have little influence in the matter. In July 1989, India, one of the developing countries, submitted a detailed paper at the negotiations expressing the developing countries' strong opposition to the inclusion of IP rights to the GATT agenda (UNCTAD-ICTSD, 2005). Although debated, the paper presented by India at the negotiations did not have the desired effect,[8] as towards the latter half of 1989 and the beginning of 1990 almost all developing countries were constrained

6 The author discusses the extensive pressure exerted on India during and after the Uruguay Round of negotiations through the United States Trade Representative (USTR) and other methods.

7 Menescal notes that a group funded by US-based TNPCs were the ones to first suggest that linking trade and IP in the GATT.

8 India had all along argued that any principle or standard relating to IP rights should be carefully tested against the needs of developing countries. It urged that the group focus on restrictive and anti-competitive practices of the owners of IP rights and evolve standards and principles for their elimination to avoid distortion of trade. It also stressed that substantive standards on IP were more in the realm of socio-economic, industrial and technological development than trade, especially in the case of developing countries.

to change their position on the inclusion of IP rights to the GATT agenda (Bird and Cahoy, 2007; Watal, 2001; Gervais, 2005).[9] With little or no opposition from the developing countries at the negotiations (Foster, 1998; Drahos, 2002),[10] the debate on the inclusion of IP rights into the GATT agenda came to an end, paving the way for the entry of the TRIPS Agreement. The leadership that India and Brazil were able to provide during the negotiations (as part of the G77 coalition) was to fade away in the post-TRIPS era. In this regard, Drahos opines that it was purely down to the perception in some quarters of India, where it is thought that India stands to gain from parts of the IP regime of the WTO. India is one of the developing countries from the BRIC alliance which has a stronger knowledge economy than other developing countries, and it can hence be argued that India will stand to gain if it were to pursue a more intense 'innovation-based' agenda as part of its economic development in the years to come.

1.2 *TNPCs and the inclusion of IP rights protection in the WTO*

A strong view exists amongst some writers that about twelve US corporations were primarily responsible for the lobbying that brought the TRIPS Agreement into existence (Sell, 2003; Drahos and Braithwaite, 2002; Matthews, 2002). The TRIPS Agreement came to be an output of private nodal governance (Drahos 2003; Weissman, 1996), with the process starting in the 1980s when one of the TNPCs took the lead in creating an agenda to include US IP rights protection abroad.[11] The pharmaceutical industry for their part engaged in aggressive lobbying campaigns on the need to secure greater patent protection abroad, and also funded academic studies aimed at proclaiming the merits of patent protection (Weissman, 1996). The US pharmaceutical industry's principle argument was that anything less than an American-style patent protection would constitute stealing by other nations (Drahos, 2003; Kosterlitz, 1993). The industry's strategy was, therefore, to persuade US policymakers to coerce Third World/developing countries to introduce restrictive patent laws into their domestic legislation

9 The shift came about due the coercive strategies adopted by the US, and as a result, India found itself isolated in the negotiations.

10 Drahos argues that developing nations had comparatively far less influence on outcomes in the international IP standard settings, at both pre-TRIPS and post-TRIPS negotiations, attributing the weak position of the developing nations to the use of coercive tactics by the United States and the European Union, who had all along stressed the need for excessively high global standards on IP protection.

11 Drahos identifies the US pharmaceutical corporation, Pfizer Inc., as taking the lead in lobbying through its well-established business networks to disseminate the idea of a trade-based approach to IP rights, and later on through interlinking the networks. The author also identifies the role played by the Advisory Committee on Trade Negotiations (ACTN), which was part of a private sector advisory committee system which was to ensure concordance between official US trade objectives and US commerce, and discusses how the CEO of Pfizer Inc. and chairman of ACTN, Mr Edmond Pratt Jr., with the help of other like-minded CEOs of leading US corporations, was able to develop a trade and investment agenda to protect US IP rights abroad.

(Drahos, 2003; Weissman, 1996; Berliner, 1990).[12] Needless to say, the lobbying was a great success, and the US government in the 1980s started introducing suitable provisions to protect IP as an investment activity in the Bilateral Investment Treaty (BIT) program, which it was negotiating with developing countries during that time (Weissman, 1996; Burgess, 1987; David, 1993).[13] The US pharmaceutical industry also succeeded in making strict international protection of IP rights a central goal of US international economic policy, and as Weissman notes, it was a great success to move the policy in the direction of strict international IP rights protection, as the traditional domain of international trade policy was primarily focused on tariff and related matters (Weissman, 1996). In February 1986, US President Reagan in a message to Congress proposed that a key item for consideration was to seek much greater protection of US IP interest in overseas territories (Drahos, 2003).[14]

The next step for the lobbyists was to move the discussion on international IP rights protection to the GATT negotiations. In 1986, a coalition of thirteen major US corporations, including Pfizer, Bristol-Meyers, Merck and Johnson & Johnson, to name a few, formed an *ad hoc* committee called Intellectual Property Committee (IPC) (Drahos, 2003; Weissman, 1990). The stated objective of the committee, in its own words, was 'dedicated to the negotiation of a comprehensive agreement on intellectual property in the current GATT round of multilateral trade negotiations' (Drahos, 2003; Weissman, 1990).[15] WIPO, created in 1967, was the first international attempt to address some of the concerns relating to an international IP rights movement, and the developing countries were, naturally, opposed to altering the WIPO system to strengthen IP rights protection (UNCTAD-ICTSD, 2005). WIPO, in the eyes of patent-holding developed nations, was incapable of responding effectively to issues relating to intellectual property rights violation (Crump and Druckman, 2012). Industry groups from patent-holding developed countries successfully created a coalition of governments that would pursue the objective of moving IP rights regulation from WIPO to the GATT (Crump and Druckman, 2012; Stewart, 1993). The

12 Starting in 1985, the USTR served notice on a number of countries, informing them about possible trade sanctions if they were to not bring their domestic patent laws into line with American laws. The USTR, acting under Section 301 of the Trade Act 1974, placed countries which did not provide adequate protection to US IP interests on its 'watch lists' and 'priority watch lists'. The primary targets were large Third World/developing countries such as India, Argentina, Brazil, Taiwan and Thailand, which had begun to develop domestic industries to compete against US pharmaceutical manufacturers in their own markets. The US Congress, in pursuit of a more combative approach to enforcing its IP rights overseas, enacted the Omnibus Trade and Competitiveness Act (Trade Act of 1988).

13 Burgess also notes that in 1984, a trade bill was passed by the US Congress, which included provisions for safeguarding IP as an important consideration in granting developing countries preferential tariff treatment.

14 In a message dated 6 February 1986 and entitled 'America's Agenda for the Future', President Reagan proposed that the key item was much greater protection for US intellectual property abroad.

15 The IPC's close relationship with the USTR permitted it to shape US proposals and negotiating positions during the course of the GATT negotiations.

move for a global IP rights protection, mooted by developed countries and led by the US, was strongly opposed by developing countries that included Argentina, Brazil, India and South Africa (Sundaram, 2014a). The developing countries were strongly in favour of a WIPO-led negotiation, as opposed to a revision of international IP rights obligations through the GATT, as the WIPO had traditionally been the forum for such matters (Edgar, 1994; Weissman, 1996, 1990).[16] Developed countries, including the US, EU and Japan acted fast to shift the global IP rights administration from the WIPO to the GATT to achieve the objective of an expanded IP property rights protection regime. Patent-holding businesses in the US, EC and Japan successfully exerted pressure on their respective governments to ensure that IP rights became a global commercial issue and also the focus of attention during the Uruguay Round of GATT negotiations (Matthews, 2002).

Most developing countries that sought membership in the WTO and entered the Uruguay Round of negotiations were not granting patent monopolies for pharmaceuticals (Correa, 2009). India's position, which was well supported by other developing countries, was that any principle or standard relating to IP rights was to be carefully tested against the needs of developing countries, and that it would be inappropriate to focus the negotiations on the protection of monopoly rights of the owners of IP rights, when almost 99 percent of the patents were owned by industrialised nations (UNCTAD-ICTSD, 2005; Sundaram, 2014a). Throughout the TRIPS negotiations, the US maintained a firm stance towards reaching a global agreement for higher levels of IP rights protection. As mentioned earlier, by the end of 1989 and the beginning of 1990 the developing countries were constrained to change their position completely due to extensive pressure – both political and economic – from the developed countries led by the US (Deere, 2009).[17] The developed countries were able to achieve their goal of higher international IP rights protection by circumventing and undermining the authority of the WIPO. The long-drawn-out Uruguay Round of negotiations produced the TRIPS Agreement, which came into force in January 1995. The Agreement can be viewed as the most important step in the globalisation of standards of patent, trade secrets and trademark protection – the three areas most relevant to the success of chemical and pharmaceutical companies (Drahos, 2003). Of major significance was the obligation on member states to make available patents for products and processes without discrimination as to the field of

16 The developing countries were distrustful of GATT, which was largely constructed and dominated by industrialised countries. They favoured discussing IP rights protection before United Nations–affiliated organizations, such as the WIPO, where the Third World countries exerted greater influence.

17 In the mid-1980s, developing countries faced pressures from both developed countries and knowledge-based multinational companies to agree to the inclusion of a stringent international IP commitment in the multilateral trading system. To break the standoff, developed countries also launched an economic and diplomatic offensive that ultimately forced developing countries to concede.

technology,[18] and requiring the introduction of product patents for chemical and pharmaceutical patents.

2 TRIPS Agreement flexibilities and the Doha Declaration

The TRIPS Agreement, which came into force on 1 January 1995, allows member states to provide for a more extensive protection of IP rights if they wish to, and a minimum standard of protection from others who may not favour the idea of an extensive protection (WIPO, 2010). The Agreement also contains flexibilities in its implementation, which is particularly aimed at developing countries and LDCs. The patent-related flexibilities identified include provision for the grant of compulsory licencing, parallel importation and provisions relating to patentable subject matter, patent rights, abuse of rights, and the control of anti-competitive practices. Flexibilities other than the ones identified above include the exhaustion of rights (Correa, 2005)[19] and parallel importation, scope of patentability and optional exclusion, exceptions to patent rights and enforcement (Deere, 2009).[20] Some developing countries feared that the extended IP rights protection granted for pharmaceutical patents under the Agreement was likely to increase dependency on TNPCs and affect the developing countries and LDCs severely, as essential medicines could become unaffordable and beyond their reach (Sundaram, 2014b).[21] The developing countries were fully aware that the patent-holding developed countries, which advocated a wider global IP rights protection and promoted the TRIPS Agreement, had a strong public healthcare system and would not be affected by the pharmaceutical patent regime of the Agreement.

The US and Switzerland (both holding a number of pharmaceutical patents), well supported by other developed countries, took the stance that the only flexibility afforded under the Agreement was its staggered implementation in certain cases, but in contrast the developing countries were of the firm view that the TRIPS Agreement did not limit their sovereign powers when addressing domestic health crises, such as HIV/AIDS (Sundaram, 2014a). In short, the impact

18 See Article 27.1 of TRIPS.

19 The 'exhaustion of patent rights' is sometimes referred to as the 'first-sale' doctrine. The TRIPS Agreement under Articles 6 and 28(6), and the Doha Declaration under Article 5(d), allow member states to determine the scope and extent of exhaustion of patent rights. This position is strongly disputed by the US Delegation to the Council of TRIPS, as it holds the view that Article 6 of the TRIPS Agreement does not allow WTO members to avail themselves of dispute settlement in relation to questions involving parallel imports, or to authorise parallel imports (Delegation of the United States, Council for TRIPS Meeting of June 1822, 2001, JOB(01)/97/Add.5, Council for TRIPS, 28 June 2001).

20 Deere suggests the development of national policies on utility models, disclosure of origin of genetic material and prior informed consent, and traditional knowledge (folklore and cultural heritage were also mentioned).

21 Sundaram (2014b) notes that in Brazil access to essential medicines is recognised as an indispensable part of the right to health guaranteed under the Constitution of the country and is considered an obligation on the part of the state.

of the TRIPS Agreement on public health in developing countries and LDCs became a serious issue. Due to growing pressure from the developing countries, and in particular from the member states from Africa, the Council for TRIPS[22] in June 2001 considered in detail the relationship between public health and TRIPS Agreement.[23] In November 2001, the Doha Declaration on TRIPS and Public Health (UNAIDS, 2011)[24] was promulgated, addressing some of the concerns of the developing countries, which also sought to clarify other divergent views held by the member states on the application and ambit of the TRIPS Agreement (Gathii, 2002). Under the Doha Declaration, the member states had the right to grant compulsory licences, to determine the grounds for the grant, and to decide what constituted a national emergency.[25] Paragraph 4 encapsulated the spirit of the Declaration in the following words:

> We agree that the TRIPS Agreement does not and should not prevent Members from taking measures to protect public health. Accordingly, while reiterating our commitment to the TRIPS Agreement, we affirm that the Agreement can and should be interpreted and implemented in a manner supportive of WTO Members' right to protect public health and, in particular, to promote access to medicines for all.

Some developing countries have made constructive use of the flexibilities while giving effect to the TRIPS Agreement into their national legislations. Some countries have delayed the introduction of product patent regime into their legislation (Sundaram, 2014a),[26] and others have used the compulsory licencing provisions to manufacture or procure generic medicines at an affordable price (Sundaram, 2014b).[27] It will not be out of place to point out that the implementation of flexibilities in key pharmaceutical markets like Brazil, India and South

22 The legal basis for the establishment of the Council is found in Article IV.5 of the WTO Agreement, which stipulates that the Council 'shall oversee the functioning' of the TRIPS Agreement.

23 In 1996, the World Health Assembly, which was mandated to report on the impact of the work of the WTO with respect to national drug policies and essential drugs, examined the relationship between public health and the TRIPS Agreement. See resolution on the Revised Drug Strategy, Resolution WHA 49.14 (25 May 1996).

24 The Doha Declaration, besides providing interpretative guidance on the policy of flexibilities embodied in the TRIPS Agreement, also sought to clarify the very scope of the TRIPS Agreement.

25 The 2001 Doha Declaration and the 2003 Decision on Implementation of paragraph 6 of the TRIPS Agreement recognises the right of a country to gain access to medicines.

26 India, one of the developing countries, has made maximum use of the flexibilities. India was able to delay the entry of the product patent regime into its patent laws and ably support its generics market, which was developed on the back of the process patent regime introduced in the Patent Act of 1970. Besides, in recent years India has also made use of the compulsory licensing provision introduced through the TRIPS-compliant legislation of 2005.

27 Brazil, one of the BRIC nations, which introduced the TRIPS-compliant patent laws into its national legislation much earlier than others, was able to use the compulsory license provisions under the TRIPS-compliant legislation to procure generic medicines at affordable prices for its much-lauded anti-AIDS programme.

Africa came at a very high price, as transnational pharmaceutical corporations, well supported by developed country participation, were able to mount oppositions and cause delays in the actual implementation (Sundaram, 2014a, 2014b; Drahos and Braithwaite, 2002).[28] If the TRIPS Agreement was a well-concerted effort by the developed countries and their TNPCs, then the Doha Declaration was a hard-fought bargain by the developing countries and LDCs, led by the African nations and well supported by the NGOs.

2.1 TRIPS implementation: the difficulties

Access to essential medicines is recognised as an indispensable part of the right to health, and it is viewed as a non-delegable obligation on the part of the state and cannot be violated based on lack of available resources (WHO Report, 2002). The developing countries were apprehensive that the IP rights standards sought to be introduced through the TRIPS Agreement would severely restrict access to essential medicines for their citizens and impede their efforts to control diseases including HIV/AIDS, tuberculosis and malaria. The developing countries also feared that the extended IP rights protection for pharmaceutical patents was likely to increase dependency on multinational pharmaceutical companies and affect the developing and the LDCs severely, as essential patented medicines would become unaffordable and beyond their reach. The Doha Declaration left unresolved the issue on how to export products manufactured under a compulsory licence to countries without domestic production capacity. The Declaration also did not address the promise of increased R&D in exchange for higher levels of IP protection, which was used as a bargaining chip by the developed countries during TRIPS negotiations ('t Hoen, 2009).

Despite having some positives (as mentioned in the earlier part of the chapter), the Doha Declaration and the UN commitments (in the form of Millennium Goals)[29] fail to deliver and much is left to be desired,[30] as the developing countries and LDCs still face big challenges in the implementation of the flexibilities due to increased IP protection introduced under the TRIPS Agreement (Deere, 2009).[31] Besides, the political and economic pressures faced from the developed countries also discourage them from implementing the flexibilities. The use of

28 TNPCs took legal action against the government of South Africa for its proposed compulsory licensing laws.

29 The United Nations Millennium Development Goal (UN MDG), Target 8.E states, 'In cooperation with pharmaceutical companies, provide access to affordable essential drugs in developing countries.' United Nations, 'Millennium Development Goals and Beyond 2015' <www.un.org/millenniumgoals/global.shtml> accessed 27 November 2017.

30 According to 2008 figures released by the WHO, approximately a third of the people worldwide lack access to medicines. Further, the high prices of essential medicines act as a barrier in the treatment of millions.

31 See also United Nations, 'The Millennium Development Goals Report 2013', which, interestingly, does not list any entries under 8.E of the Goals, which is aimed at providing access to affordable essential drugs in developing countries.

the flexibilities afforded under the Doha Declaration came under severe criticism from global pharmaceutical companies who were acting through their national governments, as they fiercely opposed the practical implementation of the TRIPS flexibilities in the case of Brazil and Thailand in 2007–2008 ('t Hoen, 2009). Nevertheless, the Doha Declaration's impact has been widespread amongst developing countries, influencing their health policies and in particular their pharmaceutical patent legislation. However, it is worth noting here that some developing countries have used the TRIPS flexibilities to produce and purchase generic ARVs. There is also evidence of donor countries now permitting the use of their funds to procure generic ARVs for least developed countries (Waning, Diedrichsen, and Moon, 2010).[32]

While the developing countries were eager to join the WTO and made to sign up to the TRIPS Agreement, most were in for a rude shock as the trade-off agreed between the developed nations and the developing nation did not materialise (Dreyfuss, 2009).[33] To a great extent, the gap in the knowledge economy between the developed and the developing countries (North–South divide) contributed to their ignorance of the TRIPS Agreement's implication and the flexibilities offered therein (Dreyfuss, 2009). Although it can be argued that all of the parties were given the opportunity to participate in the negotiations leading to the TRIPS Agreement during the Uruguay Round of negotiations, the voice of the developing countries was effectively silenced through a series of manoeuvrings – both forum shifting and economic pressure exerted through the fear of exclusion from trade and investment opportunities – by the patent-holding developed countries led by the US, EU, Switzerland and Japan (Sundaram, 2014a). A lack of clarity and consensus on the TRIPS flexibilities had hampered the efforts to widen access to ARV treatment in developing and least developed countries (UNAIDS, 2011), which affected the sub-Saharan African nations severely (UNAIDS, 2014; Haakonsson and Richey 2007).[34] The attempts by the developing countries to implement the TRIPS Agreement, through the introduction of TRIPS-compliant legislation, into their domestic legislations will be dealt with in detail in chapters 5–9, where region-specific case studies are presented. The studies cover the following developing countries, *viz.*, Brazil, China, India, South Africa and Kenya, from three different continents.

32 The value of the donor-funded developing country ARV market has had a dramatic annual growth in recent times. By 2008, Indian generic ARVs accounted for 65 percent of the total value (US$463 million) of ARV purchases reported.

33 The trade-off was access to foreign markets in exchange for raising domestic IP rights levels, which never happened.

34 Sub-Saharan Africa (SSA) has the highest incidence of HIV/AIDS in the world today. In 2013, 35 million people were living with HIV/AIDS worldwide, of which 24.7 million were from SSA. This region also accounts for almost 70 percent of global total new HIV infection. In the same year, 1.1 million people died of AIDS-related causes in SSA. Most shockingly, only 37 percent of patients in SSA received antiretroviral (ARV) treatment. Haakonsson and Richey also note that most ARVs are patented, and their high costs in developing countries limit their access to very few programmes and relatively few people.

Bibliography

1 Adede, Adronico O. 'Origins and History of the TRIPS Negotiations,' in Bellmann, Christophe, Graham Dutfield, and Ricardo Meléndez-Ortiz (eds.) *Trading in Knowledge: Development Perspectives on TRIPS, Trade and Sustainability* (ICTSD & Earthscan Publications, 2003) 23–35.

2 Bird, Robert C., and Daniel R. Cahoy. 'The Emerging BRIC Economies: Lessons from Intellectual Property Negotiation and Enforcement,' *Northwestern Journal of Technology and Intellectual Property* Vol. 5 (2007) 400, 403–404.

3 Berliner, Brian M. 'Making Intellectual Property Pirates Walk the Plank: Using Special 301 to Protect the United States' Rights,' *Loyola of Los Angeles International & Comparative Law Review* (1990) 725–752, 727.

4 Braithwaite, John, and Peter Drahos. *Global Business Regulation* (Cambridge University Press, 2000) 564–577.

5 Burgess, John. 'Fighting Trespassing on "Intellectual Property,"' *The Washington Post* (6 December 1987) <www.washingtonpost.com/archive/business/1987/12/06/fighting-trespassing-on-intellectual-property/62404fde-0ae0-4263-b5cd-77f70dd90448/> accessed 25 November 2017.

6 Correa, Carlos M. 'The TRIPS Agreement and Developing Countries,' in Macrory Patrick J., Arthur E. Appleton, and Michael P. Plummer (eds.) *The World Trade Organisation: Legal, Economic and Political Analysis* Vol. II (Springer, 2005) 447.

7 Correa, Carlos M. 'Patent Rights,' in Correa, Carlos M., and Abdulqawi A. Yusuf (eds.) *Intellectual Property and International Trade: The TRIPS Agreement* (Kluwer Law International, 2008) 227, 229.

8 Correa, Carlos M. 'Intellectual Property Rights and Inequalities in Health Outcomes,' in Ronald Labonté, and others (eds.) *Globalization and Health: Pathways, Evidence and Policy* (Routledge, 2009) 263–288, 266.

9 Crump, Larry, and Daniel Druckman. 'Turning Points in Multilateral Trade Negotiations on Intellectual property,' *International Negotiation* Vol. 17, No. 1 (2012) 9–35, 12.

10 David, Paul A. 'Intellectual Property Institutions and the Panda's Thumb: Patent, Copyrights, and the Trade Secrets in Economic Theory and History,' in Wallerstein, Mitchel B., Mary E Mogee, and Robin A. Schoen (eds.) *Global Dimensions of Intellectual Property Rights in Science and Technology* (National Academy Press, 1993) 20.

11 Deere, Carolyn. *The Implementation Game: The TRIPS Agreement and the Global Politics of Intellectual Property Reform in Developing Countries* (Oxford University Press, 2009) 8.

12 DOHA+10. *TRIPS Flexibilities and Access to Antiretroviral Therapy: Lessons from the Past, Opportunities for the Future* (UNAIDS, 2011) 6.

13 Drahos, Peter. 'Developing Countries and International Intellectual Property Standard-Setting,' *The Journal of World Intellectual Property* Vol. 5, No. 5 (2002) 765–789.

14 Drahos, Peter, and J. Braithwaite. *Information Feudalism: Who Owns the Knowledge Economy?* (Earthscan, 2002).

15 Drahos, Peter. 'Expanding Intellectual Property's Empire: The Role of FTAs,' Regulatory Institutions Network, Research School of Social Sciences, Australian National University (2003).

16 Drahos, Peter. 'Securing the Future of Intellectual Property: Intellectual Property Owners and Their Nodally Coordinated Enforcement Pyramid,' *Case Western Journal of International Law* Vol. 36 (2004) 53–77.

17 Dreyfuss, Rochelle C. 'The Role of India, China, Brazil and Other Emerging Economies in Establishing Access Norms for Intellectual Property and Intellectual Property Law Making,' *Institute for International Law and Justice Working Paper* 5 (2009) 9–53.
18 Edgar, Craig. 'Patenting Nature: GATT on a Hot Tin Roof,' *Washburn Law Journal* Vol. 34 (1994) 76–98.
19 Foster, George K. 'Opposing Forces in a Revolution in International Patent Protection: The U.S. and India in the Uruguay Round and Its Aftermath,' *UCLA Journal of International Law & Foreign Affairs* Vol. 3 (1998) 283, 317.
20 Gathii, James Thuo. 'The Legal Status of Doha Declaration on TRIPS and Public Health Under the Vienna Convention on the Law of Treaties,' *Harvard Journal of Law and Technology* Vol. 15, No. 2 (2002) 291–317, 292–293.
21 Gervais, Daniel J. 'Intellectual Property, Trade & Development: The State of Play,' *Fordham Law Review* Vol. 74, No. 2 (2005) 505–535.
22 Haakonsson, Stine Jessen, and Lisa Ann Richey. 'TRIPS and Public Health: The Doha Declaration and Africa,' *Development Policy Review* Vol. 25, No. 1 (2007) 71–90.
23 Ho, Cynthia M. *Access to Medicine in the Global Economy: International Agreement on Patents and Related Rights* (Oxford University Press, 2011) 57.
24 International Centre for Trade and Sustainable Development (ICTSD). *Resource Book on TRIPS and Development* (Cambridge University Press, 2005) 3.
25 Kosterlitz, J. 'Rx: Higher Prices,' *National Journal* Vol. 25, No. 7 (1993) 396–399.
26 Matthews, Duncan. *Globalising Intellectual Property Rights: The TRIPS Agreement* (Routledge, 2002).
27 Menescal, Andréa K. 'Those Behind the TRIPS Agreement: The Influence of the ICC and the AIPPI on International Property Decision,' *Intellectual Property Quarterly* Vol. 2 (2005) 155–182.
28 Musungu, Sisule F., and Cecilia Oh. 'The Use of Flexibilities in TRIPS by Developing Countries: Can They Promote Access to Medicines?' South Centre (2006).
29 Report of the WHO Expert Committee. 'The Selection and Use of Essential Medicines,' WHO Technical Report Series 914 (2002) <http://apps.who.int/medicinedocs/pdf/s4875e/s4875e.pdf> accessed 25 November 2017.
30 Resolution on the Revised Drug Strategy, Resolution WHA 49.14 (25 May 1996).
31 Sell, Susan K. *Power and Ideas: The North-South Politics of Intellectual Property and Antitrust* (University of New York Press, 1998) 129–139.
32 Sell, Susan K. *Private Power, Public Law: The Globalization of Intellectual Property Rights* (Cambridge University Press, 2003).
33 Sell, Susan K. 'Cat and Mouse: Forum Shifting in the Battle Over Intellectual Property Enforcement,' *American Political Science Association Meeting* Vol. 3, No. 6 (2009).
34 Stewart, Terence P. *The GATT Uruguay Round: A Negotiating History (1986–1992)*, Vol. 3 (Kluwer Law International, 1993) 1–10.
35 Sundaram, Jae. 'India's Trade-Related Aspects of Intellectual Property Rights Compliant Pharmaceutical Patent Laws: What Lessons for India and Other Developing Countries?' *Information & Communications Technology Law* Vol. 23, No. 1 (2014a) 1–30.
36 Sundaram, Jae. 'Brazil's Implementation of TRIPS Flexibilities: Ambitious Missions, Early Implementation, and the Plans for Reform,' *Information & Communications Technology Law* Vol. 23, No. 2 (2014b) 81–116.
37 't Hoen, Ellen. *The Global Politics of Pharmaceutical Monopoly Power: Drug Patents, Access, Innovation and the Application of the WTO Doha Declaration on TRIPS and Public Health* (ABM, The Netherlands, 2009) 2–3.

38 Paris Convention for the Protection of Industrial Property 1883, as amended on 28 September 1979.
39 Patent Cooperation Treaty 1970.
40 United Nations. 'Millennium Development Goals and Beyond 2015' <www.un.org/millenniumgoals/global.shtml> accessed 27 November 2017.
41 UNAIDS. 'DOHA+10, TRIPS Flexibilities and Access to Antiretroviral Therapy: Lessons from the Past, Opportunities for the Future,' UNAIDS: Technical Brief (UNAIDS, 2011) 6.
42 UNAIDS. *Factsheet 2014* (UNAIDS, 2014) <www.unaids.org/sites/default/files/documents/20141118_FS_WADreport_en.pdf> accessed 27 November 2017.
43 UNCTAD-ICTSD. *Resource Book on TRIPS and Development* (Cambridge University Press, 2005) 6.
44 United Nations. 'The Millennium Development Goals Report 2013' <www.un.org/millenniumgoals/pdf/report-2013/mdg-report-2013-english.pdf> accessed 27 November 2017.
45 Waning, Brenda, Ellen Diedrichsen, and Suerie Moon. 'A Lifeline to Treatment: The Role of Indian Generic Manufacturers in Supplying Antiretroviral Medicines to Developing Countries,' *Journal of the International AIDS Society* Vol. 13, No. 35 (2010) 1–9.
46 Watal, Jayashree. *Intellectual Property Rights in the WTO and Developing Countries* (Kluwer Law International, 2001) 21.
47 Weissman, Robert. 'Patent Plunder: TRIPing the Third World,' *Multinational Monitor*, Vol. 11, No. 11 (November 1990) <www.multinationalmonitor.org/hyper/issues/1990/11/weissman.html> accessed 25 November 2017.
48 Weissman, Robert. 'A Long, Strange TRIPS: The Pharmaceutical Industry Drive to Harmonize Global Intellectual Property Rules, and the Remaining WTO Legal Alternatives Available to Third World Countries,' *University of Pennsylvania Journal of International Economic Law* Vol. 17 (1996) 1069–1125, 1076.
49 World Intellectual Property Organization. 'Patent Related Flexibilities in the Multilateral Legal Framework and Their Legislative Implementation at the National and Regional Levels,' Committee on Development and Intellectual Property, Fifth Session, WIPO (26–30 April 2010).
50 World Trade Organization, Declaration on the TRIPS Agreement and Public Health, WT/MIN(01)/DEC/2, adopted on 20 November 2001 <www.wto.org/english/thewto_e/minist_e/min01_e/mindecl_trips_e.pdf> accessed 25 November 2017.
51 WTO General Council, 'Implementation of Paragraph 6 of the Doha Declaration on the TRIPS Agreement and Public Health,' Decision of the General Council [WT/L/540 and Corr.1] (1 September 2003).
52 Yu, Peter K. 'Currents and Crosscurrents in the International Intellectual Property Regime,' *Loyola of Los Angeles Law Review* Vol. 38 (2004) 323, 357–358.

4 Undermining TRIPS flexibilities

FTAs, RTAs, EPAs, TRIPS-plus and stoppage in transit

Contents

1 Introduction

A discussion on access to essential medicines would not be complete without mentioning the role of free trade agreements (FTAs), regional trade agreements (RTAs) economic partnership agreements and TRIPS-plus provisions – which all pose major problems to the pursuit of access to affordable medicines.[1] The threat, both actual and perceived, does not stop with the introduction of multilateral agreements which were instrumental in establishing higher international IP rights protection, but continues to grow with the forging of newer agreements. The TRIPS-plus provisions contained in FTAs/RTAs have nearly rendered useless the flexibilities contained in the TRIPS Agreement. The TRIPS-plus provisions cannot be considered as presenting a mere 'threat', as they have clearly evolved to become concrete barriers to the access to affordable medicines in developing countries and LDCs. The patent-holding developed countries have proceeded to strengthen their hold on IP rights through the introduction of TRIPS-plus provisions in the FTAs/RTAs entered into with partner countries (developed and developing countries).

1 FTAs and preferential trade agreements (PTAs) have narrower definitions than regional trade agreements (RTAs) within the WTO system. In practice, both are often used interchangeably with the term RTA. Also, in practice, an RTA need not define a geographical region, but can define relevant bilateral trade deals between geographically distant countries. While economic partnership agreements (EPAs) are not FTAs in the classic sense, they are still designed as instruments to advance the development objectives of any trade relations identified in the agreement.

In recent years, large-scale FTAs have emerged on the horizon (*e.g.*, NAFTA, TTP, TTIP – not fully ratified yet, *etc.*) led by the US. The inability of the WTO to control and question the proliferation of FTAs, and the unbridled lobbying powers enjoyed by the TNPCs to lobby their parent countries to insert TRIPS-plus provisions into the FTAs, appear to have the effect of taking away any flexibilities or advantages the developing countries may come to enjoy under the TRIPS Agreement, thus leaving them with little or no choice. The developing countries, who are parties to the FTAs, do not have the same powers as their developed country counterparts during negotiations and are forced to accept such TRIPS-plus provisions. This chapter will analyse how FTAs result in the violation of international norms on commitment to health and the status of generics in the market, which provide an effective and much more affordable alternative to patented drugs.

One of the cornerstones of the WTO is the non-discrimination principle found enshrined in the most-favoured-nation (MFN) obligation as established under Article 1 of GATT. The MFN obligation is also contained in Article 2 of GATS and Article 4 of the TRIPS Agreement. When a WTO Member State enters into an agreement with other member states, it departs from the MFN principle, as it grants a more favourable treatment to its fellow signatories under the agreement than it does to other WTO member states, multilaterally. Nonetheless, WTO member states, under certain conditions, are permitted to depart from the MFN obligation, which is outlined in paragraphs 4 to 10 of Article XXIV of GATT (as clarified in the Understanding on the Interpretation of Article XXIV of the GATT 1994), which provides for the formation and operation of customs unions and free-trade areas covering trade in goods.[2] The WTO member states, utilising the above provisions, have derogated from the MFN principle to form FTAs, which has also led to a shift in trade policies. It is to be noted here that no equivalent derogation from the MFN obligation is countenanced under the TRIPS Agreement. The WTO TRIPS Agreement has no requirement to notify relevant bilateral and regional agreements that set IP standards for their signatories, but many of those notified under other WTO Agreements have IP provisions, or provisions that indirectly touch on IP rights, such as system for bilateral dispute settlement.

2 TRIPS-plus provisions, FTAS and the WTO

The WTO does not have any control over the FTAs nor other plurilateral agreements affecting access to medicines in developing countries and LDCs. In this regard, the loss of WIPO's governance over the administration of international

2 See also Article V of GATS, governing the conclusion of economic integration agreements (EIAs) in the area of trade in services; and the Decision on Differential and More Favourable Treatment Reciprocity and Fuller Participation of Developing Countries (Enabling Clause), which provide the legal basis for preferential trade agreements between developing countries.

IP rights protection is lamentable, and the actions of the developed countries in moving the governance from the WIPO to the WTO in the late 1980s can only be perceived as a calculated move to serve the interest of 'IP rights owning' countries. As discussed in chapter 3, the developed countries led by the US engaged in 'forum shifting' to move the IP rights enforcement agenda from the WIPO to the WTO, and successfully pursued the goal of international IP rights regulation through the introduction of the TRIPS Agreement. Likewise, in the post-TRIPS era, the US has once again engaged in forum shifting by moving the negotiating agenda from the multilateral arena to FTAs to pursue its IP rights agenda through the use of TRIPS-plus provisions. Needless to say, this forum shifting is a well-tested method of improving the odds of success by not limiting efforts to a single international forum (Drahos, 2007).

It can be asserted, to a certain extent, that the developing countries and the LDCs have been traded off to benefit the IP rights holders from developed countries. The US strategy on such matters has always been to directly influence and constrain the pharmaceutical coverage programmes of its trading partners (Lopert and Gleeson, 2013). It is also argued that developed nations, led by the US, has established an 'informal empire' by dictating and interpreting the terms of international legal rules in a form suitable to their own interests without any realistic challenge, by virtue of their obvious economic supremacy (Rahmatian, 2009). In short, the international process of IP rights expansion is being achieved through the TRIPS-plus provisions by the US and the EU through FTAs.

2.1 *Nature of IP provisions in FTAs*

While the TRIPS Agreement set a minimum standard for international IP protection, the leading industries in the US were not entirely satisfied with the terms of the Agreement and sought higher standards. In the late 1990s, closed-door non-transparent FTA negotiations were developed as a means to set global IP norms (Kilic, 2014), leading to the emergence of TRIPS-plus provisions in bilateral agreements. FTAs carry TRIPS-plus obligations in exchange for trade concessions granted to the partner states. They also demonstrate how bilateral dealings permit the US to gain what it cannot easily achieve in multilateral negotiations (Feinberg, 2003).[3] Some commentators have argued that the pursuit of TRIPS-plus IP protection has been partly driven by the US desire to achieve standards of protection it anticipated from the TRIPS Agreement but failed to secure (Lopert and Gleeson, 2013). The US pharmaceutical industry, one of the largest holders of pharmaceutical patents, held the view that the TRIPS Agreement fell short of its objectives. The FTAs normally include provisions that demand an increased level of IP protection and strengthened terms of enforcement over and above

3 Feinberg notes that US leverage is more pronounced 'in bilateral or plurilateral negotiations than in larger forums where other major economic powers are present.'

the requirements of TRIPS Agreement (Fink and Reichenmiller, 2006), and are appropriately referred to as 'TRIPS-plus' in commentaries.

The US, since 1994, has entered into twenty FTAs with developed and developing countries.[4] The FTAs promoted by the US and the EU[5] contain substantive patent and enforcement rules on IP, where each subsequent agreement serves as the baseline from which to expand the ambitions of the next agreement, thereby setting the bar higher on IP rights protection. The US, through the FTAs, had gained greater influence over the domestic pharmaceutical coverage policies of its trading partners (Lopert and Gleeson, 2013). It should also be noted that although provisions affecting domestic health policy settings were included in NAFTA (which came into force in 1994), only in the post-TRIPS era have provisions affecting domestic healthcare and drug coverage programmes been developed, which potentially delay generic market entry and frustrate any efforts to exercise TRIPS flexibilities. Drahos notes that the US has emerged as 'the principal architect of the global regulatory ratchet for intellectual property', rights protection (Drahos, 2004). The US had strategically opted for bilateralism as the main route to support its industry, in its relentless campaign to increase the levels of IP protection worldwide. This bilateralism, of course, operates in a context of deep asymmetries (Correa, 2004).

3 FTAs: data exclusivity, compulsory licencing

The TRIPS Agreement, under Article 39(3),[6] requires member states to protect the test data submitted for the marketing approval of pharmaceuticals and chemical products for agriculture,[7] against any 'unfair commercial use'. Article 39(3) covers two different categories of information, *viz.*, 'trade secrets' (information including that of a technical nature) and test data, which are the results of clinical trials made to demonstrate the efficacy and safety of pharmaceutical and agrochemical products (Correa, 2011).[8] Article 39(3), while prohibiting the 'unfair' commercial use of undisclosed test data, does not specify a minimum duration for

4 Some of the countries in the list include Australia, Canada, Israel, Jordan, Mexico, Morocco and Singapore. See Free Trade Agreements, Office of the US Trade Representative <www.ustr.gov/trade-agreements/free-trade-agreements> accessed 27 November 2017.

5 EU has over twenty-nine FTAs, and is in negotiation with Canada, Australia and India for possible FTAs. <http://europa.eu/rapid/press-releaseMEMO-12-932en.htm?locale=E> accessed 27 November 2017.

6 Article 39(3) of the TRIPS Agreement reads as follows: 'Members, when requiring, as a condition of approving the marketing of pharmaceutical or of agricultural chemical products which utilize new chemical entities, the submission of undisclosed test or other data, the origination of which involves a considerable effort, shall protect such data against unfair commercial use. In addition, Members shall protect such data against disclosure, except where necessary to protect the public, or unless steps are taken to ensure that the data are protected against unfair commercial use'.

7 Test data would normally relate to the results of tests about quality, safety and efficacy of any new compounds, and such test data will need protection if national authorities require its submission.

8 The author notes that protection of test data was one of the issues that divided the North and the South during the Uruguay Round of negotiations.

the said protection. Article 39(3) requires protection be given to secret data and not to data that are already in the public domain. Thus, if the patent holder relies on an approval granted in a foreign country, the obligation under Article 39(3) does not apply. Most importantly, Article 39(3) does not impose an obligation to grant exclusivity for test data.

A number of developing countries have refused to grant data exclusivity, as it delays the entry of generics into the market.[9] India, one of the major supplier of generics in the international market, had set up a commission to investigate the question of the type of protection needed for test data for pharmaceuticals (Reddy and Sandhu, 2007). Interestingly, the commission's report from 2007 concluded that data exclusivity was neither required nor advisable for India.[10] Some developed countries, in response to strong industry lobbying, have argued that protection of test data can only be ensured if a minimum period (*e.g.*, five years) of exclusivity is granted. Despite differing views held by the member states on the interpretation of Article 39(3), there had been no efforts to establish a WTO panel to go through the issue under the Dispute Settlement Understanding (Correa, 2011).[11]

The IP template from the US FTAs specifies a minimum of five years protection of test data (Sell, 2007),[12] followed by a provision specifying a further three years' protection for new uses of existing products. Correa postulates that such practices lead to the protection of investment as such, and not of a creative or inventive outcome, which was the very purpose of IP rights (Correa, 2004). In the FTAs, entered into post-TRIPS, the protection is extended to those data already in the public domain, resulting in the creation of a 'data exclusivity' provision (Lopert and Gleeson, 2013).[13] The US has successfully pressured other countries (both developed and developing) to adopt such an approach in their bilateral agreements

9 The USTR had listed the said developing countries in its special 301 reports, identifying them as engaging in unfair trade practices.

10 Para 1.12, the report concluded as follows: 'Hence, the policy decision should be taken keeping in view the national interest of the country by making use of the flexibilities in the TRIPS Agreement, in particular, the need to ensure rapid and timely response to public health needs by facilitating timely entry of generics and encouraging competition. The ethical issues of conducting repeated human trials when data on quality and efficacy already exists should also be kept in mind. At the same time, the need to adequately promote innovation and R&D in pharmaceuticals and agrochemicals by utilizing the rich human capital and the infrastructure available in the country should also be considered. This will help build India's strength in these areas on a long term sustainable basis.'

11 Professor Correa notes that a complaint by the US before the WTO in 2000 against Argentina was settled at the consultation stage. Argentina maintained its law and did not accept the US claim that exclusive rights should be granted.

12 Sell observes that such TRIPS-plus provisions can become a real impediment to compulsory licensing, as regulatory agencies cannot assess a generic marketing application for a product which is still subject to data protection, even where a compulsory license has been granted, and thus patent infringement cannot be asserted.

13 Lopert and Gleeson note that in some jurisdictions, it may be possible for generics manufacturers to submit a literature-based application, relying on 'efficacy and safety data' that is already in the public domain, rather than on the dossier submitted by the originator. They also advance the

(Correa, 2004). Bowing to pressure from the US, Guatemala, one of the poorest countries in Latin America, enacted data exclusivity for pharmaceuticals for a period longer than that applied in the US and EU (Correa, 2011).

The TRIPS Agreement allows member states to grant compulsory licences subject to conditions contained in Article 31. To summarise, the applicant state must first attempt to obtain a voluntary licence from the patent rights holder on 'reasonable commercial terms',[14] unless the situation constitutes a 'national emergency' or other circumstance of extreme urgency or the product is intended for public non-commercial use. The US FTAs with Australia, Singapore, Jordan and Vietnam contain provisions restricting the use of compulsory licencing in emergency situations. All US FTAs, barring the Vietnam and Jordan FTAs, prevent marketing approval of generics during the patents protection period without the consent of the patent holder. This particular restriction renders compulsory licencing ineffective in those countries, including Australia and Oman. In effect, such a provision in the FTAs also restrict the entry of generics in the market well after the patent for a drug has expired, and the originators reap the benefits of exclusive marketing for an extra period (Malhotra and Grewal, 2008).

In sharp contrast in the US, generic versions of the drug were launched on the next day when the patent on Bayer's ciprofloxacin expired, pushing the price down by 95% (Malhotra and Grewal, 2008). Some US FTAs even include provisions limiting the use of compulsory licencing of drugs for certain infectious diseases – HIV/AIDS, malaria and tuberculosis. The limiting provisions at times also include restrictions to circumstances of 'extreme urgency' or 'national emergency' (Outterson, 2010). Article 31 of the TRIPS Agreement does not mention specific diseases, and references to 'national emergency' and 'other circumstances of extreme urgency' are to be considered only in relation to waiving the requirement to seek prior permission from the rights holder to obtain a voluntary licence (Lopert and Gleeson, 2013). The US, beginning with the Morocco FTA signed in 2004, has sought to clearly restrict the use of compulsory licencing by narrowing the circumstances in which it can be applied (Sell, 2007). This in effect robs the country from fully utilising the flexibilities contained in the TRIPS Agreement.

While there is a debate on whether the TRIPS Agreement provisions on data exclusivity actually introduced a regime in itself, there is little doubt that data

---

argument that a literature-based submission is not possible unless protection is limited to undisclosed data, which distinguishes a data 'protection' from a data 'exclusivity' regime.

14 TRIPS Agreement Article 31(b): 'such use may only be permitted if, prior to such use, the proposed user has made efforts to obtain authorization from the right holder on reasonable commercial terms and conditions and that such efforts have not been successful within a reasonable period of time. This requirement may be waived by a Member in the case of a national emergency or other circumstances of extreme urgency or in cases of public non-commercial use. In situations of national emergency or other circumstances of extreme urgency, the right holder shall, nevertheless, be notified as soon as reasonably practicable. In the case of public non-commercial use, where the government or contractor, without making a patent search, knows or has demonstrable grounds to know that a valid patent is or will be used by or for the government, the right holder shall be informed promptly.'

exclusivity affects access to medicines in developing countries by preventing the early entry of generics. However, the direct impact of non-disclosure of test data on access to medicines has not been comprehensively discussed in academic circles. Over two decades have passed since the TRIPS Agreement came into force, but most of the arguments opposing the entry of the Agreement under the multilateral trading system, and based primarily on the denial of access to affordable medicines, still hold good.

3.1 FTAs: *parallel imports, patent linkage*

When a patented product is re-sold by a buyer to a second buyer in another country, parallel importation occurs. Parallel importation could provide a way to access affordable medicines in low-income communities where patented medicines are highly priced, as differential pricing is very common across countries (Correa, 2002). Proponents of national exhaustion, on the other hand, argue that banning parallel importation is necessary to persuade TNPCs to implement pro-poor differential pricing of essential medicines (Lindstrom, 2010). Parallel importation reduces the profit levels of the TNPCs patent holder, as it undermines the ability of a patent holder to engage in price discrimination across national boundaries (Mercurio, 2006).

The Doha Declaration reaffirms the members' rights to use the flexibilities provided in the TRIPS Agreement not only for using compulsory licencing but also for parallel imports of drugs to 'promote access to medicines for all'. Also, the 30 August 2003 decision under the TRIPS Agreement reiterates the ability to import generics from cheaper sources, when a member state has inadequate capacity to manufacture drugs. It is to be noted that a member state can reduce drug costs by permitting the parallel importation of a patented pharmaceutical product, when the product was originally sold by the patent owner in another country (Ho, 2011).[15] However, this right may be limited through the provisions introduced in FTAs. In the case of FTAs concluded with Morocco and Australia, the US has imposed restriction and/or prohibition on parallel importation. The FTAs utilise contractual terms to limit parallel imports to prevent undesired imports, without actually addressing a nation's view on international exhaustion of patent rights (Ho, 2011). Thus, the FTAs introduce contractual restrictions – allowing TNPCs to effectively prevent unauthorised distribution *via* parallel imports.

A number of FTAs require countries to adopt 'patent linkage', which can be seen as a second requirement on regulatory laws, beyond data exclusivity. Patent linkage would require a regulatory authority to be precluded from approving a generic drug if that drug would infringe a patent (Ho, 2011).[16] Patent linkage provisions in FTAs provide ample opportunities for TNPCs to file commercial

15 IP rights are 'exhausted' once a product is placed on a market anywhere in the world. In short, the initial sale ends the patent holder's rights and control over what can be done with that product.

16 See Article 16.8(4)(c) US-Singapore FTA; Article 17.10(2)(b) US-Chile FTA; Article 17.10(5) US-Australia FTA; and Article 15.10(4) US-Morocco FTA.

litigations against governments as well as third party manufacturers. The FTAs promoted by the US not only preclude approval of a generic, but also require that the regulatory authorities notify the patent owner of the company that seeks to sell a generic version of the drug (Ho, 2011).[17] Patent linkage provisions found in FTAs promoted by the US create a presumption of validity of pharmaceutical product patents which health authorities are not empowered, or do not have the capacity to challenge (Correa, 2004). Patent linkage, in effect, seeks to establish an unnecessary nexus between the grant of marketing approval for a generic medicine and the patent status of the originator, thereby delaying generic market entry (Abbott, 2004).

Some commentators have opined that patent linkage is a US-centric phenomenon, having its origins in the US Hatch-Waxman Act (Lopert and Gleeson, 2013). Correa presents the argument that patent linkage ignores the fact that patents are private rights (as recognised in the preamble to the TRIPS Agreement), and that a patent is a legal matter entirely separate from the technical issues concerning safety and efficacy of drugs (Correa, 2004). It can also be argued that patent linkage interferes with the effective use of compulsory licencing. Importantly, the TRIPS Agreement does not require, or even suggest, a patent linkage. The point to be noted here is that the patent linkage system is a TRIPS-plus obligation that creates a new exclusive right, which is contained neither in Article 28 of the TRIPS Agreement nor in any national patent laws.

4 Conclusion

The TRIPS Agreement flexibilities and the Doha Declaration were a hard-fought bargain by the developing countries, LDCs and NGOs. One of the main concerns for some of the developing countries during the negotiations was the requirement of a sudden transition from a process patent regime to a product patent regime. The TRIPS flexibilities were built into the TRIPS Agreement to benefit the developing countries and LDCs while implementing the Agreement into their national laws. This was intended to take away the strain of imposing a higher IP rights regime upon jurisdictions which were not fully prepared to embrace a much higher standard than the one in place in the domestic legislation. The TRIPS flexibilities afforded a delayed implementation, the use of compulsory licencing, parallel imports, *etc*. In reality, it had been extremely difficult, or even impossible, for the developing countries to implement the flexibilities, as they have come to be robbed by the TRIPS-plus provisions introduced through FTAs.

A combination of factors, *viz*., the TRIPS-plus provisions introduced through FTAs, political pressure from developed countries through trade sanctions, and pressure from transnational pharmaceutical companies – either through protracted court proceedings and/or lobbying – have deprived the developing

17 See, Article 17.10(2)(c) US-Chile FTA; Article 17.10(5) US-Australia FTA; and Article 15.10(4) US-Morocco FTA.

countries and the LDCs from exercising their rights under the TRIPS Agreement. It can be argued that patent-holding developed countries have used the TRIPS Agreement to effectively set a benchmark on IP standards and have exploited the loopholes in the multilateral trading system, which allows for the creation of RTAs, to prevent the developing countries from implementing the TRIPS flexibilities.

Bibliography

1 Abbott, Frederick M. 'The Doha Declaration on the TRIPS Agreement and Public Health and the Contradictory Trend in Bilateral and Regional Trade Agreements,' Occasional Paper 14, Quaker UN Office (2004).

2 Correa, Carlos M. *Implications of the Doha Declaration on the TRIPS Agreement and Public Health* (World Health Organization, 2002).

3 Correa, Carlos M. 'Bilateralism in Intellectual Property: Defeating the WTO System for Access to Medicines,' *Case Western Reserve Journal International Law* Vol. 36 (2004) 79.

4 Correa, Carlos M. 'Test Data Protection: Rights Conferred Under the TRIPS Agreement and Some Effects of TRIPS-Plus Standards,' in Dreyfuss, Rochelle C., and Katherine J. Strandburg (eds.) *The Law and Theory of Trade Secrecy: A Handbook of Contemporary Research* (Edward Elgar Publishing, 2011) 568–590.

5 Drahos, Peter. 'Intellectual Property and Pharmaceutical Markets: A Nodal Governance Approach,' *Temple Law Review* Vol. 77 (2004) 401–424.

6 Drahos, Peter. 'Four Lessons for Developing Countries From the Trade Negotiations Over Access to Medicines,' *Liverpool Law Review* Vol. 28, No. 1 (2007) 11–39.

7 Feinberg, Richard E. 'The Political Economy of United States' Free Trade Arrangements,' *The World Economy* Vol. 26, No. 7 (2003) 1019–1040.

8 Fink, Carsten, and Patrick Reichenmiller. 'Tightening TRIPS: Intellectual Property Provisions of US Free Trade Agreements,' in Newfarmer, Richard (ed.) *Trade, Doha, and Development: Window into the Issues* (World Bank, 2006) 289–303.

9 Ho, Cynthia M. *Access to Medicine in the Global Economy: International Agreement on Patents and Related Rights* (Oxford University Press, 2011).

10 Kilic, Buruc. 'Defending the Spirit of the DOHA Declaration in Free Trade Agreements: Trans-Pacific Partnership and Access to Affordable Medicines,' *Loyola University Chicago International Law Review* Vol. 12, No. 1 (2014) 23–57.

11 Lindstrom, Beatrice. 'Scaling Back TRIPS-Plus: An Analysis of Intellectual Property Provisions in Trade Agreements and Implications for Asia and the Pacific,' *New York University Journal of International Law & Politics* Vol. 42 (2010) 917–980.

12 Lopert, Ruth, and Deborah Gleeson. 'The High Price of "Free" Trade: US Trade Agreements and Access to Medicines,' *The Journal of Law, Medicine & Ethics* Vol. 41, No. 1 (2013) 199–223.

13 Malhotra, Prabodh, and Bhajan Grewal. 'TRIPS-Plus: Free Trade Agreements Jeopardizing Public Health in Developing Nations,' in Tran, Van Hoa, and Charles Harvie (eds.) *Regional Trade Agreements in Asia* (Edward Elgar Publishing, 2008) 216–239.

14 Mercurio, Brian. 'TRIPS-Plus Provisions in FTAs: Recent Trends,' in Bartels, Lorand, and Federico Ortino (eds.) *Regional Trade Agreements and the WTO Legal System* (Oxford University Press, 2006) 215–237.

15 Outterson, Kevin. 'Disease-Based Limitations on Compulsory Licenses Under Article 31 and 31*bis*,' in Correa, Carlos M. (ed.) *Research Handbook on the Protection of*

Intellectual Property Under WTO Rules: Intellectual Property in the WTO, Vol. I (Edward Elgar Publishing, 2010) 673–697.

16 Rahmatian, Andreas. 'Neo-Colonial Aspects of Global Intellectual Property Protection,' *The Journal of World Intellectual Property* Vol. 12, No. 1 (2009) 40–74.

17 Reddy, Satwant, and Gurdial Singh Sandhu, 'Report on Steps to be Taken by Government of India in the Context of Data Protection Provisions of Article 39.3 of TRIPS Agreement,' (2007) <http://chemicals.nic.in/sites/default/files/DPBooklet.pdf> accessed 27 November 2017.

18 Sell, Susan K. 'TRIPS-Plus Free Trade Agreements and Access to Medicines,' *Liverpool Law Review* Vol. 28, No. 1 (2007) 41–75.

Part II

TRIPS and developing countries

Implementation, knowledge economy and IP policymaking

Introduction

Part II of the book presents case studies of the implementation of the TRIPS Agreement in a selection of developing countries, *viz.*, Brazil, China, India, South Africa and Kenya. The relevant chapters discuss the difficulties encountered in the implementation of the Agreement into the domestic IP legislation in the above jurisdictions. For instance, chapter 5 studies how Brazil had coped with pressure from the US whilst implementing the Agreement, ahead of its deadline. In the case of South Africa, chapter 8 takes up for analysis how it had to face an uphill task to implement some of its ambitions to allow access to ARVs in the country, and the role of the civil society and NGOs in fighting a battle against TNPCs and the US government, who were bent on blocking the passing of the legislation. The discussions will also cover the actions of TNPCs backed by patent-holding developed nations in trying to thwart the efforts of the developing countries to produce affordable medications (generics) for its own use. Part II also, in the course of the case studies, presents the advantages that some of the developing countries have over the others, especially in the areas of knowledge economy, infrastructure, stronger economy, judiciary, *etc.*, which had to some degree enabled them to stave off or tackle the intrusion of pharmaceutical corporations and developed countries from meddling with their lawmaking process. The chapter will also argue how the imposition of an enhanced IP protection through the multilateral-trading system, and the requirement to introduce a TRIPS-compliant IP regulation at the domestic level, had strained the existing legal regimes on IP rights protection and on other commitments at the policy and institutional level, *viz.*, health policies and national healthcare of developing member states of the WTO.

It is well documented that transnational pharmaceutical corporations have hindered the movement of generic drugs through the misuse of EU regulations in the past (Sundaram, 2014b; Drahos and Braithwaite, 2002),[1] although there was nothing to prove that the generic drugs transported violated any existing patent

1 TNPCs took legal action against the government of South Africa for its proposed compulsory licensing laws.

laws. In the post-TRIPS era, the transnational pharmaceutical corporations have challenged such TRIPS-compliant legislation sought to be implemented in developing countries (through the backing of developed countries), which they view as being harmful to their business interests (Sundaram, 2014a).[2] Legal actions were commenced by the TNPCs – before both the respective developing country domestic courts and the WTO Dispute Settlement Body (DSB) through developed country representation. These tactics have resulted in delaying the introduction of TRIPS-compliant patent legislation or frustrating the introduction of suitable legislation for growth and for implementation of healthcare policies in the developing countries.

2 The US Trade Representative (USTR) also used the Super 301 effectively to exert pressure on both Brazil and India to support the actions of the transnational pharmaceutical corporations. Section 301, introduced by the US under the Amended Trade Act 1974, was designed to eliminate unfair foreign trade practices that affect US trade and investment. The Omibus Trade and Competitiveness Act 1988 amended section 301 with an addition of section 310, commonly referred to as 'Super 301,'and used to accuse countries of a broad range of unfair trade practices. See Taylor (1997) for an overview of Section 301 and the WTO Dispute Settlement System.

5 Brazil

Ambitious missions and early TRIPS implementation

Contents

1 Brazil: right to health as a constitutional right

Brazil went through a phase of tumultuous change through military dictatorship in the 1960s (Skidmore, 1995),[1] which lasted for over two decades and saw the

1 On 31 March 1964, the military forces took control of key government offices in Brasilia and Rio, and power was seized by the military in a near bloodless coup. The then US president Lyndon Johnson recognised the military government within hours of the coup. As the military government had no legitimacy under the 1946 Constitution, the military high command swiftly issued a legitimizing decree on 9 April 1964, called an 'Institutional Act.' This self-proclaimed law gave the military the power to do almost anything it wished.

Constitution and the Declaration of Rights therein contained suspended for a similar period. This marked a low point in the modern history of Brazil and took the nation decades to recover from, as it caused much harm to its socio-economic conditions and left the political institutions, if not defunct, then in disarray (Baer, 2008; Skidmore, 1995).[2] Rebuilding parliamentary democracy after a hiatus of over two decades required the new government to work on the creation of a new constitution to replace the 'Institutional Acts' passed during the military rule (Mainwaring, 1986; Skidmore, 1995)[3] and thereby restore faith in democracy. The republic's seventh constitution was successfully passed on 5 October 1988 (Rosenn, 1990),[4] enshrining provisions that conferred extraordinary rights on citizens, which were not identifiable in its previous editions. One feature that stood out was the recognition of right to health as a constitutional right. Article 196 of the 1988 Constitution guarantees access to health services, which also includes access to basic medicines. An English translation of Article 196 reads as follows:

> Health is a right of all and the responsibility of the State, to be guaranteed by means of social and economic policies aimed at reducing the risk of illness and other hazards, and all the universal and equal access to actions and services for its promotion, protection and recovery.

Importantly, under the 1988 Constitution,[5] right to health is not an aspiration but a fundamental right (Silva, 2007), which creates rights in citizens and obligations in the state, professing instant application. Drawing from civil law traditions, the Constitution confers the above private right on the Brazilian citizens (Piancastelli, 2006).[6] Article 6 declares education, health, work, leisure, security, social security, protection of maternity and infancy, and assistance of the unprotected as social rights.[7] Under the 1988 Constitution, the right to health is perceived as an essential condition in preserving the constitutional principles of the dignity of the

2 By the time the military lost power in 1985, inflation was at an all-time high of 235 percent.

3 Brazil's transition from a dictatorship to a democracy took a painful and arduous ten years, starting in 1974, with the gradual liberalization of the military regime when General Ernesto Geisel assumed power. Although military rule ended in 1985, the first civilian president in over a decade, Tancredo Neves, died before assuming office. This led to the vice president, Jose Sarney, being sworn in as Brazil's transitional president.

4 The author notes that the 1988 Constitution could also be viewed as the eighth constitution, if one were to consider a constitutional amendment that redrafted the entire constitution (prior to 1988) as a new constitution.

5 Article 5, para 1: 'Rules defining fundamental rights and guarantees have instantly binding application.'

6 It is clear from a reading of Articles 1 and 2 that, besides its principle goal of legitimizing democracy and preserving sovereignty, citizenship and the dignity of human beings, the Constitution also aimed at achieving new goals in the form of improving the social conditions of its citizens.

7 Article 6 (Title II, 'Fundamental Rights and Guarantees,' chapter II, 'Social Rights'): 'Education, health, work, leisure, security, social security, protection of motherhood and childhood, and assistance to the destitute, are social rights, as set forth by this Constitution.'

human person guaranteed in Article 1(III)[8] and the right to life guaranteed under Article 5.[9] This position of right to health being recognised as a constitutional right was to later assist in the formulation of health policies in Brazil's battle against AIDS/HIV and in the implementation of TRIPS flexibilities in the late 1990s.

1.1 *Brazilian national health system:* Sistema Único de Saúde *(SUS)*

Brazil's contribution in the area of access to health and medicine is widely recognised, as the country has a well-developed national healthcare system (Rosina, Wang, and Campos, 2010), which is strongly predicated on the right to health guaranteed under its Constitution. Brazil established the National Health System, or *Sistema Único de Saúde* (SUS),[10] to implement the constitutional right to health. Though the 1988 Constitution does not identify access to medicines as a constitutional right, the legislation implementing the right to health does (Rosina, Wang, and Campos, 2010). Article 6(I) of Lei 8.080/90 specifically addresses this issue, by stating that the SUS 'must be responsible for promoting full medical assistance, which includes pharmaceutical assistance'. The setting up of the SUS enabled Brazil to bring in some 60 million citizens under the National Health System, who were excluded from the earlier centralised National Health Service operated under the military rule (Rosina, Wang, and Campos, 2010). The SUS is a publicly funded rights-based universal healthcare system, which does not restrict access to medical care and medicines to its citizens, but empowers them to seek access to healthcare and medicines. The SUS treats those who seek access to health services as rights-holding citizens rather than 'empowered clients' or passive recipients (Cornwall and Shankland, 2008).[11] Notably, the SUS has been built on the principles of universality, comprehensive care, equity, decentralisation and social oversight (*controle social*) (Cornwall and Shankland, 2008; Gragnolati, Lindelow, and Couttolenc, 2013). The pursuit of access to health started with the decentralisation of the health system and with the passing of healthcare laws in 1990, 1993 and 1996 to define more clearly the role of each level of government in delivering healthcare as envisaged under the Constitution

8 Article 1: The Federative Republic of Brazil, formed by the indissoluble union of the states and municipalities and of the Federal District, is a legal democratic state and is founded on: I. sovereignty; II. citizenship; III. the dignity of the human person; IV. the social values of labour and of free enterprise; V. political pluralism.

9 Article 5: All persons are equal before the law, without any distinction whatsoever, Brazilians and foreigners residing in the country being ensured of inviolability of the right to life, to liberty, to equality, to security and to property. . . .'

10 Brazil passed Lei 8.080/90 known as the Health Act (*Lei Orgânica da Saúde*) and Lei 8.142/90 to establish the SUS. This public health system was to deliver a guaranteed universal health care to all Brazilian citizens.

11 The authors argue that the impetus for the SUS grew out of the successful mobilisation by the *Movimento pela Reforma Sanitária* (movement for health reform) and the innovative institutional experiments in the post-dictatorship period.

(Nunn, 2009). It is to be noted here that Sao Paulo and Rio de Janeiro created free drug distribution programmes for sexually transmitted diseases, including AIDS/HIV, as early as 1983 and 1985 (Urias, 2015). The SUS, in its over twenty-five years of operations, has fundamentally transformed the Brazilian healthcare system to achieve its constitutional guarantee of right to health.

2 Response to HIV/AIDS epidemic: right to health and pharmaceutical patents

Brazil's public policy response to the AIDS epidemic preceded those of many developing countries, and it became the first developing country to provide publicly financed AIDS treatment for all citizens living with HIV/AIDS.[12] Hence, a study of Brazil's TRIPS Agreement implementations must naturally begin from Brazil's 'right to health agenda' and the fight against HIV/AIDS. Brazil had launched its anti-AIDS programme in 1983, and its response to HIV/AIDS in the years to come was positive, proactive and commendable, as the epidemic hit soon after Brazil emerged from over two decades of military rule. The 1988 Constitution, which heralded a new era by conferring the right to health as a constitutional right, and the pioneering work of Brazilian researchers under the leadership of Bernardo Galvão-Castro, in isolating the HIV virus in the 1980s, can be considered as contributing factors in the robust response of Brazil to the HIV/AIDS epidemic. Two years prior to the promulgation of the new constitution, Brazil, in response to the epidemic, established a National STD and AIDS Committee (CNAIDS), a national AIDS Committee, and a National AIDS/STD Control Programme (NAP) (Nunn, 2009). The Brazilian government developed an aggressive and innovative programme with a strong emphasis on both prevention (Marques, Guimarães, and Sternberg, 2005)[13] and treatment through early government response, effective participation of civil society and the advocacy of human rights in all strategies and actions. By 2005, Brazil's anti-AIDS programme has been implemented in over thirty developing countries (Marques, Guimarães, and Sternberg, 2005). In May 2005, Brazil courted controversy when it turned down over US$40 million worth of aid money from the US, as acceptance of the money required Brazil to condemn commercial sex workers and advocate sexual abstinence, which would have had the effect of altering its anti-AIDS programme (Marques, Guimarães, and Sternberg, 2005).[14] These

12 The former Brazilian president, Fernando Henrique Cardoso (1995–2002), makes the claim in his foreword to *The Politics and History of AIDS Treatment in Brazil* (Springer, 2009).

13 Brazil's anti-AIDS policy specifically targeted high-risk groups with safe sex advocacy, including the distribution of condoms to sex workers. Marques, Guimarães and Sternberg observe that Brazil's infection rate in the early 1980s was similar to South Africa's, but the bold health policies introduced in Brazil helped to counter the situation and minimise the ill effects.

14 The funding was provided under the US Global AIDS Bill, which has come under severe international criticism, as it requires that one-third of all AIDS funding must go to groups that promote sexual abstinence only. See also, Kaiser Health News. 'Brazil Refuses $40M in US AIDS

measures alone were not sufficient for healthcare for the individuals, as any policy drafted in this regard was strongly reliant on the right to health guaranteed under the 1988 Constitution.

As per World Bank projections made in the early 1980s, Brazil was expected to have 1.2 million people living with HIV by 2000, but statistics from 2006 on HIV prevalence showed that only an estimated 660,000 Brazilians lived with HIV/AIDS, which was purely down to Brazil's extensive HIV/AIDS programme (Marques, Guimarães, and Sternberg, 2005). Even then, Brazil had the highest absolute number of HIV cases of any country in Latin America (Nunn, 2009). The National Program for Exceptional Medicines, which was established under Ordinance 2.577/06, supplied strategic medicines for the treatment of HIV/AIDS, malaria, tuberculosis, influenza and meningitis (Rosina, Wang, and Campos, 2010). Brazil also passed Lei 9.313/96 to guarantee free and universal access to all HIV/AIDS treatments within the SUS, thereby setting up a publically funded healthcare system to provide free universal access to highly active antiretroviral therapy (HAART) for people living with HIV/AIDS (PLWHA) (Nunn, 2009; Orsi, Hasenclever, Tigre, and Coriat, 2003). Brazil was the first developing country to implement a large-scale universal ARV distribution program. In the mid-1990s, Brazil also decided to take direct action in its fight against HIV/AIDS and began producing seven non-patented antiretroviral drugs (ARVs) in the Health Ministry factories and laboratories,[15] which only produced limited results due to new patent laws introduced in 1996 (Cohen and Lybecker, 2005).[16] The new laws, which were introduced pursuant to the introduction of TRIPS Agreement, required Brazil to recognise IP rights protection for pharmaceutical products for twenty years and did not allow for the realisation of the goals set under the NAP. The success and failure of the healthcare system and the response to the HIV/AIDS epidemic cannot be judged without a study of some of the internal and external factors which had come to interfere in the realisation of the constitutional goal of right to health. The implementation of the TRIPS Agreement into Brazil's domestic laws, and the use of flexibilities afforded under the Agreement, are identified as key factors that further hindered the healthcare system delivery through the SUS and are covered in the following sections.

Grants to Protest Policy Requiring Groups to Condemn Commercial Sex Work,' *Daily Reports* (2 May 2005) <www.kaiserhealthnews.org/Daily-Reports/2005/May/02/dr00029729.aspx?p=1> accessed 27 November 2017. Pedro Chequer, the director of Brazil's AIDS programme and chair of the National Commission, who decided to refuse the grant of over US$40 million in US aid money, was quoted as saying that it viewed the Bush administration's policy as 'interference that harms the Brazilian policy regarding diversity, ethical principles and human rights.'

15 Lei 5772/1971 created the legal right for local firms to produce on-patent drugs, and as a result a number of private firms in the 1970s were able to take advantage of the law and legally reverse engineer on-patent pharmaceuticals.

16 Brazil's domestic pharmaceutical industry is a major supplier to the domestic public health system, historically benefitting from decades of a regime of non-patent protection.

3 Brazilian patent laws: from the nineteenth century *alvará* to TRIPS implementation

The origin of Brazilian patent laws can be traced back to 1809 when a system of licencing, or *alvará*,[17] was introduced by Dom João VI to stimulate invention in an economy primarily driven by agriculture (Brandão, 2012). Brazil's first constitution of 1824 recognised the right of inventors to a privilege, or remuneration, for the use of their invention, which was followed by the passing of 1830 laws recognising the rights of inventors (Drahos, 2010). Brazil introduced new patent laws in 1882, nearly sixty years after independence from Portugal. The new laws were based on universal novelty and granted patent for a period of fifteen years, with the state (under Article I, section 4) retaining the right to appropriate the patent on grounds of public necessity or utility. The laws introduced in 1882 even contemplated the possible grant of patents on chemicals and pharmaceuticals, and proceeded to set up a system of targeted examination of select areas of patents which affected public interests, namely food, chemicals and pharmaceuticals (Drahos, 2010). It is worth mentioning here that Brazil is one of the founding members of the Paris Convention and the Berne Convention, which were concluded around the time its new patent laws were introduced in 1882. The laws enacted in 1882 did not in any way contribute to the economic growth of the nation in the nineteenth century and had minimal impact, and any economic growth witnessed during that period was through agricultural exports and textiles (Drahos, 2010). Brazil adopted a policy of Import Substituting Industrialisation (ISI) in the 1950s and 1960s (Schulz and Wu, 2004),[18] which required regulation of the transfer of technology mechanism from foreign to domestic companies on terms more suitable for its own goals (Drahos, 2010; Baer, 1972).[19]

While implementing the ISI policy, Brazil undertook a review of its patent laws, as under the then-existing norms, overseas technology patent holders were in a more advantageous position as they could easily exploit the laws to create a monopoly and negotiate a better price for the use of their technology (Drahos, 2010). In response, Brazil reformed its patent laws to have better control over the technology transfer process. As part of the reformative measure, in December 1970 Brazil passed Lei 5.648 establishing the National Institute of Industrial Property (NIIP), or *Instituto Nacional da Propriedade Industrial*, which was also entrusted with the key responsibility of administering patent law and technology

17 Dom João VI set up the first license system *alvará* for inventions of new machines, following which one of the first patents was granted to a mining service machine in 1814.

18 During this period, there was limited patent protection for pharmaceutical/chemical products and processes, along with an explicit government policy of import substitution of industrialised products, which led to the expansion of important sectors such as automobile, petrochemicals, steel, *etc.*, as well as the implementation of large infrastructure projects leading to economic growth.

19 Baer notes that the Brazilian government through ISI was anxious to promote maximum vertical integration, *i.e.*, to promote both final consumer goods industries and intermediate and capital goods sectors, and that despite the promotion of ISI, over 90 percent of Brazil's exports still continued to be from the traditional sectors of food products in the late 1960s.

transfer agreements. In December 1971, Brazil made further revision to its patent laws in Lei 5.772/71, excluding several pharmaceutical processes and products from the grant of patent. Under the 1971 laws, the term of patent was to last for fifteen years, which also contained a provision for pre-grant opposition from third parties. Most notably, the 1971 laws contained provisions for the grant of compulsory licences, including on the grounds of an absence of actual working of the patent in Brazil.

In 1991, new IP legislation was presented to the Congress by President Collor de Mello for discussion, with a view to bringing Brazil's IP laws into compliance with the TRIPS Agreement. While the bill was still being debated, the Congress approved the TRIPS Agreement in Legislative Decree No. 1,355 of 30 December 1994, which became effective in Brazil on 1 January 1995 (Schulz and Wu, 2004). Although the TRIPS Agreement's transitional provisions under Article 65 permits the delayed implementation (Musungu and Oh, 2006; Chung, 2010)[20] of the product patent regime for pharmaceutical patents in developing countries, Brazil failed to take advantage and delay the implementation (Sundaram, 2014b).[21] Thus, the TRIPS Agreement was incorporated in its entirety into Brazil's legal system in 1997, bringing about a series of problems in its wake. Also, the Brazilian Patent and Trademark Office (INPI) was convinced that Brazil was not required to expressly state that it would make use of these provisions (Schulz and Wu, 2004). Notwithstanding the position taken by the INPI on the application of the TRIPS Agreement to its national laws, patent owners started lodging their applications for grant of pharmaceutical and chemical patents immediately after 1 January 1995, under Article 70(8) of the TRIPS Agreement.[22]

In 1996, the Brazilian Congress under President Cardoso passed the Industrial Property Law (LPI) Lei 9.279/96 (Law 279) to repeal the 1971 patent law, and the new laws came into force on 15 May 1997. Importantly, under the old Brazilian laws (Lei 5.772/71 Art 9c), the patenting of pharmaceuticals process and products was forbidden. The new law of 1996 introduced a higher level of protection for pharmaceutical patents, which also allowed for the patenting of chemical products. Brazil's early compliance to the TRIPS Agreement proved to be a

20 The key flexibilities built into the TRIPS Agreement are compulsory licensing under Article 31, experimental use under Article 30, parallel imports under Article 6, Bolar exceptions under Article 30, and health sector participation in analysing pharmaceutical patent claims which is implied under Article 8. Besides the above flexibilities, the TRIPS Agreement, under Articles 65(2) and 65(4), in certain cases, allows delaying the application of the provisions on product patents to such areas of technology for an additional period of five years. Musungu and Oh (2006) discuss in detail time-bound and other flexibilities available to the developing countries and the LDCs in the implementation of the TRIPS Agreement.

21 The use of Part 4 of Article 65 of the TRIPS Agreement could have enabled Brazil to extend the transitional period for yet another five years. India, another developing country and a key generics manufacturer, delayed the implementation of the product patent regime for pharmaceutical patents to gain full advantage of the transitional arrangements under Article 65 of the TRIPS Agreement.

22 The INPI ignored these applications until a 2001 law determined that all chemical and pharmaceutical product patents should be regularly examined.

costly mistake, as it witnessed the price of ARVs rise due to the elimination of the possibility of generic production of patented drugs domestically. Some writers attribute the early changes made to the Brazilian legislation to economic and political pressure exerted by US to comply with the TRIPS Agreement before the 2005 legal deadline (Orsi, Hasenclever, Tigre, and Coriat, 2003), while others attribute it to pressure from TNPCs seeking to exploit newer foreign markets through a higher level of patent protection (Rosina, Wang, and Campos, 2010). This early compliance was also to greatly disadvantage the implementation of the HIV/AIDS programme envisaged by the Brazilian government. It is understood that by virtue of Lei 9.279/96, Brazil will follow the global majority rule of a 'first to file' patent regime. Also, chapter 2 of Lei 9.279/96 contains the basic rules and exclusions regarding the types of patents allowed and also the proper subject matters for patent applications.

3.1 Key provisions 1: parallel imports, Bolar exception and compulsory licencing

In the early 1990s in the wake of the HIV/AIDS crisis, the global discussion on the grant of compulsory licences for pharmaceutical products became topical. The discussions presented a grim picture of the situation prevailing in the developing countries and LDCs (where the most affected populace is from), with access to ARV treatment becoming increasingly difficult due to exorbitant costs. In those regions, as patented drugs for the treatment of the disease became unaffordable, generic ARVs were viewed as the only affordable option/solution, for the frontline treatment of HIV/AIDS sufferers (Sundaram, 2014a). It should be borne in mind that patent protection is often cited as the key contributing factor for the non-affordability of medication for the treatment of HIV/AIDS (Waning, 2010). In such instances, the grant of compulsory licences, or the threat of such a grant by the concerned government, was considered the only option for the procurement of generic ARVs. One of the main reasons for the failure in the attempts to revise the Paris Convention 1983 in the late 1980s and early 1990s was attributed to the disagreement between the developed and developing countries on the extent of powers that a government should retain for the grant of compulsory licences, and how those powers, when retained, are to be exercised (Reichman, 2010; Reichman and Hasenzahl, 2003).

Compulsory licencing of patented drugs, which enables the access to essential medicines in times of need, is identified as one of the key features of the patent system and is recognised under the TRIPS Agreement and also under other international conventions (Bodenhausen, 1968).[23] The Doha Declaration

23 Article 31, TRIPS Agreement ('Other Use Without Authorization of Rights of Holder') and Article 30, TRIPS Agreement ('Exceptions to Rights Conferred'). The Doha Declaration, considered a corollary to the TRIPS Agreement, proclaims that each member had the right to grant compulsory licenses. The WHO has recommended the use of compulsory licenses where there is 'abuse of patent rights or a national emergency' to ensure that drug prices are consistent with the

unequivocally states that every WTO member has 'the right to grant compulsory licences and the freedom to determine the grounds upon which such licences are granted'.[24] Importantly, the text of Article 31 of the TRIPS Agreement was consciously drafted by the negotiating group to avoid any disease-based limitation being imposed on the member countries seeking to invoke the provision (Outterson, 2010).[25] Canada and the UK, both developed countries, have used compulsory licencing provisions available under their national legislations whenever possible.[26] The US has not adopted a statutory regime of granting compulsory licence, but has nevertheless allowed the practice under antitrust laws (Reichman and Hasenzahl, 2003; Correa, 2000).[27]

One of the most important features of the 1996 LPI was the introduction of provisions relating to the grant of compulsory licences. Lei 9.279/96, passed on 14 May 1996, came into force on 15 May 1997, except for 'pipeline' provisions which came into force with immediate effect. The net result was that 'pipeline' applications based on foreign patents for pharmaceuticals and chemical compounds were automatically granted, waiving the novelty requirement (Schulz and Wu, 2004). In 1998, to meet its domestic requirements, Brazil decided to increase domestic production of generic ARVs and to issue compulsory licences on patented ARVs. In 1999, the Brazilian National Congress set up an inquest committee (CPI) to investigate the reasons behind the exorbitant rise in prices

---

purchasing power of the local government. As regards other international conventions, Article 5A of the Paris Convention for the Protection of Industrial Property provides for the signatories to the Convention to have the right 'to take legislative measures providing for the grant of compulsory licenses to prevent the abuses which might result from the exercise of the exclusive rights conferred by the patent, for example, failure to work.' Under Art 5A 'failure to work,' or 'insufficient working' of a patent would tantamount to abuse of the patent rights, and can be viewed as giving rise to grounds for the grant of compulsory license.

24 *Doha Declaration on the TRIPS Agreement and Public Health* – World Trade Organization, Declaration on the TRIPS Agreement and Public Health, WT/MIN(01)/DEC/2, adopted on 20 November 2001.

25 Outterson suggests that the provision has been misunderstood (perhaps, deliberately so) in the write-ups in the *Wall Street Journal* and the *Financial Times* to imply that Article 31 is only applicable to national public health emergencies like HIV/AIDS, or only to the least-developed countries.

26 Canada, under its 1923 laws, between 1969 and 1992 issued 613 compulsory licenses for importation and/or local production of medicines as part of its cost containment measures. It changed its laws following its membership in NAFTA (1994) and the WTO (1995), but has continued to issue compulsory licenses. Likewise, the UK had invoked 'Crown Use' for the provision of generic medicines for its National Health Service (NHS), which was unsuccessfully challenged by the Pfizer Corporation in the 1960s.

27 The US had in the past granted a number of compulsory licenses to remedy anti-competitive practices and for governmental use, including national security. For instance, in the Ciba-Geigy and Sandoz merger of 1997, both pharmaceutical corporations were required to license a large portfolio of patents, haemophilia gene rights, data know-how relating to HSV-tk, *etc.*, to Rhone-Poulenc Rorer. The newly created entity, Novartis, was also required to grant such non-exclusive licenses to requesters in certain instances. In the late 1950s and early 1960s, the US also invoked government use powers on a routine basis to order generic medicines from abroad, regardless of the patent status of the products.

of the medicines sold in Brazil (Basso and Rodrigues, 2010).[28] In the same year, Brazil also introduced the National Drug Policy (Health Ministry Portaria 3.916) which was aimed at completely decentralising drug policy.[29] A combination of decreasing stocks of ARVs, devaluation of its currency and a pressing need to meet its commitment to the HIV/AIDS programme paved the way for Brazil to pass the 1999 Presidential Decree (under former President Fernando Henrique Cardoso) amending Article 71 of the LPI, relating to the issue of compulsory licences (Nunn, 2009).[30] Articles 68–74, Chapter VIII, Section III of the LPI provide for the grant of compulsory licences if the patent holder exercises the rights granted thereunder in an abusive manner, or abuses its economic power, or when the patented product is not exploited within Brazil, or when the sale of the patented product fails to satisfy the needs of the market or the 'local working' requirement (Correa, 2015).[31] Article 68, in particular, requires that the subject matter of the patent must be manufactured in Brazil within three years of receiving a patent, and failure to do so within this time frame allows Brazilian companies to apply to the government for manufacture of the patented product domestically (Nunn, 2009).[32] The Brazilian government also passed suitable legislation on the Generic Drugs Law in November 1999 to require all government purchasing contracts to be generic drugs, all packaging to carry names, and all prescriptions to be written using generic names (Cohen and Lybecker, 2005).

In 2001, four years after implementing the TRIPS Agreement, Brazil took advantage of the flexibilities and incorporated the Bolar exception, which is contained in Lei 10.196/2001 under item VII to Article 43. Incorporation of the Bolar exception had a twofold advantage for Brazil, as in addition to promoting quicker entry of generic drugs into the market, it also enabled information on the invention to be used for further research into ARVs (Chaves, Vieira, and Reis, 2008). Brazil only has a limited scope for the implementation of parallel imports, as its use is restricted to situations where a compulsory licence under Article 68, Paras 3 and 4 of LPI has been issued due to abuse of economic power by the patent holder (Chaves, Vieira, and Reis, 2008). The issue of parallel imports

28 José Serra, the then state minister for health, identified patent protection of pharmaceuticals as one of the most important factors in determining the prices of medicines. Interestingly, one of the recommendations of the CPI was the withdrawal of Brazil's membership from the Paris Convention for the Protection of Industrial Property 1883.

29 José Serra, an economist and later a politician, is seen as the key individual behind the decision to introduce the National Drug Policy and to increase the production of generic ARVs in Brazil.

30 Art. 71, Lei 9.279/1996 (enacted 15 May 1997).

31 Interestingly, under Article 70 of the LPI, compulsory licenses may also be issued in cases of dependent patents. A compulsory license may be issued under Article 71 by the Federal Executive Authorities in cases of national emergency or public interest. Professor Correa notes that the obligation to work a patent was provided for in numerous domestic patent laws in the nineteenth century. However, during the twentieth century, most industrialised countries either relaxed or eliminated such an obligation from their laws. This was done primarily to ensure that patent holders had the option of exploiting their patents merely through importation, and thereby facilitate trans-border activities in an increasingly globalized world market.

32 Arts. 68–74, Lei 9.279/ 1996 (enacted 15 May 1997).

would fall under the principles of exhaustion/first sale doctrine of patent rights, where the rights of a patent holder are exhausted as to those specific goods once it enters the market, and the patent holder cannot prevent their resale to other countries. In this regard, the TRIPS Agreement and the Doha Declaration allow member states to determine the scope and extent of exhaustion of patent rights,[33] although some developed countries, like the US, remain strongly opposed to this interpretation (Correa, 2005).[34] Parallel importation, which is considered a key legal mechanism in implementing drug access policies (and available under the TRIPS flexibilities for developing countries), has unfortunately not been effectively used by Brazil in the implementation process (Chaves, Vieira, and Reis, 2008).[35]

3.1.1 Use of price negotiation and compulsory licencing provision

Brazil's policy of combining prevention with care in the fight against the AIDS epidemic proved to have paid dividends. But the sheer increase in the number of patients and the inclusion of newer patented ARVs posed additional challenges for the Brazilian government to tackle the situation (Urias, 2015). To contain the health expenditures necessary to ensure the sustainability of the anti-AIDS program, the Brazilian Ministry of Health sought to negotiate price reductions for high-cost drugs including ARVs. One important factor that triggered the Brazilian strategy of price negotiation was the sharp rise in costs due to the high depreciation of the local currency in 1999, which saw a 64 percent rise in the cost of ARVs in Brazil between 1998 and 1999 (Urias, 2015). Brazil's successful price-negotiating strategy was defined by the WHO as a central component of the 'Brazilian model' for AIDS treatment. Even though Brazil had never used the obligatory licencing system, it adopted a strategy of threat to issue compulsory licences to pressure drug companies in price negotiations for ARV medications (Chaves, Vieira, and Reis, 2008). Following the introduction of the compulsory

33 Article 28(6) of the TRIPS Agreement states that 'This right [*i.e.*, the right of importation], like all other rights conferred under this Agreement in respect of the use, sale, importation or other distribution of goods, is subject to the provisions of Article 6.' In turn, Article 6 of the TRIPS Agreement postulates that 'nothing in this Agreement shall be used to address the issue of the exhaustion of intellectual property rights.' The Doha Declaration in Article 5(d) provides that 'the effect of the provisions of TRIPS Agreement that are relevant to the exhaustion of intellectual property rights is to leave each member free to establish its own regime for such exhaustion without challenge, subject to the MFN and national treatment.'

34 The US delegation to the Council for TRIPS, which met in June 2001, expressed the view that Article 6 of the TRIPS Agreement neither allowed WTO members to avail themselves of dispute settlement in relation to questions involving parallel imports nor authorised parallel imports. See Delegation of the United States, Council for TRIPS Meeting of June 1822, 2001, JOB(01)/97/ Add.5, Council for TRIPS, June 28, 2001.

35 Multinational pharmaceutical companies usually set different prices for the same drug in different countries, and if parallel imports are introduced as a policy mechanism, Brazil could possibly import medicines from wherever they are sold at the lowest price to benefit its HIV/AIDs programme and to honour the constitutional right to health.

licencing provisions into Brazilian laws, the US in January 2001 requested the opening of a consultation with the WTO's Dispute Settlement Body (DSU) on the basis that the obligation for local production imposed by the Brazilian law violated Articles 27 and 28 of the TRIPS Agreement. The matter never went before the panel for a full consideration of the issues identified for consultation, as the US and Brazil reached an agreement (Varella, 2004). As per terms of the agreement, both countries agreed to enter bilateral discussions before Brazil proceeded to make use of the compulsory licencing provisions under Article 68 against a US patent holder (Correa, 2015). This agreement, however, does not prevent Brazil from granting a compulsory licence based on Article 68, but only requires engaging in bilateral discussions with the US.

The critical factor in making the HIV/AIDS programme and access to medicines affordable may be the capacity to domestically produce the drugs and the credible threat of domestic production by the Brazilian government (Cohen and Lybecker, 2005). This strategy had worked well for Brazil, as the TNPCs were willing to lower the price of their products rather than have them produced domestically in Brazil (Chaves, Vieira, and Reis, 2008).[36] It had also seen the reduction in price of some of the ARVs used in the frontline treatment of HIV/AIDS. In 2005, Brazil could convince the pharmaceutical company and patent holder, Abbott Laboratories, to lower the price of ARVs lopinavir/ritonavir[37] (which was being actively used in the treatment of about 17,000 patients) by 56 percent. This was achieved through a presidential decree, declaring that the medicine was of public interest and that the patent holder Abbott was required to offer the product at a lower price. But eventually a deal was struck whereby Abbott Laboratories agreed for a fixed price of US$1,380 to be charged per patient per year until 2011, regardless of any price variation, in return for the Brazilian government guaranteeing that it will not issue any compulsory licence for the above drug (Chaves, Vieira, and Reis, 2008). Although civil society groups in Brazil were in support of the use of compulsory licencing, it considered the deal struck with Abbott Laboratories as an imposition of TRIPS-plus provisions, as it included clauses that were more restrictive than those found in the TRIPS Agreement.[38]

In 2007, for the first time, Brazil went beyond its original strategy of threatening to issue a compulsory licence. The ARV drug 'efavirenz' marketed as 'Stocrin' by its patent holder Merck Sharp & Dohme (Merck) was the most used drug in

36 The authors note that since the Brazilian government had never actually issued a compulsory license (before 2007) for domestic production of any medicines, the negotiating strategy had not been very successful and the prices agreed in later rounds were unsatisfactory. For example, the discounts secured for the new drugs 'tenofovir' and 'atazanavir' (both ARV drugs) were respectively 5.2 percent and 7.7 percent. Also, the average annual expenditure per patient in 2005 rose to R$6,124, on a par with the figure in 1998.

37 Lopinavir/ritonavir, a fixed-dose combination drug which is used in the treatment of HIV infection, is marketed by its patent holder Abbott Laboratories as Kaletra and also as Aluvia in different parts of the world.

38 It is also worth mentioning that Brazil used the threat of compulsory licensing on the patent for Glivec (marketed in the US as Gleevec) to obtain a price discount of more than 65 percent.

2007, and the going price that year was US$580 per patient.[39] Under Brazil's anti-AIDS programme, close to 77,000 patients were being treated with Efavirenz. During the negotiations, prior to the grant of the compulsory licence, Merck was selling Efavirenz at a cheaper price in countries of the same development level as Brazil but with fewer patients in need of treatment than in Brazil, and at the same time Indian generic versions of the same drug were much cheaper than Merck's and selling at US$0.45 per pill, or an annual cost of US$164.25 per patient (Correa, 2015). Around the same time, the cost of Efavirenz in Thailand was approximately US$245 per patient, and the prices for the supply of Efavirenz by WHO-prequalified laboratories, ranged around US$163. During negotiations, Merck would only offer a price reduction from US$1.59 to US$1.10 per dose, and as a result the Brazilian government was constrained to issue the Presidential Decree No 6.108, dated 4 May 2007, granting 'compulsory licence, on the ground of public interest, of Efaviren's patents, for public non-commercial use' for a period of five years, and for a fee of 1.5 percent to the patent owner of the finished product.[40] Prior to the grant of compulsory licence, Efavirenz was approximately 12 percent of the cost of the Brazilian government's expenditures for ARV drugs, and with the local production of the drug in 2009, the cost dropped to 3.9 percent (Rutledge, 2012). Following the grant of compulsory licence, a spokesperson for Merck commented that 'this expropriation of intellectual property sends a chilling signal to research-based companies about the attractiveness of undertaking risky research on diseases that affect the developing world'. Although the US criticised the action of granting compulsory licence for the drug Efavirenz as 'a major step backward', it did not pursue any trade sanctions against Brazil (Correa, 2015). As Brazil's successful anti-AIDS programme and its commitment to the constitutional right to health and access to medicines strongly hinges on the availability of affordable medicines, it may not come as a surprise if Brazil continues to explore the use of compulsory licences if the need arises.

3.1.2 Setback: seizure of generic medicines-in-transit

Between 2008 and 2009, nearly twenty shipments of generic medicines, destined to various developing countries, were intercepted and detained by the Dutch, and on one occasion by German customs officials, acting under the purported authority of BMR 1383/2003 (Miller and Anand, 2009; Khor, 2009). The shipments, which were in transit from India and not intended for sale within the EU but destined for Latin American and African countries, included generic drugs used to treat AIDS, Alzheimer's disease and heart conditions, to name a few.

39 Efavirenz is a non-nucleoside reverse transcriptase inhibitor (RTI), and the patent for it was first claimed in 1997 and automatically granted to Merck Sharp & Dohme (Merck) under the 'pipeline' provisions of the TRIPS-compliant IP laws.

40 Interestingly, Farmanguinhos, the pharmaceutical laboratory of the Oswaldo Cruz Foundation, was able to manufacture the first batch of Efavirenz in January 2009 at 45 percent of the price set by Merck prior to the grant of compulsory licence.

At the request of transnational pharmaceutical corporations, including Sanofi-Aventis SA, Novartis AG, and Eli Lilly & Co, the shipments were detained for periods extending for up to eight months (Miller and Anand, 2009; Baker, 2012). EC Regulation 1383/2003 tasks national customs offices with policing IP laws on goods entering or transiting through their ports. Using the powers under the above regulation, customs officials acted *ex officio* to initiate temporary seizures, based on fictional patent violations, to impound and thereby delay shipments of life-saving medicines bound from India to countries in Africa, Latin America and Oceania (Baker, 2012). A shipment of the generic drug losartan potassium, used in the treatment of high blood pressure and destined for Brazil, was also one of the consignments seized while in transit at Schiphol Airport in the Netherlands in December 2008 and later returned to India, the country of its origin (Kanth, 2010).

The India representative speaking at the TRIPS council meeting held on 27–28 October and 6 November 2009 deemed the seizure in transit as one of many 'serious impediments to access to medicines'.[41] It was pointed out by the India representative that the seizure in transit incident was inconsistent with the paragraph 6 system, as such seizure could prevent the hypothetical shipment of a generic drug from an exporting country to a least-developed country in a timely manner. The practice of seizure of medicines-in-transit for fictional violation of IP rights was also strongly decried by commentators (Grosse Ruse-Khan and Jaeger, 2009; Mercurio, 2012), as it violated core principles of the TRIPS Agreement. The above seizures and the EU's delayed and defensive responses to repeated expressions of diplomatic and human rights concerns led both Brazil and India to seek consultations with the EU and the Netherlands before the Dispute Settlement Body in the WTO (Baker, 2012).[42] Following negotiations amongst the parties, on 28 July 2011, the government of India announced the reaching of an 'understanding' in principle with the EU over the pending complaint before the Dispute Settlement Body challenging EU's action regarding the seizure of generic medicines-in-transit. Regardless of the outcome of the dispute before the WTO, the whole episode only succeeded in painting a very negative image of the pharmaceutical patent-holding developed countries within the EU, which were blatantly exploiting customs measures to impound generic drugs destined for developing countries and LDCs and thereby making a mockery of EU's commitment to access to affordable medicines. Unfortunately, Brazil was at the receiving end of the above events, as legally produced life-saving generic medicines

41 Minutes of Meeting of the Council for TRIPS, WTO, held on 27–28 October and 6 November 2009 <https://docs.wto.org/dol2fe/Pages/FE_Search/DDFDocuments/82087/Q/IP/C/M61.pdf> accessed 28 November 2017.

42 Communication from the Brazilian delegation requesting consultations with the EU and with the Government of the Netherlands before the Dispute Settlement Body at the WTO (12 May 2010) <www.worldtradelaw.net/cr/ds409-1(cr).pdf> accessed 28 November 2017; Communication from the Indian delegation requesting consultations with the EU and with the Government of the Netherlands before the Dispute Settlement Body at the WTO (11 May 2010) <www.worldtradelaw.net/cr/ds408-1(cr).pdf> accessed 28 November 2017.

destined to its shores were seized in transit in a developed country, through the misuse of a border control measure, thereby denying access to medicines to the vulnerable patients in a developing country.

3.2 *Key provisions 2: prior consent, ANVISA and second use medical patent*

Following the CPI recommendations, Brazil adopted provisional measures amending the Industrial Property Law, establishing the mechanism of 'prior consent' in the examination of patent applications from the pharmaceutical and chemical industry (Basso and Rodrigues, 2010). This new setup saw patent applications being scrutinised by INPI and the National Health Surveillance Agency of Brazil, or *Agência Nacional de Vigilância Sanitária* (ANVISA).[43] In December 1999, Brazil's legislature passed the 'prior consent', or *anuência prévia* rule, which is contained in Article 229-C.[44] Unfortunately, this article did not offer any guidelines as to the 'shared competence' or duties of INPI and ANVISA in the scrutiny of patent applications for pharmaceutical and chemicals (Basso and Rodrigues, 2010; Shadlen, 2011). On 14 February 2001, the Brazilian government passed Lei 10.196/2001 amending Article 229-C to make 'prior consent' a permanent feature of its LPI and included the stipulation that the grant of all patents for pharmaceutical products and processes was subject to ANVISA's prior approval (Murphy, 2005).[45] In 2008, ANVISA issued a resolution (RDC-45) to clarify its competence in such matters regarding the examination of pharmaceutical patent applications (Basso and Rodrigues, 2010).[46] The INPI, an authority created in 1970 and charged with the scrutiny of the patent applications under the Industrial Property Law, performs a different role to that of the ANVISA, and its decisions were subject to the authority of the ANVISA. This led to a cumbersome and long-drawn-out patent examination process in case of pharmaceutical and chemical patent applications. ANVISA pursues the harmonisation of

43 ANVISA is a regulatory agency with independent administration and financial autonomy. Besides coordinating with the National Sanitary Surveillance System (SNVS) and monitoring drug products and medical device prices, it is also tasked with the 'patentability' examination for pharmaceutical patents along with the INPI. Its role is akin to that of the Food and Drug Administration (FDA) of the US.

44 Article 229-C reads as follows: 'The concession of granting patents for pharmaceutical products and processes will depend on the prior consent of the National Agency of Sanitary Vigilance (ANVISA).'

45 The author refers to the creation of *anuência prévia* as a 'shotgun wedding' requiring the two distinct government agencies, INPI and ANVISA, to work together in the examination and grant of pharmaceutical patents.

46 Resolution RDC-45 was issued on 23 June 2008. Going by the explanations presented under RDC-45, INPI was charged with carrying out substantive initial assessment of the requirements and conditions of patentability and forwarding the processes it believed might be eligible for protection to ANVISA. Following which, ANVISA would then carry out an examination of the processes to satisfy the requirement of the Industrial Property Law and decide to either grant or not grant a patent to the invention.

the protection of IP rights with the protection of public health by exploiting legal flexibilities offered under the TRIPS Agreement and the Doha Declaration, while INPI follows the guidelines contained in Brazilian LPI, which was modified following Brazil's accession to the WTO (Rodrigues and Murphy, 2006; Basso and Rodrigues, 2010). Some authors posit the view that the prior consent process introduced by Brazil is in full compliance with Article 8 of the TRIPS Agreement (Chaves, Vieira, and Reis, 2008).[47]

Working of the ANVISA under the above directive demonstrated that it did not grant prior consent for (i) applications filed with insufficient description, (ii) claims from Markush groups (Cicero, 2012),[48] (iii) selections of chemical macrostructures, (iv) polymorphs, (v) raceme/isomeric mixes and (vi) second use medical patent claims (Basso and Rodrigues, 2010). ANVISA, in a report issued in 2004, clarified that it will not grant prior consent for filings related to second use patents, which is contradictory to the policy of protecting second and new use patents by the INPI (Rodrigues and Murphy, 2006).

This brings us to the discussion on granting of patents based on second and subsequent medical use. Supporters of the second and subsequent use patents argue that they protect discoveries of new uses for substances, active principles, molecules or compounds that have been previously patented, or are already in the public domain (Mitnovetski and Nicol, 2004). Subsequent patent use involves new prescribed functions of pharmaceuticals already known and used within the medical community for different purposes. In effect, a second or subsequent medical use patent, if granted, protects the discovery of a new medical application for a product that has already been recognised and utilised in the medical field (Rodrigues and Murphy, 2006). The other major argument used by supporters of second use patents is that the human and economic investment incurred by the pharmaceutical industry to discover a second use is comparable to the investment necessary to develop the product, or drug as such, and hence the need for recognition (Rodrigues and Murphy, 2006). In the UK, the position on grant of second and subsequent use pharmaceutical patent[49] was upheld in *Actavis v. Merck*,[50]

47 Article 8 of the TRIPS Agreement permits members to adopt necessary measures into their domestic laws to protect public health and promote the public interest in sectors of vital importance to their socio-economic and technological development.

48 The term 'Markush group' refers to a list of 'alternatives' set forth in a claim, and is named after Eugene Markush who successfully used a claim form that defined a genus by enumeration of the species in the 1920s [1925 CD 126 (Comm'r Pat.1925)]. Markush-style claims can be a way to explicitly claim a large number of variations of the claimed invention.

49 Second and subsequent medical use patents are now expressly permitted under section 4A (4) of the Patents Act 1977, provided the claim is in the form of 'substance x for use in the treatment of disease y', following the Enlarged Board of Appeal of the European Patent Office's G2/08 Kos decision.

50 *Actavis UK Ltd v. Merck & Co Inc.* [2008] EWCA Civ. 444. Jacob LJ observed that 'Research into new and better dosage regimes is clearly desirable, and that there is simply no policy reason why, if a novel non-obvious regime is invented, there should not be an appropriate patent reward.' See also the Court of Appeals decision in *Hospira UK Ltd and Generics UK Ltd v. Novartis* AG [2013] EWCA Civ 1663.

where the Court of Appeals came to revisit the position on patentability of dosage regime regarding Merck's patent for a drug used in male pattern baldness. The European regulatory legislation as originally drafted (The European Patent Convention, 1973) facilitated access to generic drugs within the European Union, but an interpretation of new laws from 2000 by the Enlarged Board of Appeal (EBA) does not exclude second or subsequent use pharmaceutical patent.[51]

In practice, the pharmaceutical corporations often use the second use as a tool to extend the commercial life of patents, a strategy widely referred to as evergreening, thereby maximising on the monopoly period enjoyed by the patented drug (Mueller and Chisum, 2008; Feldman, 2009; Lanjouw, 2002; Furrow, 2008). The practice of evergreening considerably delays and poses a threat for the legal entry of generics into the market, and can successfully prevent competition in the pharmaceutical market, although some pharmaceutical corporations do believe that the term evergreening is pejorative and misleading.[52] Recent Brazilian court decisions have sent out mixed signals on ANVISA's role in the scrutiny of pharmaceutical applications (Licks, 2012).[53] One decision in particular, delivered in 2013,[54] held that it is possible to grant patent protection for items not listed

51 Article 52(4) EPC 1973 and Article 53(c) EPC 2000. Under EPC 1973, inventions in order to be patentable must be 'susceptible of industrial application.' Article 52(4) clearly states the fiction that medical methods are not so susceptible. Whereas Article 54(5) provides for a special exception for medical products to the normal novelty rules by stating that if 'its use for any (medical treatment) method is not comprised in the state of the art'. EPC 2000, which came into effect from 13 December 2007, introduced changes in this regard. Article 53(c) seeks to remove the fiction about industrial applicability, and declares that patents may not be granted for medical methods. This presented a dilemma which was resolved by the EBA in G0005/83 (Eisai) and related cases. The EBA concluded that Art 54(5) of EPC did not exclude second (and further) medical indications from patent protection 'other than by a purpose-limited product claim'. In October 2004, the EPO's Technical Board of Appeal in T1020/03 in a review of G0005/83 went further, concluding that protection is not limited to new indications, which may extend to protecting a product for use in any novel and inventive therapy. The UK Patent Act 2004 implemented EPC 2000.

52 GlaxoSmithKline, 'Evergreening,' *GSK Public Policy Positions* (January 2014) <www.gsk.com/media/2949/evergreening-policy.pdf> accessed 28 November 2017.

53 On 24 January 2012, in response to a writ of *mandamus*, Judge Solange Salgado of the First Federal Court in Brasilia ruled that ANVISA, when faced with a request for prior approval while examining a pharmaceutical examination, must restrict itself only to public health issues. This decision appears to restrict the authority of ANVISA to examining patentability requirements. Similarly, on 25 January 2012, the Chief Appellate Judge Jiriar Aram Meguerian of the Court of Appeals for the first Circuit rejected ANVISA's motion regarding prior approval. The appellate court held that the greater objective of Article 229-C was to grant the possibility of ANVISA to guard against patents for pharmaceutical products and processes when faced with Article 18, Item I of the Industrial Property Laws. Both decisions seem to check the unfettered freedom of authority enjoyed by ANVISA.

54 The Brazilian Court in Rio de Janeiro, Brazil (*Primeira Seção Especializada do Tribunal Regional Federal da 2ª Região*) was deciding on an appeal against the rejection of a patent application for second use pharmaceutical patent. But the Brazilian Patent Office had not released any official statement or guidelines following the decision of the court, which makes one suspect that this could be seen as an isolated case.

as non-patentable in Lei 9.279/96, which technically threw the door open for seeking protection on second and subsequent use pharmaceutical patents. If the judicial trend of granting patents to second and subsequent use are to continue, Brazil may find itself in an untenable position, as it will potentially pose a threat to its HIV/AIDS programme, which is strongly reliant on generic drugs. Granting of second and subsequent use medical patents will see a huge price rise in pharmaceutical products and could spell the death knell of the access to medicines programme put in place by the Brazilian government following its commitment to health as a constitutional right, with the goals likely to become unachievable. As seen from several decisions made by ANVISA, its central position is clearly not in favour of granting second and subsequent use medical patents – although there is evidence that this position is changing. India, another developing country and a major generics drugs manufacturer, introduced TRIPS-compliant patent laws in 2005, thereby moving from a process patent regime to a product patent regime. The new patent law introduced by India included provisions to check the practice of evergreening, which effectively outlaws granting of second and subsequent use pharmaceutical patents.[55] The relevant provisions of the Indian Patent Act were upheld by the Supreme Court of India in the *Novartis* case[56] decided in April 2013.

From the above discussion one can conclude that the system of prior consent introduced to prevent the exploitation of the patent system by TNPCs had come under severe scrutiny, with some appreciating the measures taken by Brazil (Correa, 2007; Drahos, 2010; Shadlen, 2011; Deere, 2009), and others criticising the practice on the premise that it has led to divergent decisions being taken on pharmaceutical patent applications (Kunisawa and Yumy, 2009).[57] Although the arrangement was initially welcomed by INPI, the relationship of the two organisations was to deteriorate in the years that followed, with the INPI failing to acknowledge ANVISA's role in the 'prior consent' process (Shadlen, 2011). ANVISA, for its part, introduced measures to reassert its authority over the patent office. It also received very strong and active support from civil society groups who were, and still are, interested in furthering the cause of the Brazil's AIDS programme and the integration of the peoples' programme. The domestic pharmaceutical sector originally welcomed the 'prior consent' process when introduced in 2001, but was later not so keen to promote it (Shadlen, 2011). This change in position was clearly because of a bias against the grant of patents for incremental innovations,[58] which was detrimental to domestic

55 Discussed in detail in chapter 7.

56 *Novartis Ag v. Union of India & Others* [2013] 6 SCC 1.

57 The authors take up for study the granting of pharmaceutical patents focussing on patentability of second medical use of known substances in Brazil.

58 Article 8 Lei 9279/96 of the LPI reads as follows: 'An invention shall be patentable if it meets the requirements of novelty, inventive step and industrial application.'

Note: Article 11 states an invention or utility model shall be considered to be new if it does not form part of the state-of-the-art. An inventive step is identified in Article 14, and industrial application in Article 15. Apart from the above, Article 24 requires any application for a patent

pharmaceutical companies, as incremental innovation was seemingly the only option available for growth (Cassier and Correa, 2007).[59]

The involvement of ANVISA in the scrutiny of pharmaceutical patents has been viewed as the principle reason for the backlog before the Brazilian Patent Office, and doubtlessly this process has also slowed down the grant of patents. Although 'prior consent' as a mechanism in the scrutiny of patent application appears to be acceptable under the TRIPS Agreement, Brazil has come under tremendous external pressure due to its introduction (Shadlen, 2011).[60] One should also bear in mind that 'prior consent' was introduced by the Brazilian government into its IP legislation as part of its commitment to provide free public health at a time of crisis, on the premise that patents for pharmaceuticals are different from patents for other technologies due to their implications on public health and special relationship with society (Murphy, 2005).

Following pressure from both practitioners and pharmaceutical patent holders, ANVISA passed Resolution RDC 21/2013, which brought about significant changes to pharmaceutical patent examination. Under the above resolution, pharmaceutical cases are not sent to INPI but to ANVISA directly for examination, where the applications are scrutinised to determine if they would pose any risks to public health – depending on the outcome, there could be either a grant or a denial of 'prior consent' (Gosin, 2016). Cases which receive 'prior consent' are returned to the Brazil Patent and Trademark Office (BPTO), and the applicants of the rejected applications have a 60-day window to appeal against such decisions (Gosin, 2016).[61] The grounds of challenge to ANVISA's powers before the Brazilian courts revolve around (i) its competence to examine pharmaceutical patent applications, (ii) its action in rejecting some claims amounts to discrimination against pharmaceutical inventions and is violative of Article 27.1 of the TRIPS Agreement, and (iii) its shelving of a pharmaceutical patent application by ANVISA without prior substantive examination by the Brazilian PTO, which is unconstitutional (Gosin, 2016). The Brazilian courts, in response, have held that ANVISA must limit its review of an applicant's patent application solely to health issues (Gosin, 2016).

---

of invention or utility model to be thoroughly described, so as to allow its reproduction by one skilled in the art.

59 The authors present a study of five Brazilian pharmaceutical laboratories and are critical of the practice of generics drugs manufacturing through reverse engineering.

60 The author identifies external pressure to the use of US Special 301 reports, from the Washington-based Pharmaceutical Research and Manufacturers of America and from transnational pharmaceutical firms operating in Brazil.

61 Recent court decisions have presented a different picture, with some issuing injunctions directing ANVISA to grant 'prior consent' on the ground that it was not competent to conduct a 'patentability' examination. But in a decision handed down in 2016 by the District Court in Rio de Janeiro, a preliminary injunction was denied, ruling that ANVISA was competent to examine a pharma patent application for patentability requirements.

3.3 Mailbox legacy, backlog and the patent prosecution highway

The 'mailbox' provision was introduced in a number of jurisdictions into their IP legislations immediately after the entry of the TRIPS Agreement. In Brazil the provision was introduced under Article 40 of the Brazilian IP Law to cover patent applications filed between the dates of 1 January 1995 (the entry of TRIPS Agreement) and the date of TRIPS-compliant legislation, *viz.* 14 May 1997. All patent applications filed between the two dates, referred to as 'mailbox applications', were granted patent lasting for a period of ten years from the date of issue of patents as opposed to twenty years from the date of filing of the application. In 2016, the Brazilian Patent Office moved the Federal Court of Rio de Janeiro seeking to revoke the ten-year period of patents and replace the same with a twenty-year period of patent (Gosin, 2016). Interestingly, all patents granted under Article 40 are for pharmaceuticals and agrochemicals. Needless to say, the generics industry is opposed to the extension of the patent period from ten to twenty years for the mailbox patents.[62]

Due to the increase in the number of patent applications filed before the Brazilian Patent Office, there is an enormous backlog in the processing of patent applications. Approximately 34,000 patent applications were filed in 2014, and most interestingly an overwhelming majority were non-resident applicants (Dias, 2016).[63] In 2015, Brazil agreed with the US to the creation of a Patent Prosecution Highway (PPH) Pilot Programme to streamline the examination of patent applications, with a view to ultimately reducing the huge backlog of patent cases (Mueller and Rodrigues, 2016).[64] Interestingly, half of all the patent requests filed before the patent office are from the chemical/pharmaceutical industry, with up to 60 percent for second use patent protection (Ana, 2013). It does not come as a surprise that the majority of the non-resident pharmaceutical patent applications filed before the Brazilian Patent Office are from US-based corporations. Currently, the duration of the program is set for two years, or until 150 patent applications are received and processed (Gosin, 2016).

3.4 Access to health and medicines and judicial enforcement: trouble in paradise

Brazil's healthcare programme strongly hinges on three pillars, *viz.*, the right to health guaranteed under the Constitution, the establishment of an HIV/AIDS programme, and last but not least, a dynamic TRIPS-compliant patent law that

62 The local Brazilian chemical industry has lobbied against Article 40 through the Patent Reform Bill of 2013, which contains a number of anti-patent provisions, including one that would eliminate the ten-year minimum patent term.

63 The author argues that it is undeniable that there is a gap between applications submitted by resident and non-resident applicants in Brazil.

64 The Brazilian Patent Office, on 10 January 2016, published Resolution 154/2015 establishing the guidelines of the PPH Pilot Program between the US Patent Office and the Brazilian Patent Office.

facilitates the domestic production and purchase of generics for its health services. In the absence of any one of the aforementioned pillars, the healthcare programme is bound to fail. With a population of over 190 million and with one of the largest pharmaceutical markets in the world, Brazil spent over US$17 billion on medicines in 2009 alone (Biehl, Amon, Socal, and Petryna, 2012). Despite that, the general population's access to health services and the quality of such services varies according to geography, income and government resources (Cohen and Lybecker, 2005). The population can also be classified under three heads based on income groups, with the top earners forming only 15 percent of the population yet consuming close to half of the pharmaceuticals sold in Brazil, and the poorest forming 51 percent of the population but consuming a meagre 16 percent of the pharmaceuticals sold in Brazil (Cohen and Lybecker, 2005).[65] The middle income groups form 34 percent of the population and purchase around 36 percent of all pharmaceuticals sold (Cohen and Lybecker, 2005). The HIV/AIDS programme introduced in Brazil was a success to begin with, but strains were felt due to the uneven pace between the emergence of new pharmaceutical products within the healthcare system and the acute need for new frontline treatment for patients who were resistant to existing drugs (Chaves, Vieira, and Reis, 2008), which occurred despite Brazil using the 'national emergency' clause to facilitate local production of ARVs (Cohen and Lybecker, 2005).

As medicines became scarce or unavailable under the SUS, many Brazilians were constrained to resort to the courts to enforce their constitutional right to health, leading to an ever-increasing volume of individual right-to-health lawsuits being filed on a daily basis (Biehl, Amon, Socal, and Petryna, 2012; Hogerzeil, Samson, Casanovas, and Rahmani-Ocora, 2006). [66] The dramatic increases in lawsuits over the decade have seen the Federal Health Ministry's spending on court-attained medicines go up exponentially (Biehl, Amon, Socal, and Petryna, 2012).[67] The first of the lawsuits to be filed was in 1996, when the courts ruled in favour of the claimant/patient. In all the cases, the Brazilian courts were inclined to grant the relief claimed and order the state to provide the medicines sought, as the then-prevailing judicial consensus was that a denial of medicine was a violation of the constitutional right to health and access to medicines (Rosina, Wang, and Campos, 2010). The Brazilian courts, including the Supreme Federal Tribunal, or *Supremo Tribunal Federal* (STF), consider the right to health as an

65 The authors also mention that nearly 74 percent of the population, who are the clients of the SUS, are also the ones who cannot afford to pay for private medical care.

66 Right to health litigation is a widespread practice in southeastern and southern Brazil, where judicialisation is viewed as an alternative pathway for accessing healthcare. In 2009, 5536 cases relating to the right to health challenging high court rulings reached the Superior Court of Justice, and about half of these cases (2583) were for access to medicines. In the same year, the Federal Supreme Court of Brazil heard 806 cases related to the right to health, of which 142 were for access to medicines.

67 The authors note that the Federal Health Ministry, in 2009, spent US$47.8 million on court-attained drugs, which is a significant increase from the US$20.4 million spent in 2008 and US$4.2 million spent in 2007. The same ministry, in 2003, spent just under US$59,000.

individual entitlement to the satisfaction of all of one's health needs with the most advanced treatment available, regardless of the cost implications to the system (Ferraz, 2009). The decisions handed down by the STF portray the judiciary as a powerful tool for protecting the constitutional right to health, and in the Court's understanding of its role, such lawsuits protect citizens against government irresponsibility and omission in regards to health issues (Rosina, Wang, and Campos, 2010). Most cases that have reached the STF relate to anti-HIV treatment, followed by phenylketonuria, Duchenne muscular dystrophy and cancer treatment.

However, a slight shift in trend has been noticed in recent years in the decisions handed down by the STF, where petitions have been rejected citing public resource limitations, administrative funding allocations, *etc.* (Ferraz, 2009; Rosina, Wang, and Campos, 2010). In February and March 2007, the STF delivered two decisions denying claims for access to medicines. The then president of the STF, Ellen Gracie, was quoted as saying,

> It is my understanding that Article 196 of the Constitution, that assures the right to health, refers mostly to the carrying out of policies that reach the population as a whole, assuring them universal and equal access, and not in individual situations. The responsibility of the State to provide the resources necessary to the health care of its citizens cannot endanger the public health System.[68]

The NGOs and the civil society groups in Brazil reacted strongly to the above two decisions of the STF and advocated a strong right to health campaign, while local health officials seized the mood of the judiciary to bring court actions to interrupt medicine provisions previously ordered by the courts (Rosina, Wang, and Campos, 2010). The judicial trend that followed once again demonstrated a change, as in some cases the courts reverted to the earlier pattern of granting claims for access to medicines (Rosina, Wang, and Campos, 2010).[69] The key driving force behind the ongoing process of implementing the policy of free access to ARVs in Brazil is down to the support the policy had received from civil society groups, who have mounted a ceaseless campaign all along. The momentum generated has also helped maintain pressure on the courts in Brazil to grant judicial orders, in a majority of claims seeking access to medicines as a constitutional right.

68 As cited by Rosina, Wang, and Campos (2010) at page 176.

69 The authors observe that from mid-2007 onwards, some decisions of the STF had continued with the new approach, while others followed the pre-2007 traditional approach, demonstrating a lack of predictability in such matters. See also Biehl, Amon, Socal, and Petryna (2012), in which the authors note that 815 cases out of the 917 cases that had reached a state high court received a favourable ruling for the plaintiff (either partial or full provision of drugs), which represents a success rate of 89 percent.

3.5 Brazil's balancing act: the current state of play and proposed changes

Brazil's vision and implementation of the constitutional right to health and access to medicine, and its HIV/AIDS programme, is commendable. Brazil had held steadfastly to its stance amidst external pressure from developed countries and TNPCs to deliver its commitment to the right to health, access to medicine and the anti-AIDS programme. In the face of opposition, it had successfully manoeuvred through the troubled waters of international IP rights enforcement regime and generic medicines to make access to medicines affordable to its citizens. While the policies put in place and the actions taken pursuant to the same are laudable, one cannot fail to notice that Brazil acted hastily in its implementation of the TRIPS flexibilities, which proved to be costly. Although it managed to recover, it did not fully implement the flexibilities. For instance, it did not introduce any clear legislation to prevent/check the practice of patent evergreening by TNPCs. This is one area where Brazil will benefit by carrying out more work, as TNPCs are known for their practice of evergreening, and they have taken advantage of the TRIPS Agreement to seek extended patent protection in such fast-growing pharmaceutical markets as Brazil, India, Thailand and South Africa. It can be argued that a second and subsequent use medical patent is hardly ever granted in Brazil due to the 'prior consent' process and the involvement of ANVISA in the examination of pharmaceutical patent applications. Nevertheless, Brazil still suffers from not having a legislative framework which can lay down clear laws to protect the Brazilian jurisdiction from the abuse of patent evergreening, as the protection offered against such practices is only procedural and not contained explicitly in law. Brazil will benefit from the introduction of similar provisions as section 3(d) of the Indian Patent Act to counter the threat of the practice of evergreening.

In July 2015, a key administrative change at the INPI was announced, which saw the replacement of Otávio Brandelli with Luiz Otávio Pimentel, an academic with expertise in international law and IP laws and an arbitrator at the Ad Hoc Arbitration Court of Mercosur, as the president of INPI (Mueller, 2015a). Some of the challenges facing the president of the new INPI can be identified as providing general leadership, urgently addressing the backlog problem of patent applications through accelerating the examination process (Mueller, 2015b), and also providing leadership and support for the passage of the new IP law bill before the Parliament since 2013. On 9 October 2013, the Brazilian Parliamentary Committee released the proposals for change to its industrial property laws in a report entitled 'Brazil's Patent Reform: Innovation Towards National Competitiveness' (Lima, 2013).[70] The changes proposed in the bill are clearly influenced by the Indian Patent Act 2005 in seeking to lower the level of patent protection and at the same time raise the bar on the patentability requirement (Ali and Agarwal, 2016; Srinivasamani

70 The report was presented following extensive consultation carried out over seven workshops, conducted between 2011 and 2013.

and Ramanujan, 2013; PatLit, 2013).[71] The reforms include eliminating patent term extensions and data exclusivity, restricting patents on new forms and second and subsequent use pharmaceutical inventions, increasing the standard for inventive step,[72] and clarifying the role of Brazil's drug regulatory agency (ANVISA), besides strengthening its prior approval powers to deny pharmaceutical patents. Article 2 of Bill HR 5042/2013 restricts patent protection to a twenty-year period and seeks to scrap Article 40 of Lei 92790/1996, which grants patent protection beyond twenty years where the time taken for granting a patent exceeds ten years. This is a TRIPS-compliant provision, as Article 33 of the TRIPS Agreement does not envisage the grant of patent beyond a period of twenty years starting from the date of filing, and any further extension of patent beyond the period mentioned in Article 33 is a 'TRIPS-plus' measure (InfoJustice, 2013).[73]

The key reform proposed is under Article 3 of the above bill, which seeks to amend Articles 10 (X) and 10 (XI) to exclude certain items from patentable subject matters, restrict the patentability of second use inventions and of new forms of compounds, and raise the bar for inventive step in Brazil. The draft provision runs as follows:

> Art. 10. [The following are not considered to be inventions or utility models:]
> (X) any new property or new use of a known substance, or the mere use of a known process, unless this known process results in a new product;
> (XI) new forms of known substances that do not result in an improvement in the known efficacy of the substance.
> *For the purposes of this Article, salts, esters, ethers, polymorphs, metabolites, pure form, size of particles, isomers, mixtures of isomers, complexes, combinations and other derivatives of a known substance shall be considered the same substance, unless they significantly differ in terms of properties regarding efficacy.*

As mentioned earlier, the proposal in Article 3 is strikingly similar to section 3(d) of the Indian Patent Act 2005, which has come under severe attack and criticism from TNPCs and also from the USTR, as it is a measure introduced by the Indian legislature to counter the practice of evergreening (Sundaram, 2014a;

71 Ali and Agarwal opine that Brazil has adopted most provisions from the Indian Patent Act 2005, and posit the interesting argument that such a 'legal transplantation' of India's patent laws to a large number of countries can have far-reaching implications in international law. The other countries to amend their domestic laws on the Indian patent law model are Philippines, South Africa, Botswana and China.

72 More in line with section 3(d) of the Indian Patent Act 2005, and following the decision of the Indian Supreme Court in *Novartis Ag v. Union of India & Others* [2013] 6 SCC 1.

73 Article 33 of TRIPS Agreements reads as follows: 'The Term of protection available shall not end before the expiration of a period of twenty years counted from the filing date. There is no requirement under the TRIPS Agreement for patent term extensions to compensate for regulatory delays, either in the granting of a patent or, in the registration/marketing approval of a medicine. The term of 20 years was adopted in substantial part to compensate for customary periods of regulatory delay.'

Lima, 2013).[74] Not surprisingly, the stated purpose of the above provision in the Brazilian Parliamentary Committee's report is to prevent the practice of evergreening, used by TNPCs to extend the lifetime of patents based on minor or trivial changes to a known substance, or on easily discovered new uses of existing substances. The 'efficacy' standard suggests that there may be an inventive step worth patenting if the product shows significant or dramatic improvement in therapeutic efficacy (Romandini, 2016; Lima, 2013). The concept of invention is specified negatively in the rule, which is in sharp contrast to section 3(d) of the Indian Patent Act (Romandini, 2016).[75] The number of patents granted in Brazil from 2000 to 2011 to overseas interests stands at 197,272 (69 percent) as opposed to 88,096 to domestic interest (31percent) (Licks, 2013).

The proposal to increase the standard of inventive step through Article 3 of the bill by amending Article 31 will strengthen the patent system, and together with the introduction of changes to second and subsequent use pharmaceutical patents will see a well-protected patent regime immune to pharmaceutical patent abuse by transnational patent holders and also fewer applications from overseas patent interests. The changes mooted are similar to section 2(1)(ja) of the Indian Patent Act (Sundaram, 2014a; Matthew, 2011), and the report also refers to steps taken by other jurisdictions, namely the US, to tighten up the inventive step analysis to avoid granting twenty-year monopolies on minor or trivial advances in the art (Lima, 2013). The efforts by the Brazilian government clearly demonstrate a determination and desire to engage and collaborate with similarly placed developing countries and share valuable experience in dealing with instances of evergreening and exploitation of patent regimes by transnational corporations.

4 Conclusion

A year after the establishment of the WTO, the Joint United Nations Programme on HIV and AIDS (UNAIDS) was established,[76] as the HIV/AIDS epidemic that had spread across the globe at an alarming rate was posing further threats. The most affected regions were in developing countries and LDCs, as opposed to developed countries, which were only seeing an increase in the number of cases (Lazzarini, 2003).[77] When Brazil implemented a TRIPS-compliant patent legislation into its laws, it already had in place a policy of universal access to

74 The constitutional validity of section 3(d) of the Indian Patent Act was upheld by the Supreme Court of India in *Novartis Ag v. Union of India & Others* [2013] 6 SCC 1. See chapter 7 for a discussion.

75 In Romandini's view, the Indian Patent Act probably seeks to achieve more than the mere clarification that abstract knowledge *per se* is not eligible for protection or that finding a new property does not render new a known substance.

76 UNAIDS was established in 1994 through a resolution of the UN Economic and Social Council and launched in January 1996. A member of the United Nations Development Group, UNAIDS' primary aim is to help mount and support an expanded response to HIV/AIDS.

77 Since 1996, in developed countries, HIV/AIDS has become akin to other treatable chronic illnesses. In sharp contrast in the developing countries and LDCs, it still remains a deadly plague.

ARV treatment following the HIV/AIDS epidemic that gripped the country in the mid-1980s. The above policies read with the constitutional right to health guaranteed under the 1988 Constitution meant that the government had a herculean task, which was the production of affordable medicine, or in other words generics, to honour its commitments. Unfortunately, Brazil went ahead with the implementation of the TRIPS legislation without utilising the time-bound flexibilities afforded under the TRIPS Agreement, which saw Brazil finding itself in a very difficult situation (Ganji, 2011).[78] Its accomplishments since that time are commendable, as the country saw a decrease in mortality rates between 1997 and 2004, which continue to decrease, as well as a reduction in morbidity from 1993 to 2003. It had also witnessed a reduction in the rate of hospitalisations, which has in turn generated a cost savings of close to US$2.3 billion. These figures demonstrate that access to proper ARV treatment in Brazil over the past ten years has substantially transformed the lives of patients and the methods of controlling HIV infection, improving quality of life for people living with AIDS, increasing their life expectancy, reducing the transmissibility of the virus, and thereby causing a significant decline in mortality rates (Chaves, Vieira, and Reis, 2008).

Brazil, in its pursuit of universal health to its citizens, has followed a pattern of bold policy making backed up by legislation and the creation of appropriate institutional mechanism to implement such policies. The changes proposed to the industrial property laws in 2013 are encouraging, as they appear to address the shortcomings of some of the provisions of the existing laws – for example the practice of seeking patent protection for second and subsequent use medical use, or evergreening. This area remains a concern for Brazil's industrial property laws, as it not only currently lacks necessary legislation to check such practices, but also has a peculiar system referred to as prior consent, which has resulted in a huge backlog. Working closely with civil society groups and NGOs, Brazil has managed, so far, to ward off external pressure from TNPCs and the US in particular – which had used its Super 301[79] and the WTO's dispute settlement

78 The author notes that while legislating its TRIPS-compliant patent laws, India reacted to Western pressures by implementing the agreement in a gradual fashion, whereas Brazil enacted the Agreement in a hurried fashion. As a result, India's legal system and judiciary were better positioned to deal with new global patent laws than were Brazil's, which instead exercised its own brand of economic coercion (threat or use of compulsory licensing) to retrieve ground previously lost when it first ratified the TRIPS Agreement.

79 The US Trade Representative cites powers granted to ANVISA to review pharmaceutical patent applications for meeting patentability requirements, which regulations, according to the USTR, appear to contravene an earlier opinion of the federal attorney general that ANVISA did not have the authority, as the primary reason in its 2013 report to keep Brazil on its 'watch list' of countries whose intellectual property regimes are of concern. The US has, year after year, identified the authority granted to ANVISA as one of the reasons for having Brazil in its Special 301 'watch list.' See Office of the U.S. Trade Representative. *Special 301 Reports 1989–2017* (USTR, Washington DC, 2017) <www.keionline.org/ustr/special301> accessed 28 November 2017. The USTR has a 'priority watch list' and a 'watch list' to monitor countries around the world in their implementation of intellectual property rights. It should also be pointed out that Brazil was on the 'priority watch list' for a number of years before being put on the slightly lesser category of 'watch list.' India, another developing country, which used the TRIPS flexibilities to introduce

mechanism against it – and to successfully continue to implement its much-acclaimed anti-AIDS programme. If one were to look closely at the time line from the outbreak of the AIDS in the 1980s in Brazil to the point of the TRIPS implementation, it can be observed that all measures taken by Brazil had been within the international legal framework and were clearly TRIPS compliant. The TRIPS Agreement only recognises IP right as a private right, so that any prosecution to be launched against possible violations of IP rights are only brought by rights holders. In practice, the rights holders of TNPCs lobby their national governments to act on their behalf (Varella, 2004),[80] to either exert pressure on such national governments seeking changes or use any TRIPS-plus provision found in bilateral trade agreements to increase the level of patent protection.

Brazil's use of the compulsory licence provision is to be commended, as it was able to use the threat of granting a compulsory licence to its advantage most effectively in price negotiations with transnational pharmaceutical corporations (Chaves, Vieira, and Reis, 2008: 170–171), which has resulted in enormous savings for its anti-AIDS programme and for the SUS (Rutledge, 2012). Besides, Brazil has also issued compulsory licences when negotiations with the rights holder failed (Correa, 2013). On the one hand, it has used the threat as a bargaining chip, and when negotiations failed it has actually invoked the provision to access affordable medicines for its healthcare system. But then again, Brazil came under severe pressure from the US, as it launched a dispute before the WTO on the grounds that the Brazilian patent law provisions in this regard were not consistent with the TRIPS Agreement.[81] The use of the compulsory licencing provision by Brazil demonstrates both a hesitation in implementation (bowing to political pressure) and a willingness to engage in negotiations before implementation. A developing country, which has the flexibilities incorporated in the TRIPS Agreements for its benefit, should be able to use it for achieving its objectives without the fear of reprisal by developed countries, or for that matter rights-holding TNPCs. The sufferers are both the patients who rely upon their healthcare systems and the developing countries that administer the care for them. A study carried out by the United Nations Development Programme (UNDP) points out that the minimum standards of protection for IP rights to be

---

section 3(d) into its patent legislation to check the practice of patent evergreening, has been put on the 'priority watch list.' The USTR identifies the decision taken by the Intellectual Property Appellate Board (and confirmed by the Supreme Court of India) as one of the main reasons for putting India on the 'priority watch list.'

80 The use of Super 301 by the US is one such instance. As soon as Brazil introduced compulsory licensing provisions into its laws, the US government launched a consultation at the Dispute Settlement Body (DSU) of the WTO, on the basis that the obligation for local production imposed by the Brazilian law violated Articles 27 and 28 of the TRIPS Agreement. This could clearly be seen as an instance of a developed country acting on behalf of private rights holders (patent rights holders) to exert pressure on a developing country seeking to use the TRIPS flexibilities.

81 A compromise agreement was reached between the parties, whereby Brazil agreed to enter into bilateral discussions before proceeding to make use of the compulsory licensing provisions under Article 68 against a US patent holder. This is a perfect example of a state representing a private right interest holder, namely that of a pharmaceutical patent right holder before the WTO.

provided by each WTO member under the TRIPS Agreement were modelled on Western legal practice and are set at a level comparable to those in the developed countries and controversial, as there is an asymmetry in the level of development and research capacities between the North and the South (UNDP, 1999, 2015).

Brazil successfully lobbied for a United Nations Commission on Human Rights resolution affirming the right of access to medication. The US was the sole abstention of the 53-member body, every member of which voted to pass the resolution (Sanders, 2005). Brazil has gone to lengths to ensure access to essential pharmaceuticals for its citizens, using a combination of policies and legal framework which enables generic production of drugs through the use of compulsory licencing. It is highly unlikely that other developing countries, which lack an indigenous manufacturing capacity, can achieve similar results in their pursuit of access to medicines (Malich and Marion, 2015).[82] Brazil's success is, clearly, due to a combination of historical circumstances, constitutional rights (Paim, Travassos, Bahia, and Macinko, 2011),[83] and bold policy decisions which were put in place in the aftermath of the HIV/AIDS epidemic, which predates the WTO and the TRIPS Agreement. The transnational pharmaceutical patent holders and developed countries await the passing of new industrial property laws in the near future. As discussed, the changes proposed are unquestionably TRIPS compliant and will be beneficial to protect Brazil's jurisdiction from the abuse of patent evergreening. The new laws could potentially see the tightening up of the patent protection mechanism and could also see interference in its implementation from pharmaceutical patent holders, as it does not bode well for the practice of evergreening. Brazil reinvented itself when it came out from over two decades of military rule to make its mark in the international arena as a big player, by bravely implementing health policies through its constitutional right to health and doing battle against the scourge of HIV/AIDS. It is also to be borne in mind that Brazil did not do itself any favours with an early implementation of the TRIPS Agreement.

It will not be out of place to mention the instances in which Brazil had taken action against others before the WTO on matters relating to pharmaceutical patents. Brazil challenged before the WTO, portions of the US patent code as being non-compliant with TRIPS. The provision under challenge was Title 30, Section 202, of the United States Code, which stated that products arising from small business or non-profit patent rights in inventions made with federal assistance shall be made substantially in the United States (Bird, 2009). Not stopping there, Brazil also challenged the US provision stating that licences arising from federally owned inventions will be manufactured in the US (Bird, 2009; Mota, 2005).[84]

82 The authors note that Brazil is one of a small group of middle-income countries (which also includes India, China, Indonesia and Cuba) that has achieved near-total pharmaceutical self-sufficiency, which is attributable to a unique socio-political history. The authors also observe that Brazil viewed health as a universal right that the state had a duty to provide.

83 The authors commend Brazil for including health as a right in the Constitution, as well as the inclusion of social movements into health policy more generally, despite Brazil being in an economically weaker position when they made changes to the Constitution.

84 India joined Brazil in the dispute claiming it had a 'systemic interest' in the proceeding.

Brazil fought hard to maintain its commitment to the constitutional right to health and access to medicines, as well as its anti-AIDS campaign through the use of generics and its TRIPS-compliant industrial property laws. The proposed changes to its industrial property laws, if implemented, will only see Brazil strengthening its position amongst the developing nations that withstood pressure from pharmaceutical patent-holding corporations and developed nations. As in the case of India, when it implemented the TRIPS-compliant patent laws in 2005, Brazil can expect external pressure in its implementation of the proposed new laws relating to industrial property.

Bibliography

1 Ali, Feroz., and Radhika Agarwal 'Transplanting India's Patent Laws,' *OUPblog* (22 March 2016) <http://blog.oup.com/2016/03/transplanting-indias-patent-laws/> accessed 28 November 2017.

2 Baer, Werner. 'Import Substitution and Industrialization in Latin America: Experiences and Interpretations,' *Latin American Research Review* Vol. 7, No. 1 (1972) 95–122, 101–102.

3 Baer, Werner. *The Brazilian Economy: Growth and Development* (Lynne Rienner Publishers, 2008).

4 Baker, Brook K. 'Settlement of India/EU WTO Dispute Seizure of In-Transit Medicines: Why the Proposed EU Border Regulation Isn't Good Enough,' *Northeastern University School of Law Research Paper No. 81-2012* (2012).

5 Basso, Maristela, and Edson Beas Rodrigues Jr. *Intellectual Property Law in Brazil* (Kluwer Law International, 2010) 78.

6 Biehl, João, Joseph J. Amon, Marianna P. Socal, and Adrianna Petryna. 'Between the Court and the Clinic: Law Suits for Medicines and the Right to Health in Brazil,' *Health and Human Rights* Vol. 14, No. 1 (2012) 36–52.

7 Bird, Robert C. 'Intellectual Property Enforcement in a Global Economy: Lessons From the BRIC Nation,' in Yueh, Linda (ed.) *The Law & Economics of Globalization: New Challenges for a World in Flux* (Edward Elgar Publishing, 2009) 225–240.

8 Bodenhausen, George Hendrik Christian. *Guide to the Application of the Paris Convention for the Protection of Industrial Property, as Revised at Stockholm in 1967*, Vol. 611 (WIPO, 1968) 67–73.

9 Brandão, Rafale R. 'Brazilian Patent System: A Brief Introduction,' INPI (*Instituto Nacional da Propriedade Industrial*) (January 2012). <www.jpo.go.jp/torikumi/ibento/ibento2/pdf/brazil_seminar/tegaiyou_en.pdf> accessed 27 November 2017.

10 Cassier, Maurise, and Marilena Correa. 'Intellectual Property and Public Health: Copying of HIV/AIDS Drugs by Brazilian Public and Private Pharmaceutical Laboratories,' *Electronic Journal of Communication, Information and Innovation in Health* Vol. 1, No. 1 (2007) 83–90.

11 Chaves, Gabriela Costa, Marchell Fogaca Vieira, and Renata Reis. 'Access to Medicines and Intellectual Property in Brazil: Reflections and Strategies of Civil Society,' *SUR International Journal of Human Rights* No. 8 (2008) 163–189, 169.

12 Chung, Laura. 'Use of Paragraph 6 System for Access to Medicines,' *North Carolina Journal of International Law & Commercial Regulation* Vol. 36 (2010) 137, 174.

13 Cicero, Mike. 'Markush Groups,' *Ruttler Mills PLCC* (17 October 2012) <www.rutlerlaw.com/blog/2012/10/markush-groups/> accessed 28 November 2017.

14 Cohen, Jillian Clare, and Kristina M. Lybecker. 'AIDS Policy and Pharmaceutical Patents: Brazil's Strategy to Safeguard Public Health,' *The World Economy* Vol. 28, No. 2 (2005) 211–230, 214–215.

15 Cornwall, Andrea, and Alex Shankland. 'Engaging Citizens: Lessons from Building Brazil's National Health System,' *Social Science & Medicine* Vol. 66 (2008) 2173–2184, 2174.

16 Correa, Carlos M. *Integrating Public Health Concerns into Patent Legislation in Developing Countries* (South Centre, Geneva, 2000) 95.

17 Correa, Carlos M. 'The TRIPS Agreement and Developing Countries,' in Macrory, Patrick J., Arthur E. Appleton, and Michael P. Plummer (eds.), *The World Trade Organisation: Legal, Economic and Political Analysis* Vol. II (Springer, 2005) 447.

18 Correa, Carlos M. 'Guidelines for the Examination of Pharmaceutical Patents: Developing a Public Health Perspective,' ICTSD (2007).

19 Correa, Carlos M. 'The Use of Compulsory Licenses in Latin America,' South Views No. 60 (15 April 2013) <http://alainet.org/active/63292&lang=es> accessed 28 November 2017.

20 Correa, Carlos M. 'The Use of Compulsory Licenses in Latin America,' in Hilty, Reto M., and Kung-Chung Liu (eds.) *Compulsory Licensing: Practical Experiences and Ways Forward* (Springer, 2015) 43–60.

21 Deere, Caroline. *The Implementation Game: The TRIPS Agreement and the Global Politics of Intellectual Property Reform in Developing Countries* (Oxford University Press, 2009).

22 Dias, Vitor Martins. 'International Trade *v*. Intellectual Property Lawyers: Globalization and the Brazilian Legal Profession,' *Journal of Civil Law Studies* Vol. 9 (2016) 57–125.

23 Drahos, Peter, and J. Braithwaite. *Information Feudalism: Who Owns the Knowledge Economy?* (Earthscan, London, 2002) 6–8.

24 Drahos, Peter. *The Global Governance of Knowledge: Patent Offices and Their Clients* (Cambridge University Press, 2010) 242–243.

25 Feldman, Robin. 'Rethinking Rights in Biospace,' *Southern California Law Review* Vol. 79, No. 1 (2009) 30.

26 Ferraz, Octavia Luiz Motta. 'The Right to Health in the Courts of Brazil: Worsening Health Inequities?' *Health and Human Rights* (2009) 33–45.

27 Furrow, Michael Enzo. 'Pharmaceutical Patent Life-Cycle Management After KSR v. Teleflex,' *Food & Drug Law Journal* Vol. 63 (2008) 275.

28 Ganji, Sarath K. 'TRIPS Implementation and Strategic Health Policy in India and Brazil,' *Joseph Korbel Journal of Advanced International Studies* Vol. 3 (2011) 29–57.

29 GlaxoSmithKline. 'Evergreening,' *GSK Public Policy Positions* (January 2014) <www.gsk.com/media/2949/evergreening-policy.pdf> accessed 28 November 2017.

30 Gragnolati, Michele, Magnus Lindelow, and Bernard Couttolenc. *Twenty Years of Health System Reform in Brazil: An Assessment of the Sistema Único de Saúde* (The World Bank, 2013) 17, 25.

31 Grosse Ruse-Khan, Henning, and Thomas Jaeger. 'Policing Patents Worldwide? EC Border Measures Against Transiting Generic Drugs Under EC- and WTO Intellectual Property Regimes,' *IIC-International Review of Intellectual Property and Competition Law* Vol. 40, No. 5 (2009) 502–538.

32 Gosin, Rana. 'Update on Brazil's Pharma Patent Landscape,' *Pharmaceutical Patent Analyst* Vol. 5, No. 6 (2016) 385–390.

33 Hogerzeil, Hans V., Melanie Samson, Jaume Vidal Casanovas, and Ladan Rahmani-Ocora. 'Is Access to Essential Medicines as Part of the Fulfilment of the Right to Health Enforceable Through the Courts?' *The Lancet* Vol. 368, No. 9532 (2006) 305–311.

34 InfoJustice. 'Brief Technical Review of Brazil's Proposed Patent Law Reforms' (2013) <http://infojustice.org/wp-content/uploads/2013/10/Brief-Technical-Review-of-Brazilian-Leglislation.pdf> accessed 28 November 2017.

35 Kaiser Health News. 'Brazil Refuses $40M in US AIDS Grants To Protest Policy Requiring Groups to Condemn Commercial Sex Work,' *Daily Reports* (2 May 2005) <www.kaiserhealthnews.org/Daily-Reports/2005/May/02/dr00029729.aspx?p=1> accessed 27 November 2017.

36 Kanth, Ravi D. 'India, Brazil Drag EU to WTO,' *Business Standard* (13 May 2010) <www.business-standard.com/article/economy-policy/india-brazil-drag-eu-to-wto-110051300017_1.html> accessed 28 November 2017.

37 Khor, Martin. 'Row Over European Seizure of Low-Cost Drugs,' *Third World Resurgence No.228/229* (10 August 2009) 4–5 <www.twn.my/title2/gtrends/gtrends262.htm> accessed 28 November 2017.

38 Kunisawa, Mitsuuchi, and Viviane Yumy. 'Patenting Pharmaceutical Inventions on Second Medical Uses in Brazil,' *The Journal of World Intellectual Property* Vol. 12, No. 4 (2009) 297–316.

39 Lanjouw, Jean O. 'A New Global Patent Regime for Diseases: US and International Legal Issues,' *Harvard Journal of Law & Technology* Vol. 16 (2002) 85.

40 Lazzarini, Zita. 'Making Access to Pharmaceuticals a Reality: Legal Options Under TRIPS and the Case of Brazil,' *Yale Human Rights & Development Law Journal* Vol. 6, No. 1 (2003) 103–138, 106.

41 Licks, Otto. 'Brazilian Courts Fight to Fix TRIPS Violations,' *World Intellectual Property Review* (1 February 2012) <http://worldipreview.com/article/brazilian-courts-fight-to-fix-trips-violations> accessed 28 November 2017.

42 Licks, Otto. 'IPR Strategy in Brazil,' Licks Avagados, presentation made at the *4th LES Asia Pacific Regional Conference*, Hangzhou, Peoples Republic of China (17 October 2013) <www.leschina.cn/files/LESAP2013/2013102308.pdf> accessed 28 November 2017.

43 Lima, Newton (ed.). *Brazil's Patent Reform: Innovation Towards National Competitiveness* (Center for Strategic Studies and Debates, 2013). ISBN 978-85-402-0107-1 (e-book).

44 Mainwaring, Scott. 'The Transition to Democracy in Brazil,' *Journal of Interamerican Studies and World Affairs* Vol. 28, No.1 (1986) 149–179.

45 Malich, Erika, and Sarah Marion. 'Increasing Access to Medicines: Leveraging Brazil's Experience,' *Policy Brief, CIGI Graduate Fellows Series* (2015).

46 Mano, Ana. 'Brazilian Government Inches Closer to Reform of Patent Law and Related Legislation,' *Financial Times* (21 March 2013) <www.ft.com/cms/s/2/54ec2986-923e-11e2-a6f4-00144feabdc0.html?ft_site=falcon&desktop=true#axzz4Vf5lQm5o> accessed 28 November 2017.

47 Marques, Ubirajara Regis Quintanilha, Valeska Santos Guimarães, and Caitlin Sternberg. 'Brazil's AIDS Controversy: Antiretroviral Drugs, Breaking Patents, and Compulsory Licensing,' *Food & Drug Law Journal* Vol. 60 (2005) 471–477.

48 Matthew, Ranjan. 'Patentability Requirement in India,' *Lakshmikumaran & Sridharan* (2011) <www.lakshmisri.com/Uploads/MediaTypes/Documents/L&SWebsite_IPR_Featured_Ranjan.pdf> accessed 28 November 2017.

49 Mercurio, Brian. '"Seizing" Pharmaceuticals in Transit: Analyzing the WTO Dispute That Wasn't,' *International & Comparative Law Quarterly* Vol. 61, No. 2 (2012) 389–426.

50 Miller, John W., and Geeta Anand. 'India Prepares EU Trade Complaint,' *The Wall Street Journal* (6 August 2009) <http://online.wsj.com/article/SB124949598103308449.html?mod=googlenews_w> accessed 28 November 2017.

51 Mitnovetski, Oksana, and Dianne Nicol. 'Are Patents for Methods of Medical Treatment Contrary to the *Ordre Public* and Morality or "Generally Inconvenient?"' *Journal of Medical Ethics* Vol. 30 (2004) 470–477, 472.

52 Mota, Sue Ann. 'TRIPS: Ten Years of Disputes at the WTO,' *Computer Law Review and Technology Journal* Vol. 9, No. 3 (2005) 455–477.
53 Mueller, Janice M., and Donald Chisum. 'Enabling Patent Law's Inherent Anticipation Doctrine,' *Houston Law Review* Vol. 45 (2008) 1101, 1106–1107.
54 Mueller, Lisa L., and Robert Rodrigues. 'Brazilian Patent Office and the Patent Prosecution Highway,' *Bric Wall Blog* (16 February 2016) <https://bricwallblog.com/2016/02/16/brazilian-patent-office-and-the-patent-prosecution-highway-program/> accessed 28 November 2017.
55 Mueller, Lisa L. 'A New Beginning? Brazilian Patent and Trade Mark Office Has a New President,' *Bric Wall Blog* (29 July 2015a) <https://bricwallblog.com/2015/07/29/a-new-beginning-the-brazilian-patent-and-trademark-office-has-a-new-president/> accessed 28 November 2017.
56 Mueller, Lisa L. 'Brazilian Patent and Trade Mark Office Publishes New Rules on the Prioritization Examination of Patent Applications,' *Bric Wall Blog* (13 November 2015b) <https://bricwallblog.com/2015/11/13/brazilian-patent-and-trademark-office-publishes-new-rule-on-the-prioritization-examination-of-patent-applications/> accessed 28 November 2017.
57 Murphy, Bryan. 'Brazil's Anuência Prévia: How Brazil's Unique Pharmaceutical Patent Law Illustrates That the United States and Brazil Continue to Disagree on TRIPS' Flexibilities to Protect Access to Essential Medications' (2005) 1–16, <www.ssc.wisc.edu/~munia/467/BrazilMurphy.pdf> accessed 28 November 2017.
58 Musungu, Sisule F., and Cecilia Oh. *The Use of Flexibilities in TRIPS by Developing Countries: Can They Promote Access to Medicines* (South Centre, 2006) 8–9.
59 Norman, Helen. *Intellectual Property Law: Directions* (Oxford University Press, 2014) 92.
60 Nunn, Amy. *The Politics and History of AIDS Treatment in Brazil* (Springer, 2009) 18.
61 Novartis Ag *v. Union of India & Others* [2013] 6 SCC 1.
62 Orsi, Favienne, Lia Hasenclever, Beatriz Fialho, Paulo Tigre, and Benjamin Coriat. 'Intellectual Property Rights, Anti-AIDS Policy and Generic Drugs: Lessons From Brazil,' in Moatti, Jean-Paul, Benjamin Coriat, Yves Souteyrand, Tony Barnett, Jérôme Dumoulin, and Yves-Antoine Flori (eds.) *Economics of AIDS and Access to HIV/AIDS Care in Developing Countries, Issues and Challenges* (ANRS, Paris, 2003) 110–135, 112.
63 Outterson, Kevin. 'Disease-Based Limitations on Compulsory Licenses Under Article 31 and 31*bis*,' in Correa, Carlos M. (ed.) *Research Handbook on the Protection of Intellectual Property Under WTO Rules: Intellectual Property in the WTO*, Vol. I (Edward Elgar Publishing, 2010) 673–697.
64 Paim, Jairnilson, Claudia Travassos, Celia Almeida, Ligia Bahia, and James Macinko. 'The Brazilian Health System: History, Advances, and Challenges,' *The Lancet* Vol. 377, No. 9779 (2011) 1778–1797.
65 PatLit. 'Patents and Right to Health – Brazil and South Africa Follow in India's Footsteps,' *The Patent Litigation Weblog* (25 October 2013) <http://patlit.blogspot.co.uk/2013/10/patents-and-right-to-health-brazil-and.html> accessed 28 November 2017.
66 Piancastelli, Marcelo. 'The Federal Republic of Brazil,' in Majeed, Akhtar, Ronald L. Watts, and Douglas Brown (eds.) *Distribution of Powers and Responsibilities in Federal Countries* Vol. 2 (McGill-Queen's Press-MQUP, 2006) 67–90, 69.
67 Rosenn, Keith S. 'Brazil's New Constitution: An Exercise in Transient Constitutionalism for a Transitional Society,' *The American Journal of Comparative Law* Vol. 38 (1990) 773–802.
68 Reichman, Jerome H., and Catherine Hasenzahl. 'Non- Voluntary Licensing of Patented Inventions: Historical Perspective, Legal Framework Under TRIPS, and an

Overview of the Practice in Canada and the USA,' International Centre for Trade and Sustainable Development (2003).

69 Reichman, Jerome H. 'Compulsory Licensing of Patented Pharmaceutical Inventions: Evaluating the Options,' in Correa, Carlos M. (ed.) *Research Handbook on the Protection of Intellectual Property Under WTO Rules: Intellectual Property in the WTO*, Vol. I (Edward Elgar Publishing, 2010) 589–622.

70 Rodrigues, Edson Beans, Jr., and Bryan Murphy. 'Brazil's Prior Consent Law: A Dialogue Between Brazil and the United States Over Where the TRIPS Agreement Currently Sets the Balance Between the Protection of Pharmaceutical Patents and Access to Medicines,' *Albany Law Journal of Science & Technology* Vol. 16 (2006) 423–456, 429.

71 Romandini, Roberoto. 'Flexibilities Under TRIPS: An Analysis of the Proposal for Reforming Brazilian Patent Law,' *John Marshall Review of Intellectual Property Law* Vol. 150 (2016) 149–212.

72 Rosina, Monica Steffen Guise, Daniel Wei Liang Wang, and Thana Cristina de Campos. 'Access to Medicines: Pharmaceutical Patents and the Right to Health,' in Shaver, L. (ed.) *Access to Knowledge in Brazil: New Research on Intellectual Property, Innovation and Development* (Bloomsbury Academic, 2010) 103.

73 Rutledge, Peter B. 'TRIPS and BITS: An Essay on Compulsory Licenses, Expropriation, and International Arbitration,' *North Carolina Journal of Law & Technology* Vol. 13 (2012) 149–164.

74 Sanders, Anslem Kamperman. 'The Development Agenda for Intellectual Property: Rational Human Policy or "Modern-Day Communism"?,' Inagural Lecture Presented at Universiteit Maastricht (20 May 2005) <https://cris.maastrichtuniversity.nl/portal/files/1605396/guid-459e42d8-9b0f-41c8-aebe-ac4f83e7f631-ASSET1.0> accessed on 28 November 2017.

75 Schulz, Claudia, and Mark Wu. 'The TRIPS Agreement and Intellectual Property Protection in Brazil,' *Proceedings of the Annual Meeting (American Society of International Law)*, The American Society of International Law (March 2004) 100–106, 100.

76 Shadlen, Kenneth C. 'The Rise and Fall of 'Prior Consent' in Brazil,' *The WIPO Journal* Vol. 3, No. 1 (2011) 103–112, 104.

77 Silva, Virgílio Afonso da. 'Taking From the Poor to Give to the Rich: The Individualistic Enforcement of Social Rights,' Presented as workshop paper at *The VII World Congress of the International Association of Constitutional Law*, Athens, Greece (14 June 2007) <http://citeseerx.ist.psu.edu/viewdoc/download?doi=10.1.1.624.9890&rep=rep1&type=pdf> accessed 27 November 2017.

78 Skidmore, Thomas E. *Brazil: Five Centuries of Change* (Oxford University Press, 1995) 155–162.

79 Srinivasamani, Vindhya, and Adarsh Ramanujan. 'Brazilian Patent Law: Proposed Reforms Inspired by Indian Law,' *IPR Amicus* No. 28 (November 2013) <www.lakshmisri.com/News-and-Publications/Publications/Articles/IPR/Brazilian-patent-law-Proposed-reforms-inspired-by-Indian-law> accessed 28 November 2017.

80 Sundaram, Jae. 'India's Trade-Related Aspects of Intellectual Property Rights Compliant Pharmaceutical Patent Laws: What Lessons for India and Other Developing Countries?' *Information & Communications Technology Law* Vol. 23, No. 1 (2014a) 1–30.

81 Sundaram, Jae. 'Brazil's Implementation of TRIPS Flexibilities: Ambitious Missions, Early Implementation, and the Plans for Reform,' *Information & Communications Technology Law* Vol. 23, No. 2 (2014b) 81–116.

82 Taylor, O'Neal C. 'The Limits of Economic Power: Section 301 and the World Trade Organization Dispute Settlment System,' *Vanderbilt Journal of Transnational Law* Vol. 30 (1997) 209-348.
83 UNDP. 'Human Development Report 1999: Globalization' <http://hdr.undp.org/sites/default/files/reports/260/hdr_1999_en_nostats.pdf> accessed 28 November 2017.
84 UNDP. 'Human Development Report 2015: Work for Human Development' <http://hdr.undp.org/sites/default/files/2015_human_development_report.pdf> accessed 28 November 2017.
85 Urias, Eduordo Muriz. *Improving Access to HIV/AIDS Treatment in Brazil: When Are Compulsory Licences Effective in Price Negotiations?* Thesis submitted in fulfilment of Doctor of Philosophy Programme, Maastricht University (28 October 2015). ISBN: 9789461594761.
86 Varella, Marcelo Dias. 'WTO, Intellectual Property and AIDS: Case Studies From Brazil and South Africa,' *The Journal of World Intellectual Property* Vol. 4, No. 4 (2004) 523–547.
87 Waning, Brenda, Ellen Diedrichsen, and Suerie Moon, 'A Lifeline to Treatment: The Role of Indian Generic Manufacturers in Supplying Antiretroviral Medicines to Developing Countries,' *Journal of International AIDS Society* (2010) 1–9.
88 Waning, Brenda, Ellen Diedrichsen, and Suerie Moon. 'Latin America: Favourable Decisión of a Brazilian Court Allowing Patent Protection for Second Medical Use Claims,' *Balder IP Law* (4 August 2013) <http://balderip.com/favourable-decision-of-a-brazilan-court-allowing-patent-protection-for-second-medical-use-claims/> accessed 28 November 2017.

6 China

The uneasy transition

Contents

1 Introduction: in a league of its own

One of the world's oldest civilisations, the People's Republic of China (China)[1] is a country steeped in rich traditions that date back to well over three thousand years. During the twentieth century, China was to undergo a rough and tumultuous transformation from imperial times to the modern era. The legal codes that existed during the imperial period were drafted purely to protect the monarch's interest rather than the citizen's interest, as all power was vested in the emperor. Some commentators take the position that the role of law during the imperial period was functional and existed only as a means to preserve order (criminal law) and to garner resources to protect the state apparatus (Simon, 2013). Research carried out by scholars of the pre-imperial (2100 BCE–221 BCE) and early imperial periods show the existence of legal traditions respecting property rights, contracts, family relations, inheritance, private dispute resolution, and others from the early days of recorded history in China (Simon, 2013).

The cultural revolution of 1949 led by Chairman Mao[2] inflicted such sudden changes on the nation's culture, economy and governance, it left an indelible

1 China is officially called the People's Republic of China (PRC).

2 After overthrowing the Republic of China (ROC) in 1949, the People's Liberation Army took complete control of the government and established the People's Republic of China on 1 October 1949.

mark on the psyche of the nation. Later, under the presidency of Deng Xiaoping, from 1978, China was to undergo a series of far-reaching market economy reforms, moving the nation away from a left-leaning communist state and transforming it into one of the world's fastest-growing economies. In December 2001, China become a key member of the WTO, signalling its deeper integration into the globalised economy of the twenty-first century. China's legal system came to be judged as an instrumentalist model of the law, whereby law is viewed as a vehicle through which policy goals are achieved (Yu, 1989).[3] This raises the question of whether a civil society ever existed in China in the twenty-first century prior to the introduction of market economy reforms. The question gains in significance, as history tells us that civil society plays an important part in shaping a nation's policies and the law.[4] An investigation into such an issue, of course, is beyond the remit of the current book and will not be pursued.

2 Intellectual property laws: origins and evolution

China takes credit for developing the printing technique and the use of paper, which revolutionised the way knowledge and information is disseminated. China is also credited with the invention of gun powder. Interestingly, one does not know the individual, or individuals, behind the above inventions. Scientist and historian Joseph Needham believed that China never came to understand and/or support innovation due to 'bureaucratic feudalism' in the fourteenth century (Needham, 1956).[5] Yu notes that throughout its millennium-long imperial history, China did not develop the notion of IP rights (Yu, 2002). Yet, the earliest efforts to regulate publication and reproduction in the empire could be traced to the ninth-century Tang Dynasty, when Emperor Wengzong issued an edict in AD 835 (Alford, 1995). The edict clearly prohibited any unauthorised reproduction of calendars, almanacs and related items that might be used for predictions (Alford, 1995).[6] This imperial decree was later extended to cover the copying and distribution of state legal pronunciations. The objective of the edict was, however, to sustain imperial power rather than to promote authorship in individuals (Yu, 2002). During the Song dynasty, the Tang edict was sustained and expanded to include prepublication review and registration, but again its objective was not to promote authorship. In addition to the dynastic codes, guild

3 The author also notes that the instrumental model could be seen originating not only in the traditional Chinese legal system, but also arising from adoption of a Marxist legal model.

4 The country-specific studies presented in this book from Brazil, India, Kenya and South Africa (other than China) prove that civil society groups working alongside NGOs played an important role in shaping some of the policies on access to medicines.

5 Joseph Needham penned the extensive and detailed seven-volume work, entitled *Science and Civilization in China* in the 1950s, which is to this day considered a classic on Chinese civilization.

6 The author also notes that the emperor was more concerned with astronomy, as he was keen to assert himself as the link between humans and natural events. It was feared that any literature on prognostication could be used to predict the empire's downfall, and hence, restrictions were put in place on the reproduction of calendars, almanacs, *etc.*

regulations, local laws and clan rules were also in place to protect the producers of tea, silk, paper and medicines through the registration of brand names and symbols (Alford, 1995; Yu, 2002).[7]

Some commentators note that there were writings during the latter part of the Qing dynasty (AD 1616–1911), in which a leader of the Taiping Heavenly Kingdom, in his work *Zi Zhen Xin Pian*, suggested establishing a system of protection for inventions (Zheng, 2007),[8] leading one to assume that efforts were made to recognise works of authors during the dynastic rule. An exclusive right to an innovative technology of mechanical weaving was granted by Emperor Guangxu in 1882 (Zheng, 1999). Following the above grant, in 1898 the Qing government enacted the Reward Regulations on the Development of Technology, which unfortunately never entered into force (Liu, 2014). In 1903, the US coerced China through its military might and economic strength to sign a commercial treaty, which interestingly enough included patent protection.[9] This treaty between China and the US is one of the first efforts by the US through its strength to bring about greater IP protection in other parts of the world (Alford, 1997).

Under the Beiyang government, the Provisional Regulations on Technology Reward was promulgated in 1911, which could be considered as the first attempt in China to reward a patent, following from which patentable subject matters, first-to-file principle, patent transfer and legal liabilities were introduced (Liu, 2014). The Qing Dynasty fell in 1912, which was followed by years of political upheaval, before the Dynasty was united under the nationalist party, Kuomingtang (KMT), led by Chiang Kai-Shek, in 1927. The KMT introduced copyright laws in 1928 – largely based on the German model trademark law – and a comprehensive trademark law in 1931. In 1944, the KMT passed the first patent legislation, which recognised three types of patents, namely inventions, utility models and new designs (Liu, 2014). Disappointingly, the patent law only resulted in the grant of a handful of patents. The sluggish development of the patent system is attributable to China's economic structure and traditional culture, which was based more on values developed on the teachings of Confucius and ingrained into the societal outlook towards knowledge and learning (Liu, 2014; Yu, 2002).

Although the notion of IP rights was introduced into China in the nineteenth century, it would develop as a definite legal right only in the late 1970s, when the country reopened its market to foreign trade (Yu, 2002). It should be noted here that the legislative efforts of the KMT in the 1920s, 1930s and 1940s were not successful. Alford takes the view that the IP laws enacted during KMT's rule did not materialise, as they presumed the existence of a legal structure which was

7 Alford also notes that when China opened its coastal ports in 1840 to trade with Western nations, trade was confined to the sale of bulk commodities (tea, opium, raw silk) rather than items under brand names, which did not give rise to any violation of IP rights.

8 As cited by Liu, Wenqi, 'Evolution of Intellectual Property Protection in Post-Mao China: Law and Enforcement,' Doctoral thesis, Erasmus University, Rotterdam (2014).

9 Treaty for Extension of the Commercial Relations Between [China and the United States].

largely absent in the country during that time (Alford, 1997). When the Chairman Mao-led Communist Party of China overthrew the KMT in 1949, all laws and decrees passed during the KMT's rule were abolished, as they were perceived as tools for the repression of the masses (Blaustein, 1962). In August 1950, the Communist government promulgated the Provisional Regulations of the Guarantee of Invention Rights and Patent Rights, which closely resembled Western patent laws in force at that time (Gale, 1978).

The above laws came to be amended by the Provisional Regulations on Awards for Inventions, Technical Improvements and Rationalisation Proposals Concerning Production in 1954, which provided for monetary awards for improvements to production process, rather than the individual's right to intellectual property (Thomas, 2017). The amendments carried out to the IP legislation in 1954, and thereafter by the Communist government, were keeping in line with Marxist principles and communist ideology, where private property rights were not recognised. Guan notes that the invention award regime introduced in 1950/54 did not last very long, as by the end of 1956, 99 percent of the industrial and 85 percent of the commercial enterprises had been incorporated into the socialist public ownership system (Guan, 2014). In November 1963, China abolished the invention award system of 1950/1954, replacing it with the Regulations on Awards for Inventions and the Regulations on Awards for Technical Improvements. The 1963, Invention Regulation introduced a static one-time award, with ten thousand yuan as the top award, and the element of encouraging individual innovation and achievement was eliminated, completely (Guan, 2014). During the Cultural Revolution,[10] which began in 1966, the development of IP laws came to a complete halt, as all previously existing laws were renounced and the voices of intellectuals who advocated individualism were silenced (Gabriel, 2008).

2.1 Market economy reforms and IP laws

The IP laws introduced in 1978 saw a shift from the socialist/Marxist-influenced jurisprudence. The 1978 Invention Regulation introduced two categories of inventions, namely collective inventions and individual inventions. The IP laws developed during the communist era, until the introduction of market reforms, neither recognised innovation nor rewarded invention, as the ownership of any invention was retained by the state. Prior to the introduction of economic reforms in the late 1970s, Chinese IP laws provided little or no patent protection, as it was still struggling to emerge from a socialist/Marxist notion of property rights, which did not include individual rights to property. With the introduction of market reforms and the reopening of Chinese markets in 1979, citizens were permitted to hold limited private property (Yu, 2002), which engendered the creation of a domestic IP rights regime.

10 The Cultural Revolution, which began in 1966 and lasted for a decade, was aimed at preventing the development of a bureaucratised Soviet style of communism, resulting in the closure of schools, the mass relocation of intellectuals, *etc*.

In 1984, the Standing Committee of China's National People's Congress promulgated the first patent law legislation, which was to be later amended in 1992, 2000 and 2008. The Western notion of rewarding scientific research achievements was introduced into Chinese laws sometime between 1980 and 1983, following the visit of Chinese envoys to the US, Canada and various European nations (Sorell, 2002), and was to form the basis of the 1984 Patent Act and other subsequent IP legislations that followed. The 1984 Patent Acts's objectives were in keeping with the public interest–oriented legislation from the 1950s. Interestingly, the 1984 regulation under Article 25 excluded certain classes of items from patent protection, which included 'methods for the diagnosis or for the treatment of diseases; foods, beverages and flavorings; . . . pharmaceutical products and substances obtained by means of a chemical process'.[11] It should be noted that China's neighbour and another developing country, India, introduced patent legislation in 1970, which excluded pharmaceutical and chemical patents from the ambit of product patent regime.

It is not an exaggeration to state that trade pressure exerted by the US on China in the 1990s played a crucial role in shaping China's contemporary IP regime. Continued pressure from the US, coupled with the threat of trade sanctions by the United States Trade Representative (USTR), saw China and the US signing the 1992 'Memorandum of Understanding (MOU) on the Protection of Intellectual Property'. Under the terms of the MOU, China agreed to revamp its IP protection.[12] This resulted in the 1993 Patent Act, which extended patentable subject matter to include product patent protection to pharmaceutical products. Most importantly, the 1993 law also established an administrative protection regime to protect any foreign pharmaceutical patents granted between 1984 and 1993.[13] The administrative protection offered foreign patent holders market exclusivity for seven years and six months.[14] China was to join the Patent Cooperation Treaty in 1992, and accede to the Berne Convention and the Geneva Convention in 1993.

While still seeking membership at the WTO, China further amended its IP laws in 2000 to conform to the TRIPS Agreement (Hason and Shimotake, 2006). On 1 December 2001, China became a member of the WTO, and the TRIPS-compliant IP legislation officially came into force in China at the end of 2002.

11 Article 25. For any of the following, no patent right shall be granted: '(1) scientific discoveries; (2) rules and methods for mental activities; (3) methods for the diagnosis or for the treatment of diseases; (4) foods, beverages and flavorings; (5) pharmaceutical products and substances obtained by means of a chemical process; (6) animal and plant varieties; [and] (7) substances obtained by means of nuclear transformation.'

12 The US agreed to discontinue the investigation initiated pursuant to the 'Special 301' provisions of the US trade law in return for China's commitment to the MOU.

13 This system closely resembles the 'mailbox system' provided for under Article 70.8 of the TRIPS Agreement.

14 To be eligible for 'administrative protection' under the 1993 Patent Act, the exclusive right must have been obtained on a drug whose patent priority date was between 1 January 1986 and 1 January 1993.

While reviewing the IP laws of China in modern times, one can state that it is unavoidable to be drawn into a discussion of the various political orders that had shaped both the socio-economic and legal landscapes of China, from the early part of the twentieth century until the state's entry to the WTO in 2001. Commentators have categorised China as a 'late developing' country with regards to the establishment of a patent system, having limited awareness and operation capacity (Zhang, 2012).

3 TRIPS compliance: new laws, national IP strategy and pharmaceutical patent rights

The discussions in the preceding section demonstrated that China did not introduce patent protection for pharmaceutical products prior to 1992. It is also the case that as a direct result of bilateral trade negotiations with the US, China proceeded to change its approach towards IP rights protection, and in particular, towards pharmaceutical patent rights. The amendments made to the Patent Act in 1992 and 2000 were primarily aimed at building a legal framework to attract foreign investors to invest in China (Luginbuehl, 2014). The amendments were also in preparation for China to join the Patent Cooperation Treaty (PCT) and the WTO (Guo and Zuo, 2007). Following its accession to the WTO in December 2001, China enacted TRIPS-compliant legislation to extend all patents to twenty years, with data exclusivity for six years. It also saw a change in the law relating to infringements of process patents, resulting in the burden of proof being shifted to the alleged infringer (Hsieh, 2013).

Interestingly, pharmaceutical patent rights protection was introduced during the negotiation phase of China's membership to the WTO, although China only participated in the Uruguay Round of negotiations[15] as an 'observer' state. This status presented China with the opportunity to use the TRIPS Agreement as a model law to improve the IP legislation throughout the 1990s, before official accession. When China's pre-WTO entry compliance with IP rights were assessed, it transpired that China had already complied with less than half of the forty TRIPS requirements (Maskus, 2004). The provisions of the TRIPS Agreement greatly influenced the legal revisions of the IP laws in the 1990s and led to wide-ranging legislative changes to IP rights protection (Thomas, 2017). Commentators also note that the dispute settlement mechanism (DSU), which is part of the WTO framework, could have been a bit of a 'fear factor' for China with regard to international IP rights enforcement (Thomas, 2017).

The Chinese government in 2001 provided incentives to encourage the local pharmaceuticals' innovation of new drugs. In the same year, the State Food and Drug Administration (SFDA) extended the drug protection period for Class I drugs from eight to twelve years. For Class II drugs the period of protection was

15 The TRIPS Agreement was negotiated in the Uruguay Round of negotiations. Please see chapter 3 for a discussion.

extended from six to eight years, and for class III and new drugs from four years to eight years. Likewise, the protection period for Class IV drugs was extended from three years to six years, and for Class V new drugs was extended to six years (Lu, Bai, Tan, and Xu, 2015, 223). Guan notes that while the TRIPS regime takes a private-oriented rights approach, which is modelled on the US and Canadian systems where any alleged violations are to be challenged by the rights holders, China's implementation of the Agreement gives it a more public-oriented approach (Guan, 2014).

The Chinese State Council, in June 2008, introduced a mandatory work plan known as the National IP Strategy (NIPS), which was aimed at bringing the country's IP rights framework to the level of its EU, US and Asian counterparts by 2020 (Luginbuehl, 2014). The NIPS is the product of a National Working Group for IPR Protection, set up in 2005 to coordinate IP policies. The objectives of the strategy are the transformation of China's economic growth pattern from 'made in China' to 'invented in China', and to improve the state's core competitiveness in the international market through system reform and better enforcement (Zhang, 2010). The NIPS was followed by the National Patent Development Strategy 2011–2020 (NPDS) with a view to owning key patents in newly emerging and traditional industries.[16] The NIPS and NPDS together sought to improve patent laws through periodic revision, increase indigenous innovations and improve enforcement of patent rights (Luginbuehl, 2014).

The most important measure triggered by the NIPS was the third revision of the Chinese Patent Act, which adopted the international standard of novelty examination to conduct drug patent review and approval, parallel importing, compulsory licencing and Bolar exemption for clinical trials (Lu, Bai, Tan, and Xu 2015, 221). The newly introduced provisions to the patent laws came into effect on 1 October 2009. The revision followed China's own economic, technological and cultural interests (Zhang, 2012), with the general objectives to improve patent quality, safeguard national security, improve the balance between patent protection and public interest, and have in place measures to improve patent enforcement and prevent abuse of rights (Luginbuehl, 2014). The new laws introduced novelty standards, which allowed the State Intellectual Property Office of China (SIPO) to reject patent applications and revoke patents which are a mere copy of prior art used abroad. Importantly, the revision introduced confidentiality examination, which gives SIPO an overview of the technical areas in which research is being carried out in China and the core technical areas involved. This arrangement is applicable to inventions completed in China and before any application is sought to be filed for an overseas patent (Luginbuehl, 2014).[17]

16 See Zhang (11 November 2010).

17 Article 20(1) of the Chinese Patent Act reads as follows: 'Any entity or individual intending to file a patent application in a foreign country for an invention-creation made in China, shall apply in advance for a confidentiality examination conducted by the patent administrative department

With a view to protecting the genetic diversity of China, Article 26(5)[18] requires a mandatory declaration of the genetic sources in patent applications for inventions based on such sources (Bu, 2014; Chen, 2014). Under Article 69(5),[19] the Chinese Patent Act introduces the 'Bolar exemption'. The introduction of the provision is a significant improvement concerning access to affordable medicines, as it speeds up the process of introducing generic products after the expiry of the patent protecting the generic drug or medical apparatus. The revised Patent Act under Article 48[20] strengthens and extends the ground for granting compulsory licencing, which is identified as one of the objectives of NIPS. The new laws also vest SIPO with powers to grant compulsory licences for the manufacture and export of patented pharmaceuticals to countries or regions covered by the international treaties to which China is a signatory (Hsieh, 2013).

Under the provisions of Article 48, a compulsory licence can be sought either for non-working of the patent so granted for a period of three years from the date of grant and four years from the date of filing of the patent application, or in the event the exercise of the patent is considered a monopolistic act. Article 69(1)[21] of the amended Act introduces international exhaustion of patent rights. Hsieh notes that the number of patent applications submitted by foreign applicants after the introduction of the new patent laws in 1992 has increased steadily – from 1068 in 1993 to 3418 in 2002 (Hsieh, 2013). Further increases were noticed after the amendment in 2002 – from 3875 in 2003 to 5810 in 2006 (Hsieh, 2013). It is also noted that judicial recourse for patent infringement action is available in China, with statistics demonstrating that the enforcement

under the State Council. The procedures and duration regarding the confidentiality examination shall be enforced in accordance with the State Council regulations.'

18 Article 26(5) of the Chinese Patent Act reads as follows: 'An applicant who files a patent application for an invention-creation completed on the basis of genetic resources shall in the patent application document indicate the direct and indirect source of the genetic resources; the applicant unable to indicate the original source of the genetic resource must provide an explanation.'

19 Article 69(5) of the Chinese Patent Act reads as follows: 'None of the following shall be deemed an infringement of the patent right: . . . (5) For the purpose of providing the information needed for the administrative approval, manufacture, use, import of a drug or a medical apparatus, and exclusively for such manufacture any import of a patented drug or a patented medical apparatus.'

20 Article 48 of the Chinese Patent Act reads as follows: 'In any of the following cases, the patent administrative department under the State Council may, upon the application of that entity or individual, grant a compulsory license to exploit the patent for the invention or utility model. (1) where the patentee after the expiration of three years from the date of granting the patent right, and the expiration of four years from the date of filing, has not exploited the patent or has not sufficiently exploited the patent without any justified reasons; (2) where it has been legally determined that the enforcement of the patent right by the patentee is an act of monopoly, to avoid or to eliminate the adverse effects caused to competition.'

21 Article 69(5) of the Chinese Patent Act reads as follows: 'None of the following shall be deemed an infringement of the patent right: (1) Where, after the sale of a patented product or products directly obtained by using the patented process, which was made by the patentee or an entity/individual authorized by the patentee, any other person uses, offers to sell, sells or imports that product.'

mechanism has been used successfully by both domestic and foreign firms holding patents (Hsieh, 2013).

Despite having a substantially revised patent law, China faces challenges in implementing the amendments, as the manufacture and sale of counterfeit medicines threatens to undermine public health, besides depriving brand-name pharmaceutical firms of sales and revenue (Hason and Shimotake, 2006). It is beyond doubt that China had increased its efforts to strengthen its domestic IP laws to conform to the TRIPS Agreement and to be recognised as a key global player in the IP markets. The continuous criticism of China's efforts, though, coming from patent holders and, by default, patent-holding developed nations, is that there is no sufficient mechanism to oversee the enforcement of IP rights (Harris, 2008).[22] Some commentators argue that China is the largest producer of counterfeit pharmaceutical products, and that they pose serious health and economic dangers (Bronshtein, 2008). Although it can be argued that the implementation of TRIPS-compliant legislation in China encouraged TNPCs to seek pharmaceutical patent protection there, it should not be forgotten that the TRIPS Agreement was the brainchild of patent-holding TNPCs and developed nations who viewed emerging economies such as India, China, Brazil, *etc.*, as potentially large markets to tap into.

3.1 *Public health: TRIPS, compulsory licencing*

The Chinese healthcare system experienced a roller-coaster ride over a period of fifty years – from being among the most socialised to becoming one of the most privatised and market-driven (Wang and Tussing, 2011). Being part of the welfare system, the Chinese healthcare system has undergone transformation, both directly and indirectly, when changes were introduced to the welfare system since the beginning of the Mao era. China's public health system prior to market reforms in 1978 was organised around the work place, which was introduced during Chairman Mao's rule. Under the scheme, the Cooperative Medical Scheme (CMS) financed healthcare for members of the agricultural commune, whereas the Labour Insurance Scheme (LIS) and Government Insurance Scheme (GIS) financed healthcare for state-owned enterprise (SOE) workers and government officials, respectively (Wagstaff, Yip, Lindelow, and Hsiao, 2009).

Market reforms transformed the publicly funded healthcare system to one where healthcare financing relied on out-of-pocket payments by the individuals, leading to inequalities in healthcare utilisation (Wagstaff, Yip, Lindelow, and Hsiao, 2009). The effect of market reforms was catastrophic for the healthcare system, with the CMS collapsing due to reduction in funding for public healthcare services, and the two urban health insurance programmes going into decline (Hsieh, 2013). Qiu argues that attention was paid to economic development

22 Figures presented by the author indicate that Chinese companies produce over 30 percent of the counterfeit drugs that are in global circulation.

during the time of the market reforms at the expense of accessibility of healthcare throughout the country, which process involved the conversion of state-owned enterprises into private-owned enterprises (Qiu, 2014). One of the direct consequences of the market reform was the shift in the responsibility of providing insurance for healthcare from the state (as the employer) to the new owners of the enterprises.

China introduced compulsory licencing in the Patent Act of 1984 under Article 52, on the grounds of failure to use the patented product within three years of grant of patent. Under the 1992 Act, the above provisions were modified, which saw the cancelling of the obligation to exploit the patent in China (Shan, 2009). Under Article 51 of the 1992 Act, the Patent Office could grant compulsory licence after the expiry of three years from the grant of patent, whereas a request from an entity for a licence to exploit the invention or utility model on reasonable terms had not been successful. Under Article 52 of the 1992 Act, the Patent Office was vested with powers to grant a compulsory licence in case of a national emergency or any extraordinary state of affairs. The Patent Law of 2000, which is in line with the TRIPS Agreement, provides for the grant of compulsory licence under Article 48. The position of law, in this regard, remains unchanged from the 1992 Act. Under Article 49 of the Act, a compulsory licence can be granted in case of a national emergency or any extraordinary state of affairs – note this provision is the same as Article 52 of the 1992 Act.

Under Article 51 of the 2000 Act, anyone requesting a compulsory licence based on the three circumstances mentioned in Article 48 must furnish proof that he/she had not been able to conclude a licencing contract on reasonable terms with the patentee. Following the Doha Declaration[23] and the Decision of 30 August 2003 (WT/L/540), Implementation of paragraph 6 of the Doha Declaration on the TRIPS Agreement and Public Health (Decision of the General Council), on 29 November 2005, SIPO promulgated the Measures for Compulsory Licensing on Patent Implementation Concerning Public Health Problems 2005 (Shan, 2009). Further, the 2008 Act (the third revision) clarifies that national emergency or public interest includes a public crisis. The 2008 Act under Article 50 permits for the grant of compulsory licence of a patented pharmaceutical product for export to other countries or regions specified.[24] Article 53 provides that compulsory licences are to be used primarily for the supply of the domestic market.[25] Unlike Brazil and India, where compulsory licences have been

23 Declaration on the TRIPS Agreement and Public Health (WT/MIN(01)/DEC/2).

24 Article 50 of the Chinese Patent Act 2000 reads as follows: 'For the purpose of public health, the patent administrative department under the State Council may grant a compulsory license to manufacture a drug which has been granted a patent right in China and to export it to the countries or regions specified in related international conventions in which China is a contracting member.'

25 Article 53 of the Chinese Patent Act reads as follows: 'Except as otherwise provided for in Article 48(2) and 50 of this Law, the compulsory license is used mainly for the supply of the domestic market.'

issued in recent years,[26] no compulsory licence had been granted in China so far (Lin, 2015).[27] In 2012, the SIPO-approved amendments to the patent laws to simplify public health–related measures (such as compulsory licence procedure) were enacted on 15 March 2012 and came into effect on 1 May 2012.[28]

3.2 *Public health: access to medicines and the right to health*

The current Chinese healthcare system has its origins in a series of healthcare reforms and local experiments introduced in the 1990s. Based primarily on the *hukou*[29] system, the population was separated into two main groups, *viz.*, urban residents (U group) and rural residents (R group). The healthcare reforms announced in the twenty-first century sought to strike a balance between the socialistic model prevalent during the early years of the People's Republic and the more capitalistic model embraced in the latter part of the twentieth century in the post-market-reform era (Wang and Tussing, 2011). In 2003, the government launched a healthcare reform plan with the aim of achieving universal healthcare by 2011. Under the scheme, more public funds were allocated to the health sector (from 40 percent to 60 percent) to expand insurance coverage. Hsiao notes that the greatest discontent voiced by the public in the lead-up to China's healthcare reform concerned unaffordable access to healthcare,[30] impoverishment brought about by heavy medical expenses and inequalities across regions (Hsiao, 2004).[31]

In April 2009, further healthcare reforms were announced by President Hu with the goal to achieve equal access to affordable basic healthcare by 2012. The reforms were aimed at providing public goods and encouraging the exploration of market mechanisms to improve quality and efficiency. The scheme envisaged an investment of an additional 850 billion RMB (US$125 billion) over a period of three years in five specific areas, *viz.*, insurance coverage, increased government spending on public health services, primary healthcare facilities, reform of the pharmaceutical market and reform of public hospitals (Yip and Hsiao, 2009).

It is to be stressed here that the Chinese Constitution under Article 21[32] ensures that basic medical and health services are developed and provided for by

26 See chapters 5 and 7 for a case study of Brazil and India.

27 The author notes that there had been some unsuccessful attempts to seek compulsory licenses in China concerning hepatitis B, tuberculosis and AIDS.

28 See 'General Introduction to the Third Revision of the Patent Law of the People's Republic of China and Its Implementing Regulations' <www.bairuiip.com/index.php/Home/Newsandcases/detail/id/219.html> accessed 29 November 2017.

29 The *hukou* system is a population-registration system in which residents are designated a status based on their geographical location – being either rural or urban, based on their registered birthplace. This means, in practice, a migrant worker from the countryside may not be able to access public services (including healthcare) in Shanghai, despite working and living in the city.

30 Commonly known in China as '*kan bing nan, kan bing gui*'.

31 The author notes that the condition was brought about by two policies, *viz.*, fiscal and *laissez-faire*, adopted by the Chinese government for the rural health sector since the early 1980s.

32 Articles 21 of the Constitution of the People's Republic of China 1982 reads as follows: 'The State develops medical and health services, promotes modern medicine and traditional Chinese

the state to its citizens. Article 45 further enshrines the right of the citizen to seek 'material assistance from the State and society when they are old, ill or disabled. The State develops social insurance, social relief and medical and health services that are required for citizens to enjoy this right'.[33] What one observes from a reading of the relevant provision is that on the one hand Article 45 guarantees a right in the citizen to seek material assistance, and on the other hand obligates the State to develop social insurance, social relief, and medical and health services to facilitate the enjoyment of said right. Despite the above constitutional guarantee, health inequalities between socio-economic groups, as well as between individuals, remain in the Chinese society (Qiu, 2014).

Importantly China is a signatory to the human rights treaties (embracing equality and non-discrimination) including the Convention on the Elimination of Discrimination Against Women (CEDAW), the International Covenant on Civil and Political Rights (ICCPR), ICESCR and the Convention on the Rights of the Child (CRC).[34] Unlike the UK, China has a monist legal system with regard to international law, allowing for international treaties when ratified to automatically be national laws. Nevertheless, as Qiu notes, in practice, courts are hesitant to refer to international treaties when making decisions. Unfortunately, China's current health system is not based on the principles of equality and equity and hence not capable of addressing the disadvantages experienced by some vulnerable groups. Qiu argues that the current Chinese healthcare system only serves to deepen the existing disadvantages experienced by some vulnerable groups that lead to health disparities (Qiu, 2014).

4 Conclusion

As discussed earlier, China introduced compulsory licencing provisions into its first ever IP legislation in 1984, later updating and enhancing the provisions in

---

medicine, encourages and supports the setting up of various medical and health facilities by the rural economic collectives, State enterprises and institutions and neighbourhood organizations, and promotes health and sanitation activities of a mass character, all for the protection of the people's health.

The State develops physical culture and promotes mass sports activities to improve the people's physical fitness.'

33 Articles 45 of the Constitution of the People's Republic of China 1982 reads as follows:

> Citizens of the People's Republic of China have the right to material assistance from the State and society when they are old, ill or disabled. The State develops social insurance, social relief and medical and health services that are required for citizens to enjoy this right.
>
> The State and society ensure the livelihood of disabled members of the armed forces, provide pensions to the families of martyrs and give preferential treatment to the families of military personnel.
>
> The State and society help make arrangements for the work, livelihood and education of the blind, deaf-mutes and other handicapped citizens.

34 The International Covenant on Civil and Political Rights (adopted in 1966 by the UN General Assembly resolution 2200A(XXI)); the Convention on the Rights of the Child (adopted in 1989 by UN General Assembly resolution 44/25).

the 1992, 2000 and 2008 revisions. While the provisions for grant of compulsory licence is to be found in China's Patent Act, it has been seldom successfully utilised for issuing a compulsory licence for a pharmaceutical product. Lin notes that there had been a few attempts in the past seeking grant of compulsory licence for hepatitis B, tuberculosis and AIDS. In 2008, the Beijing Yirenping Center (BYC), collaborating with over 1800 HBV carriers and HIV-positive individuals, appealed unsuccessfully to the Ministry of Commerce for grant of compulsory licence for the drug lamivudine (Lin, 2015).

One of the reasons for the absence of equality and equity in pursuing the right to health in China is the introduction of a market economy at the cost of basic healthcare, not to mention the *hokou* system which had been an obstacle to accessing healthcare. From the foregoing discussions, one can summarise that inequalities in right to healthcare in China prevail due to unequal distribution of healthcare resources, inequitable development strategies (including the *hukou* system) and hesitation on the part of the courts to recognise the right to healthcare as a constitutional right. It can be argued that the above factors contribute directly to denying access to affordable medicines to the population at large, but not necessarily through the implementation of the TRIPS Agreement into the domestic laws.

China's IP laws are just over thirty years old and have already undergone three major revisions to keep pace with the nation's expansion economically, and have aided in the country becoming a powerhouse of manufacturing consumer durables for global consumption. China was also bold enough to introduce TRIPS-compliant patent laws even before becoming a member of the WTO, making its intention clear about being a big player on the global stage. Doubtlessly, the IP laws introduced by China since the turn of the century had given the country the necessary recognition to be considered a key player in the globalised economy. On the other hand, the IP laws relating to facilitating access to medicines, especially compulsory licencing, had been hardly utilised. Although provisions for parallel imports and Bolar exemptions have been incorporated into the Patent Laws of 2008, there is little evidence that these provisions have been fully utilised to facilitate access to affordable medicines. In the other two emerging BRICS economies taken up for study, *viz.*, Brazil and India, a clear intent to incorporate TRIPS flexibilities into domestic laws and to utilise such flexibilities for ensuring access to medicines for their citizens is observed. In the case of China, by contrast, such an assertion is impossible to make, as there is no clear evidence to show that TRIPS flexibilities had been fully utilised for accessing affordable medicines.

Bibliography

1 Alford, William P. *To Steal a Book Is an Elegant Offense: Intellectual Property Law in Chinese Civilization* (Stanford University Press, 1995) 12.

2 Alford, William P. 'Making the World Safe for What? Intellectual Property Rights, Human Rights and Foreign Economic Policy in the Post-European Cold War World,' *NYUJ International Law & Politics* (1997) 135–152.

3 Blaustein, Albert P. *Fundamental Legal Documents of Communist China* (Fred B. Rothman & Co, South Hackensack, 1962) 41.
4 Bronshtein, Dina. 'Counterfeit Pharmaceuticals in China: Could Changes Bring Stronger Protection for Intellectual Property Rights and Human Health?' *Pacific Rim Law & Policy Journal Association* Vol. 17, No. 2 (2008) 439–466.
5 Bu, Yuanshi. 'Prerequisites for Protection,' in Luginbuehl, Stefan, and Peter Ganae (eds.) *Patent Law in Greater China* (Edward Elgar Publishing, 2014) 3–24.
6 Chen, Wenping. 'Biotechnological, Chemical and Pharmaceutical Inventions I: General,' in Luginbuehl, Stefan, and Peter Ganae (eds.) *Patent Law in Greater China* (Edward Elgar Publishing, 2014) 3–24.
7 Gabriel, Raymond M. 'The Patent Revolution: Proposed Reforms in Chinese Intellectual Property Law, Policy, and Practice Are the Latest Step to Bolster Patent Protection in China,' *Asian-Pacific Law and Policy* Vol. 9, No. 2 (2008) 323–355.
8 Gale, Barden N. 'The Concept of Intellectual Property in the People's Republic of China: Inventors and Inventions,' *The China Quarterly* Vol. 74 (1978) 334–355, 336.
9 Guan, Wenwei. *Intellectual Property Theory and Practice- China's TRIPS Compliance: A Critical Examination of China's TRIPS Compliance and Beyond* (Springer, 2014) 56.
10 Guo, Shoukang, and Xiadong Zuo. 'Are Chinese Intellectual Property Laws Consistent With the TRIPS Agreement?' in Torremans, Paul, Hailing Shan, and Johan Erauw (eds.), *Intellectual Property and TRIPS Compliance in China* (Edward Elgar Publishing, 2007).
11 Harris, Donald P. 'The Honeymoon is Over: The U.S.-China WTO Intellectual Property Complaint,' *Fordham International Law Journal* Vol. 32 (2008) 96–187.
12 Hason, Averie K., and Jean E. Shimotake. 'Recent Developments in Patent Rights for Pharmaceuticals in China and India,' *Pace International Law Review* Vol. 18 (2006) 303.
13 Hsiao, William. 'Disparity in Health: The Underbelly of China's Economic Development,' *Harvard China Review* Vol. 5, No. 1 (2004) 64–70.
14 Hsieh, Chee-Ruey. 'Pharmaceutical, Health Policy and Intellectual Property Rights in China,' in Löfgren, Hans, and Owain David Williams (eds.) *The New Political Economy of Pharmaceuticals: Production, Innovation and TRIPS in the Global South* (Palgrave MacMillan, 2013).
15 Lin, Xiuqin. 'Prior Negotiation and Remuneration for Patent Compulsory Licensing: Practice, Problem, and Proposal,' in Hilty, Reto M., and Kung-Chung Liu (eds.), *Compulsory Licensing: Practical Experiences and Ways Forward* (Springer, 2015) 165–189.
16 Liu, Wenqi. 'Evolution of Intellectual Property Protection in Post-Mao China: Law and Enforcement,' Doctoral thesis, Erasmus University, Rotterdam (2014).
17 Lu, Ming Q., Sandy Bai, Yuyan Tan, and Cheng Xu. 'Pharmaceutical Intellectual Property Rights in China,' in Lu, Ming Q. (ed.) *Approaching China's Pharmaceutical Market: A Fundamental Guide to Clinical Drug Development* (Springer, 2015) 221–237, 223.
18 Luginbuehl, Stefan. 'China's Patent Policy,' in Luginbuehl, Stefan, and Peter Ganae (eds.) *Patent Law in Greater China* (Edward Elgar Publishing, 2014) 3–24.
19 Maskus, Keith E. 'Intellectual Property Rights in the WTO Accession Package: Assessing China's Reforms,' in Bhattasali, Deepak, Shantaong Li, and Will Martin (eds.), *China and the WTO: Accession, Policy Reform, and Poverty Reduction Strategies* (World Bank Publications, 2004) 49–69.
20 Needham, Joseph. *Science and Civilization in China. Vol. 2 History of Scientific Thought* (Cambridge University Press, 1956).
21 Qiu, Shengnan. 'Equality and the Right to Health: A Preliminary Assessment of China,' in Toebes, Brigit, Rhonda Ferguson, Milan M. Markovic, and Obiajulu Nnamuchi (eds.) *The Right to Health: A Multi-Country Study of Law, Policy and Practice* (Springer, 2014) 97–120.

22 Shan, Xiaoguang. 'Compulsory Licensing in Chinese Patent Law,' in Pyrmont, Wolrad Prinz zu Waldeck, Martin J. Adelman, Robert Brauneis, Joseph Drexl, and Ralph Nack (eds.) *Patents and Technological Progress in a Globalized World: Liber Amicorum Joseph Straus* (Springer, 2009) 127–133.
23 Simon, Karla W. *Civil Society in China: The Legal Framework From Ancient Times to the "New Reform"* (Oxford University Press, 2013).
24 Sorell, Louis S. 'A Comparative Analysis of Selected Aspects of Patent Law in China and the United States,' *Pacific Rim Law & Policy Journal Association* Vol. 11, No. 2 (2002) 319–338.
25 Thomas, Kristie. *Assessing Intellectual Property Compliance in Contemporary China: The World Trade Organization TRIPS Agreement* (Palgrave Macmillan, 2017) 14.
26 Wagstaff, Adam, Winnie Yip, Magnus Lindelow, and William C. Hsiao. 'China's Health System and Its Reform: A Review of Recent Studies,' *Health Economics* Vol. 18 (2009) 7–23.
27 Wang, Hongying, and Dale Tussing. 'Understanding China's Health Care Reform in a Global Context,' Paper Presented at the annual meeting of the American Political Science Association Seattle, Washington, 31 August to 2 September 2011.
28 Yip, Winnie, and William Hsiao. 'China's Health Care Reform: A Tentative Assessment,' *China Economic Review* Vol. 20 (2009) 613–619.
29 Yu, Xingzhong. 'Legal Pragmatism in the People's Republic of China,' *Journal of Chinese Law* Vol. 3 (1989) 29–51.
30 Yu, Peter K. 'The Second Coming of Intellectual Property Rights in China,' (No 11) Benjamin N Cardozo School of Law, Yeshiva University (2002).
31 Zheng, Chengsi. *Intellectual Property* [Zhi Shi Chan Quan] (Law Publishing House, Beijing, 1999) 10.
32 Zhang, Ping. 'China Sets 10-Year Plan to Boost Patent Industry,' *Embassy of the People's Republic of China in the United States of America* (11 November 2010) <www.china-embassy.org/eng/zgyw/t768465.htm> accessed 29 November 2017.
33 Zhang, Ping. 'Review and Perspective of the Chinese Patent System,' in Shimanami, Ryo (ed.) *The Future of the Patent System* (Edward Elgar Publishing, 2012) 308–366.

7 India

The transition from process to product patent

Contents

1 Introduction

India passed the Patent (Amendment) Act of 2005 to bring its patent laws in line with the TRIPS Agreement's agenda of extending international IP protection to patent rights holders, which saw the transformation of its laws from a process patent regime to a product patent regime. India, through the implementation of the TRIPS Agreement, was constrained to give up on its process patent regime introduced in 1970, which not only facilitated the development of a generics manufacturing industry but also provided better access to affordable medicines. In short, the introduction of the new patent laws witnessed a radical shift in Indian policies on pharmaceutical and chemical patenting. India also firmed up on its compulsory licencing laws, introduced direct provisions on 'exhaustion of patent rights', and 'pre-grant' and 'post-grant' opposition. Most importantly, it introduced suitable provisions to check the practice of 'evergreening' by TNPCs.

The decision to change the patent laws gained in significance, as India was one of the fastest-growing generics marketplaces, with some commentators referring to it as the 'pharmacy of the developing world' (Bazzle, 2010; MSF, 2007). The jurisprudence from the courts and quasi-judicial authorities on the Amended Act of 2005 leads one to infer the strong stance taken by India on patent evergreening, the use of pre-grant and post-grant opposition, and compulsory licencing. Although clear judicial precedent is emerging from developed countries like the US and UK, where evergreening is scorned upon, it is India that has taken the first step in introducing legislative measures to check the unethical practice of evergreening. A combined reading of the amended laws, the provisions of the TRIPS Agreement and the recent judicial and quasi-judicial renderings from India present an interesting area for study. They seem to suggest that developing countries can operate the TRIPS flexibility to their advantage, while dealing with national emergencies relating to access to affordable medicines.

In this chapter, it will be argued that the ripple effect of the 2005 Act is being felt, both domestically and globally, as several developing countries and LDCs have come to rely strongly on Indian generics. This chapter seeks to study the effectiveness of the Act of 2005 and whether it can be considered as an instance of success of the TRIPS provisions in Articles 7 and 8, read along with the Doha Declaration. It will be queried whether developing countries in the WTO can possibly benefit from the model set up by India for the issuance of compulsory licences, and to check the practice of evergreening by pharmaceutical patent holders.

2 Indian patent laws: pre-independence

Indian patent laws are steeped in the country's colonial past, as India was under British rule for close to two hundred years, between 1757 and 1947,[1] which period saw the introduction of the common law legal system in India. The Indian patent laws can be broadly categorised under two heads, *viz.*, 'pre-independence India' and 'post-independence India'. Following the debate in the mid-1800s on whether a patent granted in England would automatically extend to India, the Indian Patent Act 1856 was passed, which was in turn based on the UK Patent

1 India was under British East India Company Rule from 1757 until the transfer of power to the British Crown in 1858. Following the Great Indian Uprising of 1857–58, and Queen Victoria was proclaimed Empress of India in 1877. The British rule, referred to as 'British Raj', came to an end in August 1947. The region referred to as 'British India' consisted of the modern-day states of India, Pakistan, Bangladesh, Ceylon (modern-day Sri Lanka) and other countries.

Act 1852 (Garde, 2009). This Act granted 'exclusive privileges' to inventors for a period of fourteen years in India, and was subsequently modified in 1859, as it did not have the Queen's authority and the Indian Legislative Council was not competent to pass the legislation (Mithal, 1948; Garde, 2009). It was renamed the 'Act for granting exclusive privileges to inventors' to enable British Patent holders to acquire control over Indian markets (Judd, 2006).[2] Under the Act, novelty was regarded as anything that was not known in India or the United Kingdom of Great Britain and Ireland prior to filing of the specifications,[3] and the administration of the Act was vested in the secretary to the government of India in the Home department.

The Act of 1857 was amended in 1872 and again in 1883. In 1888, the Inventions and Designs Act was passed, consolidating and replacing the three acts of 1857, 1872 and 1883 and vesting the powers of administration in the Department of Revenue and Agriculture. Later, as the volume of work increased, 'patent secretaries' were created to examine the specifications presented by applicants (Mithal, 1948). Although UK patent laws were amended a few years before 1888, the same changes were not carried over to the Consolidation Act of 1888 in India, for the reason that the volume of patents in India were small (Garde, 2009).[4] In 1910, it was thought that India was ready for a change, and that the procedure for obtaining a patent in India should be brought in line with the British patent system (Garde, 2009), and accordingly Act II of 1911 was passed. Under the Act of 1911, the term 'patent' replaced the term 'exclusive privilege', and a patent was granted for a period of sixteen years from the date of filing of the application, with a provision to extend it a further seven years. The Act of 1911 was accompanied by a set of rules contained in Indian Patents and Design Rules 1912 (Mithal, 1948). The Act also for the first time created a system of patent administration in India under the direction of a Controller of Patents (Narayanan, 2006). In the years that followed, the above Act was amended to establish reciprocal arrangements between India and the UK, and later with Australia, Canada, Ceylon (present-day Sri Lanka), New Zealand, the State of Eire (Ireland) and the Union of South Africa. In 1930, 1099 patent applications were filed, with over 80 percent coming from foreign interests, clearly intended to establish pre-emptive claims for improvements elsewhere (Kumar and Desai, 1983). Any legislation passed (and any economic policies made) during the British Raj was primarily designed to serve and secure the interests of British patent holders in British India, and was not drafted with the native Indian in mind (Kumar and Desai, 1983). It is also safe to assume that any legislative attempts to codify a practice of granting patents commenced in India only during the British rule from the nineteenth century.

2 Between 1858 and 1905, almost 20 percent of Britain's exports were headed for India.

3 Section XIX, Indian Patent Act 1859.

4 See Objects and Reasons of the Bill Culminating in Act II of 1911, Statement of B. Robinson, Mar. 21, 1910.

2.1 *Post-independence*

At the time of independence from British rule, India was predominantly an agrarian society, with over two-thirds of its population living in rural areas. Access to medicines was scarce and much limited to the affluent, due to a lack of indigenous production of drugs (Choudhary, 2006),[5] and for want of a proper healthcare system. Post-independent India's industry sector was weak and was only contributing to a mere quarter of the national income, while also, the pharmaceutical industry was still largely controlled by multinational pharmaceutical corporations, with eight of the ten pharmaceutical companies controlled by foreign interests and holding nearly all of the pharmaceutical patents (Garde, 2009).[6] The indigenous pharmaceutical companies felt the growing need for change, as in their view the patent system in place was not capable of ensuring effective patent rights to promote industrial growth and development in India.

In 1948, the government of India appointed the Patent Enquiry Committee, which was tasked with reviewing the Patents and Designs Act 1911 and providing advice on any changes to the existing patent laws (Hamied, 2005).[7] In 1950, three years after gaining independence, India adopted its first written constitution[8] and officially became a republic (Austin, 1999).[9] The policies contained in the Indian Constitution were designed to give the state the ownership and control of key community resources.[10] It is to be noted here that India's second five-year plan had industrialisation at the heart of the agenda, with the objective of achieving self-reliance[11] and an emphasis on import substitution. In April 1950, the committee headed by Justice Bakshi Tek Chand submitted a report,

5 See also, Planning Commission of India, 'First Five Year Plan' Government of India. In the first of several five-year plans promulgated by India, one of the chief objectives sought to be achieved was identified as improvement of 'standard of living of the people by efficient exploitation of the resources of the country'.

6 In Chapter 32 of the 'First Five Year Plan,' entitled 'Health', one of the priorities listed was achieving 'self-sufficiency in drugs and equipment'. The plan clearly identified the need for 'a co-ordinated programme of development of the pharmaceutical industry'.

7 The author notes that prior to World War II, there was no basic drug manufacturer in India, and that in post-independent India, the key sectors of agriculture, medicine and education were prioritised for heavy investment to achieve self-reliance and self-sufficiency.

8 Although India gained independence from British rule on 15 August 1947, it had the status of a 'Dominion' until 1950, with George VI as head of state and Earl Mountbatten as governor general.

9 The Indian Constitution adopted in 1950 is considered the longest written constitution of any sovereign nation in the world, containing 444 articles, 22 parts and 12 schedules. The author observes the Indian Constitution as being a document primarily aimed at furthering the objective of social revolution.

10 The foundations of the policy are to be found in the Directives on State Policy in the Indian Constitution, which states, 'the ownership and control of the material resources of the community are so distributed as best to subserve the common good.' Constitution of India, Part IV, Art. 39(b).

11 The model presented by Prasanta Chandra Mahalanobis for India's second five-year plan had a nationalist approach to industrialisation, with an argument for self-reliance over foreign manufactured goods.

recommending a series of changes, including the introduction of compulsory licencing and the creation of a more stable legal framework to tackle the abuse of patents (Banerji, 2000).[12] Although a bill was tabled before the lower house of Parliament in 1953, based on the recommendations of the committee, it was to lapse due to the dissolution of Parliament.

2.2 Justice Ayyangar Committee Report

In 1957, a decade after independence, the government of India appointed yet another committee, headed by Justice N. Rajagopala Ayyangar, to review the adequacy of the Indian patent system. The committee, known as Justice Ayyangar Committee, presented its report in September 1959. The report was in two parts, with the first part dealing in general aspects of patent laws and containing recommendations, and the second part presenting comments on the lapsed bill of 1953 and suggesting improvements.[13] It is to be noted here that some of the views expressed by the committee on how food patenting and pharmaceutical inventions can affect accessibility to medicines and on compulsory licencing continued to form the basis for some part of the debates before the WTO in the run-up to the signing of the TRIPS Agreement (Ragavan, 2006).[14]

The report, which is considered as being central to the creation of patent laws in post-independent India, recommended that India should deviate from patent policies of industrialised countries and proposed radical changes to the then-existing Indian patent laws. The committee observed that the high cost of drugs in post-independent India resulted directly from the monopoly exercised by foreign-based pharmaceutical companies over drug production in India. It was of the opinion that food and medicines, which are important in daily life and vital for the health and well-being of the community, should be made available to the public at a reasonable price, and hence strongly recommended against the granting of product patents in the areas of food and medicines. The rationale behind the recommendation for a process patent regime stemmed from the premise that the recognition of the 'process of production' would accelerate research in developing alternative processes, leading to increased diversity of products at competitive prices (Ragavan, 2006). For the purposes of industrial advancement, the Ayyangar Committee favoured the 'process' rather than 'product' protection for chemicals in India.[15]

12 The committee filed a lengthy, 216-page report, with the strong recommendation that the Patents Act should contain provisions to ensure that food and medicine, and surgical and curative devices be made available to the public at the cheapest price possible, while giving reasonable compensation to the patentee.

13 Report on the Revision of the Law in India Relating to Patents for Inventions (September 1959).

14 The TRIPS Council's task was to enable local industrialisation in least developed nations, and the Ayyangar Committee Report, which also advocated self-reliance, can be considered a useful resource for the pursuit.

15 Under the German Patent Law of 1877, where patentability was restricted to novel chemical processes, a stimulated research about alternative methods for producing the same product was

The committee noted that in countries where restrictions were placed on the patents for chemical inventions by confining patentability to the invented processes, there was a similar or even greater restriction on the grant of patents to inventions in relation to articles of food and medicine. This was to be expected, as most of the pharmaceutical preparations were the products of chemical processes (Choudhary, 2006). The committee in its report had highlighted that foreign-held patents amounted to 80–90 percent of the patents granted in India, allowing the patentees to exploit the patent system to achieve a monopolistic control of the market. Around the same time, the pharmaceutical industry in India was also campaigning for changes to be brought to the patent laws, as it strongly believed that the Patents Act 1911 was not fit for purpose and had to be completely changed (Hamied, 2005).[16]

2.3 Indian Patent Act 1970

India's first post-colonial legislation on patents, the Indian Patent Act 1970, came into force on 20 April 1972. The objectives of the Act were to (i) boost Indian economic growth through indigenous technology development, (ii) make the fruits of technological innovations accessible for public purposes (particularly in public health), (iii) protect domestic enterprise and (iv) meet the constitutional obligations of the state under the fundamental rights guaranteed to the citizens found enshrined in the Constitution.[17] The Patent Act 1970 was hailed by the UNCTAD and some developing countries as a progressive statute (Choudhary, 2006).

While the Act of 1970 recognised both process and product patents, the latter was not available for food, medicine, drugs or substances produced by chemical processes, and it redefined the working of the patents. The two key features of the Act were the introduction of 'process patents' for inventions relating to food, medicine and chemical entities, and the shortening of the term of patent protection for pharmaceutical patents (Scherer and Watal, 2001).[18] Under the Act of 1970, the term of process patent protection over food, drug and medical inventions was limited to five years. The process patent regime defined under

---

witnessed. The rise of the German chemical industry dated from 1877, and during a period of thirty years, it witnessed tremendous growth and came to occupy the foremost position in Europe.

16 In 1961, the Indian Drug Manufacturers Association (IDMA) was formed for the purpose of boosting the national pharmaceutical industry. The organisation campaigned for the amendment of the patent laws then prevailing in India.

17 The objectives of the Act were in line with the State Policy contained in the Constitution of India which provided in Article 39 that the 'State shall, in particular, direct its policy towards securing . . . . . . (b) that the ownership and control of the material resources of the community are so distributed as best to serve the common good; and (c) that the operation of the economic system does not result in the concentration of wealth and means of production to the common detriment'.

18 Scherer and Watal note that many of today's developed countries excluded pharmaceutical products from patent protection until quite recently. For instance, Germany excluded pharmaceutical product patents until 1968, Italy until 1978, Spain and Portugal until 1992, Finland until 1995, Iceland and Norway until 1997 and Switzerland until 1977.

section 5(1) of the Patent Act 1970 protected the method through which the product was arrived at, *i.e.*, the process of making the product, and excluded the protection of the end product.[19] It was, therefore, perfectly possible for several manufacturers to simultaneously hold a process patent for identical products.

The process patent regime introduced under the Act of 1970 aided the Indian pharmaceutical companies to manufacture generic drugs using expired patents. The Act also introduced an automatic right to licence (compulsory licence) in the case of life-saving drugs. The above measures worked as safeguards along with the Drug Price Control Order 1970, which put a cap on the maximum price that could be charged for drugs, ensuring that life-saving medicines were available at a reasonable price in India (Das and Basu, 2012).[20] The process patent framework also enabled indigenous pharmaceutical companies to produce drugs at an affordable cost. The growth of the Indian generic pharmaceutical industry is largely attributed to the Indian Patents Act of 1970. It is to be observed that the number of patent applications filed during the operation of the Act remained stagnant (Damodaran, 2008), and arguable that the Act did not contribute to any major innovation in the pharmaceutical sector.

Aided by the 1970 Act, the domestic pharmaceutical industry in India developed over a relatively short period, making India self-sufficient in the production of basic drugs covering major therapeutic groups (Choudhary, 2006). As a result, drug prices in India ranged from five to thirty times lower than in countries where 'product patent' was in place. The next three decades saw India emerge as a globally recognised producer of low-priced generic drugs (Mueller, 2007; Grace, 2005).[21] Not surprisingly, India is currently one of the leading exporters of generic ARVs used in the treatment of HIV/AIDS to other developing countries and LDCs(Waning, Diedrichsen, and Moon, 2010). The Indian Patent Act 1970 is considered by some as a landmark in the history of industrial development in India and by some others as having a negative effect on innovation in the country (Lanjouw, 1998).

3 WTO membership and TRIPS negotiation

The well-documented negotiations on the TRIPS Agreement were conducted during the long-running Uruguay Round between 1986 and 1994. Prior to the

19 Section 5(1) of The Patents Act 1970 reads as follows: 'In the case of inventions – a. claiming substances intended for use, or capable of being used, as food or as medicine or drug, or, b. relating to substances prepared or produced by chemical processes (including alloys, optical glass, semi-conductors and inter-metallic compounds), no patent shall be granted in respect of claims for the substance themselves, but claims for the methods or processes of manufacture shall be patentable.'

20 India introduced drug price-control measures during the Chinese conflict in 1962, amidst fears that it could escalate prices of essential drugs. These measures were put in place in order to make access to medicines affordable within the country. The Drug Price Control Order, introduced in 1970, imposed an indirect control on the profitability of pharmaceutical industries.

21 By 2004, India was supplying 22 percent of the world's generic drugs and a significant amount of the vaccines to the developing world.

negotiations on the TRIPS Agreement, IP rights were principally regulated at the international level by a number of treaties administered by the WIPO, which included the Paris Convention on Industrial Property and the Berne Convention on Literary and Artistic Works. The negotiations on the TRIPS Agreement came about at a time when there was a deadlock over the revision of the Paris Convention for the Protection of Industrial Property before the WIPO.[22] Close to fifty developing countries that sought membership in the WTO were not granting patent monopolies for drugs at the time the Uruguay Round of negotiations were taking place (Correa, 2008).

India was a vocal opponent of the initiative to include IP rights in the GATT system and was the voice of the developing countries at the TRIPS negotiations. India, along with Brazil, Argentina and other developing countries, strongly criticised the proposal on the grounds that the GATT mandate did not allow for the discussion of substantive issues on IP, and it was only the WIPO that had the institutional competence to discuss such matters (Watal, 2001; Drahos, 2002). Towards this end, in July 1989, India submitted a detailed paper elaborating the developing country perspective on the negotiations (UNCTAD-ICTSD, 2005). Although the paper presented was debated extensively at the negotiations, towards the end of 1989 and the beginning of 1990 almost all developing countries had changed their position. The shift came about due to coercive strategies adopted by the US, and as a result India found itself isolated in the negotiations (Bird and Cahoy, 2007; Gervais, 2005). During the same period, India had sought assistance from the International Monetary Fund (IMF) to address depletion in its foreign currency reserves, which had brought it to the brink of an economic crisis. It is worth pointing out that the US was the chief benefactor of the IMF at that time and heavily influenced any outcomes for monetary assistance (Foster, 1998; Drahos, 2002). Due to a combination of its weak financial position and potential trade losses with the US, India relaxed its opposition to the TRIPS Agreement at the negotiations (Foster, 1998). With India agreeing to accede to the TRIPS Agreement, any opposition from the developing countries on the inclusion of IP rights protection into the WTO's covered agreements came to an end.

Following concerns raised by African groups and supported by other developing countries, the Council for TRIPS[23] agreed to deal specifically with the relationship between the TRIPS Agreement and public health. In June 2001, for the first time, the Council for TRIPS systematically considered the

22 The 1980s and 1990s saw the shift in the administration of international IP rights from the WIPO to the GATT through the lobbying of TNPCs, as they were convinced that renegotiation of the Paris Convention before the WIPO would not give them the level of protection they sought.

23 The Council for TRIPS is charged with the monitoring of WTO members' compliance with their obligations under TRIPS. The legal basis for the establishment of the Council is found in Article IV.5 of the WTO Agreement, which stipulates that the Council 'shall oversee the functioning' of the TRIPS Agreement.

relationship between public health and TRIPS.[24] The economic liberalisation policy introduced in the early 1990s was one of the factors for India relaxing its robust opposition to the inclusion of IP rights within the ambit of the WTO (Unni, 2011). India's accession to the TRIPS Agreement, and its move from being a process patent regime to a product patent regime, was viewed by some in India as a clear departure from the vision the founders had of a free India (Keayla, 2004).[25] The action was strongly criticised, as it was firstly viewed as being in violation of the fundamental rights guaranteed under Constitution of India, and secondly, the TRIPS Agreement valued and prioritised the economic gains of patent holders living in faraway countries, ahead of the millions who would suffer from non-availability of affordable medicines (Iyer, 2000).

3.1 *TRIPS compliance*

The accession to TRIPS Agreement mandated India to carry out fundamental changes to its existing IP laws, especially to recognise product patents and move away from process patents. Following the transitional arrangement provisions in the TRIPS Agreement, India was not required to comply with the product patent requirements of TRIPS immediately (Chung, 2010).[26] Nevertheless, India as per Art 70.8(a) was mandated to create a 'mailbox' for the filing of patent applications that would be examined when changes to the law were made and came into effect in 2005.[27] The mailbox facility set up by India following the Appellate Body's report,[28] allowed for the filing of pharmaceutical product patent applications pending the introduction of changes to the Patent Act of 1970.[29] Under Article 70(9) of the TRIPS Agreement, if the products featured in the mailbox

24 In 1996 the World Health Assembly examined the relationship between public health and the TRIPS Agreement, as it was mandated to report on the impact of the work of the WTO with respect to national drug policies and essential drugs. This was addressed in a resolution on the Revised Drug Strategy, Resolution WHA49.14 (25 May 1996).

25 One of the strong critics of the TRIPS Agreement was Justice VR Krishna Iyer, a former judge of the Supreme Court of India and a panel member of the People's Commission on GATT, which was to later file its report in 1996. Justice VR Krishna Iyer was of the opinion that the act of signing the TRIPS Agreement would be *ultra vires* the Constitution of India.

26 TRIPS Agreement, Articles 65(2) and 65(4), in certain cases, allows delaying the application of the provisions on product patents to such areas of technology for an additional period of five years.

27 TRIPS Agreement, Article 70.8(a), requires developing countries to set up a 'mailbox' system during the transitional period. Article 70.9 requires the grant of exclusive marketing rights in certain cases following the setting up of the 'mailbox' provision under Article 70.8(a).

28 As India failed to formally enact the 'mailbox' regime into law, the US resorted to the WTO's dispute resolution mechanism. See WTO. *India-Patent Protection for Pharmaceutical and Agricultural Chemical Products – Report of the Appellate Body* (19 December 1997) WT/DS50/AB/R, where India was directed to set up the 'mailbox'. Following the report of the Appellate Body, the 'mailbox' was implemented by the Patents (Amendment) Act, 1999, No. 17, Acts of Parliament, 1999, sections 2 and 3.

29 Around 9000 mailbox applications were filed during the transition period, of which 84 percent originated from multinational corporations, with Pfizer coming first. Indian submissions totalled

applications were granted patent and had also obtained marketing approval in any of the WTO member countries, then India was obligated to grant five-year exclusive marketing rights (EMRs) before the patent on the product was either granted or rejected in India (Dhar and Gopakumar, 2011). In March 1999, India passed the Patents (Amendment) Act 1999[30] to implement the mailbox procedure as per Article 65(4) of the TRIPS Agreement. The 1999 Act was given retroactive effect from 1 January 1995 to facilitate receipt of patent applications for pharmaceutical and agrochemical products under the mailbox procedure.

A second amendment to the 1970 Act was made in 2002, which introduced a twenty-year patent term,[31] reversed the burden of proof for process patent infringement, modified the compulsory licencing requirements, and also, for the first time introduced a definition of 'inventive step'.[32] The passing of the 2002 Amendment Act concluded India's accession to the Paris Convention for the Protection of Industrial Property 1883, and the Patent Co-operation Treaty 1970. The combined effect meant that the India had to follow the national treatment principles laid down in the Paris Convention and grant a twelve-month priority period for foreign applicants who had previously filed a patent application in their home countries.[33] One of the notable changes brought about by the 2002 Amendment was the grounds for seeking a compulsory licence on pharmaceutical patents. Broadly, a compulsory licence can be sought in the case of non-working of the patented work after three years of sealing of the patent, in the event of a national emergency (through a government notification), or in certain cases where patents are essential for the efficient working of other patented inventions.[34] In conclusion, it can be stated that the 2002 Amendment laid the groundwork for the passing of the Patent (Amendment) Act 2005.

4 The Amendment Act 2005

The membership of the WTO was expected to spur the economic growth of a nation, and India was doing as much as possible to create an environment to achieve this goal and bring in foreign investment. To this end, and to meet the obligation as a WTO member, India was to pass the Patent (Amendment) Act 2005. The efforts to make changes to the patent laws generated much controversy

---

1406, including 1300 in the pharmaceutical sector. Applications from the US topped the list, followed by India, Germany and the UK.

30 The Patents (Amendment) Act 1999, No. 17, Acts of Parliament, India (1999).

31 Prior to the 2002 Amendment, pharmaceutical process patents issued under the 1970 Act lasted for a period of five years from sealing, or seven years from the date of the patent, whichever was less.

32 See sections 27, 43, and 3(f), The Patents (Amendment) Act 2002, No. 38, Acts of Parliament, India, 2002.

33 Article 2, and Article 4(C)(1), Paris Convention for the Protection of Industrial Property 1883 (as Amended on 28 September 1979).

34 Sections, 84, 92, and 91 respectively of the Patents (Amendment) Act 2002, No. 38, Acts of Parliament, India, 2002.

even in the discussion stages (Ramesh, 2005), both in India and abroad. The efforts of the Indian government to pass the TRIPS-compliant patent legislation was considered overzealous in some quarters.[35] The NGOs and the World Health Organisation (WHO), in particular, were concerned about the plight of the HIV/AIDS sufferers in the least developed countries, who were strongly reliant on Indian generic drugs.[36] On the one hand, India was bound by its obligations to WTO, the international body facilitating multilateral trade, and on the other hand, it was strongly urged by a UN Special Envoy to ensure that India's new patent laws did not harm the supply of generic drugs to the developing countries.

The picture that emerged at that time was a collage of worry, expectation and disbelief, as it was generally perceived that any action taken to change the patent regime (other than a process patent) would have a long-lasting impact on India and its generic drug producers, on pharmaceutical patents around the world, and most importantly on millions of sufferers of HIV/AIDS living in the least developed countries,[37] who were strongly reliant on India's supply of generic ARVs. There was a growing feeling that the Indian government was working on a TRIPS-compliant patent legislation that could potentially jeopardise access to medicines for many poor patients in the developing world. Against this backdrop, India passed the Patent (Amendment) Act 2005 to bring its patent laws in line with the TRIPS Agreement, while bearing in mind its unwritten commitment to the developing and least developed countries that strongly relied on its generic drugs to do battle with the scourge of HIV/AIDS, other diseases. The 2005 Amendment Act contains a wider framework for compulsory licencing, incorporates procedures governing both 'pre-grant' and 'post-grant' opposition to patent applications, gives provisions on 'patentable subject matter' and 'exhaustion of patent rights', and most importantly carries forward the setting up of an 'inventive step' for patentability into the patent regime from the 2002 Amendment Act.

4.1 Compulsory licencing

Patent protection is cited as one of the reasons for the limited availability and affordability of medication for the treatment of HIV/AIDS. Currently, those most

35 See letter from Achmat Dangor, Director of Advocacy, Communication and Leadership for UNAIDS, to Kamal Nath, the then Minister of Commerce and Industry of India, on the Amendments to the Patents Act Under Debate, raising concerns and stating that the 'implications of the current ordinance are potentially devastating . . . urge you to consider all appropriate legal means to protect and scale up access to essential affordable medicines.' (23 February 2005) <www.cptech.org/ip/health/c/india/unaids02232005.html> accessed 28 November 2017.

36 See Letter from U.N. Special Envoys for HIV/AIDS to the then prime minister and president of India on the Amendments to the Patents Act Under Debate (11 March 2005), where India's efforts and role in promoting access to essential medicines is referred to as being crucial, and urging that no TRIPS-plus provisions be incorporated into the new Act. <www.cptech.org/ip/health/c/india/unaids03112005.html> accessed 28 November 2017.

37 See Letter from Jim Yong Kim, HIV/AIDS Director of the World Health Organization to Dr A. Ramadoss, the then Minister of Health and Family Welfare of India (17 December 2004) <www.cptech.org/ip/health/c/india/who12172004.html> accessed 28 November 2017.

affected from the crisis live in developing countries and LDCs, where generic ARVs provide the only affordable answer, as patented drugs for the treatment of the disease are unaffordable. India, as one of the leading exporters of generic ARVs, is considered a key player in providing access to affordable medicines. Compulsory licencing of patented drugs is said to be one of the essential pillars of the patent system and is found in international conventions (Bodenhausen, 1968),[38] enabling access to essential medicines in times of need, which are unaffordable otherwise. It is widely recognised that compulsory licences play an important role in preventing abuse of patent rights that may arise when a patent holder tries to pre-empt entry of competitors using its statutory rights (Dhar and Gopakumar, 2011).

Compulsory licence is considered as a mechanism through which the exclusivity associated with a patent is superseded, for reasons of failure on the part of the patent owner to perform their obligations, enabling the government to strike a balance between rewarding the inventions and, in case of need, making the product available for public use even during the term of the patent (Gopalakrishnan and Anand, 2015). Although available for use by governments, the instances when compulsory licence has been used by a government since the entry of the TRIPS Agreement in 1995 is few and far between. This position could be down to changing industry practices, the incorporation of TRIPS-plus provisions in bilateral or regional trade agreements, and trade policies of developing countries which may not want to antagonise a developed country trade partner through such practices.

The Doha Declaration states that every WTO member has 'the right to grant compulsory licences and the freedom to determine the grounds upon which such licences are granted'. As mentioned earlier, the Amendment Act 2005 contains a liberal framework for the grant of compulsory licence, and the Indian government preserved the original provisions of the 1970 Patents Act regarding compulsory licencing for use within India.[39] Under section 84 of the Act, an application for compulsory licence is sustainable three years from the grant of a patent, upon successfully satisfying the condition that the 'reasonable requirements of the public with respect to the patented invention have not been satisfied', that 'the patented invention is not available to the public at a reasonable price', and lastly the

38 Article 5A of the Paris Convention for the Protection of Industrial Property provides for the signatories to the Convention to have the right 'to take legislative measures providing for the grant of compulsory licenses to prevent the abuses which might result from the exercise of the exclusive rights conferred by the patent, for example, failure to work.' Under Art 5A 'failure to work', or 'insufficient working' of a patent would be tantamount to abuse of the patent rights, and can be viewed as giving raise to grounds for the grant of compulsory license. See also Article 31, TRIPS Agreement ('Other Use Without Authorization of Rights of Holder'), and Article 30, TRIPS Agreement ('Exceptions to Rights Conferred'). The Doha Declaration, seen as a corollary to the TRIPS Agreement, proclaims that each member had the right to grant compulsory licenses.

39 See Indian Patents (Amendment) Act 1999. Sections 84, 86, 89, 92 and 93 of the Patents Act govern domestic compulsory licenses, which remain largely unchanged by the Amendment Act of 2005.

patented invention is not worked in the territory of India.[40] The circumstances for 'reasonable requirements of the public' would arise if the patent holder refuses to grant a licence on reasonable terms. This refusal, in turn, can affect the development of new trade or industry in the country, the establishment or development of commercial activities in India and the development of the export market for a patented article manufactured in India (Dhar and Gopakumar, 2011).

The Amendment Act 2005 expanded the opportunities to obtain compulsory licences for export of patented pharmaceuticals to LDCs. The new Act confers on the government the powers to grant a compulsory licence in circumstances involving national health emergencies,[41] and also provides the mechanisms to manufacture and export patented medicines to other countries that do not have the necessary infrastructure to manufacture drugs.[42] From a reading of the relevant provisions on compulsory licencing, it is clear that the Indian government and the Controller of Patents are vested with sweeping powers to grant compulsory licences in suitable cases. The grounds of seeking a compulsory licence can include (i) if the public deems the patented invention to be unsatisfactory, (ii) if the public cannot access patented inventions at a reasonable price and (iii) if the patented invention is being worked outside the territory of India.

Under section 84, an application for compulsory licence can only be made after the expiration of three years from the date the patent was granted. Before the grant of any compulsory licence, the concerned authority is required to take into account additional factors such as (i) the nature of the invention and the measures already taken by the patentee or licencee to make full use of the invention, (ii) the ability of the applicant to work the invention to public advantage, (iii) the capacity of the applicant to undertake the risk in providing capital and working the invention, (iv) the efforts made by the applicant to obtain a licence from the patentee on reasonable terms and conditions, and that (v) such efforts were not successful within a reasonable period (Dhar and Gopakumar, 2011).

Some commentators, however, are sceptical about effectiveness of the provisions. In their view, the procedural requirements are too onerous and could result in delays, as it is not clear if the grant of a compulsory licence would be automatic if a patentee refuses to issue a voluntary licence on reasonable terms, as the grounds for determination of anti-competitive practices in India have not been spelt out clearly either in the Patents Act or in the Indian Competition Act 2002 (Dhar and Gopakumar, 2011; Jain and Darrow, 2013; Gopakumar, 2010). It can be said that the Amendment Act 2005, through its provisions, protects India's existing

40 The Act contains a list of instances where the reasonable requirements of the public shall be deemed to be unsatisfied. See sections 84(1)–(6) of the Patents Act 1970.

41 Section 55 of The Patents (Amendment) Act, 2005 (insertion of new section 92A).

42 The new section 92A titled 'Compulsory License for Export of Patented Pharmaceutical Products in Certain Exceptional Circumstances' expressly provides for the manufacture of essential medicines in response to public health crises. Section 92A(1) enjoins that the importing country must have 'insufficient' or 'no manufacturing' capacity, and allows for the importation of patented pharmaceutical products from India.

generics drugs industry, as a patentee cannot possibly bring a patent infringement action against a generic manufacturer who has been producing a patented product prior to 2005 and who continues to manufacture the product on the date of the patent grant. Since the introduction of the new laws in 2005, the offices of the Controller of Patents, in the four major cities in India, have been inundated with applications from overseas corporations. During the same period, numerous applications were received from Indian generics manufacturers for grant of compulsory licence. In this regard, decisions made by the authorities in India in recent years are taken up for study as they present an interesting picture to analyse.

4.1.1 The first compulsory licence case: Natco v. Bayer

Sorafenib tosylate is a drug used in the treatment of liver and kidney cancer. The patent holder, Bayer Corporation, was marketing the drug under the trade name of Nexavar. Bayer Corporation extended its patent application for sorafenib tosylate to India in 2001, and the registration was granted in March 2008. Further, the Indian authorities granted Bayer regulatory approval for marketing the drug under the trade name Nexavar in India in 2008. In July 2011, Natco Pharmaceuticals Ltd, an Indian generics manufacturer, lodged its application for the grant of compulsory licence to manufacture Nexavar.[43] This was considered by some industry experts as a strategic move by Natco, as there were pending infringement actions against Natco brought by Bayer. Natco argued that Bayer's patented drug, Nexavar, had not been made available to the public at a reasonably affordable price, and that the reasonable requirements of the public had not been met. It was also Natco's case that Bayer failed to work the patent in India within the specified three-year period, as it was still importing the drug into the country – although it had a manufacturing unit in India, which in turn resulted in an unaffordable price being charged for the drug in India.

It was Bayer's case that a 'reasonably affordable price' should be calculated with reference to the public as well as the patentee, and the price of the patented drugs had to be sufficient to support future drug development. Bayer also argued that 'working' in relation to patents in India meant supplying the drug to the Indian market on a commercial scale, that the relatively small market demand for Nexavar did not justify the manufacture of the product in India, and that Bayer was providing the drug only to 2 percent of the estimated number of patients in India. The Controller of Patents considered the fact that Bayer had sold no Nexavar in India in 2008, and only sold very small quantities in 2009 and 2010. The Controller of Patents found that all the necessary grounds prescribed under section 84 of the Indian Patents Act for the issuance of a compulsory licence were satisfied,

43 Prior to lodging the above application, Natco Pharmaceuticals had filed applications for grant of compulsory license under section 92A of the Indian Patent Act for two cancer drugs, namely, Suninat and Tarceva as early as 2007. Suninat and Tarceva are patented to Pfizer and Roche, respectively. Natco intended to manufacture and export them to Nepal, but later withdrew its application for issue of compulsory license.

as Bayer did not meet the reasonable requirements of the public with respect to the patented drug Nexavar, that Bayer's pricing of the drug was exorbitant and did not constitute a 'reasonably affordable' price, and that Bayer could not be said to have complied with the 'working' requirements under the Indian Patent Act, as it did not manufacture the drug Nexavar in India.[44]

On 9 March 2012, the first compulsory licence was granted by the Indian Controller of Patents at Mumbai, on the application taken out by Natco to manufacture and sell a generic version of the drug Nexavar. The drug manufactured under the compulsory licence by Natco was to cost nearly thirty times less than that being charged by the patent holder Bayer Corporation, and Natco was to pay Bayer a quarterly royalty at 6 percent of the net sales of the drug. The Controller's observations on 'local working' by Bayer on the drug Nexavar will prove controversial, as almost 90 percent of the drugs patented in India to multinationals are not manufactured in India and could be susceptible to compulsory licence (Basheer, 2012). Worthy of mention here is the fact that a compulsory licence was granted on an application taken out by a third party (market-initiated) and not by the government, and all parties concerned were heard following the principles and procedures set out under the TRIPS-compliant Indian patent legislation.

Bayer Corporation duly challenged the decision of the Controller of Patents before the IPAB (IP Appeal Board), Chennai. The IPAB, in its judgment dated 14 September 2012 confirming the order of the Controller of Patents, held that Bayer did not satisfy the reasonable requirement of the public and that the drug was not made available at a reasonably affordable price. Bayer challenged the order of the IPAB before the Bombay High Court, which confirmed the decision of the IPAB, noting that compulsory licence proceedings are in public interest.[45] The Bombay High Court observed that the 'public interest is and should always be fundamental in deciding a *lis* between the parties while granting a compulsory licence for medicines/drugs',[46] and that 'medicine has to be made available to every patient and this cannot be deprived/scarified at the altar of rights of patent holder'.[47] On 12 December 2014, the Supreme Court of India dismissed the special leave sought by Bayer to challenge the decision of the Bombay High Court, thereby bringing the judicial saga of *Natco v. Bayer* to close.

4.1.2 BDR v. Bristol-Myers Squibb

Dasatinib, which is used in the treatment of chronic myeloid leukaemia (CML), is marketed by the patent holder Bristol-Myers Squibb (hereafter Bristol-Myers)

44 In the proceedings, Bayer argued that Cipla, another Indian generics manufacturer, had been marketing a generic version of Nexavar in India at a much lower price since April–May 2010, such that no objection regarding the medicine's availability could be legitimately raised. However, the Controller noted that Bayer had commenced infringement proceedings against Cipla, and thus the sales carried out by an alleged infringer should not be considered to support Bayer's case.

45 *Bayer Corpn. v. Union of India*, (2014) SCC OnLine Bom 963: AIR 2014 Bom 178.

46 *Ibid.*, para 19.

47 *Ibid.*, para 13(f).

under the brand name Sprycel. In March 2013, the Mumbai-based BDR Pharmaceuticals filed an application under section 84 of the Indian Patent Act before the Controller of Patents, Mumbai, for the grant of compulsory licence to manufacture a generic version of the drug Dasatinib. BDR Pharmaceuticals (BDR) argued that the drug had received 'orphan drug designation'[48] in the US, Europe and Switzerland, and that it had the capacity to manufacture and supply the drugs in India. It was also contended by BDR that its efforts to engage the patentee in a dialogue for the purposes of securing a grant of a voluntary licence were fruitless, and hence it was constrained to approach the Controller of Patents with an application for grant of compulsory licence for the drug Dasatinib. The patentee Bristol-Myers, in contrast, was able to demonstrate that it did respond in time to the applicant's request for voluntary licence and sought additional information regarding BDR's capabilities, intent, *etc.*, but did not receive any response from the applicant.

The Controller of Patents, while concluding that BDR failed to satisfy the requirements for grant of a compulsory licence under section 84, observed that the stage to make a decision on the merits of the case presented under section 84 had not arrived yet, as the applicant deliberately refrained from engaging in any kind of dialogue with the patentee for the purposes of securing the grant of a voluntary licence, and that the applicant did not follow the scheme of law and the procedure mandated for the grant of a compulsory licence under section 84 of the Indian Patent Act.[49]

4.1.3 Lee Pharma v. AstraZeneca

Saxagliptin is used in the treatment of Type-II Diabetes Mellitus, and the patent for the drug was granted to Bristol-Myers Squibb in 2007. The said patent right was later assigned to AstraZeneca by way of a Deed of Assignment. In June 2015, Lee Pharma, an Indian pharmaceutical company, had taken out an application for the grant of compulsory licence under section 84 of the Patent Act. The stated grounds were that Saxagliptin was not manufactured in India even after eight years of grant of patent, that it was being imported into India at a cost of Rs. 0.80 per tablet and sold at a market price of Rs. 41–45, and that the patentee had not taken adequate steps to manufacture Saxagliptin in India. It is to be noted here that Saxagliptin is usually a drug used in 'life management', unlike the case of a cancer drug which is used in 'life threatening' situations.

The Indian Patent Office (IPO), Mumbai, while rejecting the application by Lee Pharma, held that the applicant for compulsory licence had 'failed to satisfy

48 Orphan drugs are used in the treatment of patients with rare diseases. The term orphan drug is used in both US and EU legislations to describe a drug that is indicated for a rare disease, or 'orphan disease'. Under the US Orphan Drug Act, 'orphan drug' designation is accorded if the drug is intended to treat a condition affecting fewer than 200,000 of the population in the US, or which will not be profitable within seven years following approval by the FDA. In the EU, it is intended to treat a disease affecting fewer than five per 10,000 of the population.

49 *BDR Pharmaceuticals International Pvt Ltd v. Bristol-Myers Squibb Co* CLA No. 1 of 2013, Controller of Patents, Patent Office, Mumbai (29 October 2013).

the controller regarding any of the grounds as specified in Section 84(1) of the Act', and that 'a *prima facie* case has not been made out for making of an order under Section 84 of the Act'.[50]

4.1.4 A closer look at the compulsory licence provision

The procedure laid down for the grant of compulsory licence under the Act of 2005 is cumbersome and long drawn, with no time limit specified in the Act or the Rules for the disposal of an application that is lodged before the authorities. Lack of clarity in this regard could see the compulsory licence provision becoming redundant and unusable for the purposes for which it was incorporated into the Act. Further, the Act does not fully utilise the TRIPS flexibilities, as any final decision regarding the use of a patented invention under compulsory licence can be challenged in a court of law and an injunction sought to prevent the use of a patented invention (Gopakumar, 2010). Under Article 44 of the TRIPS Agreement, there is no obligation on the part of a member state to provide for the remedy of injunction against government use. The practices in the US and UK in this respect are different and less cumbersome, as the governments in both countries can take over the patent invention without seeking a licence or engage in lengthy negotiations with the patent holder. The only remedy available for the patent holder is to sue the government for compensation and not for an injunction (Correa, 1999). Some commentators opine that India, with its public sector pharmaceutical industry, should strengthen the government use provisions in its Patent Act (Basheer, 2012) and remove any uncertainties.

The question that comes to haunt us is whether such a grant of compulsory licences will in any way fail to provide incentives to innovate in India and drive away international corporations from the country. Critics of the compulsory licence regime have always argued that grant of compulsory licence discourages innovation. Issuing of patent is strongly predicated on the premise that it encourages innovation by offering a limited monopoly to the patentee, which presents the argument that compulsory licences will kill off innovation. There is no strong empirical evidence to suggest that compulsory licences do have a negative effect on innovation (Basheer, 2012). In contrast, the studies available only indicate that licences do not have any significant demonstrable effects on the rate and pace of innovation (Chien, 2003). There are also others who seriously question the efficacy of the compulsory licencing system under the TRIPS Agreement, which they think has not helped in achieving the goal of access to affordable medicines (Paas, 2009). For now, the evidence seems to suggest that grant of compulsory licence does not affect innovation in the Indian pharmaceutical sector, which is dominated by generics manufacturers.

50 *Lee Pharma Ltd. v. AstraZeneca*, CLA No 1 of 2015, The Controller of Patents, Patent Office, Mumbai (19 January 2016).

5 The aftermath

Commentators have expressed differing views on the outcome of *Natco v. Bayer* case, with some expressing the opinion that India might possibly be in violation of the non-discrimination principle mandated under Article 27(1) of TRIPS (Bonadio, 2012), and others taking the position that the grant of compulsory licence is unlikely to constitute any violation (Basheer, 2012), going by the WTO decision in *Canada – Patent Protection of Pharmaceutical Products*.[51] In the aftermath, the originator company Hoffmann La-Roche (hereafter Roche) entered into a manufacturing contract with Emcure, a local generic manufacturer, to satisfy the 'working requirement' for their drug patent, and Cipla reduced the price of its generic version of sorafenib to INR 6,840 (US$ 130). Patent-holding multinationals are seeking to forge marketing alliances (not to include technology transfer) with local manufacturers in India, as they consider voluntary licencing to local partners under mutually agreeable terms as an effective way to avoid compulsory licencing, and at the same time expand their market presence in the region (Unnikrishnan, 2013). The swiftness with which the multinational pharmaceutical corporations are reacting to the decision, in order to avoid any further losses to their patent rights and market share, is striking.

With regards the outcome of the proceedings in *BDR v. Bristol-Myers Squibb* is concerned, it comes as a relief for the patentee, as it did not lose any revenue on its patent, but on the other hand the decision is a big disappointment to millions of patients suffering from CML, as the drug will not be accessible due to its very high price. In India, a month's dose of the drug costs about INR 100,000, and BDR's application for compulsory licence was based on the premise that it will be able to sell a month's dose of the drug for a mere INR 8,100. In sharp contrast to the response to the decision made in the *Natco v. Bayer* case, which was received with shock by multinational drug manufacturers operating in India, the decision in the *BDR v. Bristol-Myers Squibb* case was received in muted silence. Both applications for grant of compulsory licences were made under section 84 of the Indian Patent Act. The above decisions demonstrate that Indian authorities are keen to interpret the law in the light of its true purport, and compulsory licence will not be granted on all applications. As regards the case of *Lee Pharma v. AstraZeneca* is concerned, it is not surprising that the application for the grant of compulsory licence did not succeed.

In a separate development, the Swiss drug manufacturer Roche decided not to seek extension of its patent for the cancer drug Herceptin in India, which expired in May 2013 (Rajagopal, 2013), but due to its complex chemical combinations, it is unlikely that generics manufacturers will be able to make a copy soon. Roche had come under severe pressure from the Indian government to cut the prices of key anti-cancer drugs, as it is beyond the reach of many cancer patients in the country. It is to be noted that Biocon-Mylan, Reliance Life Sciences and BDR

51 WTO. *Canada – Patent Protection of Pharmaceutical Products* – Report of the Panel (17 March 2000) WT/DS114/R.

Pharmaceuticals are some of the companies who are currently working on a copy of Herceptin in India.

5.1 *Pre-grant and post-grant opposition*

Section 25 of the Patent (Amendment) Act 2005 provides for pre-grant opposition of patents in India. Under this provision, any third party can challenge the application for grant of patent. Section 25(1) lists eleven grounds for lodging a pre-grant opposition and challenging the grant of a frivolous or invalid patent. The introduction of pre-grant and post-grant opposition under the amended patent laws is considered by some developed countries as a controversial step, as it slows down the grant of patents. The Patent (Amendment) Act 2005 also provides for taking out a post-grant opposition within one year from the date of publication of the grant of patent, and the same can be considered as a second window of opportunity for lodging any opposition.[52] Under this provision, any 'interested person' may give notice of opposition to the Controller in the prescribed manner on any of the grounds mentioned in section 25 of the Patent (Amendment) Act 2005. The grounds for both pre-grant and post-grant opposition are identical, and there is nothing in the Act to preclude a pre-grant opponent from subsequently filing a post-grant opposition on the same patent.

The opposition at the pre-grant stage is more by way of representation as opposed to notice of opposition, and further, there is no scope for an appeal against the decision of the Controller on any pre-grant opposition.[53] The only remedy that is open to the aggrieved party in such circumstances is to seek judicial review under the Constitution of India,[54] which can be a lengthy procedure allowing the patent holder to enjoy a wrongful monopoly during the pendency of such proceedings before the court. Some generic drug manufacturers and public interest groups have utilised the pre-grant provisions to prevent frivolous patents, but the provision remains underutilised due to barriers in accessing information (Gopakumar, 2010). Denial of access to or non-disclosure of information on pending applications pose a serious threat, as the Indian Patent Office does not publish full details of pending applications. It is important to clarify this provision, especially when India has introduced measures to check

52 Article 99 of the European Patent Convention (EPC) allows an opposition to be filed by any person within nine months of the publication of the grant of the European Patent (EP) in the European Patent Bulletin (EPB). Any opposition lodged applies to the EP patent in all contracting states where the EP patent has effect. The US has a provision for re-examination to challenge the validity of a granted patent. Here again, the re-examination procedure can be invoked by any person at any time during the period of enforceability of a patent. The US re-examination procedures are detailed and fall under two categories, namely, *ex parte* re-examination and *inter partes* re-examination.

53 However, it is to be pointed out that the Madras High Court allowed *Novartis* to challenge the order passed by the Controller under the pre-grant procedure before the IP Appellate Board.

54 Judicial review is available under Article 226 of the Constitution of India, before a High Court, and under Article 32 before the Supreme Court of India.

the practice of patent evergreening. The Novartis case, discussed in section 6 of the chapter, arose out of pre-grant oppositions lodged by generic drug manufacturers and NGOs.

5.2 *Patentability and patent evergreening*

Earlier, the Justice Ayyangar Committee Report had recommended the introduction of process patents into the patent laws in India. The recommendations were based on a detailed, in-depth study of post-independent India's socio-economic conditions and the need to develop a self-reliant and self-sufficient nation. After the introduction of the process patent system under the Patent Act 1970, India has moved towards a product patent system, which embraces the opposite of what was recommended by the Justice Ayyangar Committee in 1959. One of the important changes made to the laws is the introduction of 'patent eligibility' under section 3(d) of the Act of 2005. Section 3(d) prohibits the grant of patents on derivatives of known substances, unless such derivatives display significantly enhanced efficacy. Section 3(d) spells out such instances which will not be considered 'inventions' under the Act. The text of section 3(d) reads as follows:

> the mere discovery of a new form of a known substance which does not result in the enhancement of the known efficacy of that substance or the mere discovery of any new property or new use for a known substance or of the mere use of a known process, machine or apparatus unless such process results in a new product or employs at least one new reactant.
>
> Explanation: For the purposes of this clause, salts, esters, ethers, polymorphs, metabolites, pure form, particle size, isomers, mixtures of isomers, complexes, combicountries and other derivatives of known substance shall be considered to be the same substance, unless they differ significantly in properties with regard to efficacy.

Section 3(d) is aimed at denying patent for trivial modifications on existing patents and preventing the practice of evergreening. As described in chapter 1, the expression evergreening (Glasgow, 2001) is used to identify the practice of obtaining multiple patents that cover different aspects of the same product, and is also known variously as 'stockpiling', 'life-cycle management', 'patent-layering', and 'line-extension'. Evergreening, in effect, refers to the attempts by pharmaceutical patent owners to extend the term of patents they already hold, through the adoption of modified forms of the same drug, new delivery systems and new uses for the drug (Mueller and Chisum, 2008; Feldman, 2005). Pharmaceutical companies resort to the practice with a view to maximising on the monopoly period enjoyed by the patented drug (Furrow, 2008), with commentators expressing serious concerns about the same (Lanjouw, 2002). Multiple patenting of known substances, or evergreening, considerably delays and poses a threat for the legal entry of generics into the market and can successfully prevent competition in the pharmaceutical market.

When India set up the 'mailbox' under the transitional arrangements in 1999, it received close to 9000 applications. It could be argued that several overseas applications that were lodged by TNPCs through the system were an attempt at evergreening their patents (Dhar and Gopakumar, 2011).[55] India's pharmaceutical industry, being strongly driven by generic drug manufacturers, required a strict patentability criterion to ensure the early entry of generics into the market. The introduction of section 3(d) was the answer, as it aimed to both increase the threshold limit of patentability criteria and exclude certain types of inventions from the ambit of the Patent Act. This section seeks to disallow the patenting of a known substance unless it results in an enhancement of the efficacy of that substance, and it constitutes a bold legislative step to curb the practice of evergreening (Sen and Ramanujan, 2010). Importantly, section 3(d) applies to both pharmaceutical patents and chemical patents.

The section encourages sequential developments of existing products or technologies that help bring improved products to the market, as opposed to evergreening which is considered the improper extension of patent monopoly of a pharmaceutical product (Basheer, 2005).[56] The introduction of the pre-grant inspection was the first step in bringing about a fundamental shift in the way pharmaceutical patent applications were to be scrutinised in India. Judicial precedent has been set in the US[57] and the UK,[58] both common law countries holding a substantial number of pharmaceutical patents, to discourage the practice of evergreening. Introduction of section 3(d) into the patent laws is to be considered a definitive legislative measure taken by India to tackle the menace of evergreening and is to be commended. Interestingly, the US topped the list of pharmaceutical patent applications lodged when India set up the mailbox under the transitional arrangement, with the UK coming fourth in the list behind Germany (Narendranath, 2005).

55 The authors refer to the practice of granting patents to IMDs (incrementally modified drugs) in the US, and how an overwhelming majority of the applications received by the Patent Office in India through the 'mailbox' set-up would fall under the IMDs category.

56 The author notes that incremental innovations are not the same as evergreening, and section 3(d) of the Act of 2005 draws a distinction between the two.

57 The courts in the United States rely on the doctrine of inherent anticipation to deal with instances of 'patent evergreening', which was demonstrated in the judgment handed down by the Court of Appeals for the Federal Circuit (CAFC) in *Schering Corp. v. Geneva Pharm., Inc.*, 339 F.3d 1373 (Fed Cir 2003). Also, the US Hatch-Waxman Act 1984 provides for financial incentives and encourages generic firms to identify and challenge improperly issued secondary patents. That said, the provisions of the Hatch-Waxman Act cannot be equated to the Indian Patent Act, which also provides for pre-grant opposition under the 2005 Amendment.

58 The courts in the UK follow similar principles as prevalent in the US to discourage patent evergreening. See the Court of Appeal decision in *Les Laboratoires Servier v. Apotex Inc.* [2008] EWCA Civ 445. Lord Justice Jacob while dismissing the appeal and holding that Servier's patent was invalid for lack of novelty and obviousness, observed that 'It is the sort of patent which can give the patent system a bad name. . . . The only solution to this type of undesirable patent is a rapid and efficient method for obtaining its revocation. Then it can be got rid of before it does too much harm to the public interest.'

6 Interpreting section 3(d): the Novartis saga

In 1993, Novartis AG (Novartis) filed a patent in the US covering the free base[59] imatinib and other pharmaceutically acceptable salts. Later, Novartis derived the drug Glivec, which is the beta-crystalline form of imatinib mesylat. This drug is known to make chronic myeloid leukaemia a manageable disease by controlling cellular action that allows the cancer to grow. Although it does not cure the disease, it is considered a step forward in the treatment of cancer. Novartis also marketed glivec in the US under the trade name Gleevec.

On 17 July 1998, Novartis lodged its application for a patent in India through the 'mailbox', and applied for an exclusive marketing right (EMR). With the grant of the EMR in 2003, consumers in India saw a ten-fold increase in the price of glivec. Novartis's patent application for glivec faced severe opposition from Indian generic manufacturers (against which Novartis had filed infringement suits) and the NGO, Cancer Patients Aid Association (CPAA). The main grounds for opposition were that the application lacked novelty, as it did not demonstrate any significant 'efficacy' to satisfy the requirement of section 3(d) and have any obviousness, and it had a wrongful priority. The opposition could be heard at a stage prior to the grant of patent, under section 23 of the 2005 Amendment. On 8 March 2006, agreeing with the arguments of the opponents to the patent, the Assistant Controller of Patents rejected the application taken out by Novartis, holding that the new version of glivec was not sufficiently different from the old unprotected version to warrant a patent. Novartis filed two petitions before the Madras High Court, seeking to reverse the decision of the Assistant Controller of Patent and to declare section 3(d) of the Amendment Act unconstitutional and in violation of India's obligation under the TRIPS Agreement. Pending proceedings, the government constituted the IP Appellate Board, and the first of the petitions mentioned above was transferred to the IPAB.

Novartis also argued that section 3(d) violated Article 14[60] of the Constitution of India, as it vested unbridled powers on the patent controller, leading to discriminatory results. The petition challenging the TRIPS compliance and the constitutional validity of section 3(d) was heard first, and by judgment dated 6 August 2007, the court held that the provision in question was not in violation of Article 14 of the Constitution of India,[61] and that it did not confer the Controller of Patents with uncontrolled powers. The court held that it did not have the jurisdiction to decide on the compliance of a domestic Indian law to that of an international treaty, and refused to grant a declaratory relief as sought for by Novartis. Accordingly, the court declined to go into the question if section 3(d)

59 The expression 'free base' is commonly used in organic chemistry and pharmaceutical research to describe the 'deprotonated' amine form of a chemical compound. It refers to the pure basic form of an amine, as opposed to the salt form.

60 Article 14, of the Constitution of India reads as follows: 'The State shall not deny to any person equality before the law or the equal protection of the laws within the territory of India.'

61 *Novartis Ag v. Union of India and Others* (2007) 4 MLJ 1153.

of the Indian Patent Act was consistent with Article 27 of the TRIPS Agreement. The court also observed that the government had a constitutional duty to provide good healthcare to its citizens through access to medicines, and for that purpose there should be suitable legislative measures in place to prevent the practice of evergreening, which has a negative impact on the availability of affordable medicines. The petition challenging the decision of the Controller of Patents dealing with patentability of glivec was heard by the IPAB, at Chennai, which also ruled against Novartis.[62]

Novartis was granted special leave to appeal against the above decisions to the Supreme Court of India. A total of five appeals were lodged before the Supreme Court, and on 1 April 2013, the Court delivered a detailed judgment.[63] One of the key legal issues before the Supreme Court was whether the mesylate salt form of imatinib had been disclosed, was publicly known, prior to 1997. To satisfy the requirement of 'enhanced efficacy' in section 3(d), Novartis compared the beta crystalline with the already known mesylate salt. It was Novartis's case that the beta crystalline form showed an increase of 30 percent in terms of 'bioavailability', which was not in comparison to the known and previously marketed mesylate salt form of the drug. In short, Novartis was not comparing its 'new' form of salt to its 'old' marketed form of salt, but rather to what it knew would be a much less 'bioavailable' form (Abbott, 2013). The Supreme Court ruled that imatinib mesylate was a known substance since 1994 and does not qualify as an 'invention' in terms of clauses (j) and (ja) of section 2(1).[64] In doing so, the Court also held that the beta crystalline form does not satisfy the requirements of the criterion set under section 3(d), concluding that section 3(d) was meant to create a 'second tier of qualifying standards' for chemical substances to combat 'any attempt at repetitive patenting or extension of the patent term on spurious grounds'. Most importantly, the Supreme Court interpreted efficacy to mean therapeutic efficacy. Here, the Court sought to link patenting to therapeutic benefit, or more precisely net benefits to society, thereby highlighting the relevance of specific conditions prevalent in a country for deciding the appropriate patent regime to adopt (Chaudhuri, 2013), within the parameters of IP rights regime laid out under the TRIPS Agreement. The court rejected the appeal, as in its view Novartis could not demonstrate that the new form of the known substance could enhance the therapeutic efficacy of the drug.

When Novartis made its application through the mailbox, it was not required to make a case for therapeutic benefit, as section 3(d) was non-existent at that

62 Judgment of the IPAB in *Novartis Ag v. Union of India & Others* (26 June 2009) <www.lawyerscollective.org/files/novartis/IIIIPAB/Novartis%20AG%20v.%20UoI%20and%20others%20[IPAB%20order].pdf> accessed 28 November 2017.

63 *Novartis Ag v. Union of India & Others* (2013) 6 SCC 1.

64 The Patents (Amendment) Act 2005, section 2(1)(ja) defines inventive step as 'a feature of an invention that involves technical advance as compared to the existing knowledge or having economic significance or both and that makes the invention not obvious to a person skilled in the art.'

time and was only to be introduced later in 2005. Nevertheless, when Novartis was given the opportunity to produce evidence to demonstrate the therapeutic efficacy of beta crystalline at the 'pre-grant opposition' stage, it did not do so, as there was no study available to that effect.[65] Novartis also argued that its research and development had to be recouped and hence the high price for the drug (Love, 2013).[66] Interestingly, the patent that was at issue before the Indian Supreme Court was also the target of a Hatch-Waxman challenge in the US in 2007 (Sampat, Shadlen, and Amin, 2012), and Novartis did not appear to be litigating in response to this challenge, suggesting that it accepted the patent as questionable even in the US.

While Novartis has, naturally, not welcomed the decision, the Indian public, health economists and other interest groups have all welcomed the decision and consider it a landmark judgment, as the generic drug makers can continue to sell copies of the drug at an affordable price in India. The Novartis case, through its legal debate on section 3(d), has brought into sharp focus the rights of a sovereign country to build safeguards into its patent laws for protecting public interest and on the issue of access to affordable medicines, which is vital for the realisation of health as a human right (Chandra, 2010a). The judgment links the key question of patenting with net benefits to society, thereby emphasising the importance of socio-economic conditions in a country while deciding on the appropriate patent regime to adopt (Chaudhuri, 2013). The Supreme Court was unequivocal in stating that the purpose of section 3(d) was to prevent the practice of evergreening.[67] The case will be a legacy of the TRIPS Agreement and its flawed vision for the creation of a globally harmonised IP protection (Rangnekar, 2013).

6.1 *Case analysis*

Although section 3(d) is aimed at preventing the practice of evergreening, the scheme of the Act does not completely rule out the possibility of evergreening of patents (Gopakumar, 2013).[68] The definitions on the criteria of patentability and exclusions of patentability provide scope for pharmaceutical companies to work their way around section 3(d) and obtain patents for known substances (Gopakumar, 2010, 335). Empirical evidence also suggests that the Indian Patent Office may have failed to carry out strict scrutiny of patent applications and unwittingly granted patents to known substances (Gopakumar, 2013), which demonstrates a

65 Novartis opted to file a few affidavits before the IPAB, Chennai, to prove the efficacy of beta crystalline, instead of presenting any scientific data from clinical studies to that effect.

66 The author argues that Novartis was ably supported by significant contributions from philanthropic sources in the US, while only spending a fraction on the R&D for the development of 'Gleevec,' or glivec.

67 *Novartis Ag v. Union of India & Others*, paras 100–102.

68 In the author's estimation, close to 3500 product patents have been granted by the Indian Patent Office between 2007 and 2010, of which many are likely to have been granted in violation of section 3(d). The author also advocates a review of all these patents in the light of the Supreme Court judgment in the Novartis case.

weakness on the procedural side of the Indian Patent Office. The US-India Business Chamber has criticised section 3(d) as capable of barring inventions that may otherwise meet the requirement of patentability and considered truly inventive. It has further stated that the removal of section 3(d) from the Amended Act would allow all incremental innovations to undergo examination and be treated in the same manner regardless of industry or field of technology (White and Case, 2009). Much criticism had also flown from the US on India's new patent laws, especially aimed at section 3(d),[69] whereas UNAIDS recognised India's new patent laws as a model for developing countries to embrace on the use of the TRIPS flexibilities (UNAIDS, 2011). In sum, the introduction of section 3(d) is a positive step taken by the Indian lawmakers to tackle the menace of evergreening practiced by pharmaceutical patent holders.

The Indian Supreme Court, while delivering the judgment in the Novartis case, observed that it did not wish the Indian patent laws to

> develop on lines where the scope of the patent is determined not on intrinsic worth of the invention but by the artful drafting of its claims, and where patents are traded as a commodity not for production and marketing of the patented products but to search for someone who may be sued for infringement of the patent.[70]

This observation was obviously aimed at the modern-day practices of multinational pharmaceutical corporations. The interpretation of the provision, *i.e.*, section 3(d) in the judgment, clearly demonstrates that India has adopted a standard of pharmaceutical patenting that is stricter than that followed by the US or the EU (Abbott, 2013). Most importantly, the patent application must show that the modification will result in an improvement in the treatment of the patient, and it was not enough to merely show that the compound was different from the old one. Here the Court was seeking to introduce the social welfare theory in the interpretation of 'efficacy', as opposed to therapeutic efficacy.

Some commentators have argued that the underlying policy/theory behind the judgment of the Supreme Court cannot be one to check the practice of evergreening, as it does not explain the distinction between therapeutic efficacy and other types of improvements to drugs, and that it can only be the promotion of access to life-saving generic medicines, which accords more with the social welfare theory (Du, 2014, 34). Abbott notes that the Supreme Court left open the question of whether 'enhanced efficacy' refers to the curative effect of the drug or more broadly to improved safety profile and reduced toxicity (Abbott, 2013). The questions that need answering are not only about the Indian patent laws, but also about the actions of multinational corporations who, well supported by their national governments (through lobbying), have sought to exploit new and

69 The US Trade Representative cites section 3(d) of the Indian Patent Act as one of the reasons to keep India on its 'priority watch list' of countries whose IP regimes are of concern.

70 Para 156 of the judgment of the Indian Supreme Court in *Novartis Ag v. Uion of India & Others*.

emerging patent legislations in the post-TRIPS era to their advantage, and also the actions of patent-holding developed countries in exerting pressure on developing countries/emerging economies to change their domestic laws and policies on IP rights (Grace, 2004), which continue to have a devastating impact on access to affordable medicines. Commenting on the outcome of the *Novartis* case, the free trade economist Panagariya notes that the USTR, while complaining about the flaws of the Indian Patent Act, had not chosen to challenge it before the WTO, as the chances of success were very slim (Panagariya, 2014). This leads us to the next inevitable question, For how long will WTO permit developed countries to negotiate on access to medicines with IP rights?

7 Exhaustion of patent rights and parallel imports

India took advantage of the TRIPS flexibility to introduce key provisions into its patent laws which included, amongst others, the exhaustion of patent rights and parallel importation. India viewed this as an important step, as it had emerged as a key player in producing and exporting generic drugs with the introduction of process patents under the 1970 Act. The TRIPS Agreement allows member states to determine the scope and extent of exhaustion of patent rights. Article 28(6) of the TRIPS Agreement states that 'This right [*i.e.*, the right of importation], like all other rights conferred under this Agreement in respect of the use, sale, importation or other distribution of goods, is subject to the provisions of Article 6'. In turn, Article 6 of the TRIPS Agreement postulates that 'nothing in this Agreement shall be used to address the issue of the exhaustion of IP rights'. Article 5(d) of the Doha Declaration provides that 'the effect of the provisions of TRIPS Agreement that are relevant to the exhaustion of IP rights is to leave each member free to establish its own regime for such exhaustion without challenge, subject to the MFN and national treatment'. In other words, the TRIPS Agreement does not pose any restrictions on the application of the doctrine of exhaustion in domestic patent laws, despite dissenting views (Correa, 2005).[71]

The Indian Patent Amendment Act recognises and implements the principle of international exhaustion (or, first sale doctrine) of patent rights. This principle imposes certain limits on the patentee's exclusive rights, in that the patentee cannot control the resale or redistribution of the particular product that has already been sold. Under this provision, once a patented product has been sold with the patentee's approval outside India, the subsequent importation of that same patented item into India will not amount to infringement of the Indian patent (Basheer and Kochupillai, 2008). This principle is recognised in countries such as India, Japan, Taiwan, Kenya, Andean Group countries, Australia and New

71 The US delegation to the Council for TRIPS, which met in June 2001, was of the firm view that Article 6 allowed WTO members neither to avail themselves of dispute settlement in relation to questions involving parallel imports nor to authorise parallel imports. See Delegation of the United States, Council for TRIPS Meeting of June 1822, 2001, JOB(01)/97/Add.5, Council for TRIPS, (28 June 2001).

Zealand, but is not recognised in several other jurisdictions including the US, EU, Brazil and China. The provision was first introduced under section 107(A)(b) of the Patents (Amendment) Act 2002, which provided that the 'importation of patented products by any person from a person who is duly authorised by the patentee to sell or distribute the product, shall not be considered as an infringement of patent rights'. It was considered restrictive in scope and was amended by the Patents (Amendment) Act 2005, which states that 'importation of patented products by any person from a person who is duly authorised under the law to produce and sell or distribute the product, shall not be considered as an infringement of patent rights'.[72]

Parallel imports, which are but a natural corollary of the doctrine of exhaustion, helps in the increased allocation of products at the lowest possible price. It is likened to compulsory licences and can act as an important device to discipline the markets and to induce suppliers to commercialise their pharmaceutical products on reasonable conditions (Correa, 2005). Some writers even opine that parallel imports through compulsory licences may in some cases be the only way to gain access to affordable medicine, especially when the TRIPS Agreement is fully implemented (Correa, 2005). Recognition of parallel imports is an emerging trend amongst developing countries that have proceeded to introduce an express statutory provision incorporating international exhaustion of patent rights into their national laws with the aim of ensuring their citizens' access to lower-cost medicines (Wise, 2006).

7.1 *Indian pharmaceutical policy*

The new patent regime introduced under Amendment Act 2005 gives India the necessary legal framework to protect its patent system from practice of patent evergreening and expands the scope of granting compulsory licences in the event of any emergencies. Before the introduction of TRIPS-compliant patent laws into the domestic legislation, there were intense debates in the Indian Parliament and in other public forums across the country, which demonstrated the elaborate democratic process the proposals went through. India has witnessed very little R&D investment from the TNPCs, and the figures released by PhRMA, from 2014 (released in 2016), show that only US$25.8 million (0.0 percent share) was invested in India.[73] Although it was hoped that the new laws based on product patents would stimulate both domestic and foreign firms to engage in R&D activities in India, it has not materialised (Mondal and Pingali, 2017). Around the same time, several drugs were coming off patent protection in the US, which

72 Section 58, the Patents (Amendment) Act 2005.

73 For the same period the members invested over US$40.7 billion (76.5 percent share) in the US, US$2.5 billion (4.8 percent share) in the UK, and US$4.6 billion (8.7 percent share) in other western European countries. Interestingly, a sum of US$35.5 million was spent in South Africa (0.1 percent share), and only US$36.3 million (0.1 percent share) for the rest of Africa was invested (PhRMA, 2016).

permitted the Indian companies to sell generic drugs in the USA, provided they were able to obtain regulatory approval (Mondal and Pingali, 2017). The Indian pharmaceutical industry has continued to grow, mostly fuelled by exports of global generics. If the new patent laws were to work to India's benefit in the longer term, it will have to address a few shortcomings in the 2005 legislation, the accompanying procedures and the national drug policy.

In 2002, in anticipation of the new patent laws, India introduced a Pharmaceutical Policy[74] aimed at improving incentives for research and development within the Indian pharmaceutical industry to achieve sustainable growth. This policy proposed the reduction of the number of drugs under price control, but came to be stayed by the Indian Supreme Court. The price control mechanism is one of the flexibilities available under the TRIPS Agreement to ensure access to medicines (Gopakumar, 2010), which can assist developing countries to make access to medicines affordable. India announced a revised National Pharmaceutical Pricing Policy (NPPP) in November 2012, which sought to cap the price of 348 drugs. The NPPP and the Drugs (Prices Control) Order 2013 came to be challenged before the Supreme Court by the All India Drug Action Network (AIDAN). In July 2016, the Supreme Court directed the Indian government to re-examine the NPPP of 2012 and the Drug Pricing Control Order (DPCO) of 2013, considering the recommendations made by AIDAN.[75] Following the Supreme Court's directive, the government of India has been working on a new policy to check the excessive controls that thwart both competitiveness and innovation in the sector. A significant part of the Indian pharmaceutical market is regulated by direct pricing as opposed to competition policies (Mondal and Pingali, 2017). As of March 2016, the DPCO has brought 376 domestic generic formulations under the ambit of price regulation covering an estimated 30 percent of the overall market. It has also brought 700 drugs under price control, which are used in the treatment of major diseases. In a separate development, it is understood that Prime Minister Narendra Modi–led Indian government was considering the introduction of a 'generics-only' drugs plan to achieve access to affordable medicines.

India cannot afford to indulge in arbitrary drug price policies if it were to take full advantage of the TRIPS flexibilities and implement the new patent laws. Since the passing of the new patent laws in 2005, India has witnessed the acquisition of several generic pharmaceutical companies by multinational corporations (Singh, 2010).[76] These acquisitions do not bode well for India and other developing

74 Section 11 of the Indian Pharmaceutical Policy 2002 states that the span of price control over drugs and pharmaceuticals would be reduced substantially. <http://nppaindia.nic.in/may-2002/policy-02.html> accessed 28 November 2017.

75 Legal Correspondent, 'SC Asks Govt. to Review Drug Pricing Policy,' *The Hindu* (16 July 2015) <www.thehindu.com/news/national/sc-asks-govt-to-review-drug-pricing-policy/article7426659.ece> accessed 28 November 2017.

76 The author notes that in the last decade, six Indian generic companies were merged with or acquired by foreign entities: Matrix Lab, Dabur Pharma, Ranbaxy Labs, Shanta Biotech, Orchid Chemicals and Piramal Healthcare. The total cost of the takeover is estimated at US$1.58 billion.

countries, as they undermine the future availability of affordable medicines as well as the effective use of the WTO TRIPS flexibilities, including pre-grant opposition and compulsory licence under the new Act. A study carried out by India's Parliamentary Standing Committee on Commerce recommended a blanket ban[77] on the acquisition[78] of Indian pharmaceutical companies by multinational corporations. The committee noted that the multinational corporations have encroached upon the Indian generic industry base, and was unanimous in its view in seeking a ban on foreign direct investment in the existing pharmaceutical sector.

External factors too can pose threats to the full implementation of the new patent laws. The US is critical of the 2005 patent laws introduced in India, and the US Trade Representative (USTR) has repeatedly identified India's introduction of section 3(d) as the reason for putting it on the priority watch list, which is to be considered a tactic adopted by the US to exert pressure on India to change its patent laws. This is interesting, as the US has the Hatch-Waxman Act within its patent legislation, which aims to produce a result similar to section 3(d), but albeit at a later stage. The US and EU have through the incorporation of TRIPS-plus provisions in regional trade agreements (RTAs) preserved the practice of evergreening for their multinationals in other jurisdictions.[79] India is party to over twenty-five FTAs, and has been in negotiations with the EU since 2007 for the creation of another FTA. It is reliably understood that the EU has demanded extended terms of patent protection from India, which could potentially undermine India's efforts in putting an end to the practice of evergreening. It is abundantly clear that TRIPS-plus provisions in RTAs and FTAs can pose a major challenge to India in the full realisation of its TRIPS-compliant patent laws, and India may be pressured through negotiation to let evergreening through its backdoor (Gopakumar, 2013).[80]

On 12 May 2016, India published its National Intellectual Property Rights Policy (National IPR Policy). The policy, drafted by an independent IP rights think tank consisting of six members and chaired by retired Justice Prabha Sridevan, has as its objective to raise awareness of the importance of IP rights as a tool for financial and economic advancement. It seeks to present IP rights as a marketable financial asset and promote innovation and entrepreneurship, while

---

Ranbaxy was purchased by Japan-based Daiichi Sankyo Co. in June 2008; Piramal Healthcare was bought by US-based Abbott Laboratories; Matrix Lab was acquired by Mylan Inc. and Dabur Pharma was acquired by German Fresenius Kabl, to name a few.

77 Parliament of India, 'One Hundred and Tenth Report on FDI in Pharmaceutical Sector' (13 August 2011) <http://164.100.47.5/newcommittee/reports/EnglishCommittees/Committee%20on%20Commerce/110.pdf> accessed 28 November 2017.

78 India introduced changes to its FDI policy relating to the pharmaceutical sector in 2011, which allowed 100 percent FDI in both new and existing pharmaceutical business.

79 See discussion in chapter 4.

80 The author is of the view that Bilateral Investment Treaties (BITs) may prevent India from taking effective measures to curb patents on known substances, and strongly advocates the removal of IP rights from the definition of investments.

protecting public interest. The policy is considered as being TRIPS compliant and seeks to facilitate domestic IP rights filings. The critics of the policy are apprehensive of the weak provisions of affordable medicines and agro seeds in the IPR policy document (Gopakumar, 2016), and some have commented that it is tailor-made to suit the requirements of the Western governments (Mani, 2016).

8 Conclusion

Through the new patent law framework introduced in 2005, India has once again demonstrated it can take the lead role in presenting a patent law regime which can serve as a useful model for other developing countries to emulate (UNAIDS, 2011). Since its introduction in 2005, the patent law provisions have been frequently invoked by TNPCs seeking the grant of patents, on other occasions by generic drug manufacturers and NGOs seeking the pre-grant and post-grant opposition, besides the odd occasion for the grant of compulsory licences. The decisions taken serve as a stark warning of the bumpy road ahead for the TNPCs seeking to extend the life span of patents through evergreening, and to the Indian generic pharmaceutical industry seeking grant of compulsory licences. The interpretation of section 3(d) of the Patent Act by the Indian Supreme Court in the *Novartis* case demonstrates the unequivocal position taken by India to protect its own patent jurisdiction from being subjected to abuse by TNPCs through the practice of evergreening. The Supreme Court's judgment sets the boundaries on granting patents and on the practice of patent evergreening, and the judgment is widely considered a landmark amongst patent law practitioners in India.

Some commentators have expressed the strong opinion that the patenting trend prevalent in developed countries is not in the interest of the consumers (Chaudhuri, 2013)[81] and makes medicines unaffordable, and have suggested that developing countries follow in the footsteps of India by introducing provisions similar to section 3(d) into their patent legislations to make medicines more affordable (Chaudhuri, 2013). The provision, as incorporated by the Indian legislation, may suit India's requirements, as it has a robust judiciary to interpret the provisions justly in the light of the objectives of the amendment, and also a good infrastructure for manufacturing generics drugs. Besides, India does not face the same problems as other developing countries and least developed countries in the knowledge economy. At this point, the judgment of the Indian Supreme Court can only be seen as the outcome of the first of the few battles to come on Indian patent laws, and that the Indian courtrooms will not be the only domain where they will be played out.

India's decision to introduce a product patent regime into its laws in 1970, on the back of the Justice Ayyangar Committee Report, was a reformative measure, as it was in response to internal factors, *i.e.*, the socio-economic conditions then

81 The author is critical of the trend prevalent in developed nations like the US, where in the name of innovation 'mindless patenting' takes place much against the interest of the consumer. This model, in his opinion, is followed by several developing countries either willingly or unwillingly.

prevailing in the country. This measure not only helped India to achieve more self-sufficiency in access to medicines through generics drug manufacturing, but helped other developing countries in the fight against HIV/AIDS in the years to follow. In sharp contrast, the introduction of the product patent system in 2005 was more a response to external factors, *i.e.*, TRIPS compliance, and if the same were not to be administered properly, can become counterproductive to both India's interests and that of other developing countries that strongly rely on it for generics supply. The problems identified in the Justice Ayyangar Committee Report, especially on access to medicines, have not been fully addressed, and the reasons for the introduction of process patent in the 1970s have not been fully realised, but India, nevertheless, has moved towards a new patent law regime. This transformation in India will be felt around the globe (Mueller, 2007), and it will also have to be observed how India endeavours to maintain its stance in the face of stiff challenges from developed countries and multinational pharmaceutical patent holders alike.

Bibliography

1 Abbott, Frederick M. 'The Judgment in Novartis v. India: What the Supreme Court of India Said,' *Inside Views, Intellectual Property Watch* (2013).
2 Austin, Granville. *The Indian Constitution: Cornerstone of a Nation* (Oxford University Press, 1999).
3 Banerji, Shondeep. 'The Indian Intellectual Property Rights Regime and the TRIPs Agreement,' in Long, Clarisa (ed.), *Intellectual Property Rights in Emerging Markets* (American Enterprise Institute Press, 2000) 47–95, 63.
4 Basheer, Shamnad. 'Limiting the Scope of Pharmaceutical Patents and Micro-organisms: A TRIPS Compatibility Review,' IP Institute (2005) 47–49.
5 Basheer, Shamnad, and Mrinalini Kochupillai. 'Exhausting Patent Rights in India: Parallel Imports and TRIPS Compliance,' *Journal of Intellectual Property Rights* Vol. 13 (2008) 486, 487–488.
6 Basheer, Shamnad. 'India's First Compulsory License: Patents vs. Public Health?' *IP Osgoode* (2 April 2012) <www.iposgoode.ca/2012/04/india%E2%80%99s-first-compulsory-license-patents-vs-public-health/> accessed 28 November 2017.
7 *Bayer Corpn. v. Union of India*, (2014) SCC OnLine Bom 963: AIR 2014 Bom 178.
8 Bazzle, Timothy. 'Pharmacy of the Developing World: Reconciling Intellectual Property Rights in India With the Right to Health: TRIPS, India's Patent System and Essential Medicines,' *Georgetown Journal of International Law* Vol. 42 (2010) 785–815.
9 *BDR Pharmaceuticals International Pvt Ltd v Bristol-Myers Squibb Co* CLA No. 1 of 2013, Controller of Patents, Patent Office, Mumbai (29 October 2013) <https://spicyip.com/wp-content/uploads/2017/07/CLA1of2013.pdf > accessed 28 November 2017.
10 Bodenhausen, George Hendrik Christian. *Guide to the Application of the Paris Convention for the Protection of Industrial Property, as Revised at Stockholm in 1967*, Vol. 611 (WIPO, 1968) 67–73.
11 Bird, Robert C., and Daniel R. Cahoy. 'The Emerging BRIC Economies: Lessons From Intellectual Property Negotiation and Enforcement,' *Northwestern Journal of Technology and Intellectual Property* Vol. 5 (2007) 400, 403–404.

12 Bonadio, Enrico. 'Compulsory Licensing of Patents: The Bayer/Natco Case,' *European Intellectual Property Review* Vol. 34, No. 10 (2012) 719–728, 720.

13 Chandra, Rajshree. 'The Role of National Laws in Reconciling Constitutional Right to Health With TRIPS Obligations: An Examination of the Glivec Patent Case in India,' in Pogge, Thomas, Matthew Rimme, and Kim Rubenstein (eds.), *Incentives for Global Public Health: Patent Law and Access to Essential Medicines* (Cambridge University Press, 2010a) 381–405, 389.

14 Chien, Colleen. 'Cheap Drugs at What Price to Innovation: Does Compulsory Licensing of Pharmaceuticals Hurt Innovation?' *Berkeley Tech Law Journal* Vol. 18 (2003) 853, 896–907.

15 Choudhary, D.N. *Evolution of Patent Laws: Developing Countries Perspective* (Capital Law House, 2006) 13.

16 Chaudhuri, Sudip. 'The Larger Implications of the Novartis-Glivec Judgment,' *Economic and Political Weekly* Vol. 48, No. 17 (2013) 10–12.

17 Chung, Laura. 'Use of Paragraph 6 System for Access to Medicines,' *North Carolina Journal of International Law and Commercial Regulation* Vol. 36 (2010) 137.

18 Correa, Carlos M. *IP Rights and the Use of Compulsory Licenses: Options for Developing Countries* (South Centre, 1999).

19 Correa, Carlos M. 'The TRIPS Agreement and Developing Countries,' in Macrory Patrick J., Arthur E. Appleton, and Michael P. Plummer (eds.), *The World Trade Organisation: Legal, Economic and Political Analysis* Vol. II (Springer, 2005) 447, 449.

20 Correa, Carlos M. 'Patent Rights,' in Correa, Carlos M., and Abdulqawi Yusuf (eds.), *Intellectual Property and International Trade: The TRIPS Agreement* (Kluwer, 2008) 227, 229.

21 Damodaran, A.D. 'Indian Patent Law in the Post-TRIPS Decade: S&T Policy Appraisal,' *Journal of Intellectual Property Rights* Vol. 13 (2008) 414–423.

22 Das, Moumita, and Sanat Kumar Basu. 'Drug Price Control in India: "The Past and the Present,"' *NSHM Journal of Pharmacy and Healthcare Management* Vol. 3 (2012) 41–47, 41.

23 Dhar, Biswajit, and K.M. Gopakumar. *Effect of Product Patents on the Indian Pharmaceutical Industry* (Center for WTO Studies, 2011).

24 Drahos, Peter. 'Developing Countries and International Intellectual Property Standard-Setting,' *The Journal of World Intellectual Property* Vol. 5, No. 5 (2002) 765–789.

25 Du, Dorothy. 'Novartis Ag v. Union of India: "Evergreening," TRIPS, and "Enhanced Efficacy" Under Section 3(d),' *Journal of Intellectual Property Law* Vol. 21, No. 2 (2014) 223–263.

26 Feldman, Robin. 'Rethinking Rights in Biospace,' *Southern California Law Review* Vol. 79 (2005) 1–44, 30.

27 Foster, George K. 'Opposing Forces in a Revolution in International Patent Protection: The U.S. and India in the Uruguay Round and Its Aftermath,' *UCLA Journal of International Law & Foreign Affairs* Vol. 3 (1998) 283.

28 Furrow, Michael Enzo. 'Pharmaceutical Patent Life-Cycle Management after *KSR v. Teleflex*,' *Food & Drug Law Journal* Vol. 63 (2008) 275-320.

29 Garde, Tanuj V. 'India,' in Goldstein, Paul, and Joseph Strauss (eds.) *Intellectual Property in Asia: Law, Economics, History and Politics* (Springer, 2009) 55–86.

30 Gervais, Daniel J. 'Intellectual Property, Trade & Development: The State of Play,' *Fordham Law Review* Vol. 74, No. 2 (2005) 505–535.

31 Glasgow, Lara J. 'Stretching the Limits of Intellectual Property Rights: Has the Pharmaceutical Industry Gone Too Far?' *IDEA* Vol. 41 (2001) 227.

32 Gopakumar, K.M. 'Product Patents and Access to Medicines in India: A Critical Review of the Implementation of TRIPS Patent Regime,' *The Law and Development Review* Vol. 3, No. 2, (2010) 325–368, 340–341.
33 Gopakumar, K.M. 'The Need to Curb Patents of Known Substances,' *Economic & Political Weekly* Vol. 48, No. 32 (10 August 2013) 56.
34 Gopakumar, K.M. 'Why New IPR Policy Is Inadequate,' *Economic & Political Weekly* Vol. 51, No. 21 (21 May 2016) 16–18.
35 Gopalakrishnan, N.S., and Madhuri Anand. 'Compulsory Licence Under Indian Patent Law,' in Hilty, Reto M., and Kung-Chung Liu (eds.) *Compulsory Licensing: Practical Experiences and Ways Forward* (Springer, 2015) 11–42.
36 Grace, Cheri. 'The Effect of Changing IP on Pharmaceutical Industry Prospects in India and China: Considerations for Access to Medicines,' *DFID Health Systems Resource Centre* (2004) 1–68, 35.
37 Grace, Cheri. 'A Briefing Paper for DFID: Update on China and India and Access to Medicines,' *DFID Briefing Paper No* 8 (2005).
38 Hamied, Y.K. 'Indian Pharma Industry: Decades of Struggle and Achievements.' On the Occasion of Dr AV Rama Rao's 70th Birthday, Hyderabad (2005).
39 Iyer, V.R. Krishna. 'Human Health and Patent Law,' *Frontline* Vol. 17, No. 21 (14–27 October 2000) <www.frontline.in/static/html/fl1721/17210790.htm> accessed 28 November 2017.
40 Jain, Dipika., and Jonathan J. Darrow, 'An Exploration of Compulsory Licensing as an Effecive Policy Tool for Antiretroviral Drugs in India,' *Health Matrix* Vol. 23, Issue 2 (2013) 425–457.
41 Judd, Denis. *The Lion and the Tiger: The Rise and Fall of the British Raj* (Oxford University Press, 2006) 6.
42 Keayla, B.K. 'TRIPS Patent System and Doha Declaration: Implementation Process by India' Rajiv Gandhi Institute for Contemporary Studies (2004).
43 Kumar, Dharma, and Meghnad Desai (eds.). *The Cambridge Economic History of India Vol. II: c. 1757–1970* (Cambridge University Press, 1983).
44 Lanjouw, Jean O. 'The Introduction of Pharmaceutical Product Patents in India: "Heartless Exploitation of the Poor and Suffering,"' No. W6366, National Bureau of Economic Research (1998).
45 Lanjouw, Jean O. 'A New Global Patent Regime for Diseases: US and International Legal Issues,' *Harvard Journal of Law & Technology* Vol. 16 (2002) 85.
46 *Lee Pharma Ltd. v. AstraZeneca*, CLA No 1 of 2015, The Controller of Patents, Patent Office, Mumbai (19 January 2016) <www.jetro.go.jp/ext_images/world/asia/in/ip/pdf/Lee-prima-facie-notice_en20160119.pdf> accessed 28 November 2017.
47 Love, James. 'R&D Costs for Gleevec,' *Knowledge Ecology International* (3 April 2013) <http://www.keionline.org/22170> accessed 28 November 2017.
48 MSF, 'Indian Court Ruling in Novartis Case Protects India as the "Pharmacy of the World"' (6 August 2007) <www.doctorswithoutborders.org/news-stories/press-release/indian-court-ruling-novartis-case-protects-india-pharmacy-developing> accessed 28 November 2017.
49 Mani, Sunil. 'New IPR Policy 2016,' *Economic & Political Weekly* Vol. 51, No. 38 (17 September 2016).
50 Mithal, Ved P. 'Patents in India,' *Journal of the Patent Office* Vol. XXX, No. 1 (1948).
51 Mondal, Shamim S., and Viswanath Pingali. 'Competition and Intellectual Property Policies in the Indian Pharmaceutical Sector,' *VIKALPA* Vol. 42, No. 2 (2017).

52 Mueller, Janice M. 'The Tiger Awakens: The Tumultuous Transformation of India's Patent System and the Rise of Indian Pharmaceutical Innovation,' *University of Pittsburgh Law Review* Vol. 68, No. 3 (2007) 491.

53 Mueller, Janice M., and Donald Chisum. 'Enabling Patent Law's Inherent Anticipation Doctrine,' *Houston Law Review* Vol. 45, No. 4 (2008) 1101, 1106–1107.

54 Narayanan, Parameswaran. *Patent Law* (4th ed, Eastern Law House, New Delhi, 2006).

55 Narendranath, K.G. 'Patent Mailbox Opens, Pfizer Is Top Applicant,' *The Financial Express* (21 March 2005) <www.financialexpress.com/archive/patent-mailbox-opens-pfizer-is-top-applicant/129581/> accessed 28 November 2017.

56 Paas, Katri. 'Compulsory Licensing Under the TRIPS Agreement – A Cruel Taunt for Developing Countries?,' *European Intellectual Property Review* Vol. 31, No. 12 (2009) 609–613.

57 Panagariya, Arvind. 'India Must Call the US' Bluff on Patents,' *Business Standard*, New Delhi (4 March 2014) <www.business-standard.com/article/opinion/arvind-panagariyaindia-must-call-the-us-bluff-on-patents-114030401221_1.html> accessed 28 November 2017.

58 Planning Commission of India. 'First Five Year Plan,' Government of India <http://planningcommission.nic.in/plans/planrel/fiveyr/default.html> accessed 28 November 2017.

59 Ragavan, Srividhya. 'Of the Inequals of the Uruguay Round,' *Marquette Intellectual Property Law Review* Vol. 10, No. 2 (2006) 273.

60 Rajagopal, Divya. 'Swiss Drug Major Roche to Drop Anti-Cancer Drug Herceptin Patent in India,' *The Economic Times* (16 August 2013) <http://articles.economictimes.indiatimes.com/2013-08-16/news/41417840_1_major-roche-herceptin-patent-office> accessed 28 November 2017.

61 Ramesh, Randeep. 'Cheap AIDS Drugs Under Threat,' *The Guardian, UK* (London, 23 March 2005) <www.theguardian.com/world/2005/mar/23/india.aids1?INTCMP=SRCH> accessed 28 November 2017.

62 Rangnekar, Dwijen. 'The Supreme Court Judgment,' *Economic & Political Weekly* Vol. 48, No. 32 (2013) 39.

63 A Report on the Revision of the Law in India Relating to Patents for Inventions (September 1959) <http://spicyip.com/wp-content/uploads/2013/10/ayyangar_committee_report.pdf> accessed 28 November 2017.

64 Sampat, Bhaven N., Kenneth C. Shadlen, and Tahir M. Amin. 'Challenges to India's Pharmaceutical Patent Laws,' *Science* Vol. 337, No. 6093 (2012) 414–415.

65 Scherer, Frederic M., and Jayashree Watal. 'Post-TRIPS Options for Access to Patented Medicines in Developing Countries,' *Commission on Macroeconomics and Health Working Paper Series* (20 November 2001) <http://icrier.org/pdf/jayawatal%20.pdf> accessed 28 November 2017.

66 Sen, Rajarshi, and Adarsh Ramanujan. 'Pruning the Evergreen Tree or Tripping Up Over TRIPS? Section 3(d) of the Indian Patents Act 1970,' *International Review of Intellectual Property & Competition Law* Vol. 41, No. 2 (2010) 170–186.

67 Singh, Madhur. 'India May Issue Compulsory Licenses to Control Drug Prices,' *WTO Reporter* (27 August 2010).

68 UNAIDS. 'DOHA+10, TRIPS Flexibilities and Access to Antiretroviral Therapy: Lessons From the Past, Opportunities for the Future,' *UNAIDS Technical Brief*, Geneva (2011).

69 UNCTAD-ICTSD. *Resource Book on TRIPS and Development* (Cambridge University Press, 2005).

70 Unni, V.K. 'Indian Patent Law and TRIPS: Redrawing the Flexibility Framework,' *Global Business & Development Law Journal* Vol. 25 (2011) 323, 330.
71 Unnikrishnan, C.H. 'Compulsory License May Spur More Voluntary Licensing Deals,' *Livemint* (24 January 2013) <www.livemint.com/Home-Page/f0R9060osU7bENFNwlnx5O/Compulsory-licences-may-spur-more-voluntary-licensing-deals.html> accessed 28 November 2017.
72 US-India Business Council. 'The Value of Incremental Pharmaceutical Innovations – Benefits for Indian Patients and Indian Business,' White & Case and DUA Consulting (June 2009) <www.indiaenvironmentportal.org.in/files/USIBCIncrementalInnovationReportFinal.pd> accessed 28 November 2017.
73 WTO, *India-Patent Protection for Pharmaceutical and Agricultural Chemical Products – Report of the Appellate Body* (19 December 1997) WT/DS50/AB/R.
74 Waning, Brenda, Ellen Diedrichsen, and Suerie Moon. 'A Lifeline to Treatment: The Role of Indian Generic Manufacturer in Supplying Antiretroviral Medicines to Developing Countries,' *Journal of International AIDS Society* Vol. 13, No. 35 (2010) 1–9.
75 Watal, Jayashree. *Intellectual Property Rights in the WTO and Developing Countries* (Kluwer Law International, 2001).
76 Wise, Jacqui. 'Access to AIDS Medicines Stumbles on Trade Rules,' *World Health Organization Bulletin* Vol. 84, No. 5 (2006) 342–344 <www.ncbi.nlm.nih.gov/pmc/articles/PMC2627352/pdf/16710536.pdf> accessed 28 November 2017.

8 South Africa

Against all odds

Contents

1 Sub-Saharan Africa: the Uruguay Round and IP rights

Chapters 8 and 9 take up for study the key reasons behind the continued inability of South Africa and Kenya, two sub-Saharan African (SSA) countries, to access affordable medicines and their difficulty in utilising flexibilities found in the TRIPS Agreement. This raises the inevitable question as to what is keeping the SSA countries from seeking an amendment of the TRIPS Agreement to remove pharmaceutical patents from the ambit of its operation. The two countries taken up for study have varied socio-economic conditions, infrastructure to manufacture medicines, knowledge economy, *etc.*, presenting the opportunity to analyse difficulties that the countries have encountered in implementing the TRIPS Agreement, while continuing to deal with one major problem, *i.e.*, barriers to access to affordable medicines in their efforts to find healthcare for their poor and needy. It is essential to understand the position of SSA countries during the trade negotiations at the Uruguay Round, before we embark on case studies of TRIPS implementation in South Africa and Kenya.

The Uruguay Round of trade negotiations was dominated by the 'Quad', *viz.*, the US, the EU, Japan and Canada (Drahos and Braithwaite, 2002; Harris, 2006). The developing countries, realising the difficulties the Agreement would present them with, had vigorously campaigned against the inclusion of IP rights protection within the multilateral trading system. One of the chief areas of concern for them was the near impossibility of accessing affordable medicines under the proposed international IP rights regime of the WTO. The African Group, primarily consisting of countries from SSA – both developing and LDC – was largely absent from the Uruguay Round of trade negotiations (Drahos, 2003). Adusei argues that the SSA countries became political inferiors who played little or no meaningful role in the Uruguay Round of negotiations, as they were absent at both the negotiations and the consensus-building activities (Adusei, 2013). Ogunkola, on the other hand, notes that less than 3 percent of the written proposals and comments circulated during the Uruguay Round were submitted by SSA countries (Ogunkola, 1999; Blackhurst, Lyakurwa, and Oyejide, 1999). Although the Uruguay Round of negotiations commenced in 1986, the SSA countries' voice would only be heard in 1989, when Nigeria and Tanzania joined the group of ten developing countries to object to the inclusion of IP rights protection in the multilateral trading system ('t Hoen, 2009).[1] African states in the post-colonial era have sought, to varying degrees, to revise existing IP laws or enact new IP laws into their domestic legislations (Okediji, 2003). But the efforts have been stymied by the introduction of the international IP framework under the TRIPS Agreement. Some commentators view the TRIPS Agreement as a 'device that drives economic neo-colonialism forward', and the very process of the making of TRIPS Agreement demonstrates the same (Rahmatian, 2009). Some commentators identify TRIPS as a powerful mechanism through which European and American laws have been transplanted into other jurisdictions around the world (Seuba, 2014).

The negotiators from SSA did not possess the necessary expertise to engage in international negotiations involving IP matters (Adusei, 2013, Kongolo, 2013), which did not help to further their cause. This position, coupled with the costs of being involved in a lengthy negotiation at the Uruguay Round, had effectively blocked the SSA countries from any meaningful engagement at the negotiating table (Blackhurst, Lyakurwa, and Oyejide, 1999). Many African countries signed the WTO agreements without fully understanding their objectives and remits, or their long-term potential impact for that matter (Mshomba, 2009). As with the TRIPS Agreement, the SSA countries were totally oblivious to its impact on their citizens' health (Adusei, 2013). Drahos and Braithwaite note that the South African trade negotiators simply did not realise that they were in fact signing an agreement that would contribute to a situation by 2001 in which a 15-year-old would have greater than a 50 percent chance of dying from HIV/AIDS-related illness (Drahos and Braithwaite, 2002). Regardless, the proposal for an international IP rights regime went ahead, resulting in the introduction of the TRIPS Agreement in the multilateral trading system. The main reason TRIPS is considered a serious threat to access to medicines is the twenty-year product patent

1 It is to be noted that there are 48 countries in sub-Saharan Africa.

protection granted to pharmaceutical patents under the Agreement,[2] which outlaws process patents and effectively delays the entry of affordable generics in the market. Process patent paved the way for generic drugs and is much more affordable than patented/brand-name drugs produced by transnational pharmaceutical corporations (Sundaram, 2014).[3] Importantly, most SSA countries rely on generic drugs (Joncheere, Rietveld, and Huttin, 2003),[4] which are free of patent and hence more affordable (Norris, 2015; Rajeshwari, 2016).[5]

Developing countries and least developed countries (LDCs) had little or no involvement in the development of the international IP conventions/treaties, as most were negotiated in the colonial era (Deere, 2009, 8), almost a century before the Uruguay Round of negotiations took place in the 1980s–1990s. A number of SSA countries (and some of the former colonies in South America and Asia) were made signatories to international conventions during the colonial period, without the need for them to be parties.[6] It should also be added here that participation in GATT 1947 (the precursor to the WTO) was extended to the former colonies of the GATT members under Article XXXVI:5 of the GATT, resulting in the inclusion of all African countries, with the exception of Morocco (Mshomba, 2009).

The TRIPS Agreement, most importantly, contains flexibilities in its implementation, which are primarily aimed at benefitting the developing countries and LDCs, and helps them in the pursuit of access to affordable medicines. Sadly, SSA still remains the epicentre of the global AIDS epidemic, with 76 percent of AIDS-related deaths occurring in the region (Cann, 2004). In SSA, the main mode of HIV transmission is through heterosexual sex with a concomitant

2 Under the Paris Convention for Protection of Industrial Property 1883, contracting parties were permitted to exclude patent protection in certain sectors such as pharmaceuticals, and permitted to determine the duration of patent rights, and grant compulsory license for a variety of reasons. Most of these flexibilities are not available under the TRIPS Agreement.

3 India, seen as the leading manufacturer of generic drugs in the world, introduced process patent into its legislation in the 1970s, which helped in the production of cheaper medicines for its own use and for export to other developing countries and LDCs. Pharmaceutical products became patentable in France and Germany in 1967, in Italy in 1979 and in Spain in 1992.

4 Generic drugs contain the same active ingredient as the original patented brand-name products upon which they are based. In short, generics are identical to the branded product in its chemical composition, and good generics are viewed as an affordable alternative to the costlier brand-name products. Note, the World Health Organization (WHO) has avoided the use of the term 'generic product' as much as possible, and instead uses the expression 'multisource pharmaceutical product'.

5 Indian manufactured ARVs dominate the ARV market, accounting for over 80 percent of global sales. According to WHO, estimates of close to 12 million AIDS patients source their ARVs from India, which is often referred to as the 'pharmacy of the developing world'.

6 Through the mechanism established under Article 19 of the Berne Convention, the former colonial powers of Britain, France, Italy, Belgium and Spain acceded a choice of their colonies to the Convention. The original Article 19 of the Berne Convention 1886 reads: '[1] Countries acceding to this Convention shall also have the right to accede thereto at any time on behalf of their colonies or foreign possessions. [2] They may for this purpose make either a general declaration of adhesion that includes all their colonies or possessions, or expressly indicate only those which are included, or which are excluded.'

epidemic in children through vertical transmission. As such, women are disproportionately affected, accounting for 58 percent of the total number of people living with HIV. SSA also has the highest number of children living with HIV and the highest number of AIDS-related deaths. Scholarly discourse on TRIPS flexibilities clearly allude to the WTO's failure to address the problem of access to medicines in developing countries and LDCs (Sundaram, 2015) in the negotiation and implementation of the international IP rights regime. With the entry of the TRIPS Agreement in 1995, developing countries from SSA were required to implement the Agreement through the introduction of TRIPS-compliant IP legislation into the legal system. The overreach of TRIPS presented formidable constraints to the developing economies and the LDCs, as it has been an uphill task for SSA states to implement the Agreement.

2 South Africa: an introduction

The history of South Africa does not start with the arrival of European colonial powers, but stretches back thousands of years in time (Thompson, 2014). While colonisation introduced South Africa (and SSA) to the civilisations outside Africa, it also led to the unchecked exploitation of its abundant wealth by colonising powers. Colonisation, primarily by the Dutch and the English (Thompson, 2014),[7] brought with it various customs and values from mainland Europe which were alien to the region. It also resulted in the introduction of laws and regulation into the territory, as the colonial powers sought to replicate the institutional structure of their native countries for the purposes of governance. In the coming years, the traditional values of the native South Africans were systematically eroded (Thompson, 2014), while the two colonial powers sought to establish their hegemony in the occupied territory. One of the mechanisms introduced by the colonial powers was the legal system – which to this day remains in place. South Africa's legal system, at best can be classified as hybrid, with a blend of Roman-Dutch civil law (through the Dutch), Common law (through the English) and customary laws inherited from the indigenous South Africans (Lewis, 2005).[8]

7 The first European explorer to set foot in South Africa was the Portuguese explorer Bartolomeu Dias, in 1488. Bartolomeu was to reach the eastern coast and name it *Cabo das Tomentas* (Cape of Storm) in May 1488. This was to be later renamed by John II as *Cabo da Boa Esperança*, or Cape of Good Hope. Vasco Da Gama was to later take a direct route to the Cape of Good Hope in 1497–98. With the decline of Portugal's maritime power in the seventeenth century, the British East India Company and the Dutch East India Company made frequent stops at the Cape of Good Hope. The Dutch and the English were later to create settlements in parts of South Africa in the nineteenth century. The discovery of diamonds and gold in the latter part of the nineteenth century saw an increase in both economic growth of the settlers and immigration from Europe.

8 The author, a judge of the Supreme Court of Appeal, notes that various features of the common law were superimposed onto the Roman-Dutch law, and in several areas of the law English principles and rules predominated, some eventually becoming incorporated through statute. With the advent of democracy in 1994, the legal system, although left intact, was turned upside down. The revised constitution of 1996 made all laws subordinate to the South African Constitution.

Although colonialism was to recede in the twentieth century, South Africa continued to be ruled by the National Party through a policy of segregation along racial lines,[9] which continued to be in force until 1994. The policies introduced during the apartheid era linger as a dark legacy haunting the country to this date.

2.1 Democratic South Africa: hopes and setbacks

A multi-ethnic country,[10] the Republic of South Africa holds an important position in international politics with significant regional influence. Its economy is based on mining, agricultural exports and financial services, all largely established during the apartheid era. It is well documented that South Africa's transition from apartheid to democracy formally began in 1990 with the release of Nelson Mandela from prison and the 'un-banning' of the liberation movement led by him. When Nelson Mandela assumed office in 1994, leading the first ever democratically elected government in South Africa, he was not only faced with the task of healing the wounds and scars of decades of racial segregation, but also with a multitude of problems associated with the provisions of healthcare in the country. One of the major problems relating to healthcare was the high price of medicines in an unregulated medicines market, against the backdrop of a country whose population was in the grips of an HIV/AIDS epidemic. Highly priced ARVs[11] made access to affordable medicines an unreal goal and good medical treatment a distant dream in South Africa. In 1994, the South African healthcare system was based on a two-tiered approach,[12] with many South Africans having no healthcare, which made the system a priority for reform in the post-apartheid era (Fisher III and Rigamonti, 2005; Schneider, Barron and Fonn, 2007).[13] Unfortunately, the new government created superfluous institutions and

9 The National Party, founded in 1915, assumed power in 1948 and introduced apartheid, or racial segregation in all walks of life. It was in power for 46 years until 1994, when Nelson Mandela, belonging to the African National Congress (ANC), was democratically elected to power. The last of the National Party presidents, FW de Klerk was instrumental in ending apartheid in South Africa through sustained negotiations with the ANC, culminating in the ANC coming to power in 1994.

10 The ethnic groups in South Africa comprise of black (native) South Africans 80.2 percent, white Caucasian South Africans 8.4 percent, and Indian/Asian South Africans 2.5 percent.

11 Antiretroviral drugs (ARVs) do not offer a cure but slow down the reproduction of HIV in the body by reducing the amount of the virus in the bloodstream, which in turn reduces the progression of the disease.

12 Approximately 20 percent of the population (mostly white Caucasian) had private health care, and the black majority relied purely on public sector care. Sadly, the public sector health care was blighted by irrational use of resources, poor working conditions and inadequate infrastructure.

13 Schneider, Barron and Fonn note that the health care system that the ANC inherited in 1994 was divided into two parallel sectors, with the public sector financed through general taxation for the majority and the private sector funded mainly through medical aids for a largely white minority. Racially fragmented into 14 different operating authorities, the health care in place was highly inequitable, expensive and inefficient. Writing in 2007, the authors note that the South African health care system was as problematic then as it was in 1994.

wasted money on replicating various state infrastructures (Fourie and Meyer, 2010). In 1996, the National Drug Policy (NDP) was created after a full review process, with the objective of making available safe and effective drugs at a low cost, which was to be achieved through the guarantee of healthcare enshrined in the Constitution.

Due to a combination of international sanctions and the impact of high interest rates on sovereign debt from the fiscal expenditures of the apartheid regime, the democratic government was in fiscal crisis and its capacity was limited (Klug, 2012). The old apartheid government, at the same time, was putting forth the case for an end to South Africa's international isolation and commenced negotiations for the terms of South Africa's re-entry into the world economy by participating in the trade negotiations to form the WTO (Klug, 2012). This was also the time when the Uruguay Round of negotiations was taking place in which international IP rights protection was being seriously debated, wherein the old government presented South African as a 'developed country', which status it held in the GATT (Klug, 2012). This, it should be mentioned, was not South Africa's true position post-apartheid. However, this assumed status of a 'developed country' was to pose a serious problem, as by doing so South Africa would be required to implement all its WTO obligations, including TRIPS Agreement by the beginning of 1995. This meant South Africa was giving up on the status of being a developing country before the WTO – a beneficial position, which allowed countries with weaker economies (weak infrastructure and knowledge economy) the opportunity of a staggered implementation of the TRIPS Agreement. The decision to maintain the developed country status was taken not by a democratically elected government but by the apartheid government before the elections in 1994, and South Africa unwittingly became a founding member of the new WTO. Most shockingly, the officials handling IP issues merely asserted that South African law had long protected patents and other forms of IP; therefore, they argued, the TRIPS Agreement held no significant consequences for the country (Klug, 2012).

Investigations in the lead-up to the creation of the NDP revealed serious anomalies, especially the inequity in the access to essential medicines, the high price of pharmaceuticals in the private sector and the loss of drugs due to poor security in the public sector (National Drug Policy for South Africa, 1996).[14] During this time, South Africa also witnessed a tremendous increase in the HIV/AIDS infection rate (Russell, 1999),[15] in comparison to other SSA countries. Spurred on by the involvement of AIDS activists, and with the growing prices of ARVs, the government's response was to demand a reduction in the price charged

14 Figures from 1990 show that the private sector accounted for 80 percent of South Africa's total expenditures on drugs, even though 60–70 percent of the total volume of pharmaceuticals were sold to the public sector.

15 Almost overnight, South Africa become the country with the most infected by the HIV virus. Approximately 45 percent of military personnel were infected with the HIV virus.

by the pharmaceutical manufacturers of ARVs.[16] This situation saw the Minister of Health pitted against a powerful opponent, *viz.*, the Pharmaceutical Manufacturers Association of South Africa (PMA). In the Minister of Health's view, both the shortage of prescription drugs in the public sector and the high prices for the same in the private sector were down to the pricing strategies adopted by the TNPCs which held the pharmaceutical patents for ARVs (Attaran, 2001). The PMA's interpretation of the situation was different, with theft to blame for the high price of ARVs as opposed to its own pricing strategy (Fisher III and Rigamonti, 2005). It also held the position that a reduction in drug prices would not solve the problem that South Africa faced as it did not have the necessary infrastructure for the distribution of medicines.

3 The Medicines Act: the court and street battles

The consequences of the decision not to classify itself as a 'developing country' became evident in 1997, when the government attempted to adopt a domestic version of the WHO's essential medicines program, only to face enormous opposition from the PMA, the Pharmaceutical Manufacturers of America (PhRMA) and the US (Klug 2012). In 1997, the PMA took matters into its hands by filing a complaint with the Public Protector of South Africa alleging that the Department of Health had made statements creating a perception that medicines in South Africa was expensive, for which the pharmaceutical companies were to blame. The PMA, besides launching a media battle to exert pressure on the South African government, also brought a complaint against the government regarding the provisions of parallel importation contained in the pending legislation (based on a draft WIPO patent treaty) before the Parliament (Abbott, 2002a). To coincide with the PMA's actions, the US also started exerting trade pressure on South Africa. However, the South African parliamentary subcommittee, dominated by the ANC, was to swiftly pass legislation containing provisions for parallel importation. In 1997, the South African Parliament amended the Medicines and Related Substance Act 101 of 1965 (Medicines Act). Section 15C of the amended Act[17] gave the government powers to revoke patents on medicines, which allowed for broad-based compulsory licencing to manufacture

16 Many South Africans were constrained to use the private health sector as they either did not live close to an adequate public health facility or such services were inaccessible in the region. Many users of the public health system often had no choice but to purchase medicines from private pharmacies or their doctors. Most often, the reason was that the medicines that they needed were not available in the public sector.

17 Section 15C reads as follows: 'Measures to Ensure Supply of more Affordable Medicines:

The Minister may prescribe conditions for the supply of more affordable medicines in certain circumstances so as to protect the health of the public, and in particular may –

(a) notwithstanding anything to the contrary contained in the Patents Act 1978 (Act No. 57 of 1978), determine that the rights with regard to any medicine under a patent granted in the Republic shall not extend to acts in respect of such medicine which has been put onto the market by the owner of the medicine, or with his or her consent;

generic versions of HIV/AIDS drugs, besides also allowing for parallel imports to enable South Africa to benefit from importing lower-priced patented drugs. Most of the drugs flagged for compulsory licencing was developed by the US National Institute of Health.

The legality of the amended Medicines Act was challenged by the members of PhRMA before the Pretoria High Court, which was well supported by the US government (Sell, 2001; Abbott, 2002c; Marcellin, 2010; Sell, 2006). The South African government was drawn into a legal battle with the TNPCs, which almost derailed the plans it had in place to address the AIDS epidemic that was sweeping through the country. The US, as a developed nation and holder of numerous pharmaceutical patents, and the TNPCs desired a stronger enforcement of the IP rights in South Africa, and considered the Medicines Act as a huge threat to their interests. It is well documented that the USTR, the Patent and Trademark Office, Cabinet officials, and then Vice President Gore (who was also the Democratic party candidate for the next US presidency) actively participated in pressuring the South African government along with PhRMA to scrap the newly introduced provisions of the Medicines Act.

The TNPCs challenged the constitutionality of the amended Medicines Act on the grounds that section 15C (i) delegated powers from the legislative to the executive branch of government, which was impermissible, as it authorised the Minister of Health to determine the application of patent rights and the conditions for the supply of more affordable medicines without any limiting guidelines; (ii) enabled the Minister of Health to deprive IP rights holders of their lawful property rights without compensation in flagrant violation of Article 25 of the South African Constitution; and (iii) was also a violation of Article 27 of the TRIPS Agreement, as South Africa was bound by the TRIPS Agreement, and that the relevant provision of the Amended Act was also a violation of Articles 44(4) and 231(2)–(3) of the South African Constitution (Fisher III and Rigamonti, 2005).

The South African government's legal position was that section 15C was constitutionally sound, as it did not grant the Minister of Health broad powers to abrogate patent rights, and fully complied with the TRIPS Agreement. They further argued that the TRIPS Agreement did not prohibit parallel imports and that section 15C[18] did not address the controversial issue of compulsory licencing. South Africa believed that a much higher standard than the expected TRIPS

(b) prescribe the conditions on which any medicine which is identical in composition, meets the same quality standard and is intended to have the same proprietary name as that of another medicine already registered in the Republic, but which is imported by a person other than the person who is the holder of the registration certificate of the medicine already registered and which originates from any site of manufacture of the original manufacturer as approved by the council in the prescribed manner, may be imported;

(c) prescribe the registration procedure for, as well as the use of, the medicine referred to in paragraph (b).'

18 See WTO and WHO, *WTO Agreements and Public Health* (WTO-WHO 2002) 106.

threshold was being sought to be imposed on it, *i.e.*, a TRIPS-plus standard by both the US and the TNPCs through the court action which challenged the constitutionality of section 15C of the Medicines Act 1997.[19] The TNPCs firmly held on to the position that parallel imports of pharmaceutical products undermined the ability of pharmaceutical companies to be able to charge different prices in different parts of the world, and they advocated a tiered price strategy (Baleta, 2001).

Pending the legal challenges to section 15C before the South African court, PhRMA urged the USTR in February 1998 to name South Africa as a 'Priority Foreign Country', as the Medicines Act 1997 posed a direct challenge to the achievements of the Uruguay Round, and that South Africa offered no protection for test data and had introduced price controls (Sell, 2001). The USTR placed South Africa under the Super 301 'Watch List' and urged the South African government to repeal the Medicines Act 1997.[20] In 1998, then US Vice President Al Gore and other US officials, including the US Embassy staff stationed in South Africa, directly conveyed US concerns over Article 15C of the Medicines Act 1997, and stated categorically that serious consequences would ensue if South Africa used Article 15C to 'abrogate patents or open the floodgates to parallel imports' (Bond, 1999; Abbott, 2002b).[21] It is to be noted here that Al Gore as the co-chairman of the US/South Africa Binational Commission was able to exert pressure on South Africa on the issue of pharmaceutical patents. Despite the sustained pressure from the USTR and others, South Africa refused to repeal the Medicines Act, which allowed it to gain support for its actions from activist groups. This led to the involvement of the AIDS Coalition to Unleash Power (ACT UP)[22] in the medicines campaign.

ACT UP decided to target Al Gore as someone closely linked with PhRMA and its lobbyists. ACT UP's group members repeatedly disrupted Al Gore's campaign appearances in the summer of 1999 (Sell, 2001).[23] In 2000, after lengthy discussions with representatives of the activist groups, PhRMA and the South

19 See Statement by the South African Delegation, Minutes of the Council for TRIPS Special Discussions on Intellectual Property and Access to Medicines, IP/C/M/31 (10 July 2001), p 27.

20 The USTR placed both Brazil and India under a Super 301 'watch list' when they sought to pass IP legislation containing provisions for compulsory licensing and parallel importation. The implementations of the TRIPS Agreement in the said jurisdictions are discussed in chapters 5 and 7 respectively.

21 Abbott in the concluding paragraphs observes as follows: 'The United States has gone to an extreme, threatening to impose trade sanctions on developing countries that attempt to address one of the worst public health crises ever faced by human civilization. . . . The TRIPS Agreement is not only about protecting pharmaceutical industry profits. It is also about the health of the global economy, and about the health of individuals.'

22 Founded in 1987, AIDS Coalition to Unleash Power is an international direct-action advocacy group, with branches in key cities around the world. In 1987, ACT UP held a demonstration on Wall Street and Broadway demanding greater access to experimental AIDS drugs and for a coordinated national policy to fight the disease.

23 The ACT UP activists were present when Gore announced his bid for the presidency and held banners that read 'Gore's Greed Kills', which had quite an impact on live television.

African government, Gore announced the change of policy supporting compulsory licencing and parallel importation in South Africa (Sell, 2001). Following which, the US withdrew its two years of objections to the South African Medicines Act, and shortly thereafter South Africa was removed from the USTR watch list (Nader, Love and Weissman, 1999; Weissman, 1999).[24] The news came as a huge relief to South Africa. In the absence of ACT UPs actions in the US and the access campaign, South Africa would not have won the battle. The TNPCs announced the suspension of the case before the courts in South Africa. Shortly thereafter, in May 2000, President Bill Clinton formally announced that the US would not revoke or revise any IP law policy of a beneficiary SSA country that regulates HIV/AIDS pharmaceuticals or medical technologies.[25] It took another whole year of bad press for Bristol-Myers Squibb (BMS) to announce that it would not enforce a critical patent in SSA on part of a three-drug HIV cocktail.[26] Eventually, in April 2001, the TNPCs dropped the court case challenging the constitutional validity of section 15C of the Medicines Act (Fisher III and Rigamonti, 2005),[27] and also agreed to cover South Africa's legal costs incurred in defending the court case (Ho, 2011).

In sum, it can be said that the TNPCs were averse to the idea of a developing country introducing parallel importation and of compulsory licencing of pharmaceutical patents into the domestic laws, which would have given them the authority to invoke the provisions to make access to ARVs a reality. This episode, played out in the full media glare, showcased how ill-prepared the member states of the WTO were to the implementation of a covered agreement of the WTO, *viz.*, the TRIPS Agreement, and also exposed the glaring inequities in the negotiating process in the lead-up to the introduction of the international IP regime. It will not be out of context to state here that the members of the African Groups were either ill-informed or not able to comprehend the gravity of the IP regime's remit and were totally oblivious to its consequences. South Africa is one of the countries in SSA which has a better capability and infrastructure (together with a knowledge economy) to produce pharmaceutical products than other SSA countries have.

24 The campaign was successfully led by Ralf Nader, James Love and Robert Weissman, who all later addressed a letter to USTR expressing pleasure with the outcome in South Africa's case and urging the USTR to extend its policy in the South African case to all developing countries. Weissman cites then US Surgeon General David Satcher of having likened the HIV/AIDS epidemic in Africa to the plague that decimated Europe in the fourteenth century.

25 See Exec. Order No. 13,155, 65 Fed. Reg. 30,521 (12 May 2000), §§ 1(a) and 3(a).

26 Cynthia Ho (2011) notes that although the US government stopped exerting pressure on South Africa, the TNPCs did not immediately follow suit.

27 Fisher and Rigamonti note that the talks to withdraw the court case involved Kofi Annan, then secretary general of the UN, who was contacted by Jean-Pierre Garnier, the CEO of GlaxoSmith-Kline (on behalf of the TNPCs) to broker a deal with Thabo Mbeki, then president of South Africa.

4 TRIPS flexibilities, the Doha Declaration and sub-Saharan Africa

Although the NDP is the centrepiece of South Africa's policy framework on medicines, one should note that it was developed at a time when South Africa believed that its regulatory options were significantly narrower than they are today (Schneider, Barron and Fonn, 2007). The battle for South Africa was not over yet with the withdrawal of the court case challenging the constitutional validity of section 15C. The late 1990s and early 2000s were to witness important domestic and international struggles around access to essential medicines, which highlighted the deficiencies of the patent system and the legal means to limit its abuses. Not all developing countries were aware that the developed countries (the advocates of a wider global IP rights protection) had a strong public healthcare system and would be unaffected by the pharmaceutical patent regime of the TRIPS Agreement (Sundaram, 2015), and that it would be the developing countries and the LDCs left to face the enormous burden of a higher IP rights protection.

As the public health challenges were explicitly linked to the regulation of international trade (Haakonsson and Richey, 2007) conducted through the WTO, it became increasingly clear to the developing countries that the Agreement would severely restrict access to essential medicines for their citizens, and thus impede any efforts to control diseases including HIV/AIDS, tuberculosis and malaria. The inclusion of pharmaceutical patents under the extended IP rights protection of the TRIPS Agreement had only increased the dependency on brand-name pharmaceutical products, resulting in essential medicines becoming unaffordable and beyond the reach of a developing country's populace.[28] To complicate matters, the flexibilities afforded under the Agreement to the developing countries and the LDCs were viewed very narrowly by patent-holding developed countries, taking the stance that the only flexibility afforded under the Agreement was its staggered implementation in certain cases. This was in stark contrast to the assumed position of the developing countries, *i.e.*, that the Agreement did not limit their sovereign powers when addressing domestic health crises, such as HIV/AIDS (Sundaram, 2014). The impact of the TRIPS Agreement on public health in developing countries and LDCs became a serious issue.

It should be borne in mind that a lack of clarity and consensus on the TRIPS flexibilities had hampered the efforts to widen access to ARV treatment in both developing countries and the LDCs (UNAIDS, 2011), which factor severely affected the SSA nations (UNAIDS, 2016)[29] particularly South Africa. Most

28 Access to essential medicines is recognised as an indispensable part of the right to health and is considered a non-delegable obligation on the part of the state and cannot be violated based on lack of available resources.

29 SSA has the highest incidence of HIV/AIDS in the world today. At the end of 2015, 36.7 million people were living with HIV/AIDS worldwide, of which 25.5 million were from SSA. This region also accounts for almost 70 percent of global total new HIV infection. Most shockingly, only 37 percent of patients in SSA receive ARV treatment.

ARVs are patented, and their high costs in developing countries limit their access to a very few programmes and to relatively few patients (Haakonsson and Richey 2007). The concerns of the SSA countries and other developing countries only intensified when the US and EU, along with the TNPCs, commenced an aggressive campaign against countries that proceeded to take advantage of the IP rights policy options contained in the TRIPS Agreement (Abbott, 2002c), with the most notable legal action being launched against South Africa, Brazil and India. The court cases not only prised open the debate on the precise meaning of the flexibilities contained in the TRIPS Agreement, but also the principles and objectives embodied in Articles 7 and 8 of the Agreement (Marcellin, 2010), besides raising questions on the appropriateness of Article 31 in general, and Article 31(f) in particular (Bartlett, 2003).

With growing pressure from the African Group, the Council for TRIPS[30] in June 2001 considered in detail the relationship between public health and the TRIPS Agreement.[31] In November 2001, the Doha Declaration on TRIPS and Public Health[32] (Doha Declaration) was promulgated to address the concerns of the developing countries and also to clarify other divergent views held by the developed nations and developing nations on the application and ambit of the TRIPS Agreement (Gathii, 2002). The Doha Declaration recognised the right of a member state to grant compulsory licences, determine the grounds for the grant, and also define what constituted a national emergency.[33] The Doha Declaration and the 2003 Decision on Implementation of paragraph 6[34] of the TRIPS Agreement, also allowed access to generic medicines for HIV/AIDS, malaria and tuberculosis (Haakonsson and Richey, 2007).

The Declaration, for the first time since negotiations began for the introduction of IP rights in the multilateral trading system, recognised that IP and trade rules had a negative impact on access to medicines. Paragraph 4 of the Declaration states that '. . . we affirm that the Agreement can and should be interpreted and implemented in a manner supportive of WTO Members' right to protect public health and, in particular, to promote access to medicines for all.' Despite a Declaration coming from the highest trading body, and with a UN commitment in the form of Millennium Goals (UN, 2015),[35] much is still desired from the

30 The Council for TRIPS is also charged with the monitoring of WTO members' compliance with their obligations under the TRIPS Agreement.

31 See resolution on the Revised Drug Strategy, Resolution WHA49.14 (25 May 1996).

32 WHO, Declaration on the TRIPS Agreement and Public Health, WT/MIN(01)/DEC/2, adopted on 20 November 2001.

33 The 2001 Doha Declaration and the 2003 Decision on Implementation of paragraph 6 of the TRIPS Agreement recognises the right of a country to gain access to medicines.

34 World Trade Organization, Implementation of paragraph 6 of the Doha Declaration on the TRIPS Agreement and Public Health, WT/L/540 and Corr.1 (1 September 2003).

35 The United Nations Millennium Development Goal (UN MDG), Target 8.E states as follows: 'In cooperation with pharmaceutical companies, provide access to affordable essential drugs in developing countries.' See also United Nations, 'The Millennium Development Goals Report

TRIPS Agreement in terms of access to medicines,[36] as close to a third of the people worldwide lack affordable essential medicines due to exorbitant prices. The developing countries and LDCs still face big challenges when trying to implement the TRIPS flexibilities due to increased IP rights protection introduced under the TRIPS Agreement (Deere, 2009) and through TRIPS-plus provisions introduced under free trade agreements (FTAs).[37]

The Doha Declaration was a hard-fought bargain that came about through the combined efforts of developing countries, LDCs (led by the African nations) and well-supported by the NGOs. The Doha Declaration has impacted the developing countries, as it has influenced their health policies and, in particular, their pharmaceutical patent legislation. The Doha Declaration, to a certain extent, clarified the scope of the TRIPS Agreement and provided interpretive guidance and political space for the use of the flexibility policy embodied in the TRIPS Agreement. Unfortunately, the Declaration left unresolved the key issue of exporting products manufactured under a compulsory licence to countries without domestic production capacity, besides not addressing the promise of increased R&D in exchange for higher levels of IP protection, which was used as a bargaining chip by the developed countries during the Uruguay Round of negotiations on extended IP rights protection ('t Hoen, 2009).

4.1 *Post-apartheid South Africa and the healthcare system*

The 'disastrous influenza epidemic of 1918' led to the adoption of the first national public health legislation, *viz.*, the Public Health Act of 1919, which created a three-tier system of healthcare management in South Africa (Van Rensburg, 2004). The racial segregation of healthcare under apartheid only formalised what had been practiced from the earliest of colonial times. Reform proposals to overhaul the health policies were rejected during the 1950s apartheid era, which in turn heralded a phase when little thinking went into the creation of any health policy or action to improve existing health services available to the majority of the South African population (De Beer, 1986, 29). All these meant that the first democratically elected government inherited a completely fragmented healthcare system (Klug, 2012). Nelson Mandela, on assuming power in 1994, declared that one of the priorities of the new government would be to provide free health service to pregnant women and all children under the age of six.

2013'. Interestingly, the report does not list any entries under 8E of the Goals, which is aimed at providing access to affordable essential drugs in developing countries.

36 According to 2008 figures released by the WHO, approximately a third of the people worldwide lack access to medicines. Further, the high prices of essential medicines act as a barrier in the treatment of millions.

37 The TRIPS-plus provisions embedded in FTAs prove access to affordable medicines to be a difficult task, as it effectively outlaws generics and also requires extended protection to pharmaceutical patents beyond the period prescribed under the TRIPS Agreement.

The South African public healthcare system primarily caters to the poor black majority (Day and Gray, 2008),[38] while the private healthcare system is unevenly distributed nationally, catering to the needs of the more affluent population (Coovadia, Jewkes, Barron, Sanders, and McIntyre, 2009).[39] The South African healthcare system, both in its structure and population health outcomes, clearly reflects the apartheid legacy of inequality (Giaimo, 2016). A classic example would be the health expenditure for the year 1992/93, where the private sector consumed 48.5 percent of total healthcare expenditure, while nearly 80 percent of the population did not have access to private healthcare (South African Department of Health, 1996). The structure of the South African pharmaceutical industry, and as well as the pharmaceutical supply system, reflect the apartheid divide. As the industry was dominated by subsidiaries of the TNPCs, the market also reflect the apartheid divide (Klug, 2012). It will not be an exaggeration to state that the levels of healthcare in South Africa are largely socially determined, and that poverty, inequality and their effects on ill health are much more deeply ingrained in the South African society than in the richer industrialised democracies (Giaimo, 2016). Some of the challenges facing South Africa, in this regard, are traceable to government policies devised during the post-apartheid era.

One must note that South Africa has the highest *per capita* care spending level – both public and private, but where spending is unequally distributed (Ataguba and Akazili, 2010). The shambolic distribution of resources across public and private healthcare is one of the major barriers in achieving the goal of providing healthcare guaranteed under the post-apartheid constitution. While the well-stocked private healthcare system met the needs of the wealthy minority, the under-resourced public healthcare system barely met the health requirements of the poor, and at times impoverished, majority. Even in the post-apartheid era, the South African healthcare system is two-tiered and continues to be highly inequitable (Schneider, Barron, and Fonn, 2007).[40] The South African disease has been described as a fourfold burden, which is (i) the burden of HIV and related diseases; (ii) the diseases of inequality, poverty and underdevelopment – notably infectious diseases; (iii) the chronic diseases of lifestyle; and (iv) that of a high fatality rate related to injury and violence (Redelinghuys, 2012). Analysing the infection rate of HIV and TB across the population, Giaimo notes that the figures significantly mask the racial and income disparities in the experience of disease, and that the black South African population bears the brunt of these illnesses (Giaimo, 2016).[41]

38 About 82 percent of the general population of almost 50 million was dependent on the public health care sector, and within that population approximately 86 percent are black.

39 Figures from 2008 show that 70 percent of the private hospitals were in three of the country's nine provinces, with 38 percent in Gauteng province.

40 The authors note that the apartheid-era private system received the majority of resources (56 percent of total health care expenditure), while servicing only 23 percent of the population who had access to health insurance. The private sector employed 85 percent of the dentists and more than 60 percent of all doctors, physiotherapists, nurses and other health care personnel.

41 HIV/AIDS and tuberculosis (TB) are considered as the twin scourges that sharply reduce life expectancy in South Africa. The country's rate of new HIV infection ranks first in the world, and its infection rate for TB, at 860 per 100,000 people in 2013, is among the highest in the world.

Even before the first democratically elected new government under Nelson Mandela started addressing some of the then-existing health policies and system that were in place in South Africa, it began work on drawing up a national constitution. This was with a clear view to start eradicating the inequalities brought about under the apartheid era. South Africa's Constitution, while brimming with human rights principles, also has entrenched within it an enforceable right to access healthcare services (Forman and Singh, 2014). It should be remembered that the entry into the WTO and the birth of post-apartheid South Africa coincided, and it would be preposterous to say that the country was well prepared to embrace the IP protection regime under the TRIPS Agreement. In 1994, when the new government under Nelson Mandela came to power, the country was institutionally isolated from external sources of liquidity, and close to insolvency (Fourie and Meyer, 2010). The Mandela government was instrumental in forging AIDS policymaking, spanning three phases. The first phase was between 1994 and early 1996, when the Reconstruction and Development Programme (RDP) was presented as the broad policy blueprint to improve the socio-political equity. The RDP was abandoned in April 1996 in favour of the Growth, Employment and Redistribution Programme (GEAR), which was only to be followed by a series of 'AIDS scandals' in the country (Fourie and Meyer, 2010). The shift in policy under the GEAR programme dramatically changed the macroeconomic direction of policy and provided openings for greater internationalisation as well as a range of new market-oriented initiatives (Klug, 2012).

One will have to engage in enquiring if the constitutional guarantee for healthcare has helped South Africa in finding solutions to its long-standing problems of access to medicines in the post-apartheid era. This enquiry will take into consideration the extent of the right contained in the Constitution, and if and how the South African judiciary has helped in facilitating the public to access the right through the court system. Under the 1996 Constitution of the Republic of South Africa (Hoexter, 2004),[42] the state has a duty to take steps to put in place a legal framework to facilitate access to such healthcare services (Hassim, Heywood, and Berger, 2007).[43] The duty cast on the government refers directly to the government's role as a regulator, rather than as a provider, and requires having in place a legal framework that individuals can utilise to realise their rights through their own actions.[44] To address the inequity in the health service, the government issued

42 In Hoexter's opinion, the Constitution of South Africa is a 'voluminous document fairly bristling with human rights, including the right to administrative justice'.

43 The Constitutional Court in *Minister of Health v. Treatment Action Campaign (No 2)* 2002 (5) SA 721 (CC), held that access to health care services included access to medicines.

44 See section 33(3) of the Constitution, which calls for the enactment of national legislation to give effect to the right to administrative justice, and to provide for judicial review of administrative action. Section 33 reads as follows: 'Just administrative action: (1) Everyone has the right to administrative action that is lawful, reasonable and procedurally fair. (2) Everyone whose rights have been adversely affected by administrative action has the right to be given written reasons. (3) National legislation must be enacted to give effect to these rights, and must – (a) provide for

a white paper in 1997 (South African Department of Health, 1997). The *White Paper for the Transformation of the Health System of South Africa* is doubtlessly the key policy document for the healthcare sector in the post-apartheid era (Department of Health, 1997). The white paper aimed at addressing the inequity in the health service by seeking to increase access to primary healthcare, creating a unified national system, developing a district health system, ensuring the availability of safe, good-quality essential drugs and rationalising health financing through budget reprioritisation. Two main strategies of the white paper are worth identifying, *viz.*, reformation of the healthcare system – a paradigm shift toward primary healthcare, and remedying the legacy of gross inequality that was ingrained in the edifice of the healthcare system from the apartheid era through the introduction of the district health system (Ngwena, Cook, and Durojaye, 2013).

Achieving equity was a tall order, as South Africa suffered (and continues to suffer) from an unequal distribution of wealth (Statistics South Africa, 2008, 2012).[45] This position is well captured by the fact that despite there being growth since 1994 of the black middle class and affluent sector, the vast majority of poverty is still concentrated amongst black South Africans (Armstrong, Lekezwa, and Siebrits, 2008). As far as South African healthcare financing is concerned, it is highly fragmented, with little or no pooling of funds for financial risk protection (Ataguba and Akazili, 2010).

On the back of economic growth in 2001, the health spending increased (Schneider, Barron, and Fonn, 2007), but this increased spending had not kept pace with population growth and the increase in new users of the system (McIntyre, 2004). The objective of the National Health Act 61 of 2003 (NHA) is outlined in section 2 as 'to regulate national health and provide uniformity in respect of health services across the nation'. It goes further in 2(c) to state that the objective includes the 'protecting, respecting, promoting and fulfilling the right of – (i) people of South Africa to the progressive realisation of the constitutional right to access to healthcare services, including reproductive healthcare', which provision reiterates the guarantee to healthcare found in the Constitution. Section 3(1)(d) of the NHA, on the other hand, requires the Minister of Health to ensure the provision of essential health services within the limits of available resources. This saw the mandatory healthcare being provided to pregnant women and lactating mothers, as well as children under the age of six to cover primary

---

the review of administrative action by a court or, where appropriate, an independent and impartial tribunal; (b) impose a duty on the state to give effect to the rights in subsections (1) and (2); and (c) promote an efficient administration.'

The scheme contained in the above provision of the Constitution was later to be codified in the Promotion of Administrative Justice Act 2000. See, for a general discourse, Hoexter (2012) chapter 7.

45 The poorest 10 percent of the country's population receive approximately 0.1 percent of total income, while the top 10 percent of the country's population receive approximately 51 percent of the total income. It is noted that change in health expenditure is tough to measure/interpret, since all expenditure on medical aid and medical insurance is classified as 'miscellaneous expenditure' according to COICOP.

healthcare services without costs. Unfortunately for South Africa, the problems have not gone away, as statistics reveal that the nation's growth of the pandemic is unchecked and is also the largest in the world (Statistics South Africa, 2016).[46] This state of affairs can be attributed to lack of progress in implementing the health policies developed by the African National Congress (Coovadia, Jewkes, Barron, Sanders, and McIntyre, 2009).

4.2 Healthcare, human rights and the constitutional court

It is well known that the first task undertaken by the post-apartheid government was the drafting of a new constitution, which strongly advocated for constitutional supremacy over any other form of law. Section 7(1) of the Constitution identifies the Bill of Rights as the 'cornerstone of democracy', placing human rights at the apex of governance.[47] As mentioned earlier, the key right of 'universal healthcare' is to be found contained in section 27 of the Constitution. Sections 28(1)(c) and 35(2)(e) of the Constitution confers health rights on children and incarcerated individuals, respectively. Under sections 27 and 28 (Functions of Provincial Health Council), the Constitution embodies social and economic rights, which include the rights to food, healthcare, water, social security, housing and education and children's rights. Section 27 provides a direct right to health, the text of which reads as follows:

27 (1) Everyone has the right to have access to –

- (a) healthcare services, including reproductive healthcare;
- (b) sufficient food and water; and
- (c) social security, including, if they are unable to support themselves and their dependants, appropriate social assistance.

(2) The state must take reasonable legislative and other measures, within its available resources, to achieve the progressive realisation of each of these rights.
(3) No one may be refused emergency medical treatment.

The right to health manifests in several provisions of the South African Constitution, and section 27 is unequivocal and the most universal of them all. It is clear from a reading of section 27 that it confers equal treatment on anyone wishing to access healthcare services. The section is about a positive entitlement, which confers on everyone the right to access health services based on need (Ngwena,

46 An estimated 1.8 million people were infected in 1996, which has risen to 7.03 million in 2016, which is the equivalent of 12.7 percent of the total South African population.
47 'Section 7. Rights: (1) This Bill of Rights is a cornerstone of democracy in South Africa. It enshrines the rights of all people in our country and affirms the democratic values of human dignity, equality and freedom. (2) The state must respect, protect, promote and fulfil the rights in the Bill of Rights. (3) The rights in the Bill of Rights are subject to the limitations contained or referred to in section 36, or elsewhere in the Bill.'

2000), and 27(2) simultaneously imposes a positive corresponding duty upon the state to provide health services (Ngwena, Cook, and Durojaye, 2013). The right to health found in section 27 is limited by section 36, which allows for limits on the rights identified in the Bill of Rights to the extent that such limitations are reasonable and justifiable in a democratic society based on human dignity, equality and freedom. It is also to be noted that section 27(2) limits the state's duty to the use of the resources that are available to meet the health needs on a progressive basis (Ngwena, Cook, and Durojaye, 2013). The section bears a strong resemblance to Article 2(1) of the International Covenant on Economic, Social and Cultural Rights (ICESCR).

Forman and Singh argue that the guarantee of universal healthcare contained in section 27 is far narrower than the international 'human rights to the highest attainable standard of health' found enshrined in the Universal Declaration of Human Rights 1948, and that the Constitution does not make any provisions for the government's broader public health responsibilities (Forman and Singh, 2014). Forman and Singh are also critical of the section 27 guarantee, as in their view the provision provides very little indication of what is encompassed within the entitlement of healthcare services, and the task of interpretation falls to the government and the judiciary.

5 Judicial interpretation of constitutional rights

The limits of section 27 were tested in *Soobramoney v. Minister of Health, KwaZulu-Natal* case[48] (hereafter *Soobramoney*). The claimant, who was a diabetic, experienced renal failure and faced imminent death in the absence of renal dialysis. As he did not meet the criteria for access to dialysis, medical treatment was refused, and the claimant moved the High Court challenging the refusal for treatment. The claimant's case was premised on the argument that the refusal for treatment infringed his right to life guaranteed under section 11 and that of section 27(3) of the Constitution. The High Court rejected the claimant's case on the ground that the claimant did not meet the guidelines laid down for determining eligibility for dialysis. The High Court also observed that 'emergency medical treatment' was to be interpreted in the context of finite resources, and ruled that the function of the court was not to direct the state to make additional funds available. On appeal, the Constitutional Court held that section 27(3) had a narrow constitutional meaning and could not be invoked to access ongoing treatment for chronic ailments. While dismissing the appeal, the Constitutional Court held that the right to treatment could not be construed outside the context of the availability of health services generally. The Constitutional Court also held that the hospital authorities could not be expected to provide treatment to all patients matching the appellant's health profile, and that drawing an appropriate policy lay with the hospital authorities, who had acted in good faith.

48 *Soobramoney v. Minister of Health, KwaZulu-Natal* (1997) (12) BCLR 1696 (CC).

Some commentators take the view that the decision of the Constitutional Court in *Soobramoney* does not thoroughly illuminate the normative content of section 27 as a socio-economic right (Ngwena, Cook, and Durojaye, 2013), and some others have expressed the opinion that the court was slow to interfere with the decisions made by the hospital authorities, holding that determination of an appropriate policy lay with the hospital authorities, who had acted in good faith (Davis, 2004). It should not be forgotten that *Soobramoney* was the first decision of the Constitutional Court, both from the perspective of interpretation of the right to access to healthcare services and on the interpretation of a socio-economic right as a justiciable right. Although the first of its kind, one of the major shortcomings in the ruling is the absence of a systematic approach to the determination of a socio-economic right, which in effect does not offer any clear interpretive assistance on the normative content of the right to healthcare services guaranteed under the Constitution.

The Constitutional Court once again had the occasion to deal with and determine the socio-economic rights contained in the Constitution in *Minister of Health and Others v. Treatment Action Campaign and Others*[49] (hereafter TAC). This case is relevant to our discussions, as it concerned the refusal to make the ARV drug nevirapine available in the public sector to prevent the mother-to-child transmission of HIV. The applicants challenged the government's decision to restrict the dispensation of the ARV drug Nevirapine to only 18 pilot sites, which constituted a breach of section 27 – right of access to healthcare, and section 28(1)(c) – the right of the child to basic healthcare services. The applicants were successful before the High Court, which held that the government's ARV dispensation programme clearly fell short of a reasonable measure to realise the right of access to healthcare under section 27 of the Constitution. On appeal the Constitutional Court modified the judgment of the High Court and refused to recognise section 27(1) as giving rise to a self-standing independent positive right (para 39). The Constitutional Court ordered the government to remove any restrictions limiting the dispensation of Nevirapine to only pilot sites, and further directed the government to expedite the use of Nevirapine at public health facilities. In concluding as above, it followed the reasoning applied in the case of *Grootboom*[50] in interpreting section 27(2) and found as follows:

> the policy of confining Nevirapine to research and training sites fails to address the needs of mothers and their newborn children who did not have

49 *Minister of Health and Others v. Treatment Action Campaign and Others* (2002), (10) BCLR 1033 (CC).

50 *Government of the Republic of South Africa and Others v. Grootboom and Others* (2000), (11) BCLR 1169 (CC). The respondents were evicted from their informal superstructures erected on the lands earmarked by the government for low-cost housing. The case revolved around the interpretation and application of the right of access to housing under section 26, or other alternative basic shelter under section 28 of the Constitution. The Constitutional Court, while holding in favour of the respondents, drew inspiration from international conventions. The Court particularly cited Articles 11(1) and 2(1) of the ICESCR and their interpretation by the Committee on Economic, Social and Cultural Rights (CESCR). Although not relating to 'access to health care', *Grootboom*

> access to these sites. It fails to distinguish between the evaluation of programmes for reducing mother-to-child transmission and the need to provide access to health care services required by those who do not have access to these sites.
>
> (Para 67)

5.1 *The implications of the court decisions*

The inclusion of positive obligations on the state to provide access to health care has developed a significant scope to seek court intervention to force the state to implement such policies to realise the constitutional rights (Broster, 2015). For instance, in the TAC judgment, the Constitutional Court refused to hold that section 27(1) constituted a self-standing right and to grant a structural interdict. The Court in most cases demonstrated a reluctance to follow a 'minimum core' approach to socio-economic rights, and was also not prepared to grant an injunctive remedy (Ngwena, Cook, and Durojaye, 2013). One of the criticisms of the Constitutional Court's jurisprudence on the area of socio-economic rights is its failure to create a minimum core content. But on the other hand, the court has also provided instances where the court will intervene to compel the state to comply with its constitutional obligation (Broster, 2015). Some writers have criticised the Constitutional Court in *Soobramoney* for unduly limiting the court's role in deciding on allocation of health care resources and in the protection of socio-economic rights in general (Ngwena, 2013).

Importantly, the South African Constitutional Court, while interpreting the rights contained in section 28 of the Constitution, drew inspiration from the wording and interpretive jurisprudence of Articles 11(1) and 2(1) of the ICESCR. Shinn notes that the term 'right to health', when used in international human rights discourses, is understood in a much wider sense than it is understood in a domestic law sense. Shinn further notes that this right would invariably cover the right of access to a range of facilities, goods and services, including health services, and also the right to the underlying determinants of health such as food, housing, safe water, sanitation, healthy working conditions, and an environment that is safe and free from hazards such as pollutants (Shinn, 1999). The right to health under the South African Constitution is to be viewed much more narrowly to mean only a legally enforceable right of access to health services for the 'attainment of health'. Buchanan is of the opinion that the 'attainment of health' cannot be guaranteed irrespective of the term that one uses to convey a notion of entitlement to services for attaining health (Buchanan, 1984).

One should bear in mind that constitutionally guaranteed rights are subject to jurisprudential interpretation, or justiciability of a constitutional court of the respective state. Ngwena interprets 'justiciability' to mean the constitutional

---

is the Constitutional Court's most important decision on the interpretation and application of socio-economic rights contained in the South African Constitution.

competence of the courts to adjudicate a claim that seeks to enforce a state obligation (Ngwena, 2013), and in our case the obligation of the state to provide health service. Ngwena further classifies judicial competence as being both in the constitutional sense and that of institutional competence. South Africa in Ngwena's opinion presents an ideal jurisdiction to test the justiciability of the right to health, as it has a transformative constitution, which contains within it the commitment to substantive equality, respect of human dignity and an explicit recognition of socio-economic rights including the right to health (Ngwena, 2013). For instance, in *Soobramoney*, the court observed that section 27(3) was designed for a sudden catastrophe that calls for immediate medical attention, and that the applicant had a long-standing health condition, and a broader interpretation to suit his requirement was untenable. In the court's considered view, the relevant sections only obliged the state to provide health care services to all citizens within its available resources, and if the appellant's relief were only to be granted it would have the consequence of prioritising the treatment of terminal illnesses over other forms of care (para 19).[51]

Some commentators opine that the state's obligation is 'positive', which includes appropriate regulation of the private sector. The Constitution clearly obligates the government to take all reasonable steps to have in place a legal framework that facilitates access to essential medicines (Hassim, Heywood, and Berger, 2007). This obligation includes not only the government being a provider of goods and services, but also a place to have a legal framework to assist individuals to realise their rights through their own action (Hassim, Heywood, and Berger, 2007). Whether this view is well captured in the Constitutional Court's interpretation of the right to health provisions of the South African Constitution is debatable. For instance, the court in *Soobramoney* decided to limit the realisation of the constitutional right of access to health care, once it became apparent that the state resources were unavailable. The judicial interpretation of the relevant provisions of the Constitution shows both a hesitation in following a minimum core approach for the recognition and grant of socio-economic rights and in the grant of an injunctive remedy. It can be concluded from the discussions that the state's powers in this case are limited to providing diagnostic, curative and rehabilitative services towards achieving the goal of 'right to health'.

In 2005, in *Minister of Health v. New Clicks South Africa (Pty) Ltd*, the court held that any regulation that sought to limit pharmaceutical profit margins was unconstitutional for a number of reasons. The findings of the court were premised on the understanding that the regulations would harm the right of access to health care services due to closure of rural and courier pharmacies, which was primarily serving the poor and vulnerable of the population.[52] Interestingly, the above case did

51 The claimant relied on the judgment of the Indian Supreme Court in *Paschim Banga Khet Mazdoor Samity and others v. State of West Bengal* (1996) AIR SC 2426. The claimant in the Indian case was refused medical treatment by the hospitals and successfully pursued his right for life under Article 21 of the Indian Constitution.

52 *Minister of Health v. New Clicks South Africa (Pty) Ltd* 2006 (2) SA 311 (CC) paras 1, 16, 19, and 32.

not explicitly relate to socio-economic rights or the reasonableness of the policy (Pieterse, 2014). Although the South African Constitutional Court is now more open to the idea of enforcing socio-economic rights, including health-related rights, some commentators remain disappointed by the scarcity of standard-setting on the enforcement of socio-economic rights (Pieterse, 2014). Commentators have expressed the view that the socio-economic rights guaranteed in the Constitution will remain conceptually empty, and be of little use to citizens, if the Constitutional Court continues to decline to grant concrete content to socio-economic rights through its judgments (Mubangizi and Twinomugisha, 2010). Liebenberg takes the stance that realising the socio-economic rights depends on the willingness of the South African judges, practitioners and participants in socio-economic rights litigation in reshaping traditional concepts of liberal legalism that pose impediments to creative and innovative responses to socio-economic rights claims (Liebenberg, 2010). The view expressed by Liebenberg shines a light on the state of affairs on the uphill task faced by South Africans in realising socio-economic rights, due to the hesitation on the part of the South African Constitutional Court, which appears to be hamstrung by the views of a bygone era.

5.2 The national health insurance and the National Health Act 2013

In 2011, the National Health Insurance Committee produced a policy paper on National Health Insurance (NHI).[53] The NHI intends to cover all South Africans free of charge at the point of care, as it envisages universal coverage and equitable access to care. The NHI represents a policy shift, calculated to eliminate disparities and inequities in health care, which will necessitate reorganisation of the existing health care system (Fusheini and Eyles, 2016). According to the policy paper, the implementation of the NHI is 'consistent with the Constitutional commitment of the state to take reasonable legislative and other measures, within its available resources, to achieve the progressive realisation of the right to all for access to health care services including reproductive health care'.[54]

One important feature of the NHI is the pooling of funds to offer health services to all South African citizens (and permanent residents) based on their health needs, regardless of their socio-economic status. In July 2013, President Jacob Zuma signed the National Health Amendment Act No 12 of 2013 into law. The Amendment Act intends to establish monitoring bodies to ensure quality assurance and to address human rights violations in the healthcare sector. The Act seeks to establish an ombudsman to receive complaints from patients and to ensure that necessary remedies are provided to the complainants in a fair, economical and expeditious manner (Ngwena, Cook, and Durojaye, 2013). Hence, the successful implementation of the NHI would require the re-engineering of

53 Republic of South Africa, 'National Health Insurance in South Africa: A Policy Paper,' *Government Gazette* (12 August 2011).

54 *Ibid.*

the public health care (PHC) to strengthen its capacity and broaden its reach (Van Rensburg, 2004). In the ANC's view, the single-payer NHI is the solution for many of the shortcomings of the current dual health care system, but unfortunately, the most important questions, *viz.*, the financing of health care, are not yet settled in the proposal (Giaimo, 2016).

6 Conclusion

While the South African government is taking steps to make access to health care more practicable, the key question of access to medicines lingers in the background. The funding is to come from the government for the transformative agenda that the state has embarked on – which will be met through taxation, *etc.*, but the fact that the cost of medicines will be determined and set by TNPCs to suit their requirements remains unresolved. This again will be based on profit margins and private gains, not premised on public welfare. One can definitely argue that in the post-apartheid era, the democratically elected government has certainly taken a few major steps to transform the health service, including the introduction of the Medicines Act, implementation of the NHI, *etc.* Nevertheless, the results present a mixed picture, clearly indicating there is a long way to go before South Africa can claim it had made significant progress. It is no longer the creation of a legal or policy framework, or even having in place an institutional framework, but the actual implementation of the vision to provide access to health care to a nation which is divided on racial lines, where basic human needs are available only to a select few. South Africa's problem of access to medicines is multifaceted and cannot be solved through the constitutional guarantee of right to health, or through the creation of a legal framework to enforce the same, but requires a multi-pronged approach.

Bibliography

1 Abbott, Frederick M. 'WTO TRIPS Agreement and its Implications for Access to Medicines in Developing Countries,' *Study Paper 2a*, United Kingdom Commission on Intellectual Property Rights (2002a).

2 Abbott, Frederick M. 'The TRIPS-Legality of Measures Taken to Address Public Health Crises: Responding to USTR-State-Industry Positions that Undermine the WTO,' in Kennedy, Daniel L.M., and James D. Southwick (eds.) *Political Economy of International Trade: Essays in Honor of Robert E. Hudec* (Cambridge University Press, 2002b) 311–342.

3 Abbott, Frederick M. 'The Doha Declaration on the TRIPS Agreement and Public Health: Lighting a Dark Corner at the WTO,' *Journal of International Economic Law* Vol. 5 (2002c) 469–505.

4 Adusei, Poku. *Patenting of Pharmaceuticals and Development in Sub-Saharan Africa: Laws, Institutions, Practices, and Politics* (Springer Science & Business Media, 2013) 80–85.

5 Armstrong, Paula, Bongisa Lekezwa, and Krige Siebrits, 'Poverty in South Africa: A Profile Based on Recent Household Surveys,' *Matieland: Stellenbosch Economic Working Paper* 4, No. 8 (2008) <www.ekon.sun.ac.za/wpapers/2008/wp042008/wp-04-2008.pdf> accessed 29 November 2017.

6 Ataguba, John Ele-Ojo, and James Akazili. 'Health Care Financing in South Africa: Moving Towards Universal Coverage,' *CME: Your SA Journal of CPD* Vol. 28 No. 2 (2010) 74–78, 75.

7 Attaran, Amir, and Lee Gillespie-White. 'Do Patent for ARVs Constrain Access to AIDS Treatment in Africa?' *Journal of American Medical Association* Vol. 286, No. 15 (2001) 1886–1892.

8 Baleta, Adele. 'Drug Firms Take South Africa's Government to Court,' *Lancet* Vol. 357, No. 9258 (2001) 775.

9 Bartlett, Sandra. 'Compulsory Licenses Pursuant to TRIPS Article 31 in Light of the Doha Declaration on the TRIPS Agreement and Public Health,' *Journal of World Intellectual Property* Vol. 6, No. 2 (2003) 283–310.

10 Blackhurst, Richard, Bill Lyakurwa, and Ademola Oyejide. 'Improving African Participation in the WTO,' Paper Commissioned by the *World Bank for a Conference* at the WTO (1999) 1–45.

11 Bond, Patrick. 'Globalization, Pharmaceutical Pricing, and South African Health Policy: Managing Confrontation with US Firms and Politicians,' *International Journal of Health Services* Vol. 29, No. 4 (1999) 765–792.

12 Broster, Emma Justine. 'Litigating the Right to Health Care in South Africa,' in Durojaye, Ebenezer (ed.), *Litigating the Right to Health in Africa: Challenges and Prospects* (Routledge, 2015) 99–118.

13 Buchanan, Allan. 'The Right to a Decent Minimum of Health Care,' *Philosophy and Public Affairs* Vol. 13, No. 1 (1984) 55–78, 56.

14 CIA. *The World Factbook* <www.cia.gov/library/publications/the-world-factbook/geos/print_sf.html> accessed 29 November 2017.

15 Cann, Wesley A., Jr., 'On the Relationship Between Intellectual Property Rights and the Need of Less-Developed Countries for Access to Pharmaceuticals: Creating a Legal Duty to Supply Under a Theory of Progressive Global Constitutionalism,' *University of Pennsylvania Journal of International Economic Law* Vol. 25 (2004) 755.

16 Coovadia, Hoosen, Rachel Jewkes, Peter Barron, David Sanders, and Diane McIntyre, 'The Health and Health System of South Africa: Historical Roots of Current Public Health Challenges,' *The Lancet* Vol. 374, No. 9692 (2009) 817–834.

17 Council WTO General. 'Implementation of Paragraph 6 of the Doha Declaration on the TRIPS Agreement and Public Health,' *Decision of the General Council* [WT/L/540 and Corr.1] (1 September 2003).

18 Davis, Dennis. 'Socio-Economic Rights in South Africa: The Record of the Constitutional Court after Ten Years: Feature,' *ESR Review: Economic and Social Rights in South Africa* Vol. 5, No. 5 (2004) 3–7.

19 Day, Candy, and Andy Gray. 'Health and Related Indicators,' *South African Health Review* (2008) 239–395.

20 De Beer, Cedric. *The South African Disease: Apartheid, Health and Health Services* (Africa World Press, 1986) 29.

21 Deere, Carolyn. *The Implementation Game: The TRIPS Agreement and the Global Politics of Intellectual Property Reform in Developing Countries* (Oxford University Press, 2009).

22 Drahos, Peter, and John Braithwaite. *Information Feudalism: Who Owns the Knowledge Economy?* (Earthscan, 2002).

23 Drahos, Peter. 'When the Weak Bargain With the Strong: Negotiation in the World Trade Organization,' *International Negotiation* Vol. 8, No. 1 (2003) 79–109.

24 Fisher III, William W., and Cyrill P Rigamonti. 'The South Africa AIDS Controversy: A Case Study in Patent Law and Policy,' *The Law and Business of Patents* (2005) 1–56.

25 Forman, Lisa, and Jerome Amir Singh. 'The Role of Rights and Litigation in Assuring More Equitable Access to Health Care in South Africa,' in Flood, Colleen M., and Aeyal Gross (eds.) *The Right to Health at the Public/Private Divide: A Global Comparative Study* (Cambridge University Press, 2014) 288–318.

26 Fourie, Pieter, and Melissa Meyer. *The Politics of AIDS Denialism: South Africa's Failure to Respond* (Ashgate Publishing, 2010) 77–78.

27 Fusheini, Adam, and John Eyles. 'Achieving Universal Health Coverage in South Africa Through a District Health System Approach: Conflicting Ideologies of Health Care Provision,' *BMC Health Services Research* Vol. 16, No. 1 (2016) 558.

28 Gathii, James Thuo. 'The Legal Status of Doha Declaration on TRIPS and Public Health Under the Vienna Convention on the Law of Treaties,' *Harvard Journal of Law & Technology* Vol. 15 (2002) 291–317, 292–293.

29 Giaimo, Susan. *Reforming Health Care in the United States, Germany, and South Africa: Comparative Perspectives on Health* (Palgrave Macmillan, 2016) 143–182.

30 Government *of the Republic of South Africa and Others v. Grootboom and Others* (2000), (11) BCLR 1169 (CC).

31 Haakonsson, Stine Jessen, and Lisa Ann Richey. 'TRIPS and Public Health: The Doha Declaration and Africa,' *Development Policy Review* Vol. 25, No. 1 (2007) 71–90.

32 Harris, Donald P. 'Carrying a Good Joke Too Far: TRIPS and Treaties of Adhesion,' *University of Pennsylvania Journal of International Economic Law* Vol. 27, No. 3 (2006) 681–755.

33 Hassim, Adil, Mark Heywood, and Jonathan Berger (eds.) *Health and Democracy: A Guide to Human Rights, Health Law and Policy in Post-Apartheid South Africa* (Siber Ink, 2007) 444–445.

34 Ho, Cynthia M. *Access to Medicines in the Global Economy: International Agreements and Related Rights* (Oxford University Press, 2011) 330–333.

35 Hoexter, Cora. 'The Principle of Legality in South African Administrative Law,' *Macquarie Law Journal* Vol. 4 (2004) 165, 166.

36 Hoexter, Cora. *Administrative Law in South Africa* (Claremont, 2012).

37 Joncheere, Kees de, Ad H. Rietveld, and Christine Huttin, 'Experience With Generics,' in Dukes, Graham M.N., Flora M. Haaijer-Ruskamp, Kees de Joncheere, and Ad H. Rietveld (eds.). *Drugs and Money: Prices, Affordability and Cost Containment* (WHO, 2003).

38 Klug, Heinz. 'Access to Medicines and the Transformation of the South African State: Exploring the Interaction of Legal and Policy Changes in Health, Intellectual Property, Trade, and Competition Law in the Context of South Africa's HIV/AIDS Pandemic,' *Law & Social Enquiry* Vol. 37, No. 2 (2012) 297–329.

39 Kongolo, Tshimanga. *The African Contributions in Shaping the Worldwide Intellectual Property System* (Ashgate, 2013).

40 Letter from Nader, Love and Weissman to Ambassador Charlene Barshefsky (6 October 1999), <www.cptech.org/ip/health/country/cb-oct6-99.html> accessed 29 November 2017.

41 Liebenberg, Sandra. *Socio-Economic Rights: Adjudication Under a Transformative Constitution* (Juta and Company Ltd, 2010) 43, 66–71.

42 Lewis, Carole. 'A Mixed Legal System with a Constitution on Top: South African Law in the Era of Democracy,' *Amicus Curiae Issue* Vol. 57 (2005).

43 Marcellin, Sherry S. *The Political Economy of Pharmaceutical Patents: US Sectional Interests and the African Group at the WTO* (Ashgate, 2010) 134.

44 McIntyre, Diane. 'The Nature and State of Health Care Financing and Deliver in South Africa: The Obstacles to Realizing the Right to Health,' Presentation at Seminar on *Health Sector Transformation*, Vol. 10 (February 2004) 269–270.
45 *Minister of Health and Others v. Treatment Action Campaign and Others* (2002), (10) BCLR 1033 (CC).
46 *Minister of Health v. New Clicks South Africa (Pty) Ltd* 2006 (2) SA 311 (CC).
47 Mshomba, Richard E. *Africa and the World Trade Organization* (Cambridge University Press, 2009).
48 Mubangizi, John C., and Ben K. Twinomugisha. 'The Right to Health Care in the Specific Context of Access to HIV/AIDS Medicines: What Can South Africa and Uganda Learn From Each Other?' *African Human Rights Law Journal* Vol. 10, No. 1 (2010) 105 128–129.
49 Nader, Love, and Weissman, Letter to Ambassador Charlene Barshefsky (6 October 1999), available at <www.cptech.org/ip/health/country/cb-oct6-99.html> accessed 29 November 2017.
50 National Drug Policy for South Africa, 1996.
51 Ngwena, Charles. 'The Recognition of Access to Health Care as a Human Right in South Africa: Is It Enough?' *Health and Human Rights* (2000) 26–44.
52 Ngwena, Charles. 'Scope and Limits of Judicialisation of the Constitutional Right to Health in South Africa: An Appraisal of Key Cases with Particular Reference to Justiciability,' *Revista de Direito Sanitário* Vol. 14, No. 2 (2013) 43–64.
53 Ngwena, Charles, Rebecca Cook, and Ebenezer Durojaye. 'The Right to Health in Post-Apartheid Era South Africa,' in Zuniga, Jose M., Stephen P. Marks, Lawrence O. Gostin (eds.) *Advancing the Human Rights to Health* (Oxford University Press, 2013).
54 Norris, Jeremiah. 'India's Role as Pharmacy of the Developing World,' *The Financial Times* (18 September 2015) <www.ft.com/content/d4951900-5aea-11e5-9846-de406ccb37f2> accessed 29 November 2017.
55 Ogunkola, E. Olawale. 'African Capacity for Compliance and Defense of WTO Rights,' *Dissemination Workshop of Africa and the World Trading System Project*, Yaounde Vol. 17 (1999).
56 Okediji, Ruth L. 'The International Relations of Intellectual Property: Narratives of Developing Country Participation in the Global Intellectual Property System,' *Singapore Journal of International & Comparative Law* Vol. 7 (2003) 315–385.
57 *Paschim Banga Khet Mazdoor Samity and others v. State of West Bengal* (1996) AIR SC 2426.
58 Pieterse, Marius. *Can Rights Cure? The Impact of Human Rights Litigation on South Africa's Health System* (Pretoria University Law Press, 2014).
59 Rahmatian, Andreas. 'Neo-Colonial Aspects of Global Intellectual Property Protection,' *The Journal of World Intellectual Property* Vol. 12, No. 1 (2009) 40–74.
60 Rajeshwari, Sreelekshmi. 'India – No Longer the Pharmacy of the Developing World?' *Cambridge Globalist* (30 January 2016) <http://cambridgeglobalist.org/2016/01/30/india-no-longer-the-pharmacy-of-the-developing-world/> accessed 29 November 2017.
61 Redelinghuys, Nola. 'Health and Health Status of the South African Population,' in van Rensburg, H.C.J. (ed.), *Health and Health Care in South Africa* (Van Schaik, 2012) 237–292.
62 Republic of South Africa. 'National Health Insurance in South Africa: A Policy Paper,' *Government Gazette* (12 August 2011).
63 Russell, Veja Sabin. 'New Crusade to Lower AIDS Drug Costs: Africa's Needs at Odds with Firms' Profit Motive,' *San Francisco Chronicle* (24 May 1999) <www.sfgate.com/

health/article/New-Crusade-To-Lower-AIDS-Drug-Costs-Africa-s-2929307.php> accessed 29 November 2017.

64 Schneider, Helen, Peter Barron, and Sharon Fonn. 'The Promise and the Practice of Transformation in South Africa's Health System,' in Buhlungu, Shakela, John Daniel, Roger Southall, and Jessica Lutchman (eds.) *State of the Nation: South Africa 2007* (HSRC Press, 2007) 289–311.

65 Sell, Susan K. 'TRIPS and the Access to Medicines Campaign,' *Wisconsin International Law Journal* Vol. 20, No. 3 (2001) 481–522.

66 Sell, Susan K. 'Books, Drugs and Seeds: The Politics of Access,' Prepared for the Transatlantic Consumer Dialogue, "The Politics and Ideology of Intellectual Property" (Brussels, March 20–21, 2006) 1–80.

67 Seuba, Xavier. 'International Regulation of Pharmaceuticals: Codification by Means of Legal Transplantation,' *Information Note*, ICTSD Programme on Innovation, Technology and Intellectual Property' (July 2014) 3.

68 Shinn, Carolynne. 'The Right to the Highest Attainable Standard of Health: Public Health's Opportunity to Reframe Human Rights Debate in the United States,' *Health and Human Rights* Vol. 4, No. 1 (1999) 114–133, 119.

69 *Soobramoney v. Minister of Health, KwaZulu-Natal* (1997) (12) BCLR 1696 (CC).

70 South African Department of Health. 'National Drug Policy of South Africa 3,' (1996).

71 South African Department of Health. 'White Paper for the Transformation of the Health System in South Africa' (Notice 667 of 1997). <www.gov.za/sites/www.gov.za/files/17910_gen667_0.pdf> accessed on 29 November 2017.

72 Statistics South Africa. 'Income and Expenditure of Households 2005/2006: Analysis of Results (2008)' <www.statssa.gov.za/publications/Report-01-00-01/Report-01-00-012005.pdf> accessed on 29 November 2017.

73 Statistics South Africa. 'Income and Expenditure of Households 2010/2011 (2012)' <www.statssa.gov.za/publications/P0100/P01002011.pdf> accessed on 29 November 2017.

74 Statistics South Africa. 'Mid Year Population Estimates 2016,' (August 2016). <www.statssa.gov.za/publications/P0302/P03022016.pdf> accessed on 29 November 2017.

75 Sundaram, Jae. 'India's Trade-Related Aspects of Intellectual Property Rights Compliant Pharmaceutical Patent Laws: What Lessons for India and Other Developing Countries?' *Information & Communications Technology Law* Vol. 23, No. 1 (2014) 1–30.

76 Sundaram, Jae. 'Analysis of TRIPS Agreement and the Justification of International IP Rights Protection in the WTO's Multilateral Trading System, With Particular Reference to Pharmaceutical Patents,' *Information & Communications Technology Law* Vol. 24, No. 2 (2015) 1–43.

77 't Hoen, Ellen F.M. *The Global Politics of Pharmaceutical Monopoly Power: Drug Patents, Access, Innovation and the Application of WTO Declaration on TRIPS and Public Health* (AMB, Amsterdam, 2009).

78 Thompson, Leonard M. *A History of South Africa* (Yale University Press, 2014).

79 United Nations. 'The Millennium Development Goals Report 2013' <www.un.org/millenniumgoals/pdf/report-2013/mdg-report-2013-english.pdf> accessed 29 November 2017.

80 United Nations. 'Millennium Development Goals and Beyond 2015' <www.un.org/millenniumgoals/global.shtml> accessed 29 November 2017.

81 UNAIDS. *DOHA+10, TRIPS Flexibilities and Access to Antiretroviral Therapy: Lessons From the Past, Opportunities for the Future* (UNAIDS, Geneva, 2011) 6.

82 UNAIDS. 'Factsheet November 2016' (UNAIDS 2016) <www.unaids.org/sites/default/files/media_asset/UNAIDS_FactSheet_en.pdf> accessed 29 November 2017.

83 UNCTAD-ICTSD. *Resource Book on TRIPS and Development* (Cambridge University Press, 2005) 739.

84 Van Rensburg, H.C.J. 'National Health Systems: Structure, Types and Dynamics,' in van Rensburg, H.C.J. (ed.) *Health and Health Care in South Africa* (Van Schaik Publishers, 2004) 1–44.

85 WHO. 'The Selection and Use of Essential Medicines,' *WHO Technical Report Series 914* (2002) <http://apps.who.int/medicinedocs/pdf/s4875e/s4875e.pdf> accessed 29 November 2017.

86 WHO. Declaration on the TRIPS Agreement and Public Health, WT/MIN(01)/DEC/2, adopted on 20 November 2001 <www.wto.org/english/thewto_e/minist_e/min01_e/mindecl_trips_e.pdf> accessed 29 November 2017.

87 WIPO. *Guide to the Berne Convention for the Protection of Literary and Artistic Works (Paris Act, 1971)*, WIPO Publication No 615 (E), ISBN 92-805-0002-3 (1978) <www.wipo.int/edocs/pubdocs/en/copyright/615/wipo_pub_615.pdf> accessed 29 November 2017.

88 Weissman, Robert. 'Aids Drugs for Africa: Grassroots Pressure Overcomes U.S.-Industry "Full Court Press" to Block South Africa's Affordable Medicine Program,' *Multinational Monitor* Vol. 20, No. 9 (1999).

9 Kenya

Can generics still reach the needy?

Contents

1 Kenya: an introduction

Kenya is one of the SSA countries, geographically located in the eastern part of Africa, sharing its borders with Ethiopia, Somalia, South Sudan, Tanzania and Uganda. Kenya boasts a population of over 46 million people.[1] Kenya was under British rule between 1895 and 1963 as East Africa Protectorate and later as Kenya Colony (Hornsby, 2012),[2] gaining independence in December 1963 following a

1 The population comprises four ethnicities, *viz*., African, non-African (Asian), non-African (European), and non-African (Arab). Christianity is professed among the majority of the population (83 percent), with Islam coming second. It is noted that Kenya has experienced an increase in population growth since the mid-twentieth century because of its high birth rate and declining mortality rate. See Central Intelligence Agency, 'The World FactBook, Africa: Kenya.'

2 The author opines that Kenya was a colonial invention, and that its post-colonial history has been dominated by disruptive changes.

protracted and violent struggle (Anderson, 2005).[3] The biggest economy in East Africa and one of the key players in the SSA, Kenya is a founding member of the WTO[4] and took part in the key negotiations leading to the formation and launch of the WTO in 1995. As a developing country member, Kenya was obligated to implement the TRIPS Agreement in January 2000.[5]

As discussed in earlier chapters, several former colonies inherited the legal systems, including IP laws, from the European colonial powers. In Kenya's case, the English legal system was introduced during colonial rule and continues to form the basis of its legal structure and judicial system in the post-colonial era. IP laws were introduced in Kenya by the British colonial power with the objective of advancing and protecting imperialist interests, as at the time of its introduction the literacy levels of the natives were very low and local innovation was non-existent (Kameri-Mbote, 2005).[6] For instance, the extension of the amended UK Copyright Act 1956 to Kenya in 1963 was for the sole purpose of protecting the monopoly rights of British publishers in Kenya, and it introduced censorship to prevent the publication of material deemed to be anti-colonial (Chege, 1978).[7] Due to low literacy rates, there was an increased reliance on English language publications from the UK and the US, for educational and other purposes.

In post-independent Kenya, much of the population still lives in poor conditions. The 2016 figures released by The World Bank shows that 33.6 percent of Kenyans were living on US$1.90 in 2005 (World Bank, 2017). The economy has shown improvement, with a projected growth of 6 percent in 2017, which is attributed to a combination of factors, *viz.*, low oil prices (in 2015), good agricultural performance, supportive monetary policy and ongoing infrastructure investments (World Bank, 2016). The report also notes that the Kenyan economy is creating new jobs, albeit in the informal service sector and of a low productivity in nature. On the social front, Kenya has met some of the Millennium Development Goals (MDGs),[8] *viz.*, reduced child mortality, near universal

3 The Mau Mau Rebellion, which started in the 1950s, was defeated by the ruling British colonial power through a brutal campaign of military action and widespread detention of the Kikuyu clan. Later, the colonial power worked with the native Africans and white settlers to plan the country's transition.

4 Kenya was a founding member of the WHO and WIPO, and took part in some of the TRIPS negotiations and other processes leading to the formation of the WTO.

5 Being classified as a developing country put Kenya at a disadvantage. Kenya contemplated joining the LDC category in the past, as in the case of Zimbabwe, which devolved from being a developing country to a *de facto* LDC.

6 The East African Order in Council 1897 extended the application of the English Copyright Act 1842, the International Copyright Act of 1844, the Fine Arts Copyright Act of 1862 and the Copyright (Musical Composition) Act of 1888 to Kenya.

7 Chege also notes that though the Act of 1963 was superseded by chapter 130 of the Laws of Kenya 1966, there was very little change in substance of the law. The 1966 Act was later amended in 1975, 1982 and 1989.

8 The eight Millennium Development Goals are (1) eradication of extreme poverty, (2) achieving universal primary education, (3) promote gender equality and empower women, (4) reduce child mortality, (5) improve maternal health, (6) combat HIV/AIDS, malaria and other diseases, (7) ensure environmental sustainability and (8) develop a global partnership for development.

primary school enrolment and narrowing gender gaps in education (Republic of Kenya, 2014).

2 HIV/AIDS and other health care woes

The major diseases that afflict Kenya are HIV/AIDS, malaria, tuberculosis and other neglected diseases (Mey, 2013; UNIDO, 2010).[9] HIV/AIDS was first diagnosed in Kenya in 1984 (Kawewa, 2005),[10] and in the 1990s it became one of the major causes for mortality in the country. HIV/AIDS remains the chief health problem for the country, despite the fact that much progress has been made by the government in response to the situation brought out by the disease. According to the National AIDS Control Council (NACC), over 1.6 million people were living with the disease in 2013 (Ministry of Devolution and Planning, 2014). Apart from HIV/AIDS, malaria and tuberculosis are identified as posing major health problems. In 2006, an estimated 15 million malaria cases were reported in the country, and according to WHO figures from 2009, Kenya is ranked thirteenth in the list of twenty-two high-burden tuberculosis countries in the world.

Coming back to the chief health concern, in 1999, the adult HIV prevalence was estimated to be over 10 percent, and the Kenyan government in response declared HIV/AIDS a national disaster. These rates were to come down in 2005 to 6.7 percent (WHO, 2005). According to figures presented by UNAIDS, Kenya has the joint fourth-largest HIV epidemic in the world, alongside Mozambique and Uganda (UNAIDS, 2016). These figures are again based on the number of people living with HIV, which was 1.5 million in 2015. Roughly 36,000 people died from AIDS-related illnesses in the same year, which is less than the figure of 51,000 who died in 2010. Statistics from 2008–2009 reveal that about 1.2 million Kenyan children were orphaned by the disease (KNBS and ICF Macro, 2010). According to the NACC, the incidence of HIV peaked at 10.5 percent in 1996 and fell to 5.9 percent by 2014, which was largely due to a rapid scaling up of the treatment and care for HIV patients (NACC, 2014).

The HIV epidemic is referred to as 'generalised' in Kenya, as it affects all sections of the population – children, young adults, adults, women and men. However, recent studies have indicated that the trend has changed, as it is more concentrated in some key populations that are more vulnerable to HIV transmission (NACC, 2014).[11] Pharmaceutical services are provided in the context of the Kenya Pharmaceutical Policy (KNPP); as the Kenyan pharmaceutical sector is complex and multi-faceted, and several factors influence access to essential

9 Based on outpatient data from 2008, Kenyan demand for essential medicines falls under ten disease categories, representing an average of 79.2 percent of all disease incidents causing morbidity. Data from the same year also showed that malaria and respiratory diseases accounted for more than 57 percent of outpatient morbidity.

10 According to Kawewa, the first HIV/AIDS infection occurred in 1978 in the communities living around Lake Victoria.

11 Figures presented by NACC also indicate that an estimated 30 percent of the new infections in Kenya are among individuals from key populations.

medicines. The state's response to the HIV/AIDS crisis was to scale up the treatment and care in over the last decade. Access to ARVs have improved from as low as 11,000 persons in 2003, to 138,000 in 2007 and 250,000 by March 2009 (UNIDO, 2010).

3 IP legislative framework: pre- and post-TRIPS era

As mentioned earlier, Kenya's IP laws were an extension of the British colonial past, and continued to apply even after independence, as the substance of the laws did not change much (Kameri-Mbote, 2005). Although the laws introduced by Britain were changed in 1975, 1982 and 1989, the most radical of changes was to take place only in 2001 with the introduction of the Industrial Property Act. In 1973, the African Regional Intellectual Property Organisation (ARIPO) was created by Anglophile African countries, of which Kenya is a founding member.[12] ARIPO, while entrusted with administering the member states' IP law needs, also strongly advocated that its members adopt independent IP systems (Mey, 2013).

ARIPO's objectives contained in Article 3 of the Lusaka Agreement are the harmonisation and development of industrial property laws to suit the needs of its member states and to steer them towards technological, economic and industrial development.[13] The objectives reflected the fact that the member states of ARIPO were still dependent on an IP legal format largely based on the British system, which was more beneficial to the colonial masters, and that there was a need to move away from the colonial past into a model more suitable to the member states and their interests. The revised Lusaka Agreement enlarges the functions to be discharged by ARIPO on behalf of its member states. Most notably, under section 2.1 of the Harare Protocol (to which Kenya is a signatory), the ARIPO office can process, grant or register patents and industrial designs on behalf of the states that are party to the Protocol (Antons, Blakeney, and Heath, 2004, 238).

3.1 *The Industrial Property Act 1989*

Following the recommendations from ARIPO to its member states to review their inherited IP laws, Kenya embarked on a path of reform of its own IP laws to suit the needs of local innovators and researchers, with the economic and social needs of its own people in mind (Mey, 2013). By the mid-1980s, the HIV/AIDS

12 ARIPO is one of the sub-regional IP organisation in SSA. The other sub-regional IP organisations comprise Francophile nations, *viz.*, *Organisation Africaine de la Propriété Intellectuelle* (OAPI). The OAPI member states share the same body of IP laws as provided for in the Bangui Agreement Relating to the Creation of an African Intellectual Property Organization of 1977. ARIPO's Protocols, in contrast, do not have direct application in member states, and each member state has its own national IP framework.

13 WIPO Treaty 1976.

pandemic had peaked and there arose an urgent need to have in place, in the domestic patent law framework, stronger safeguards for protecting public health and for improving access to essential medicines (Mey, 2013). In short, a new regime with an emphasis on local needs, with a transparent evaluation of patent applications that made it possible to contest the validity of any patent rights, was desired. Kenya enacted its Industrial Property Act 1989 (IPA, 1989) to address the above concerns.

The IPA 1989 was aimed at providing a cost-effective, flexible and predictable framework needed for obtaining, managing, protecting and enforcing various forms of IP rights in Kenya and abroad. According to the lawmakers, the framework was intended to facilitate the growth of IP-related technology transfer; incentivise R&D to stimulate local research and innovation; and diffuse knowledge leading to economic growth (Nyakundi and Mnjama, 2007). The IPA 1989, the first post-independent IP legislation, repealed the Patent Registration Act, created the Kenya Industrial Property Office (KIPO) and at the same time provided for the establishment of the Industrial Property Tribunal (IPT) (Dutfield, 2004).[14] After a series of amendments, the IPA 1989, was eventually repealed and replaced by the IPA 2001. The IPA 2001 was TRIPS compliant and brought about changes to the existing laws, including confirming the IPT's mandate to hear all IP-related disputes arising from the implementation of the IPA 2001 and changing KIPO's name to the Kenya Industrial Property Institute (KIPI).

3.2 *The Industrial Property Act 2001*

In the post-TRIPS era, Kenya was required to introduce a TRIPS-compliant domestic IP legislation as per its commitment to the WTO. The combined effect of the heavy burden of dealing with a large disease-ridden society with a weak health care system and pockets of its population living in abject poverty was not going to make the task easier. To implement a TRIPS-compliant IP legislation would threaten the measures put in place to address the problem of access to affordable medicines and health care, as the price of essential medicines and ARVs would sharply increase. In 2001, as a developing country member of the WTO, Kenya introduced TRIPS-compliant domestic IP legislation through the Industrial Property Act 2001. Taking advantage of the flexibilities available for developing countries under the Agreement, Kenya introduced provisions in an expansive manner to allow for access to essential medicines, including the importation of generic medicines (Sihanya, 2005). Harrington notes that the passage of the legislation can also be considered the first phase in the struggle over access to

14 See sections 2 and 118 of the IPA, 1989 (repealed), and now sections 2 and 113 of the IPA, 2001. The KIPO's duties, as identified, included scrutinising applications for and grant industrial property rights, and administering IP rights, promoting creativity, inventiveness and innovation among local actors. Apart from the above, the KIPO was also charged with the task of training and equipping the public with industrial property information for technological and economic development.

essential medicines (Harrington, 2014), while some others have opined that the Industrial Property Act 2001, along with the TRIPS Agreement, was a stumbling block in the pursuit of access to affordable medicines (Sihanya, 2005).

In the lead-up to the passing of IPA 2001, a coalition of local and international NGOs working in Kenya with people affected by HIV/AIDS and other medical organisations had formed the Kenya Coalition for Access to Essential Medicines.[15] The Coalition sought to convince the legislators to use flexibilities contained in the TRIPS Agreement to factor in provisions to ensure better access to affordable medicines and to not offer any patent protection in excess of the TRIPS requirements (Lewis-Lettington and Musungu, 2000). The Coalition's efforts were supported by the KIPI, the key administrators from the Ministry of Trade, and importantly Minister of Trade Nicholas Biwott, who was in turn a close ally of then President Moi.[16] The Coalition carried out a detailed legal analysis of the draft bill, prior to the same being debated before Parliament, and brought forth its own proposals to safeguard access to medicines and the interest of the public.[17] As the human right to health was not recognised by the Kenyan Constitution that was in force at that time, the Coalition's arguments/proposals were not premised on human right to health but on starker political messages through members of Parliament who were sympathetic and supportive of the Coalition's cause (Lewis-Lettington and Munyi, 2004).

The executives of TNPCs from developed countries lobbied and exerted pressure on the Kenyan government to weaken the IP bill that was being debated (Ford, 2004; Sihanya, 2005). The then health minister Sam Ongeri, in an interview with the BBC, expressed the opinion that brand-name drugs protected by 'unrealistic' laws were 'unaffordable'.[18] The move by Kenya to introduce the IPA 2001 came shortly after TNPCs dropped court action in South Africa against the government of South Africa.[19] Around the time the bill was being debated, generics companies were selling ARV combinations to Cameroon and Nigeria for as little as $350 per patient per year, while, in contrast, TNPCs were selling their branded products in Kenya for as high as $1,620 per patient per year to a limited number of hospitals (Ford, 2004). The bill was passed in June 2001 with the stated objective of promoting inventive and innovative endeavours and facilitating technology transfer and acquisition; the regulation and grant of patents; industrial designs; utility models and the dissemination of IP-related information.

15 The Coalition counted amongst its members 15 NGOs and medical organisations, including Kenya Treatment Action Movement, Kenya Medical Association, Action Aid, Médecins Sans Frontières, Nyumbani, The Association of People Living With Aids, Women Fighting Aids in Kenya, Care International and Health Action International. See also Anon, 'Lobby Launches AIDS Bill Drive,' *Daily Nation* (30 May 2001).

16 Interview with Robert Lewis-Lettington, Legal Consultant (9 May 2012), as cited by Harrington 2014.

17 *Ibid.*

18 Anon. 'Kenya Readies Aids Drugs Law,' *BBC News* (22 April 2001) <http://news.bbc.co.uk/1/hi/world/africa/1291200.stm> accessed 29 November 2017.

19 See chapter 8 for a discussion on the South Africa court action.

With a clear focus on public health, the Act included provisions on government use,[20] compulsory licencing[21] and the Bolar exception[22] and contained such provisions to protect interests that are crucial for the development of new and improved medicines.[23]

Section 2 of the IPA 2001, unlike its predecessor,[24] refines and expands on the definition of invention as follows:

> A new and useful art (whether producing a physical effect or not), process, machine, manufacture or composition of matter which is not obvious, or any new and useful improvement thereof which is not obvious, capable of being used or applied in trade or industry and includes an alleged invention.

The remit of section 2 is further enhanced by sections 21 and 22 of the IPA 2001. Section 21, contained in Part III (Patentability), presents the meaning of 'invention' as a solution to a specific problem in the field of technology, and may be, or may relate to, a product or a process. It provides further guidance and clarity by stating what is not considered a discovery.[25] Part III also contains section 22, which provides that an invention is patentable provided it can meet the three-part test of being novel, involving an inventive step and having either industrial applicability or a new use (Mey, 2013).[26] In section 2, the IPA 2001 uses the phrase 'IP rights' instead of 'industrial property right', with respect to innovation, to include utility models, technovation models, industrial designs and other non-patentable creations of improvements.[27] Although yet to be fully utilised in Kenya, it can still be considered a potent tool for generic manufacturers (Lewis-Lettington and Munyi, 2004). Section 3 of the IPA 2001 establishes

20 See section 80, Industrial Property Act 2001.

21 See sections 76–78, Industrial Property Act 2001.

22 See section 54(2), Industrial Property Act 2001.

23 See sections 54 and 55, Industrial Property Act 2001, which strengthen the patent holders' rights as articulated in Article 28 of the TRIPS Agreement.

24 Section 7 of the Industrial Property Act 1989 (repealed) merely provided that 'an invention is patentable if it is new, involves an inventive step and is industrially applicable'.

25 Section 21(3) identifies the following as not falling within the meaning of inventions and will not be accorded patent protection: discoveries, scientific theories and mathematical methods, schemes, rules or methods for doing business, performing purely mental acts or playing games, methods for treatment of the human or animal body by surgery or therapy, as well as diagnostic methods practised in relation thereto, except products for use in any such methods, mere presentation of information, and public health–related methods of use or uses of any molecule or other substance whatsoever used for the prevention or treatment of any disease which the Minister responsible for matters relating to health may designate as a serious health hazard or as a life-threatening disease. In short, the section presents a non-inclusive checklist of inventions that are excluded from the ambit of patentability, which is in compliance with Article 1 and paragraphs 2 and 3 of Article 27 of the TRIPS Agreement.

26 Mey argues that the definition of the term 'invention' as found in IPA 2001 is not overreaching but reflects the commonly accepted interpretation of the term, especially in common law countries, and cites a number of court decisions from UK and Australia to support the arguments.

27 See section 2, Industrial Property Act 2001.

and empowers the authority of KIPI to administer, protect and enforce IP rights in Kenya and to participate in global efforts to improve access to essential medicines (Mey, 2013).

Section 54 of the IPA 2001 gives patent holders the right to exclude others from making, using, selling or importing the patented object and from using a patented process, or making, using, selling or importing the product of a patented process.[28] Under the TRIPS-compliant Act, the protection is granted for a period of twenty years from the date of filing of the patent application.[29] As mentioned earlier, the Act provides for the grant of compulsory licence under section 58(5) for 'reasons of public interest or based on interdependence of patents and by the provisions on State exploitation of patented inventions'.[30] Under the said provisions, any person can apply for a compulsory licence after a lapse of four years from the date of filing, or three years from the grant of the patent, whichever period is longer, with a view to exploit the invention on the grounds that the market is not being supplied on reasonable terms in Kenya.[31] The scheme envisaged requires that the applicant seeking a grant of compulsory licence show that he or she has been unable to attain a voluntary licence on reasonable commercial terms from the owner of the patent.[32] But, in the event of a 'national emergency or other circumstances of extreme urgency', the above requirement is waived, while the owner of the patent is notified of the grant of such compulsory licence.[33]

The question that is still to be answered is how a 'national emergency' will be designated, and what constitutes an 'other circumstance of extreme urgency' under section 74(2) of the Act (Lewis-Lettington and Munyi, 2004).[34] Part XI of the Act, which deals with the 'exploitation of patented inventions', however, authorises the government, upon application, to grant permission for the exploitation of the protected invention by the government or a designated third party with adequate compensation being paid to the patent holder.[35] The Act further authorises the concerned government minister to import, manufacture or supply, or utilise a patented substance, without notice to the patent holder, and without requiring payment of any compensation to the owner of the patent.[36]

Under the erstwhile regime of IPA 1989, branded drugs marketed elsewhere in the world more cheaply by the patent holder could not be imported and sold

28 Section 54(1), Industrial Property Act 2001.
29 Section 60, Industrial Property Act 2001.
30 Section 58(5), Industrial Property Act 2001.
31 Section 72(1), Industrial Property Act 2001.
32 Section 74(1), Industrial Property Act 2001.
33 Section 74(2), Industrial Property Act 2001.
34 See also O'Carroll, Sorcha. 'Importing Indian Generic Drugs Following TRIPS: Case Studies from Zambia and Kenya,' *Unpublished Paper* (2005), where the author argues that (i) suspension of payment provision contained in section 74(2) of the Act is unlikely to be useful for the purposes of importing patented drugs under a compulsory licence and (ii) when applied to drugs manufactured domestically, the provision would violate TRIPS if it denied adequate remuneration to patent holders with respect to compulsory licences granted under Article 31.
35 Section 80(1), Industrial Property Act 2001.
36 Section 80.1A and 80.1B, Industrial Property Act 2001.

at a lower price in Kenya without the consent of the patent holder (Harrington, 2014). Article 6 of the TRIPS Agreement does not require a particular patent exhaustion regime to be in place in the domestic law. Taking advantage of the position, Kenya introduced an international regime of exhaustion under section 58(2).[37] The Coalition was to play an important role in the introduction of the exhaustion provision into the IPA 2001. The IPA 2001 came into force on 1 May 2002, and in June 2002, an amendment was made to section 58(2) to introduce the qualification that the products were originally marketed 'by the owner of the patent, or with his express consent' (Lewis-Lettington and Munyi, 2004). The amendment had the effect of allowing only the parallel import of branded products, and thereby blocking the planned import of generics from India by the activists (Lewis-Lettington and Munyi, 2004).[38] As the amendment was contrary to Kenyan Parliamentary rule, the Kenyan Parliament voted to restore the original version of section 58(2) of IPA 2001 (Lewis-Lettington and Munyi, 2004).[39]

While on the one hand the IPA 2001 incorporates provisions to ensure better access to essential medicines, it also ensures the position of the rights holder in line with the objectives of the TRIPS Agreement, besides also recognising and encouraging innovation through the introduction of appropriate provisions.[40] Keeping in line with the extended protection offered under the TRIPS Agreement, section 60 of the IPA 2001 affords a uniform patent term protection of twenty years for all categories of inventions. The WTO members, on 6 December 2005, approved changes to the TRIPS Agreement, making permanent a decision on patents and public health originally adopted in 2003 (WTO, 2005). This amendment was later formally built into the TRIPS Agreement after acceptance of the Protocol amending the Agreement by two-thirds of the WTO's members (Sundaram, 2015). On 15 July 2015, Kenya signed the Protocol to amend the TRIPS Agreement (WTO, 2017).

4 Kenya: the pharmaceutical hub of EAC

Kenya has been recognised as the East African hub for pharmaceutical production and import/distribution into the region (Khan, 2015). It is the largest producer of pharmaceutical products in the Common Market for Eastern and Southern Africa (COMESA), and has shown progressive development besides

37 Section 58(2), Industrial Property Act 2001, reads as follows: 'The rights under the patent shall not extend to acts in respect of articles which have been put on the market in Kenya or in any other country or imported into Kenya.'

38 The authors note that the amendment was passed in haste during a late-night session of Parliament, as part of an omnibus bill to amend diverse pieces of legislation in the Statute Law (Miscellaneous Amendments) Act, 2002.

39 The authors also note that the amendment was contrary to the Kenyan Parliamentary rule that no amendments should be permitted to any Act prior to six months after its entry into force, and that the Minister for Trade and Industry, KIPI and the Attorney General's Chambers all stating that they were not the source of the amendment.

40 Section 110, Industrial Property Act 2001 shifts the burden of proof in case of infringement of patent rights from the owner of a patent to the infringer as required by Article 34 of TRIPS.

making significant progress in fighting malaria, tuberculosis, cholera, HIV/AIDS and other communicable diseases (Export Processing Zones Authority, 2005). It is also noted that 50 percent of the region's pharmaceutical products come from Kenya (Kalunda, Nduku, and Kabiru, 2012). Kenya's pharmaceutical sector has also greatly benefited from licencing agreements with multinational corporations (Khan, 2015). Kenya is forecast to have a compound annual growth rate (CAGR) of 17 percent through 2016–2017, with public-private partnerships (PPPs) shaping the healthcare sector of the East African Community (Odongo, 2011; EAC, 2017; Gastorn and Masinde, 2017).[41] The expansion of the EAC block of countries (from three to five) has seen Kenya benefit from the supply of pharmaceuticals to a larger market. Kenya's pharmaceutical imports in 2008 were valued at US$240 million (UNIDO, 2010), and the country was the third largest importer of generic medicines from India in the same year, valued at US$70 million (Mey, 2010).

The continued expansion of the EAC and an increased participation in its affairs augurs well for Kenya. Currently, Kenya exports its pharmaceutical products to Tanzania, Uganda, Democratic Republic of Congo, Rwanda, Burundi, the Comoros, Ethiopia and Malawi, among other destinations. A UNIDO survey also revealed that local manufacture of pharmaceuticals accounted only for a small share of donor-funded drug procurement in SSA, as it requires WHO prequalification in donor sourcing, which has not been achieved by local manufacturers (UNIDO, 2010).

Despite being the key supplier of pharmaceutical products in the EAC, the Kenyan health care system, as in the case of South Africa, suffers from inequalities. The country does not have a compulsory health insurance mechanism for the poor, which means that most of the population will have to pay out of their pockets for any health care bills (Mey, 2013).[42] There is a high demand for pharmaceutical products in Kenya, which is derived from a high disease incidence. Abject poverty prevailing in sections of the Kenyan community (UNICEF, 2013)[43] does not allow for access to branded medicine. Statistics produced by WHO in 2013 appear to show that 59 percent of HIV-infected individuals and 37 percent of infected pregnant women did not receive any ARV treatment (WHO, 2015). Kenya's spending on essential medicines is reliant on the US

41 Although founded in 1967 by Kenya, Uganda and Tanzania, the East African Community (EAC) collapsed in 1977 and was recreated by the same three states in 1999. The membership expanded to five countries in 2007, with the accession of Rwanda and Burundi. EAC's membership was further expanded in 2016, when the Republic of South Sudan became the sixth member. The EAC is currently home to 150 million citizens, with a combined gross domestic product of US$146 billion. In July 2010, the EAC created a common market in the region, with Kenya, Uganda, Tanzania, Rwanda and Burundi as members. The markets outlined in the Protocol's Articles 4, 16 and 24 identify the sustenance of economic growth and development of the member states through the free flow of goods (including medicines), services, capital and people across the five countries.

42 Figures from Central Bank of Kenya released in 2010 show that only 1.3 million of the total population had some form of health insurance cover.

43 Over 20 percent of Kenya's population live on under $1.25 per day.

President's Emergency Plan for AIDS Relief (PEPFASR) (UNICEF, 2013) and to some extent on the Global Fund to Fight AIDS, Tuberculosis and Malaria (GFATM) (UNIDO, 2010; Osewe, Nkrumah, and Sackey, 2008).

As discussed earlier, the IPA 2001 substantially incorporated the flexibilities afforded under the TRIPS Agreement. But how much of it was utilised to access affordable medicines is still to be determined. Although legally provided for under the IPA 2001, Kenya has not issued a compulsory licence with regards to pharmaceutical patents (Osewe, Nkrumah, and Sackey, 2008). Although orientation towards local manufacturing of pharmaceutical production is well captured in the policies of the government, the strategy adopted is one of voluntary licencing. GlaxoSmithKline (GSK) and Boehringer Ingelheim (BI), had controlled the ARV markets in Kenya and relied on importation of their branded products for sale, as they had no local manufacturing facilities. Between 1995 and 2003, six Kenyan generic manufacturers attempted to negotiate voluntary licences with the originator companies GSK and BI to locally produce the first-line ARVs zidovudine, lamivudine and nevirapine. The conditions set by both GSK and BI made local manufacturing impracticable (Osewe, Nkrumah, and Sackey, 2008).

After successfully winning a government tender to produce first-line ARVs, Cosmos Pharmaceuticals in 2004 announced its intention to start producing the generic versions of the frontline ARVs for the EAC market.[44] As the Ministry of Trade and Industry refused to issue a compulsory licence (Avafia, 2015), discussions took place between Cosmos and GSK, resulting in a licencing agreement between the parties in September 2004 for the local production of zidovudine, lamivudine and the combination of the two, combivir by Cosmos.[45] The local production of ARVs by Cosmos was rendered untenable, as GSK reduced its prices of the ARVs in Kenya. Avafia notes that Cosmos did not challenge the action of GSK, as it would not have constituted a ground for anti-competitive behaviour under applicable legislation in Kenya (Avafia, 2015).[46] Nevertheless, consumers benefited from the lower ARV prices by GSK (Avafia, Berger, and Hartzenberg, 2006). In short, the TRIPS flexibilities incorporated into the IPA 2001 were being tested but were not yielding the desired results, and thereby defeating the objectives. The legal landscape was to be further distorted by the government with the introduction of another legislation which seriously undermined the TRIPS flexibilities incorporated in the IPA 2001.

44 Anon. 'Kenyan Firm to Make AIDS Drugs,' *BBC News* (22 September 2004).

45 In 2007, Boehringer Ingelheim declared that it would not seek to enforce its patents for nevirapine in 70 countries, including countries classified by the World Bank as Low Income Countries (LICs), those classified by the UN as LDCs, and all countries in Africa regardless of their classification as a developing country or Middle Income Country. The policy was extended to a second-line ARV, tipranavir, for which Bayer is the patent holder.

46 Avafia notes that the case, from the perspective of increasing treatment access, illustrates how the adoption and potential use of public health–related TRIPS flexibilities can lead to reduced treatment costs, even if it does not always result in increased local pharmaceutical production.

5 The right to life: Anti-Counterfeit Act 2008, the new constitution and *Patricia Asero Ochieng & 2 Others v. Attorney General & Another* [2012]

While the IPA 2001 substantially incorporated the TRIPS flexibilities into the domestic IP legislation, the implementation of such flexibilities was hindered with the passing of the Anti-Counterfeit Act 2008 (ACA). Bowing down to the relentless campaign carried out by manufacturers for a better and more effective enforcement of IPRs, the Kenyan government took up for debate the Anti-Counterfeit Bill. The reasons for such a campaign were due to weak civil remedies and insufficient criminal penalties, amongst others (Sihanya, 2005). There was a general dissatisfaction with the Pharmacy and Poisons Board (PPB), as it was felt that it did not have stringent oversight of parallel importation, which allowed for counterfeit products, including drugs, to enter the market (Mbogo, 2008). During the legislative process, the Kenyan Association of Manufacturers (KAM), with a strong membership of over 700 manufacturers, played a significant role in the drafting of the bill and also influencing the outcome of the debate (Harrington, 2014).[47] The civil society groups were concerned that the Anti-Counterfeit Bill, if passed into law, would introduce a TRIPS-plus regime and undo any benefits to access to medicines brought into the legal framework by IPA 2001.

KAM's lobbyists presented the Anti-Counterfeit Bill as a facilitator to promote economic growth of the nation and to enforce IP rights in Kenya to attract foreign direct investment (FDI) into the country. As KAM enjoyed a long-running close relation with the Ministry of Trade (Mbatiah, 2010), it was also able to help frame the issues for debate and retain an upper hand through its lobby. Although civil society groups such as Health Action International (HAI) Africa and Kenya Treatment Action Movement were opposed to the bill, they did not have the resources that KAM had at its disposal. KAM, while acknowledging the need for low-cost medicines, argued that counterfeiting itself was a threat to the health of ordinary Kenyans (Harrington, 2014).[48] Not surprisingly, a number of pharmaceutical members took the lead within KAM in pushing for much greater IP enforcement (Mbatiah, 2010). It became an uphill task for the activists to argue their principal point that if the Anti-Counterfeit Bill were passed into law, it would make access to generic medicines difficult and could also be easily misused by corporate interests, as it did not distinguish sub-standard medicines from counterfeit medicines.

5.1 *The Anti-Counterfeit Act 2008*

The Anti-Counterfeit Act (ACA) was passed on 10 December 2008 and came into effect on 7 July 2009. Intense lobbying from industry associations preceded

47 KAM established an Anti-Counterfeit and Illicit Trade Committee and campaigned and lobbied vigorously throughout 2008. Interestingly, the membership of KAM comprises both national and international pharmaceutical industrial entities.

48 Harrington argues that the position adopted by KAM was the same ideological ground occupied by activists.

the Act's implementation (Wadhams, 2009).[49] It was well supported by KAM, the Pharmaceutical Society of Kenya Private Sector Alliance (KEPSA), the American Chamber of Commerce of Kenya (ACCK) and the World Customs Organisation's Regional Intelligence Liaison Office for Eastern and Southern Africa. It is to be emphasised here that the origins of the ACA are to be found in the Anti-Counterfeit Trade Agreement (ACTA), which was negotiated behind closed doors, with a strong TRIPS-plus agenda (MSF, 2012).[50] Section 2 of the ACA defined 'counterfeiting' as the manufacture, packaging, re-packaging or labelling of goods that are identical to, substantially similar to or calculated to be confused with goods subject to an IP right.[51] The ACA under section 3 established the Anti-Counterfeit Agency, which is tasked *inter alia* to 'combat counterfeiting, trade and other dealings in counterfeit goods in Kenya in accordance with this Act',[52] and to 'perform any other duty that may directly or indirectly contribute to the attainment'[53] of its function. Under section 32, it is an offence to possess, manufacture, sell, distribute, import, export or tranship counterfeit goods.[54]

The inspection powers of the Anti-Counterfeiting Agency, especially the powers contained under sections 22 and 23, drew much attention. Under section 6, the management of the Agency is vested in a board, with section 22 empowering the board to 'appoint such number of inspectors as it may consider appropriate'. ACA also vests the inspectors functioning under the Act with broad powers to be used at any reasonable time and for a reasonable cause; to enter and search suspected premises and vehicles; seize and detain goods suspected to be counterfeit; and arrest, without warrant, any person suspected to have committed an offence under the ACA.[55] Further, the Act also envisaged harsh penalties of a five-year imprisonment and fine for a first-time offence,[56] and fifteen years for a second-time offence,[57] if found guilty. Critics viewed the above provisions as ambiguous, arbitrary, prone to be misinterpreted or abused, and potentially detrimental to the government's efforts to ensure access to essential medicines. Besides civil society members and human rights advocates, Indian generics manufacturers too joined

49 The lobby was well supported by some from the pharmaceutical industry, including GlaxoSmithKline.

50 ACTA was promoted as a multilateral treaty to establish international standards for IP rights enforcement, and it sought to establish an international legal framework to target counterfeit goods, generic medicines and copyright infringement. It also sought to create a governing body, similar to the WTO, to oversee the implementation of the above objectives. Although the agreement was signed in October 2011 by Australia, Canada, Japan, Morocco, New Zealand, Singapore, South Korea, the US, Mexico and twenty-two Member States of the EU, it has yet to enter into force. The EU Parliament, on 4 July 2012, overwhelmingly rejected the agreement. Most interestingly, none from SSA either participated in the negotiations, or signed the ACTA.

51 Section 2, Anti-Counterfeit Act 2008.

52 Section 5(b), Anti-Counterfeit Act 2008.

53 Section 5(f), Anti-Counterfeit Act 2008.

54 Section 32, Anti-Counterfeit Act 2008.

55 Section 23, Anti-Counterfeit Act 2008.

56 Section 35(1), Anti-Counterfeit Act 2008.

57 Section 35(2), Anti-Counterfeit Act 2008.

the chorus of opposition to ACA (Kimani, 2009; Unnikrishnan, 2010), as they feared the generics they supplied to Kenya could be confused for 'counterfeit' medicine. Some commentators have even opined that ACA was more TRIPS-plus, as it offered wider protection to IP rights holders than what was on offer under the TRIPS Agreement (Von Braun and Munyi, 2010) and imposed criminal penalties for patent infringement (Harrington, 2014).

5.2 Patricia Asero Ochieng & 2 Others v. Attorney General & Another, *and the 'right to health' under the new constitution*

The constitutional validity of the ACA was challenged shortly after it came into force in July 2009. Three claimants who had been living with HIV/AIDS and receiving ARVs, supplied through the Kenyan government's programme and Médecins Sans Frontières (MSF), approached the court, on the premise that the provisions of ACA, especially the definitions, enforcement powers and criminal penalties, threatened their right to life guaranteed under sections 70 and 71 of the Kenyan Constitution, which was in force then.[58] An interim order was made by Justice Rosalyn Wendoh in April 2010, suspending the operation of ACA as regards the importation of generic medicine, as there was a real threat the Act would be used to seize generics and thereby deprive the petitioners from accessing ARVs, leading to the risk of irreparable harm.

During the pendency of the case in August 2010, the Kenyan Parliament enacted a revised constitution, which contained much wider and enforceable social and economic rights. Briefly, Article 43(1)(a) of the new constitution enshrines the right to health (including reproductive health care), while Article 53(1)(c) secures the right to health for children, Article 46(1)(c) obligates the government to protect the health of consumers in Kenya, and Article 2(4) clearly lays down that any laws that are inconsistent to its provisions are void to that extent.[59] Most importantly, the Sixth Schedule of the new constitution brought the entire 2010 Constitution into force with immediate effect, after promulgation. As a result, the pleadings in the above case came to be amended to include the plea that the provisions of the ACA seriously threatened their rights to life, dignity and health, as protected under the new constitution. Later, the AIDS Law Project (ALP) joined the petitioners as an interested party to the court action (Ongoya, 2010; Harrington, 2014).[60] The court also appointed Anand Grover,

58 One of the litigants was a 5-year-old, who was infected and receiving ARV treatment.

59 Article 2(4), reads as follows: 'Any law, including customary law, that is inconsistent with this Constitution is void to the extent of the inconsistency, and any act or omission in contravention of this Constitution is invalid.'

60 Only in the decade before the drafting of the new constitution did the Kenyan courts began to consider applications on the grounds of interested parties. Harrington (2014) also notes that the new constitution entrenched broad rules of standing for interested parties, such as the Kenya AIDS Law Project, in Article 2(2)(c).

then UN Special Rapporteur on the Right of Everyone to Highest Attainable Standard of Physical and Mental Health, as *amicus curiae* to the proceedings.[61]

Apart from the above provisions of the new constitution, the HIV and AIDS Prevention and Control Act (HAPCA) guarantees the right to health care services, which includes the right of access to medicines for individuals infected/living with HIV and AIDS.[62] The case revolved around the key legal issue of the constitutionality of the ACA, in which the petitioners had averred that the provisions of the ACA, and in particular sections 2, 32 and 34, as being unconstitutional. The premise of the argument was that if given effect to, the provisions of ACA would deny the petitioners access to essential medicines, thereby infringing their constitutional right to life, health and dignity as contained in Articles 26(1), 28 and 43(1), besides infringing the right to basic health care for children contained in Article 53. Interestingly, the issues raised by the petitioners in the case before the court were also raised as genuine concerns during the debate before the Kenyan Parliament by the civil society organisations who opposed the ACA bill (Nyachae and Ogendi, 2015).

The case was eventually heard and decided in April 2012, almost after three years from the date of filing, with the long delay to some degree attributable to Kenya's transition from its old constitution to the new constitution. It is not an exaggeration to state that the new constitution could not have come at a better time for the petitioners and other interested parties, as the provisions of the new constitution helped them immensely in their legal challenge of the ACA. It was the petitioners' case that their economic conditions did not permit them the luxury of accessing branded drugs for their treatment, and they were reliant on free medicines distributed by the government with partners such as MSF; that any disruption to the supply of cheaper generics would deprive them of their right to enjoy the highest attainable standard of health; that the enforcement of ACA would lead to the denial of essential medicines and the guarantees contained in the HAPCA; and that the non-exemption of generics from the operation of ACA imposed an heavy burden on consumers of generics to prove they were not counterfeit. It was also the case of the petitioners that section 2 of ACA was too widely drafted and allowed for extra-territorial enforcement of IP rights.

The ALP for their part pleaded that ACA violated the right to equality for those living with HIV to enjoy a right to life, health and dignity; that ACA as laid out violated the right to family life as guaranteed under Article 45(1) of the Constitution; and that ACA posed a major threat to the right of a child to basic health care as guaranteed under Article 53(2) of the Constitution. Anand Grover, the *amicus curiae* in the matter, was to submit an elaborate brief detailing the position of law, more in support of the petitioners' plea. The *amicus curiae* took the position that the failure to exempt generic medicines from the ambit of ACA would affect the manufacture, sale and distribution of generic equivalent

61 Anand Grover appeared as *amicus curiae* under Article 22(3)(e) of the Kenyan Constitution.

62 Section 19, HIV and AIDS Prevention and Control Act 2006. Likewise, section 9 of the Children's Act 2006 guarantees the right to health of children under the age of 18 years in Kenya.

of patented medicines; that conflating generics with counterfeit medicines would result in legitimate generics being confiscated, leading to a spike in the prices of medicines in Kenya and resulting in limited access to essential medicines; and that such a result would qualify as a violation of the constitutional and international right to health.[63] In contrast, the respondents took the position that section 2 of ACA did not target generics, and no case was made to question the definition of 'counterfeit' as it was clear and unambiguous; that there were sufficient safeguards contained in the Act as regards access to generics; that ACA was primarily aimed at protecting the consumers from using counterfeit products; and that the Act was indeed an enabler of human rights.

5.3 The judgment and findings

After considering the arguments of the parties concerned, and as well as the brief of the *amicus curiae*, Lady Justice Mumbi Ngugi proceeded to decide the case in favour of the petitioners. While deciding the case, the court relied considerably on international law, especially while dealing with the issue of right to health. Until the passing of the new constitution, Kenya was a dualist state, requiring all international law to be implemented domestically through legislative enactment (Viljoen, 2012; Ambani, 2010).[64] The 2010 Constitution, however, under Article 2(6), envisaged the direct application of international law as contained in ratified treaties into the Kenyan domestic legal system, bringing about a significant change (Ambani, 2010).[65] The new constitution facilitated the transition of Kenya from a 'dualist' to a 'monist' state, and immediately witnessed the application of the principles to the case under discussion. The court in the instant case treated Article 2(6) to mean that the court was 'bound by the Constitution to have regard to these treaties' (Nyachae and Ogendi, 2015).[66]

63 See Nyachae and Ogendi (2015) for a discussion of the pleadings in the case.

64 The Independence Constitution, from 1963, did not provide for direct application of international law in the Kenyan legal system. Kenya, like most other common law countries (former colonies of Britain), had adopted a dualist approach to international law. Under the dualist approach, based on the doctrine of transformation, international law could only be applicable in the domestic legal system if it had been 'domesticated' by parliamentary legislation. Ambani (2010) makes the point that while Kenya's decision to adopt the dualist approach may in itself not be retrogressive, its practice led to the relegation of the often fairly progressive international human rights instruments. See also *Okunda & Another v. Republic* [1970] EA 453, while dealing with the question of the supremacy of East African Community law over Kenyan law, the court confirmed the position that Kenya was a dualist state under the then constitution.

65 Article 2(6) reads as follows: 'Any treaty or convention ratified by Kenya shall form part of the law of Kenya under this Constitution'. See also Article 2(5), which reads as follows: 'The general rules of international law shall form part of the law of Kenya'. Ambani argues that Article 2(5) also allows for the application of those international norms that have gained customary international status in municipal courts.

66 *PAO & 2 Others v. Attorney General* [2012] eKLR (para 55). Nyachae and Ogendi question whether 'to have regard' satisfies the standards set in the 2010 Constitution.

The court, while discussing the extent to which the said constitutional right is to be applied, relied on Article 12 of the International Convention on Economic, Social, and Cultural Rights (ICESCR),[67] which was ratified by Kenya in 1972. The court relied on the jurisprudence of the Committee on Economic, Social, and Cultural Rights (CESCR) and the General Comment 14 to interpret the provisions of the Constitution dealing with the right to health,[68] and General Comment 17 to interpret on the right of everyone to benefit from the protection of the moral and material interests resulting from any scientific, literary or artistic production of which he or she is the author.[69] Article 43(1)(e) of the Constitution states that 'Every person has the right to the highest attainable standard of health, which includes the right to health care services, including reproductive health care', and the greater part of the judicial discussion focussed on the scope of the provision, considering the broader social and policy context of the case. The court made a significant observation that the right to life, right to dignity and right to health were all 'inextricably bound' with one another.[70] The court also noted that the implementation of IPA 2001 with the TRIPS flexibility helped reduce the price of ARVs, thereby widening access to medicines for the poor and needy,[71] and that the uncertainty surrounding the interpretation of 'counterfeit' as contained in section 2 threatened access to affordable medicines.[72] It is to be noted here that the *amicus curiae* had submitted in his brief that although generics are identical copies of the original branded drugs, they can be confiscated as per definition of 'counterfeit' found in section 2 of ACA. The court, concurring with the submissions of both the petitioners and the *amicus curiae*, held that broad enforcement powers contained in ACA, coupled with ambiguous definitions and followed by exorbitant criminal sanctions, would have a negative effect on the production, importation and distribution of generic medicines.[73] The court found that sections 2, 32 and 34 of the impugned Act were inconsistent with Articles 26(1), 28 and 43 of the Kenyan Constitution, and that the government was found to be in violation of its constitutional and international law obligations to the right to health through the enactment of the Anti-Counterfeit Act 2008. The judge, while arriving at the above conclusion, referred to the judgment delivered by the

67 Article 12(1) of ICESCR reads as follows: 'The States Parties to the present Covenant recognize the right of everyone to the enjoyment of the highest attainable standard of physical and mental health.'

68 CESCR, General Comment No 14, 'The right to the Highest Attainable Standard of Health (2000) UN Doc E/C.12/2000/4.

69 CESCR, General Comment No 17, 'The right of everyone to benefit from the protection of the moral and material interests resulting from any scientific, literary or artistic production of which he or she is the author (Article 15, paragraph 1(c), of the Covenant)' (2005) UN Doc E/C.12/GC/17.

70 *PAO & 2 Others v. Attorney General* [2012] eKLR (para 56).

71 *Ibid.* (para 51).

72 *Ibid.* (paras 73–76).

73 *Ibid.* (para 78).

South African Constitutional Court in *Minister of Health and Others v. Treatment Action Campaign and Others*.[74]

6 What was achieved?

The judgment was a clear step in the right direction, as the Kenyan government through the passing of ACA was in serious jeopardy of undoing all the good work that had gone into the passing of IPA 2001 and the HIV and AIDS Prevention and Control Act 2006 (HAPCA), both of which had paved the way for establishing a clear mechanism to access essential medicines for the poor and needy. The incorporation of flexibilities into the IPA 2001 and the passing of the HAPCA were indeed a collective effort, through the participation of NGOs (both national and international), the parties affected by a lack of access to medicines, and other like-minded organisations coming together to find a solution to the long-standing problem of access to medicines in the country. It can be argued that the Kenyan legislative mechanism was clearly influenced by powerful lobbying from the industrial forces (importantly, pharmaceutical patent rights holders) into taking the decision to pass ACA. It is also clear that the roots of ACA are to be found in the plurilateral ACTA, which was negotiated and put together by developed countries in secrecy. As mentioned earlier, the new constitution could have not have come at a better time for those litigants who sought to challenge the validity of ACA as being in violation of their fundamental rights to life, health and dignity.

The judgment delivered in *PAO v. Attorney General* not only struck down legislation which threatened to derail the TRIPS flexibilities build into IPA 2001, but also the public mechanisms put in place following the passing of the Act of 2001 to facilitate access to medicines. By striking down the ACA, the Kenyan court ensured that TRIPS-plus provisions were not brought into the country through the backdoor under the pretext of establishing a legal mechanism to prevent the entry of counterfeit goods into the territory. The judgment also demonstrates the good use of international law jurisprudence by the Kenyan court in establishing the rights to life, health and dignity, which although contained in the Kenyan Constitution, was not well supported by judicial precedence in the country. One of the key reasons for the Kenyan judiciary's inability to use international jurisprudence in its decision-making process was its status as a dualist state. As outlined earlier, this position was to change with the passing of the 2010 Constitution, which transformed Kenya to a monist state, and in that process allowed the courts to have immediate access to international jurisprudence in its decision-making process. This status of Kenya becoming a monist state proved

74 *Minister of Health and Others v. Treatment Action Campaign and Others* (2002), (10) BCLR 1033 (CC). The applicants in the case challenged the South African government's decision to restrict the dispensation of the ARV drug nevirapine to only 18 pilot sites, which they argued was clear breach of the right of access to healthcare and the right of the child to basic healthcare services, as contained in sections 27 and 28(1)(c) of the Constitution of South Africa.

to have a profound effect, as the court could draw from both international and SSA jurisprudence (South Africa) alike in deciding the rights of its citizen to life, health and dignity. On the other hand, the Kenyan judiciary's reluctance to use regional instruments (to which Kenya has signed up), as opposed to international instruments (and jurisprudence) is unclear. Nyachae and Ogendi argue that this practice is partly down to a lack of dissemination of such content, and partly down to being attitudinal, *i.e.*, litigants regarding regional instruments as inferior to international standards (Nyachae and Ogendi, 2015).

7 Conclusion: way forward

With the introduction of the IPA 2001, Kenya took the first legislative step to not only implement a TRIPS-compliant domestic legislation, but also to incorporate such TRIPS flexibilities into the IPA 2001 to make access to affordable medicines realisable. Some of the flexibilities contained in the Act include compulsory licencing the Bolar exception, *etc.* The lack of a national health law and a clear health care policy is a key challenge still facing Kenya. Although being negotiated, it has yet to come to fruition, as the process had been met with delays. This means that the right to health as contained in Article 43(1)(a) of the Constitution remains vague (Nyachae and Ogendi, 2015), unsupported and compromised. One of the essentials in a constitutional democracy is the establishment of appropriate institutions supported by a well-crafted legal mechanism to monitor any development goals, and to ensure those rights are protected and that there is proper recourse available for redress in the event of a denial or breach of such rights. In the case of Kenya, the institutional edifice needs to be well grounded, giving the citizens the confidence that their socio-economic rights as guaranteed under the Constitution will not be jeopardised by maverick legislation like the ACA.

Although Kenya is seen as a pharmaceutical hub for importation, distribution and manufacturing in the East African Community, the market forces have not been able to satisfy the requirements of basic healthcare in the country. As a result, Kenya's HIV response is still reliant on external funding – 70 percent, with the remaining 30 percent coming from the government (17 percent) and by private individuals (13 percent) (NACC, 2014). While the government has doubled its spending from $US57.49 million in 2006 to $US153 in 2012, it is still a long way to go, as there has been a drop in overseas funding (NACC, 2014). Although Kenya is widely seen as one of SSA's HIV prevention success stories, its HIV response cost is expected to increase by 114 percent between 2010 and 2020, which represents a funding of US$1.75 billion (NACC, 2014). In its continuing fight against HIV/AIDS, in 2016 Kenya became the second country in SSA to issue full regulatory approval of pre-exposure prophylaxis (PrEP), which uses antiretroviral drugs to protect HIV-negative people from HIV before potential exposure to the virus as a preventive measure (UNAIDS, 2016).

Mey, while stressing self-sufficiency in the manufacturing sector as one of the key building blocks in the pursuit of access to affordable medicines, also notes that due to multiple problems faced by Kenya, the task may not be easy to achieve (Mey, 2013). It is to be noted that the infrastructure needed to develop a proper pharmaceutical manufacturing base for delivery of health outcomes is clearly missing in Kenya. Amongst the shortcomings, Mey identifies deficiencies in good manufacturing practices (GMP), to ensure that products are consistently produced and controlled to the quality standards appropriate to their intended use, and high-level of corruption in Kenya, which can scupper any efforts to establish long-lasting sites for the manufacture of basic medicines. Figures presented above show that there is an over-reliance by Kenya on donor aid from developed countries, which is useful in controlling an endemic disease, but may fail to achieve the goal set by the Kenyan government.

Overseas funding is often uncertain and unreliable, as it is based on consumption (rather than investments) and the imposition of unfair trade practices and policies of the donor developed nations (Andrews, 2009). Mey argues that drug donations have their own shortcomings, as they do not solve the problem of drug access in the long term, but have the potential to impact on the development of local drug manufacturers, whose products cannot compete against donated pharmaceuticals. Often the donated drugs have 'either just expired or have short shelf lives making them unusable by the prospective recipient' (Mey, 2013). In terms of health research investments by TNPCs in Kenya, there is a big gap in comparison to other regions of the world. The figures released by PhRMA, from 2014 (released in 2016), which presents a breakdown of member companies' health R&D investment by geographic area, a sum of US$35.5 million was spent in South Africa (0.1 percent share), and only US$36.3 million (0.1 percent share) for the rest of Africa was invested (PhRMA, 2016). One could argue that Kenya is a least-health R&D-intensive country (Mey, 2013). One other area that Kenya needs to invest in and develop is the knowledge economy, as any research initiative is strongly hinged on having a good knowledge base.

Bibliography

1 Ambani, Osogo J. 'Navigating Past the "Dualist Doctrine": The Case for Progressive Jurisprudence on the Application of International Human Rights Norms in Kenya,' in Killander, Magnus (ed.) *International Law and Domestic Human Rights Litigation in Africa* (Pretoria University Law Press, 2010) 26, 32.

2 Anderson, David. *Histories of the Hanged: Britain's Dirty War in Kenya and the End of Empire* (WW Norton & Company, 2005).

3 Andrews, Nathan. 'Foreign Aid and Development in Africa: What the Literature Says and What the Reality Is,' *Journal of African Studies and Development* Vol. 1, No. 1 (2009) 8–15.

4 Antons, Christoph, Michael Blakeney, and Christopher Heath (eds.) *Intellectual Property Harmonisation Within ASEAN and APEC* (Kluwer International, 2004) 238.

5 Avafia, Tenu, Jonathan Berger, and Trudi Hartzenberg. 'The Ability of Select Sub-Saharan African Countries to Utilise TRIPS Flexibilities and Competition Law to Ensure a Sustainable Supply of Essential Medicines: A Study of Producing and Importing Countries,' *Tralac Documento de Trabajo* 12 (2006).

6 Avafia, Tenu. 'Public Health Related TRIPS Flexibilities and South-South Co-Operation as Enablers of Treatment Access in Eastern and Southern Africa: Perspectives from Producing and Importing Countries,' Doctoral dissertation (Queen Mary University of London, 2015).

7 Beyer, Peter. 'Developing Socially Responsible Intellectual Property Licensing Policies: Non- Exclusive Licensing Initiatives in the Pharmaceutical Sector,' in Werra, Jacques de (ed.) *Research Handbook on Intellectual Property Licensing* (Edward Elgar Publishing, 2012) 227–256.

8 Central Intelligence Agency. 'The World FactBook, Africa: Kenya,' <www.cia.gov/library/publications/the-world-factbook/geos/ke.html> accessed 29 November 2017.

9 Chege, John Waruingi. *Copyright Law and Publishing in Kenya* (Kenya Literature Bureau, 1978).

10 Dutfield, Graham. *Intellectual Property, Biogenetic Resources and Traditional Knowledge* (Earthscan, 2004) 212.

11 East African Community. 'Overview of EAC,' (2017) <www.eac.int/about/overview> accessed 29 November 2017.

12 Export Processing Zones Authority, 'Kenya's Pharmaceutical Industry 2005,' (2005) <http://www.epzakenya.com/UserFiles/files/Pharmaceutical.pdf> accessed 29 November 2017.

13 Ford, Nathan. 'Patents, Access to Medicines and the Role of Non-Governmental Organisations,' *Journal of Generic Medicines* Vol. 1, No. 2 (2004) 137–145.

14 Gastorn, Kennedy, Wanyama Masinde. 'The EAC Common Market,' in Ugirashebuja, Emmanuel, John Eudes Ruhangisa, Tom Ottervanger, and Armin Cuyvers (eds.) *East African Community Law: Institutional, Substantive and Comparative EU Aspects* (Brill Nijhoff, 2017) 285–292.

15 Harrington, John. 'Access to Essential Medicines in Kenya: Intellectual Property, Anti-Counterfeiting, and the Right to Health,' in Freeman, Michael, Sarah Hawkes, and Belinda Bennett (eds.) *Law and Global Health: Current Legal Issues* (Oxford University Press, 2014) 94–119.

16 Harrington, John. 'Intellectual Property and the Life Sciences in Kenya: Enforcement and Access to Medicines,' in Matthews, Duncan, and Herbert Zech (eds.) *Research Handbook on Intellectual Property and the Life Science* (Edward Elgar Publishing, 2017) 395–407.

17 Hornsby, Charles. *Kenya: A History Since Independence* (I.B. Tauris & Co Ltd, 2012).

18 Kalunda, Elizabeth, Beatrice Nduku, and John Kabiru. 'Pharmaceutical Manufacturing Companies in Kenya and Their Credit Risk Management Practices,' *Research Journal of Finance and Accounting* Vol. 3, No. 5 (2012).

19 Kameri-Mbote, Patricia. 'Intellectual Property Protection in Africa: An Assessment of the Status of Laws, Research and Policy Analysis on Intellectual Property Rights in Kenya,' *IELRC Working Paper No. 2* (2005).

20 Kawewa, Janet. 'Situational Analysis of HIV/AIDS in Kenya,' UNESCO, Department of Adult Education (2005) <www.unesco.org/education/uie/pdf/Kawewa.pdf> accessed 29 November 2017.

21 Kenya National Bureau of Statistics (KNBS) and ICF Macro. 'Kenya Demographic and Health Survey 2008–2009' (KNBS and ICF Macro, 2010).

22 Kenya National AIDS Control Council. 'Kenya AIDS Strategic Framework 2014/2015–2018/2019,' (NACC, 2014).

23 Khan, Jibran. 'KENYA Snow-Capped Mountains on the Equator and Pharmaceutical Industry,' (16 September 2015) <www.linkedin.com/pulse/kenya-snow-capped-mountains-equator-pharmaceutical-dr> accessed 29 November 2017.

24 Kimani, Dagi. 'Indian Drug Makers Say Kenya's Counterfeit Law Will Wipe Out Their Market,' *The East African* (23 January 2009) <www.theeastafrican.co.ke/news/2558-519156-uyynffz/index.html> accessed 29 November 2017.

25 Lewis-Lettington, Robert J., and Sisule F. Musungu. 'In Defence of Kenya's Health: Proposed Amendments to the Industrial Property Bill 2000,' Kenya Coalition for Access to Essential Medicines, Nairobi (2000).

26 Lewis-Lettington, Robert, and Peter Munyi. 'Willingness and Ability to Use TRIPS Flexibilities: Kenya Case Study,' Department of International Development (2004).

27 MSF. 'A Blank Cheque for Abuse: The Anti-Counterfeiting Trade Agreement (ACTA) and Its Impact on Access to Medicines,' *MSF Briefing Document* (February 2012) <www.msfaccess.org/sites/default/files/MSF_assets/Access/Docs/Access_Briefing_ACTABlankCheque_ENG_2012.pdf > accessed 29 November 2017.

28 Mbatiah, Suleiman. 'Kenya: Pharmaceutical Companies Pushing Anti-Counterfeit Law,' *Inter Press Service* (14 June 2010) <www.ipsnews.net/2010/06/kenya-pharmaceutical-companies-pushing-anti-counterfeit-law/> accessed 29 November 2017.

29 Mbogo, Steven. 'Why We Are Losing the War Against Fake Drugs,' *Business Daily* (1 May 2008).

30 Mey, Brenda P. 'Unfettered Consumer Access to Affordable Therapies in the Post-TRIPS Era: A Dead- End Journey for Patients? Kenya and India Case Studies,' *The Journal of World Intellectual Property* Vol. 13, No. 3 (2010) 403–473.

31 Mey, Brenda P. *The Legal Dual: The TRIPS Agreement and Drug Access Issues* (Peter Lang GmBH, 2013).

32 Nyachae, Jacinta, and Paul Ogendi. 'Litigating the Right to Health in Kenya: An Analysis of Selected Cases,' in Durojaye, Ebenezer (ed.) *Litigating the Right to Health in Africa: Challenges and Prospects* (Routledge, 2015) 177–194.

33 Nyakundi, Joshua, and Nathan Mnjama, 'Management of Patent Information in Kenya,' *Open Journal Systems* Vol. 17, No. 1 (2007).

34 O'Carroll, Sorcha. 'Importing Indian Generic Drugs Following TRIPS: Case Studies from Zambia and Kenya,' *Unpublished Paper* (2005) <www.lmls.com/files/socarroll_importingindiangenericdrugs.pdf> accessed 29 November 2017.

35 Odongo, Mary. 'Towards an East African Community Common Market: Challenges and Opportunities,' *Institute of Economic Studies*, *Trade Notes*, No. 33 (2011).

36 Ongoya, Elisha Z. 'The Law, the Procedures and the Trends in Jurisprudence on Constitutional and Fundamental Rights Litigation in Kenya,' *KLR Journal* Vol. 2 (2010) <http://kenyalaw.org/kl/index.php?id=1925> accessed 29 November 2017.

37 Osewe, Patrick Lumumba, Yvonne Korkoi Nkrumah, and Emmanuel K. Sackey (eds.) *Improving Access to HIV/AIDS Medicines in Africa: Trade-Related Aspects of Intellectual Property Rights Flexibilities* (World Bank Publications, 2008) 33.

38 PhRMA. '2016 PhRMA Annual Membership Survey' (2016) <http://phrma-docs.phrma.org/sites/default/files/pdf/annual-membership-survey-results.pdf> accessed 29 November 2017.

39 Republic of Kenya. *Millennium Development Goals: Status Report for Kenya 2013* (Ministry of Devolution and Planning, 2014).

40 Sihanya, Ben. 'Patents, Parallel Importation and Compulsory Licensing of HIV/AIDS Drugs: The Experience of Kenya,' in Gallegher, Pete, Patrick Low, and Andrew L. Stoler (eds.) *Managing the Challenges of WTO Participation: 45 Case Studies* (Cambridge University Press, 2005) 264–283.

41 Sundaram, Jae. 'Access to Medicines and the TRIPS Agreement: What Next for Sub-Saharan Africa?' *Information & Communications Technology Law* Vol. 24, No. 3 (2015) 242–261.

42 UNAIDS. 'Prevention Gap Report,' (2016).
43 UNICEF. 'Kenya-Statistics' (27 December 2013) <www.unicef.org/infobycountry/kenya_statistics.html> accessed 29 November 2017.
44 United Nations Industrial Development Organisation. *Pharmaceutical Sector Profile: Kenya* (UNIDO, 2010).
45 Unnikrishnan, C.H. 'Indian Drug Makers Worried by East Africa's Legal Proposals,' *Live Mint* (16 February 2010) <www.livemint.com/2010/02/15221607/Indian-drug-makers-worried-by.html> accessed 29 November 2017.
46 Viljoen, Frans. *International Human Rights Law in Africa* (Oxford University Press, 2012) 522.
47 Von Braun, Johanna, and Peter Munyi. 'New Enforcement Mechanisms Challenge the Legality of Generics in the Name of Public Health: The Emergence of Anti-Counterfeiting Legislation in East Africa,' *African Journal of International and Comparative Law* Vol. 18, No. 2 (2010) 238–253.
48 WTO. 'Members OK Amendment to Make Health Flexibility Permanent,' (6 December 2005) <www.wto.org/english/news_e/pres05_e/pr426_e.htm> accessed 29 November 2017.
49 WTO, 'Amendment of the TRIPS Agreement,' (23 January 2017) <www.wto.org/english/tratop_e/trips_e/amendment_e.htm> accessed 29 November 2017.
50 Wadhams, Nicholas. 'Kenya Pressured to Implement Anti-Counterfeit Law Despite Access Fears,' *Intellectual Property Watch* (2 July 2009) <www.ip-watch.org/2009/07/02/kenya-pressured-to-implement-anti-counterfeit-law-despite-access-fears/> accessed 29 November 2017.
51 World Bank Group. 'Kenya Economic Update: Kazi ni Kazi – Informal Should Not Be Normal,' (March 2016) <http://documents.worldbank.org/curated/en/888091467988907587/pdf/104289-NWP-PUBLIC-Kenya-Economic-Update-Copy.pdf> accessed 29 November 2017.
52 World Bank. 'Poverty & Equity: Country Dashboard, Kenya' (2017) <http://povertydata.worldbank.org/poverty/country/KEN> accessed 29 November 2017.
53 World Health Organisation. 'HIV/AIDS in Kenya,' (WHO, 2005) <www.who.int/hiv/HIVCP_KEN.pdf> accessed 29 November 2017.
54 World Health Organisation, 'World Health Statistics 2015,' (WHO, 2015) <http://apps.who.int/iris/bitstream/10665/170250/1/9789240694439_eng.pdf> accessed 29 November 2017.
55 Anon. 'Lobby Launches AIDS Bill Drive,' *Daily Nation* (30 May 2001) <www.nation.co.ke/news/1056-339908-laarbnz/index.html> accessed 29 November 2017.
56 Anon. 'Kenya Readies Aids Drugs Law,' *BBC News* (22 April 2001) <http://news.bbc.co.uk/1/hi/world/africa/1291200.stm> accessed 29 November 2017.
57 Anon. 'Kenyan Firm to Make AIDS Drugs,' *BBC News* (22 September 2004) <http://news.bbc.co.uk/2/hi/africa/3680672.stm> accessed 29 November 2017.

Part III

TRIPS at what cost?

Introduction

The country-specific studies coupled with an enquiry of the IP rights protection (more specifically to pharmaceutical patents), and a study of the ill-effects of FTAs and TRIPS-plus provisions, presented us with a scenario, where TNPCs along with the developed nations have systematically used the institutions and trade agreements and policies to push the agenda for a bigger pharmaceutical market share in both developing countries and LDCs. This may appear, on the surface, to be a perfectly legitimate action. But unfortunately, it comes at a cost, *viz.*, human lives.

The closing chapter of the book looks at the continuing struggle for access to medicines in developing countries and LDCs in an ever-changing landscape of FTAs and TRIPS-plus provisions, which appear to set the goal post further away from reach, and suggests possible solutions to the problem. The chapter is also a stark reminder to the governing bodies and trade policymakers that patients in developing countries have continued to suffer, the problem of access to medicines has only worsened, and it is time for some concrete measures to be put in place to save the unnecessary suffering and deaths of innocent lives.

10 TRIPS Agreement and the future of access to affordable medicines

Contents

1 Introduction

Through the TRIPS Agreement, the WTO rolled out the global IP protection, which ushered in major changes to the international IP rights enforcement. The Agreement, by reference, incorporates a number of WIPO conventions[1] and hence its scope is broad,[2] encompassing almost all types of IP rights.[3] Being part of the global 'rules-based' multilateral trading system, disputes between WTO members with regard to IP rights violations could only be settled before the Dispute Settlement Body (DSU) following the WTO rules. Above all, the TRIPS Agreement contains detailed rules on enforcement, including civil and administrative procedures. Importantly, for our purposes, the protection envisaged under the Agreement includes pharmaceutical patent rights. Although the preamble to the Agreement recognises the public policy underpinnings of the Agreement, including development and technological transfer,[4] in reality the Agreement stands to protect and enforce the private rights of individual IP rights holders. The Agreement, while receiving the greatest critical scrutiny, has also generated

1 Paris Convention, the Berne Convention, the Rome Convention, and the Treaty on Intellectual Property in Respect of Integrated Circuits (1989).

2 The initial objective identified during the TRIPS Agreement negotiations was the development of a multilateral framework 'dealing with international trade in counterfeit goods'. See the Punta del Este Declaration in 1986 launching the Uruguay Round, MIN.DEC, 20 Sept. 1986.

3 See Articles 9–39 of the TRIPS Agreement. However, authors' moral rights, utility model protection and protection against unfair competition are excluded.

4 The preamble to the TRIPS Agreement reads as follows: 'Recognizing the underlying public policy objectives of national systems for the protection of intellectual property, including developmental and technological objectives.'

the fiercest opposition in the area of pharmaceutical innovation and access to medicines (Williams and Löfgren, 2013).

The TRIPS Agreement has gone on to shape the political economy of pharmaceuticals. It expressly acknowledges the competing interest of private rights and that of public health concerns. In Article 7, the objectives of the Agreement are delineated as follows:

> The protection and enforcement of intellectual property rights should contribute to the promotion of technological innovation and to the transfer and dissemination of technology, to the mutual advantage of producers and users of technological knowledge and in a manner conducive to social and economic welfare, and to a balance of rights and obligations.

As regards public health, Article 8.1 sets out the following principle:

> Members may, in formulating or amending their laws and regulations, adopt measures necessary to protect public health and nutrition, and to promote the public interest in sectors of vital importance to their socio-economic and technological development, provided that such measures are consistent with the provisions of this Agreement.

Mitchell and Voon posit the argument that Articles 7 and 8 are aspirational provisions and hence unlikely to resolve difficulties, as is arguably the case for compulsory licencing in connection with patented pharmaceuticals (Mitchell and Voon, 2010). It is doubtless that patent protection for pharmaceutical products as mandated under the TRIPS Agreement presents a major obstacle to public health measures in developing countries. The implementation of the Agreement has posed serious problems to those developing countries with little or no manufacturing capacity, that look to import medicines to deal with public health concerns. This leaves us with the questions, Has the implementation of the Agreement taken the public policy objectives seriously? Who benefits from the TRIPS Agreement – the patent-holding developed countries or the IP importing developing countries and LDCs who need life-saving medicines at affordable prices? Have the proponents of the TRIPS Agreement lost sight of the public policy underpinnings/undertakings contained in the TRIPS Agreement? There is no doubt that access to affordable medicines is more threatened now than before, as a direct result of the introduction of the extended pharmaceutical patent protection under the TRIPS Agreement. With over twenty years of implementation of the TRIPS regime, the water has only muddied further, in an ever-changing landscape brought about by FTAs and TRIPS-plus provisions.

1.1 The costs and benefits of TRIPS to developing countries

It has been argued, and demonstrated, that the cost of implementing TRIPS on the developing countries is enormous. The TRIPS Agreement has proven to be one of the most politically charged and divisive multilateral agreements yet negotiated in the post-WWII era. Powerful critiques of the IP rights system in general, and those opposed to extension of patent protection to pharmaceutical patents in particular, have articulated clearly the negative impact of TRIPS on developing countries and LDCs (Pogge, Rimmer, and Rubenstein, 2010). In the earlier chapters, the developing country experience, or difficulties, in implementing the TRIPS Agreement was taken up for study. It was noted that Brazil, India and Kenya had, prior to 1995, framed national IP rights legislation based on sovereignty (based on social and economic developmental goals), and did not recognise pharmaceutical product patents. India, in particular, had a significant local pharmaceutical industry, and continues to have a strong generics industry (Sundaram, 2014a).

It is well documented that the TRIPS Agreement was influenced by the US IP legal regime, and it did not come as a surprise that the US had to introduce the fewest changes to conform to the TRIPS Agreement, incurring very little additional costs. In contrast, the additional costs of implementing TRIPS in a developing country are difficult to estimate accurately, as there are both economic costs and associated human and social costs to be considered (Lopert and Gleeson, 2013). Very few expert studies have been undertaken to estimate the costs of implementing TRIPS in developing nations. One study, carried out by Oxfam in 2007, estimated the annual cost of implementation of TRIPS in developing countries would exceed US$40 billion (Malpani, 2007). The study suggests that the additional costs would come from developing countries, as developed nations already had in place TRIPS-conforming IP legislation. Set against this backdrop, the developing countries will also have to cope with another threat, *viz.*, TRIPS-plus provisions, which are sought to be introduced by developed countries through FTAs.

The case studies of implementation of TRIPS Agreement in developing countries, carried out in earlier chapters, also demonstrated the crippling effect of the pharmaceutical patent protection on health policy initiatives and access to medicines. The TRIPS implementation process was an enormous drain on the resources of developing countries, who were already under tremendous domestic pressure to meet the healthcare needs of their citizens. It also established that pharmaceutical patent rights could not be the sole determinant of the political economy of global drug production. Through the implementation of TRIPS Agreement, and TRIPS-plus provisions, pharmaceutical patents (and exclusive marketing rights) have enabled TNPCs to charge exorbitant prices(Williams and Löfgren, 2013). Further, the extension of patent protection often translates into many millions or even billions of dollars to TNPCs. That said, currently the boundary between the R&D-based and the generics segments of the pharmaceutical industry is blurring, as a number of TNPCs also supply generics (Löfgren, 2007).[5] With the implementation of the TRIPS Agreement, a two-tier system of

5 It is also true that some generics producers supply patented products.

nation states has been firmly established, *viz.*, IP producers/exporters and IP consumers/importers. This development, forged through the WTO, has now allowed developed nations to further introduce TRIPS-plus provision through FTAs, which is now slowly becoming the norm.

While resisting the call to relax patent protection for pharmaceutical products, proponents of the IP regime have repeatedly argued that patent protection was necessary for the financing of the discovery and commercialisation of new drugs. Interestingly, many of the new medicines commercialised post-1945 were discovered and introduced into the market before product patents were available in most countries (Munos, 2009). At the end of the 1980s, at least forty developing countries, including the most populous, provided no protection for pharmaceuticals (Chien, 2003, 864). As discussed in earlier chapters, the notion of product patents as a basic requirement for pharmaceutical innovation gained the status of common sense only during the Uruguay Round of negotiations, where the international IP rights regime was discussed, leading to the introduction of TRIPS Agreement. Before the advent of the WTO, the laws of approximately fifty states excluded pharmaceutical products from patent protection. To demonstrate, one can take the case of Japan, which did not introduce product patents for drugs until 1976.[6]

The country-specific studies presented in earlier chapters demonstrate that generics continue to remain the chief source of affordable medicine. It is obvious that the TNPCs also want to have a major share of the generics market wherever possible – in short, they are keen to muscle out any generics challenge that may arise in both the developed and developing country markets. It was noted in the earlier chapters that TNPCs have taken steps to collaborate with generics producers in India, which is a major player in the generics market. The TNPCs view the developing country markets – with bigger disease-prone populations – as new revenue streams. In the global political economy of pharmaceuticals, the TRIPS regime coupled with TRIPS-plus provisions contained in FTAs provide a pivotal strategic tool for the TNPCs and the governments of the US and EU. The role of TRIPS-plus is paramount in enforcing the IP rights vision of the developed nations on the rest of the players, as it has the effect of extending the patent protection, and thus delaying the market entry of more affordable generic drugs (UNDP, UNAIDS, 2012). In the post-TRIPS era, the pharmaceutical patent landscape has changed to the benefit of patent-holding TNPCs and developed countries, and many now question the basic rationale behind the international IP rights regime rolled out under the auspices of the WTO.

If solutions for the continuing problem of access to medicines (made acute by the introduction of global IP protection of pharmaceutical patents in the WTO) are to be explored at an institutional level, then the answers are to be found only at the institutional level by forming a clearer agenda on global health and access to medicines. It can only be achieved by engaging the primary actors, namely the

6 Product patents in the pharmaceutical sector is relatively new to many developed countries. Switzerland waited until 1977 to introduce patents covering pharmaceutical products. Spain, Portugal, Greece and Norway introduced product patents covering drugs as recently as 1992.

WHO, the WTO and the World Bank, to find a workable solution by forging a new global health governance model, which should be partly funded by the TNPCs. This argument is put forth, as the laws drafted clearly appear to be one-sided and favouring the pharmaceutical patent holder, while the consumer in the developing countries are denied access to affordable medicines – both patented and generic.

2 The promise of TRIPS: will it ever be realised?

The entry of the TRIPS Agreement through the multilateral trading system marked the high point of neoliberalism, besides also triggering a global counter-movement which sought to protect and extend local production of affordable generics and define access to essential medicines as a human right (Williams and Löfgren, 2013). As a next step, some developing country governments also sought to pursue their citizens' rights by demanding expanded market competition for such medicines in order to bring down drug prices.[7] The TRIPS Agreement guarantees, protects and presents a mechanism to enforce that right. TRIPS also contain flexibilities, including the grant of compulsory licencing and parallel importation. It is well known that many developing countries and LDCs do not have the manufacturing capacity and/or the economic viability to produce either active ingredients or formulations, and as a result cannot avail the provision of 'compulsory licences' under the TRIPS Agreement. For instance, most of the SSA countries suffer due to lack of access to medicines. As they do not possess the necessary infrastructure to manufacture any generic drugs for frontline treatment, they rely solely on imported generics for treatment.

The TRIPS Agreement, and the Doha Declaration, sought to balance international trade with public health through the inclusion of flexibilities, such as compulsory licencing, to expand domestic production and to permit the export of low-cost generics. The option of importing generic medicines from other countries is restricted in the Agreement, which requires production under compulsory licence to be predominantly for the supply of the domestic market. Grant of compulsory licence would authorise a third party to manufacture and sell a pharmaceutical product without the consent of the patent holder in return for 'adequate' compensation. The Doha Declaration of 2001 confirms this position in the following words: '[e]ach member [country] has the right to grant compulsory licences and the freedom to determine the grounds upon which such licences are granted'. After nearly two years of negotiations, on 30 August 2003,[8] the General Council of the WTO finally adopted the Decision on Implementation

7 Williams and Löfgren also posit the argument that in the process, the global IP rights regime promoted by the TNPCs as 'the guarantor of good governance in pharmaceutical market was thus unmasked as the protector of their anti-competitive, monopoly rents.'

8 Implementation of paragraph 6 of the Doha Declaration on the TRIPS Agreement and Public Health WT/L/540 (30 August 2003). Paragraph 6 of the Doha Declaration reads as follows: 'WTO members with insufficient or no manufacturing capacities in the pharmaceutical sector could face difficulties in making effective use of compulsory licensing under the TRIPS Agreement.'

of paragraph 6 of the Doha Declaration on the TRIPS Agreement and Public Health (the August Decision).

The proliferation of FTAs had seen the use of TRIPS-plus provisions, which effectively negates the use of any TRIPS flexibilities by developing country partners (Correa, 2004).[9] The US and other patent-holding developed nations exercise strong pressures for compulsory licences to be considered legitimate only in extreme circumstances of national emergency. Beall and Kuhn note that between January 1995 and June 2011, there were only about twenty-four compulsory licencing episodes spread across seventeen nations, mostly for HIV/AIDS medications (Beall and Kuhn, 2012). The case studies presented earlier demonstrated that in most cases the member states had found it extremely difficult to utilise the compulsory licencing provisions of the TRIPS Agreement. The strategy to use compulsory licencing, or the threat of issue of compulsory licence, has not yet acquired sufficient momentum to seriously shift market dynamics in the Global South (Khor, 2010). With the exception of countries like Brazil and India, it had been impossible for developing countries to invoke the compulsory licencing provision for purposes of accessing affordable medicines.[10] The question that keeps coming back is whether the flexibilities enshrined in the TRIPS Agreement had ever been allowed a smooth implementation, without the intervention of patent rights holders. This brings into focus the discussion of balancing public health with private rights, and whether the TRIPS Agreement accomplishes the task.

Löfgren and Williams warn that pessimism should be tempered by optimistic signals, as resistance to the new political economy of pharmaceuticals is ongoing, and equally multi-levelled and complex are the sources of pressures to conform and align (Williams and Löfgren, 2013). A number of developing countries have responded to the new political economy of pharmaceuticals through policy moves and insulating their populations from some of the most negative effects of the global IP rights regime (Williams and Löfgren, 2013).

Discussions focussing on India and Brazil clearly highlighted the battle of two developing countries against the might of TNPCs backed by the US and other developed nations. The discussions also underpinned the fact that India, with its manufacturing infrastructure, generics industry and a stronger knowledge economy, was far better prepared than any other developing country to resist the TNPCs and the US. India, while implementing TRIPS through the Indian Patents (Amendment) Act 2005, introduced section 3(d) to counter the practice of patent evergreening in the pharmaceutical sector. India also successfully staved off challenges from the pharmaceutical sector to section 3(d) of the Patent Act 2005 in the *Novartis* case.[11] India also made better use of TRIPS flexibilities

9 The author notes that bilateral agreements established by the US with some developing and developed countries (*e.g.*, Australia, the Central American countries, Chile, Jordan, Morocco) require the protection of data under a *sui generis* regime of data exclusivity for at least five years from the date of the first approval of a pharmaceutical product in the country.

10 In the case of China, a late comer to the WTO fold, the provision was not sought to be utilised.

11 Indian Supreme Court Judgment in *Novartis Ag v. Union of India & Others* (2013) 6 SCC 1. See chapter 7 for a discussion on TRIPS implementation in India.

than any other similarly placed developing country – including the grant of compulsory licence. India is now being seen as the fulcrum of global political and social struggles over pharmaceutical policy and access to medicines, as evidenced through the high-profile cases (Williams and Löfgren, 2013). Next to India, Brazil had also shown resolve in its push to establish its right to grant of compulsory licence, and in the drafting of a new patent legislation to support its policy of free access to medicines.[12] While India and Brazil through their bold legal measures have cleverly navigated through the pitfalls of implementing TRIPS, the same cannot be said about other developing countries.

3 The role of non-state actors

Numerous studies into the political economy of pharmaceutical patent protection and access to medicines identify the key players as IP producing nations, IP consuming nations, patent holders and non-governmental organizations (NGOs). The NGOs have played, and continue to play a significant role in the struggle for access to medicines in the developing countries and the LDCs, challenging both TNPCs and the patent-holding developed countries. The NGOs, including Treatment Action Campaign, Knowledge Ecology International, ACT UP and MSF, revolutionised advocacy dramatically with regards to access to ARVs used in the treatment of HIV/AIDS (Novogrodsky, 2010).[13] When the developed nations led by the US sought to introduce IP rights protection in the multilateral trading system at the Uruguay Round of negotiations, the NGOs were conspicuously absent from the national debates. As discussed in earlier chapters, well-financed TNPCs and other IP producing industries played a pivotal role in the creation of TRIPS Agreement, which was well supported by developed countries.

Both NGOs and IP producing industries are considered as non-state actors. While NGOs fell within the category of civil society groups with a more human rights agenda as their centre piece, the IP producing industries had their focus on protecting private rights worth billions of US dollars (as opposed to human rights), with the full support of developed nations who had everything to gain at the negotiations in the lead-up to the TRIPS Agreement. The IP producers/ patent holders were successful in shaping trade law through the expansion of IP rights at the international level. In the post-TRIPS era, the NGOs had always been the voice of the needy in the battle for access to medicines. Civil society groups were instrumental in warding off the threat from TNPCs when the legal challenge was brought before the South African Courts challenging the new patent legislation. It is well documented that they not only fought the battle in

12 See chapter 5 for a discussion on TRIPS implementation in Brazil.

13 Both brand and generic pharmaceutical manufacturers have played their part in the development of global rules and incentives for production. Philanthropic foundations, such as the Bill & Melinda Gates Foundation, have pledged close to US$8 billion to global health initiatives, and the William J. Clinton Foundation has been instrumental in negotiating price reduction for bulk purchasing, preferential pricing and the rollout of ARVs to developing countries and communities in need.

South Africa, but also took it to the US by threatening to derail the election campaign of Al Gore.[14] The civil society groups were in full swing when Novartis launched its campaign to challenge the validity of section 3(d) of the Indian Patent (Amendment) Act 2005,[15] besides being in the forefront of providing treatment, education and prevention services in many parts of the developing world. In short, they have revolutionised AIDS service delivery by training community health workers called 'accompagnateurs' to distribute ARVs, supervise home-based therapy and ensure adequate feeding (Farmer, 2007). It is doubtless that the role of the NGOs in this regard is unmatched, and without their unique contributions, we might have witnessed a more asymmetric rights regime, with significantly more suffering. Importantly, the NGOs do not consider their task as being over, and they continue to work tirelessly in pursuit of justice.

4 Conclusion: the forgotten right to health

The central theme of the current study is the continuing problem of access to affordable medicines in the developing countries and LDCs in the post-TRIPS era. One of the earlier chapters of the study had noted that the failure to strike a balance between the right to health and the private right (negative right) to hold a patent to the exclusion of the others had led to the worsening of the situation of access to medicines in economically weaker nations. Case studies of Brazil, China, India, South Africa and Kenya, presented in earlier chapters, all support this position. The need and necessity to give primacy to patent right over the right to access affordable medicines in an environment which begs affordable treatment and care is the antithesis of the objectives of a welfare state. The current status of access to medicines around the globe in developing countries and LDCs capture an uncomfortable truth, *i.e.*, that people die not from the non-availability of a cure, but due to inaccessibility to existing drugs, as they are beyond their economic reach.

In the twenty-first century globalised economy, promoted by the multilateral trading system, having a strong knowledge economy translates into a stronger economy. One is made to wonder whether the fruits of the medical sciences are to serve humanity as a whole or only those human populations that control scientific knowledge. What was demonstrated in the case studies was that those developing countries with a stronger knowledge economy were better equipped to cope with the demands of the TRIPS Agreement. In the implementation process, one noticed the unnecessary tensions brought about between the need to meet the basic right to health and the necessity to implement and give effect to an international private right. The failure of the WTO to strike a clear balance between the right to health *vis-à-vis* innovators' rights had led to an overemphasis of IP rights – in terms of both trade policy development and enforcement mechanism before the multilateral trading system. Huge gaps exist between the health needs

14 See chapter 8 for a discussion on TRIPS implementation in South Africa.
15 See chapter 7 for a discussion on TRIPS implementation in India.

confronting citizens in the developed countries and those confronting citizens in the developing countries and LDCs. One factor that sets apart the two sides of the divide is the means that are available to access affordable medicines, not the availability of a cure.

The elevated status of IP rights before the international trade body had resulted in allowing developed countries with stronger knowledge economies to set TRIPS as a benchmark in their bilateral trade agreements with developing nations and introduce TRIPS-plus provisions into FTAs. This has resulted in the developing countries having to surrender the TRIPS flexibilities (which they fought hard for at the negotiations) in return for access to developed country markets. As discussed in earlier,[16] the developed countries have made, in most instances, their developing country partners in FTAs give up on TRIPS flexibilities. Where the developing countries resisted such incursions from developed countries, they were challenged before domestic courts and the WTO Dispute Settlement Body, besides incurring the wrath of USTR. We live in the TRIPS-plus world, where the TRIPS Agreement was only the starting point for further expansion of IP rights, and the voice of the human rights lawyers and civil society activists are drowned. The expansion of IP rights, initially through TRIPS (with the blessing of the WTO), and later through TRIPS-plus provisions, has allowed the exclusive rights and remedies of patent holders to completely negate the health rights of communities in developing countries and LDCs.

Chandra argues that it is no longer an option to plead the case of health as a basic right, as its primacy is unquestionable and goes beyond the innovators' rights, which are more in the nature of economic rewards stimulating innovation and not, generally, preconditioning survival (Chandra, 2010). Chandra further argues that the legal terms of adjudication between the two competing rights ought to be based on a cognisance of their distinction. Chandra also advocates that right to health must be linked with human right discourses as well as the discourse on global justice, as addressing health needs is critical for poverty alleviation and human development (Chandra, 2010). This argument gains in significance, as the WTO has a social agenda at the heart of its multilateral trading system. When the right to health is discussed alongside IP rights, it remains more a statement of intent, or remains at the entry level of purpose and objective, and does not mature into a justiciable right as do IP rights (Chandra, 2010). While there is evidence that superior courts from countries like India, South Africa and Brazil are now prepared to interpret right to health as a right to life, there is still a long way to go, and the WTO through the promotion of TRIPS has not done any favours for the cause. National laws passed in countries such as Brazil[17] and India[18] demonstrate the intent to introduce health safeguards into domestic legislation.

Chandra notes that the state provides an institutional context within the domestic sphere, where rights are formulated and recognised, and is the agency

16 See chapter 4 for a discussion on the use of TRIPS-plus provisions in FTAs.

17 See chapter 5 for a discussion on the changes made to the Brazilian constitution and IP legislation.

18 See chapter 7 for a discussion on section 3(d) of the Indian Patent Act 2005.

through which a commitment to rights may become tangible (Chandra, 2010). Although universal human rights and claim to health have been recognised in international treaties, the major problem appears to be the non-existence of a central agency (like the WTO) to assume ownership of the right to health (human right), to provide oversight and having the teeth to enforce the same, as in the case of IP rights. There is now an imminent need for an institutional context in which these rights are formally grounded. The above study has presented a stark scenario, in which the TRIPS Agreement while recognising and extending IP rights protection, has also created a two-tier system of IP producers and IP consumers, dividing the populations into the haves and have-nots of the knowledge economy. The study of the implementation of the TRIPS Agreement in different jurisdictions of the developing world also makes the case for a radical policy change with regards to IP rights protection, and in particular to patent protection afforded to pharmaceutical products. TRIPS, has in effect exacerbated the problem of access to medicines and serves only as an obstacle to the human right to health. The introduction of TRIPS not only caused problems in access to affordable medicines but also to other rights touching upon agriculture, traditional knowledge, *etc*. This leads one to conclude that there should be a complete rethink of the IP rights protection resting with the multilateral trading system, as there are more public rights involved in the discourse than the protection of private rights. As a first step, an amendment to remove pharmaceutical patent protection from the ambit of TRIPS is desirable.

Bibliography

1 Beall, Reed, and Randall Kuhn. 'Trends in Compulsory Licensing of Pharmaceuticals Since the Doha Declaration: A Database Analysis,' *PLoS Medicine* Vol. 9, No. 1 (2012) e1001154.
2 Chandra, Rajshree. *Knowledge as Property: Issues in the Moral Grounding of Intellectual Property Rights* (Oxford University Press, 2010).
3 Chien, Colleen. 'Cheap Drugs at What Price to Innovation: Does Compulsory Licensing of Pharmaceuticals Hurt Innovation?' *Berkeley Tech Law Journal* Vol. 18 (2003) 853.
4 Correa, Carlos M. 'Bilateralism in Intellectual Property: Defeating the WTO System for Access to Medicines,' *Case Western Reserve Journal International Law* Vol. 36 (2004) 79.
5 Farmer, Paul. 'From "Marvelous Momentum" to Health Care for All,' *Foreign Affairs* Vol. 86 (2007) 155, 156.
6 Khor, Martin. 'Patents, Compulsory Licenses and Access to Medicines: Some Recent Experiences,' in *Intellectual Property and Access to Medicines: Papers and Perspectives* (WHO, 2010) 87–105.
7 Löfgren, Hans. 'The Global Biopharma Industry and the Rise of Indian Drug Multinationals: Implications for Australian Generics Policy,' *Australia New Zealand Health Policy* Vol. 4 (2007) 10.
8 Lopert, Ruth, and Deborah Gleeson. 'The High Price of "Free" Trade: US Trade Agreements and Access to Medicines,' *The Journal of Law, Medicine & Ethics* Vol. 41, No. 1 (2013) 199–223.
9 Malpani, Rohit. 'All Costs, No Benefits: How TRIPS-Plus Intellectual Property Rules in the US-Jordan FTA Affect Access to Medicines,' *Oxfam Briefing Paper* (2007).

10 Mitchell, Andrew D., and Tania Voon. 'The TRIPS Waiver as a Recognition of Public Health Concerns in the WTO,' in Pogge, Thomas, Matthew Rimmer, and Kim Rubenstein (eds.) *Incentives for Global Public Health* (Cambridge University Press, 2010) 56–76.
11 Munos, Bernard. 'Lessons from 60 Years of Pharmaceutical Innovation,' *Nature Reviews Drug Discovery* Vol. 8 (2009) 959–968.
12 Novogrodsky, Noah Benjamin. 'Beyond TRIPS: The Role of Non-State Actors and Access to Essential Medicines,' in Pogge, Thomas, Matthew Rimmer, and Kim Rubenstein (eds.) *Incentives for Global Public Health: Patents and Access to Medicines* (Cambridge University Press, 2010) 343–356.
13 Pogge, Thomas, Matthew Rimmer, and Kim Rubenstein (eds.) *Incentives for Global Public Health* (Cambridge University Press, 2010).
14 Sundaram, Jae. 'India's Trade-Related Aspects of Intellectual Property Rights Compliant Pharmaceutical Patent Laws: What Lessons for India and Other Developing Countries?' *Information & Communications Technology Law* Vol. 23, No. 1 (2014a) 1–30.
15 UNDP, UNAIDS. 'The Potential Impact of Free Trade Agreements on Public Health,' *Issue Brief* (2012).
16 Williams, Owain Davis, and Hans Löfgren. 'The Political Economy of Pharmaceuticals: Conformity and Resistance in the Global South,' in Löfgren, Hans, and Owain Davis Williams (eds.) *The New Political Econ of Pharmaceuticals* (Palgrave Macmillan, 2013) 1–28.1

Index

For Product Safety Concerns and Information please contact our EU representative GPSR@taylorandfrancis.com
Taylor & Francis Verlag GmbH, Kaufingerstraße 24, 80331 München, Germany

www.ingramcontent.com/pod-product-compliance
Ingram Content Group UK Ltd.
Pitfield, Milton Keynes, MK11 3LW, UK
UKHW011001180926
475701UK00004B/490
9780367590918